Environmental

Environmental Economics

Theory and Applications

Katar Singh
Anil Shishodia

SAGE Publications
Los Angeles • London • New Delhi • Singapore

First published in 2007 by

 Sage Publications India Pvt Ltd
B 1/I-1, Mohan Cooperative Industrial Area
Mathura Road, New Delhi 110 044
www.sagepub.in

Sage Publications Inc
2455 Teller Road
Thousand Oaks, California 91320

Sage Publications Ltd
1 Oliver's Yard
55 City Road
London EC1Y 1SP

Sage Publications Asia-Pacific Pte Ltd
33 Pekin Street
#02-01 Far East Square
Singapore 048763

Published by Vivek Mehra for Sage Publications India Pvt Ltd, typeset in 10/12 pt Palatino by Quick Sort (India) Private Limited, Chennai and printed at Chaman Enterprises, New Delhi.

Library of Congress Cataloging-in-Publication Data

Singh, Katar, 1939–
  Environmental economics : theory and applications / Katar Singh, Anil Shishodia.
    p. cm.
Includes bibliographical references and index.
  1. Environmental economics. 2. Environmental policy. 3. Environmental management. 4. Natural resources—Management. I. Shishodia, Anil, 1962– II. Title.
HC79.E5S4454   333.7—dc22   2007   2007036650

ISBN: 978-0-7619-3597-1 (PB)   978-81-7829-760-6 (India-PB)

The Sage Team: Sugata Ghosh, Neha Kohli and Sanjeev Sharma

Contents

List of Tables

List of Figures

List of Boxes

Preface

In India, more than three-quarters of the population depends directly for its livelihoods on activities based on natural resources, through agriculture, animal husbandry, forestry and fisheries. The remainder of the population relies on these resources indirectly, for food, fuel, industrial output and recreation. Their economic well-being is inextricably tied to the productivity of natural resources. Sadly, most of the natural resources and the environment in India are in a serious state of degradation. For example, forest land has been degraded and productivity of forests has been declining over time. Agricultural lands suffer from erosion, waterlogging, salinity and general loss of fertility, making them less productive. Water for drinking and irrigation is increasingly getting scarce and polluted. Fishery yields are falling, and air quality is deteriorating. All this poses a serious threat to the survival of millions of rural people in general and the poor in particular. In view of this, restoration and judicious use and management of natural resources and the environment are essential to ensure sustainable livelihoods and the well-being of people.

Of the various disciplines that might help identify and analyse the problems of degradation of natural resources and the environment, environmental economics is perhaps best able to provide insights critical to understanding and resolving natural resource and environment policy and management issues. Economic analysis can identify productive patterns of natural resource use; it can assess the economic incentives that guide people toward or away from such patterns; and it can evaluate their implications for equity and sustainability. It is, in fact, an essential tool for designing environment policy and management strategies.

The field of economics is well established in India but in the past there has been little focus on the economic aspects of environmental and natural resource management. Interest in these problems is now increasing, as is evident from the initiation of natural resource and environmental economics teaching and research programmes in many universities and research institutes. At most of these institutions, however, natural resource and environmental economics programmes are in their infancy. Qualified teachers and teaching materials are scarce and capability to conduct research is limited. In view of this, there is need to develop teaching, training and research skills and capability in the field of natural resource and environmental economics and management.

There are many good books on environmental economics available in the market now. But in our opinion none of those books is suitable for use as a textbook in Indian universities and colleges. This book is intended to fill in that void. This book is primarily written to cater to the needs of Indian students, teachers, researchers, environment managers, and policy makers. The main objective of the book is to enhance their knowledge of the basic concepts, theories, tools and techniques of environmental economics so as to enable them to diagnose the root causes of environmental problems and identify practicable alternatives for their resolution. This, we hope, will help improve the teaching, training and research in environmental economics and assist resource owners and managers, policy makers and governmental and non-governmental organisations (NGOs) in judiciously using and managing India's natural resources and environment. This is critical to achieving the environmentally sustainable use of natural resources and the environment, which is so essential for sustaining and improving the livelihoods of millions of rural people, especially the poor.

The book comprises 14 chapters; together they present a fairly comprehensive yet crisp treatment of both the theoretical and applied aspects of environmental economics, keeping in view the Indian context. Chapter 1 introduces the subject matter of environmental economics to the reader and deals with its definition, scope, distinguishing features, rationale, as well as its growth and development over time. It also presents a glimpse of certain serious environmental problems that India is currently facing and outlines a generic approach to resolve them. In Chapter 2, we explore and discuss the relations and interactions between economy, environment and development. Chapters 3 and 4 present certain basic concepts and theories underlying individual and collective choices vis-à-vis the environment. Chapter 5 is devoted to the discussion of the meaning, types and methods of valuation of environmental assets, goods and functions. In Chapter 6, the basics of environmental accounting are presented with a case study of the existing system of forest resource accounting in a forest division in Madhya Pradesh. Policy instruments useful for environment management are presented in Chapter 7. Chapters 8 to 11 deal with environmental problems of land, water, forests and fisheries, respectively, and explore their root causes identifying alternatives for their resolution. In Chapter 12, we discuss the main functions and benefits of biodiversity conservation, diagnose the causes of loss of biodiversity and identify policy instruments of biodiversity conservation. Chapter 13 is devoted to the discussion of climatic changes, such as acid rain, global warming, depletion of ozone layer, floods and drought, and their impact on the environment. Finally, Chapter 14 presents the basic elements of an ideal environment management policy and a critique of India's National Environment Policy 2006. A glossary of important technical terms used in environmental economics literature is also included.

While finalising the contents of this book, we have taken into account the curricula of environmental economics courses offered at the Bachelor's and Master's levels by reputed institutions in India. At the end of each chapter, we have summed up the main points made in the chapter and included a few discussion questions to encourage the student to think through the content of the chapter and relate it to real world situations.

We do not claim any originality of the ideas, concepts and theories of environmental economics presented in the book. But what is new and original in the book is the way we have synthesised, organised and presented the material in a form that is, in our opinion, easy to comprehend and apply. In writing this book, and in the development of our thoughts and ideas about environmental economics, we have benefited a great deal from our interactions with our students, colleagues, environment policy makers and managers, and last, but not the least, from the writings of eminent natural resource and environmental economists. To name them all would be impossible and to mention a few invidious. We extend our sincere thanks to them all.

We would, however, like to place on record our utmost thanks to Tejeshwar Singh, formerly Managing Director and now Chairman, Sage, who, at a time when the first author had almost given up the project, exhorted him to pick up the courage and complete it. We are also thankful to Mimi Choudhury, formerly Commissioning Editor, Sage, for encouraging us to take up the project and for providing us with the curricula of environmental economics courses followed in a few Indian universities and colleges. Sadly for us, she left Sage without seeing this work through. But Sugata Ghosh, Vice President, Commissioning, who took over the charge from Mimi Choudhury, more than compensated us for the loss through expediting the processing of the manuscript most professionally and speedily. Neha Kohli, the production editor, speeded up the entire process and brought out the book in a relatively short period of time.

We are also thankful to an anonymous reviewer of the manuscript of the book for his/her valuable comments and suggestions.

Finally, we are thankful to the India Natural Resource Economics and Management (INREM) Foundation and the Department of Economics, Sardar Patel University, for providing us the necessary facilities and a congenial environment for writing this book. In particular, we want to thank Jose S., Office Manager, INREM Foundation, for his help in word-processing, formatting and printing the manuscript of the book.

Katar Singh
Anil Shishodia

1 Introduction

1.1 MEANING AND IMPORTANCE OF ENVIRONMENT

Environment connotes the sum total of the things or circumstances surrounding an organism including humans (Cunningham et al. 1999: 343). In this book, by the term 'environment', we mean the natural environment, which encompasses all the biotic and abiotic elements that form our surroundings, that is, air, land, water, forests, seas, animals and all other living and non-living elements on Planet Earth. Without the environment, none of us can survive. In short, the following are the main functions of the environment: *(i)* provision of 'natural goods' such as lakes, landscape, wildlife; *(ii)* supplying natural resources such as land, water, forests, and minerals, which are used to create economic goods; *(iii)* functioning as a 'sink' into which the by-products of economic activities are dumped/discarded; and *(iv)* providing environmental services and amenities such as the maintenance of a habitable biosphere, including the stratospheric ozone layer, climate stability and genetic diversity, and recreation and aesthetic appreciation.

Environment has multiple dimensions: physical, chemical and biological. It could be both natural and man-made. The natural environment keeps changing over time naturally and it is also amenable to changes by human beings. Thanks to scientific and technological developments, our ability to alter the environment has increased tremendously, whereas the capacity of the environment to cope with those alterations is limited. The challenge of creating and maintaining a sustainable environment is probably the single most pressing issue confronting us today and will remain so in the foreseeable future (Raven et al. 1998: v).

We interact daily with the environment around us. We inhale oxygen from the environment, drink water obtained from it, eat food directly produced by it (or produced by human beings using its resources), exhale carbon dioxide (CO_2) into it, and dispose wastes and by-products in it. Throughout most of our history, we have taken the environment for granted; it provided us with food, fuel and shelter with little or no complaint. Over the past century or so, however, the situation has undergone a sea-change. The environment can no longer satisfy our growing demands, and after using and spending resources extravagantly for so long man has realised that, like economic goods and services, most environmental resources and services are also scarce and exhaustible. Thanks to a growing population, urbanisation, industrialisation, liberalised international trade, and the consequent problems of congestion, degradation of natural resources, and pollution of air and water, more and more people, now than in the past, are forced to breathe foul air, drink contaminated water and eat hazardous food. Nature's bounty and abundance are disappearing at a rapid rate in many regions of the World due to the human alterations of the environment. All this has brought to the fore the need for protection and preservation of the environment and the urgency of developing sound environmental policies and programmes. Without them, development would not only be unsustainable, rather it would be tantamount to retrogression.

This chapter is devoted to define and elaborate the basic concepts used in environmental economics including its definition and scope. It presents an overview of the role of environmental economics, its growth and development as a discipline, and environmental problems of India. The main objective of the chapter is to familiarise the student with the types and nature of environmental problems, their root causes, and how environmental economics can address them.

1.2 DEFINITION AND SCOPE OF ENVIRONMENTAL ECONOMICS

Environmental economics is a nascent sub-discipline of economics. It would therefore be in order if we first define its parent discipline, that is economics. Economics is best defined as a social science that deals with the explanation and prediction of economic behaviour of rational individuals, groups of individuals, or other economic decision-making entities. Economic behaviour is revealed in terms of choices that people, or groups of people make. So, economics is also called a science of making choices. One of the most commonly accepted definitions of economics is given by Lionel Robbins. According to him: 'Economics is the science which studies human behaviour as a relationship between ends and means which have alternative uses' (Robbins 1935). This definition implies the fact that human beings have many ends, or wants and that the means available to achieve the ends, or satisfy the wants are scarce and have alternative uses. In a nutshell, it is the multiplicity of ends/wants and limited availability and existence of alternative uses of means that give rise to the problem of choice, or the need for economising. Hence, it is clear that if the means were not scarcely relative to ends, there would be no need for making choices or economising and no need for economics.

Environmental economics deals with the application of the principles of economics to study why and how human beings interact with their environment the way they do, how they use and manage the environmental resources, and what are the impacts of human activities on the environment. It draws from all other sub-disciplines of economics such as microeconomics, macroeconomics, and welfare economics, as well as from natural sciences including environment science. It attempts to explain the economic aspects of attitude and behaviour of people with regards to the natural environment. It is also concerned with how economic institutions and policies can be changed to bring the environmental impacts of human activities into balance with human desires and the needs of the ecosystems.

Environmental economics seeks to analyse environmental issues, which are complex and multidisciplinary in nature. Consequently, it represents an inter-section of several social science and natural science disciplines. In its formative years in the 1960s, it encompassed a diversity of economic doctrines and a pluralistic view (Pearce and Turner 1990). Many economic concepts and tools such as marginalism, consumer's surplus, producer's surplus, opportunity cost, externalities, subsidies, taxes, social welfare function, Pareto optimality, and cost-benefit analysis have relevance and applications in analysing environmental problems.

Environmental economics deals with economic aspects of interdependence and interactions between human beings and the environment. Since many environmental assets, goods, amenities, and services have no markets and hence either have no prices, or have prices that are distorted, most environmental problems could be considered as problems of non-optimal pricing (Pearce 1976: 3). In other words, environmental problems arise either from non-existence or failure of markets. Environmental economics deals with non-market goods, amenities and services provided by Mother Nature.

The definition of environmental economics as a discipline dealing with the relationship between economic activities and the environment focuses attention on economic development and its effects on environment. Man has been tampering with the ecosphere for a very long time, presuming that environmental resources and amenities are inexhaustible. But now he is forced to recognise that, like other economic goods, environmental goods and services are also scarce, and exhaustible. This is where economics enters the scene as it is a science of 'allocating scarce resources among competing uses'. Economics thus has a vital role to play in finding solutions of environmental problems. As environmental goods and services are scarce, society can have more of them only by giving up significant amounts of other desirable goods and services, that is, there is a trade-off between environmental goods and other economic goods.

Like its parent discipline, environmental economics also has two branches, namely, positive environmental economics, and normative environmental economics. The positive environmental economics draws upon microeconomic theories and macroeconomic theories to describe and explain the ways in which economic factors influence the consumption and production of environmental goods and services. It is largely descriptive and predictive. The normative environmental economics is largely prescriptive, that is, it attempts to prescribe what ought to be done to protect and conserve the environment. It applies the principles of welfare economics to determine the socially optimum allocation of environmental goods and services currently and over time that maximises the net social welfare of present as well as future generations.

1.3 ENVIRONMENTAL ECONOMICS vs. TRADITIONAL ECONOMICS

Before we proceed further, it would be good to understand the distinction between traditional economics and environmental economics. According to Lesser et al. (1997: 5–20), the following points are the major differences between environmental economics and traditional economics (see Table 1.1):

Table 1.1 Similarities and Differences between Traditional Economics and Environmental Economics

Traditional Economics	Environmental Economics
1. It does not deal with the inter-relationship and interactions between the environment and economic activities.	1. A nascent sub-discipline of economics that deals with the inter-relationship and interactions between the environment and economic activities.
2. Deals with private goods that are bought and sold in markets.	2. Deals with public or collective goods for which either no markets exists or the markets are imperfect.
3. Does not take into account externalities associated with the actions of individuals, groups of individuals and organisations.	3. Takes into account the externalities associated with the actions of individuals, groups of individuals and organisations.
4. Time-related decisions such as allocations of resources over time and inter-generational equity do not receive much attention.	4. Time-related decisions and inter-generational equity receive high attention.
5. Often does not consider the limited capacity of environment to provide inputs for production and absorb wastes produced in the process of production.	5. Limited capacity of the environment is explicitly considered.

Source: Lesser et al. (1997).

1. The fundamental presumption of environmental economics is that the environment and economy are inter-linked and inter-dependent entities and, therefore, changes in one affect the other. Traditional economics does not explicitly take into consideration the interdependence between economy and the environment and does not seek to explain how economic decisions affect the environment and vice versa.

2. Environmental goods are often 'public goods' in the sense that they can be enjoyed, or consumed by many individuals simultaneously without affecting others' consumption. This attribute of environmental goods frequently involves a breakdown in the way markets work or a complete absence of markets. Thus, for environmental goods and amenities like clean air, solar radiation, natural scenic beauty, and biodiversity, there exist no markets, whereas for traditional 'economic goods' such as clothes, cars, television, and books, there are well-defined markets.

3. In many cases of consumption and production of economic goods and services, especially environmental goods and services, there are unintended side effects, or externalities that affect others. Environmental economics deals with those externalities whereas traditional economics does not.

4. Time often plays a crucial and defining role in environmental economics. Traditional economics can determine efficient ways to allocate resources for producing goods and services. The allocation is, however, simplified and confined to a single period of time with the underlying presumption that the production of an additional unit of a commodity today does not preclude producing one tomorrow. In the case of many environmental goods, allocation of resources over time is critical. For example, while burning fossil fuels and polluting the environment today, we may be creating problems for future generations for years or forever. Similarly, if we harvest all prawns today, the supply will be gone forever. Our consumption decisions of some environmental goods may be 'irreversible' and may have a profound impact on the well-being of future generations.

5. Traditional economics does not explicitly take into account the fact that the capacity of the environment to provide production inputs and to assimilate the wastes produced in the processes of production and consumption is limited whereas environmental economics does not ignore this constraint of the environment.

Natural resource economics and ecological economics are the two other sister sub-disciplines of environmental economics. Natural resource economics is a sub-discipline of economics concerned with the allocation and use of renewable and non-renewable resources such as land, water, forests, minerals and fish. It does not explicitly deal with the problems of interactions between human activities and the environment and issues of inter-generational equity. Environmental economics differs from resource economics in that it focuses on the valuation and management of environmental quality, and not just on the allocation and use of resource stocks.

Ecological economics is also a branch of economics that explicitly recognises the limits of the environment and the interactions between human activities and the environment. It is a trans-disciplinary field that addresses the relationship between ecosystems and economic systems. It goes beyond normal conceptions of scientific disciplines and attempts to integrate and synthesise many different disciplinary perspectives in order to achieve an ecologically and economically sustainable world. It deals with the interactions between human activities and the environment and highlights the need for understanding of ecological processes, systems, causes and effects in addressing economic and environmental problems.

1.4 THE RATIONALE OF ENVIRONMENTAL ECONOMICS

Environmental economics links broad concepts of how the environment works with fundamental economic concepts like demand and supply. Because humans interact with the environment, and because humans allocate scarce resources applying economic principles and tools, study of environmental economics can lead to greater insights about why environmental problems exist and what the best solutions to those problems are. Why is the air polluted? Why are rivers and lakes polluted? What is the right amount of carbon dioxide in the atmosphere? Answers to these and other similar questions can serve as the basis of sound policies that can eliminate or at least lessen the severity of environmental problems. Environmental policy makers need to be concerned with the economic aspects of both environmental problems and making policies to remedy them. Environmental economics cannot answer all environmental policy questions, but still will be the only source of answers for many.

All environmental problems can be traced to the fundamental economic problem of 'scarcity', that is, we cannot have everything we want because our resources are limited. Environmental problems arise when the use of the environment for one set of functions interferes with, or prevents, the operation of other functions. For example, using the atmosphere as a dumping ground for chlorofluorocarbons (CFCs) or carbon dioxide (CO_2) damages the ozone shield and reduces climate stability; damming a river to provide hydropower destroys riparian habitations and agriculture and, possibly, a whole range of associated cultural and recreational activities; quarrying of minerals destroys land and constructing big reservoirs submerges landscapes of historic, recreational or aesthetic value. It can be seen from these examples that environmental problems occur mainly when the use of the environment to supply resources to, or disposal of wastes from, economic activity reduces its ability to supply other environmental services. In addition the environmental problems have a negative impact on economic activity.

Determining the most reasonable trade-offs among various uses of the environment is where the study of environmental economics is important. Solving environmental problems requires an understanding of fundamental economic concepts such as scarcity. Traditional economics begins with the interaction of supply and demand. With the help of these, it can be explained how well-established markets function. But for many environmental goods and services, such as clean air, there is 'not a direct market' that can mediate between buyers and sellers. No one has distinct ownership of clean air supplies (all of us—and none of us—own the atmosphere). But the principle that determines the price of economic goods can also apply to non-market goods like clean air, which like apples, requires resources to produce. As apple production needs land, water, fertilisers and labour among others, 'clean air' production requires that the atmosphere not be used as waste dump or at least used less so. That means waste must be diverted elsewhere which also requires scarce resources. One solution, at least for some environmental problems, is to introduce some market interactions where none had existed previously. That is one key goal of environmental economics.

Much of environmental economics has focused on the relative merits and demerits of different policy responses to various flaws of market mechanism in the areas of environmental degradation and pollutions, for example, should emissions be stopped by regulation or should they be taxed? In fact, environmental economics provides a solid foundation for most of the policy measures designed to address environmental problems. It seeks to compare the expected social benefits and social costs of policy measures and advocates the promulgation of only those measures which promise to enhance the net social welfare.

1.5 THE EVOLUTION AND GROWTH OF ENVIRONMENTAL ECONOMICS

Classical economists such as Adam Smith (1723–1790), Thomas Malthus (1766–1834), David Ricardo (1772–1823) and John Stuart Mill (1806–1873) did not explicitly address the environmental aspects of economic growth but they left a legacy of ideas many of which are relevant to, and have been re-introduced into, contemporary environmental debates. For example, Ricardo argued that economic growth would peter out in the long-run because of scarcity of natural resources and diminishing returns to land that would set in as society is forced to move on to bring under cultivation successively less productive land to produce food enough to feed its increasing population. John Stuart Mill conceived of economic progress in terms of a race between technical change and diminishing returns in agriculture. Classical theory of political economy highlighted the importance of the market as an instrument of stimulating both growth and innovation, but remained essentially pessimistic about long-run economic growth prospects. The growth economy was thought to be merely a temporary phase between two stable equilibrium positions, with the final position representing a barren subsistence level existence—the stationary state.

Starting around 1870, neoclassical economic thought began to develop within the mainstream economics profession. The neoclassical economists introduced a new methodology of marginal analysis, which dealt with the study of the relationships between small or incremental changes in inputs and outputs. The 'rational and egotistic person' constituted the 'hard core' of the neoclassical economic theory, which postulated that a rational individual tries to maximise his satisfaction, or utility subject to his income (budget) constraints. According to the mainstream neoclassical system of thought the economic value of marketable commodities, unpriced environmental goods and services, or sympathy for future generations is determined based on the amount of personal utility yielded.

The experiences of the inter-war years (1920s and 1930s), when mass unemployment became a reality, contrary to what the neoclassical economists had presumed, led to the formulation of Keynesian economics with its emphasis on government intervention and deficit spending. Thus during the 1950s, growth of economics as a discipline got back onto both the economic and political agendas. Subsequently, during the 1960s, environmental pollution caused mainly by rapid economic growth in developed countries intensified and became widespread. This led to the emergence of new environmental ideologies and mass awareness about the need and importance of keeping the quality of the environment intact. A number of these new ideologies were basically anti-economic growth.

Since 1970, a number of 'world views' have crystallised within environmentalism, providing a rationale for the emergence of environmental economics as a sub-discipline of economics. Four basic world views can be distinguished, ranging from support for a market and technology-driven growth process which is environmentally damaging, through a position favouring managed resource conservation and growth, to 'eco-preservationist' positions which explicitly reject the economic growth paradigm. The need of the 21st century and beyond is self sustainable development. In this context, it is of vital importance to allocate the planet's scarce resources such that the goal of sustainable development is attained.

In many developing countries including India, pollution is still seen as a necessary price for economic growth. As a result, some cities such as Mexico City, São Paulo, Delhi and Kolkata regularly suffer air pollution levels that are far more severe than those in developed countries. Worst of all, many of the poorest nations seem stuck in an unending cycle of poverty and economic degradation; they are unable to devote the necessary resources to secure tomorrow's economic interests because they are too concerned with survival today. No more do these nations have the resources to combat major environmental concerns like global climate change than they have to launch probes to distant planets. Their's is a daily struggle to provide enough food, shelter, and uncontaminated water, all the while watching their rapidly growing populations overburdening their limited natural resources and the environment.

One reason for the relatively recent emergence of environmental economics is the change in our society's attitude toward the environment over time. Before the American Revolution, there was a colonial tradition of social control that provided a great deal of environmental protection. Common Law at that time imposed a lot of legal restrictions on the ability of landowners to pollute streams used by their neighbours. By about 1820, the whole landscape of Common Law changed to that of a free-market or 'laissez-faire' economic system. Under this, only economic development was emphasised upon and no questions were asked, whether trees were felled or mines quarried, rivers dammed as long as it was in the interest of economic growth.

Until the 1960s, a view prevailed that the environment was capable of absorbing all the unwanted by-products of the human pursuits of economic well-being. Economists concentrated on reallocation of scarce land and labour and did not consider environment as a scarce resource. Then, there began a widespread shift in values and expectations, which represented a sort of return to the pre-Revolutionary colonial tradition of social control. We began to notice the effects of our economic actions on the environment. We discovered that our air and water had become filthy. Our society then started looking for its response toward environmental protection, combining everything from legislation, mandating improvements in air and water quality, to agitations protesting against wasteful and profligate use of our natural resources and the environment. Economists responded by studying the causes of degradation of the environment and seeking alternatives for preserving the quality and integrity of the environment.

With the end of the Cold War and the collapse of the Soviet Union, the world discovered that environmental degradation was not a unique attribute of the 'capitalist' Western world. Quite the contrary, in many formerly Communist countries, including Poland, Russia and Czech Republic, pollution existed at levels unimaginable in the West. Decades of heavy industrialisation had led to crippling declines in air and water quality. Water pollution levels in some rivers and lakes in eastern Europe were very high. Unfortunately these environmental problems were compounded by an overarching silence, in the belief that no physical price was too great to pay to seek economic and military parity with the West.

To sum up, the major landmarks in the growth and development of environmental economics are as follows (Dixon et al. 1994):

- **1972:** The Stockholm conference on Human Environment created formal international awareness of the need for maintaining the quality and integrity of environment.
- **1987:** Brundtland Commission's Report, *Our Common Future*, popularised the concept of sustainable development.
- **1992:** World Bank's *World Development Report* highlighted the links between development and environment and opportunities for 'win-win' policies.
- **1992:** Setting up of the Global Environment Fund (GEF) provided grant funds for activities such as biodiversity protection, reduction of greenhouse gas emissions, and reduction of (CFC) emissions to protect the ozone layer.
- **1992:** Agenda 21 of the United Nations Conference on Environment and Development (Earth Summit) in Rio de Janeiro prompted the United Nations Statistics Division (UNSD) to prepare and publish, in 1993, a Handbook of National Accounting entitled *Integrated Environmental and Economic Accounting* (SEEA).
- **1992:** Convention on Biological Diversity highlighted the need for biodiversity conservation.
- **1993:** Development of a Forest Resource Accounting (FRA) system by the International Institute of Environment and Development (IIED) and the United Nations Environment Programme-World Conservation and Monitoring Centre (UNEP-WCMC) for the International Tropical Timber Organisation (ITTO).
- **1990s and beyond:** Growth and development of theoretical and applied economic analyses of environmental issues.

These and other related developments led to the setting up of several specialised institutes, departments and professional bodies including the IIED, Swedish Royal Academy's Beijer Institute, International Society for Ecological Economics and Indian Society for Ecological Economics. Besides, several professional journals have also been launched and national and international conferences and training courses in environmental economics organised. This trend is continuing and is likely to gain momentum as awareness about the need to protect and conserve the environment grows in developing countries.

In India, although the field of economics is well established, there had been little focus in the past on the economic aspects of environmental and natural resource management. But interest in these problems is increasing now, as is evident from the initiation of natural resource and environmental economics teaching and research programmes in many universities and research institutes. At most of these institutions, however, natural resource and environmental economics programmes are in their infancy. Qualified teachers and teaching materials are scarce, and capability to conduct research is limited. There is only a weak link between the research conducted and the needs of policy makers, managers and resource users in solving critical natural resource management problems. An institutional mechanism is needed in India to help develop teaching, training and research skills and capability in the field of natural resource and environmental economics and management.

Some of the major developments in the field of natural resource and environmental economics in India are summed up below.

In 1992, a programme called India Natural Resource Economics Programme (INREP) was launched and based in the International Crops Research Institute for the Semi-Arid Tropics (ICRISAT), Patencheru, Andhra Pradesh. After some time of its existence and operation, it was decided in a meeting held on 6–7 August 1992 at Hotel Quality Inn, Hyderabad that a new organisation should be created for taking up the activities of INREP. The meeting was convened by the Ford Foundation, New Delhi and attended by 10 eminent agricultural and natural resources economists and William R. Bentley from Winrock International, and John Ambler from the Ford Foundation, New Delhi. A Steering Committee was constituted under the chairmanship of Katar Singh, then RBI Chair Professor, Institute of Rural Management, Anand to guide and facilitate the process of creating the proposed organisation. This meeting also decided to name the new organisation as India Natural Resource Economics and Management (INREM) Foundation. Subsequently, the INREM Foundation was registered on 16 April 1994 under the Societies

Registration Act, 1860 bearing No. GUJ 4365/Ahmedabad and the Bombay Public Trust Act, 1950 bearing No. F/4226/Ahmedabad. It is also registered under Section 6 (1) (a) of the Foreign Contribution (Regulation) Act 1976 with Registration No. 042040119 (Educational). The mission of INREM Foundation is to promote sustainable use and management of natural resources and environment in India. Its main objective is to promote teaching, training and research in natural resources and environmental economics in Indian universities and help improve natural resources policies and programmes.

Since its inception in 1994, INREM Foundation has undertaken several research projects and conducted several training programmes. One of its major contributions is the publication of a text book, *Natural Resource Economics: Theory and Application in India,* 1997, edited by John Kerr, Dinesh K. Marothia, Katar Singh, C. Ramasamy and William Bentley and published by Oxford and India Book House Publishing Company Private Limited, New Delhi in 1997. This is the most comprehensive and the only text book of its kind on the subject of natural resource economics ever published in India. With a grant from Winrock International Institute for Agricultural Development, USA, INREM Foundation purchased 300 copies of the book and distributed all the copies *gratis* to various Indian Universities and selected agricultural and natural resource economists.

The Indian Society for Ecological Economics (INSEE) is a professional society registered under the Indian Societies Act in 1999. It is affiliated to the International Society for Ecological Economics. INSEE aims to further the cause of sustainable development by providing a forum for continuous dialogue between scholars, practitioners and policy analysts working on different aspects of environment and ecology. It seeks to disseminate the results of research and its policy implications through multiple avenues such as conferences, workshops, networking and the sponsoring of research and publications. It has published several books brought under its auspices by its members based on the papers contributed to its biennial conferences.

Beginning 2000–2001, the Ministry of Environment and Forests (MoEF), Government of India (GoI) implemented, with World Bank's assistance, a five-year programme called, 'India: Environmental Management Capacity Building Technical Assistance Project'.[1] The Madras School of Economics, Chennai was the Executing Agency. The specific objective of the project was to enhance environmental management capacity in

---

[1]The details of the programme are available at the Website of the Madras School of Economics, Chennai: http://www.mse.ac.in.

selected areas of environmental management. An important area or component so identified for such capacity building or enhancement relates to environmental economics. The objective was to increase the capacity for the application of economic principles and tools to environmental management in India across the full range of issues such as priority-setting, cost-benefit analysis of alternative policies for pollution control, resource management and biodiversity conservation. Achievement of this objective was sought to be measured in terms of the additional number of students at the under-graduate and post-graduate level trained in environmental economics; the number of officials, industrial managers, NGOs and others trained in environmental economics; the reach and quality of research in the field of environmental economics; and the integration of the research recommendations into environmental decision-making at the various levels of government.

The environmental economics programme consisted of:

1. Establishing an Environmental Economics Indicators and Project Planning Cell (EEIPPC) in the Ministry of Environment and Forests.
2. Establishment of project units in environmental economics in four core institutions.
3. Support to developing an environmental economics curriculum and to preparing teaching materials, case studies and textbooks combining India-specific case studies with examples of 'best practices' from other countries for diploma and degree programmes.
4. A faculty-upgradation programme, designed to train economics faculty members from across India in basic environmental economics to better equip them to introduce the environmental economics curriculum in their respective colleges and universities. This was designed to consist primarily of short courses offered in India, but was supplemented by a few fellowships at prominent environmental economics faculty in other countries.
5. A Ph.D. Scholars Workshop programme to provide an opportunity for the scholars to present their results and get feedback from experts in environmental economics and also to provide access to the library, computer and faculty resources in well established centres in environmental economics.
6. A programme to invite environmental economics faculty from other countries to teach and conduct research on India-specific topics.

7. Training programmes for practising economists and non-economists on the applications of the principles of environmental economics, mainly to pollution control policy, environmental costs and benefits, environmental assessments, cost-effectiveness and trade-offs between environment and economic growth.

8. Short-term overseas training programme for Indian Economic Service (IES) candidates.

9. Support to selected university, institute and college libraries to expand their collections of important books, journals and data bases in environmental economics.

10. Support to applied research, case studies and analysis of best practices in the area of environmental economics. A tentative list of themes included: Economic Analysis of Policies in Natural Resource Management, Environmental Pollution, Role of Institutions in Environmental Management, Valuation Methods, International Environmental Issues, Environmental Technologies, and Clean Production Technologies.

11. Short-term (2–3 months) overseas research grants for researchers to enable them to visit well-known centres in environmental economics for consultations with the experts and use the library facilities.

12. Travel grants for presenting papers in international environmental economics conferences. The training component of the programme envisaged training of economics faculty (200 persons, 4 weeks duration), training of non-economists (800 persons, 5 days duration), Ph.D. Scholars (60 persons, 3 days) and overseas fellowships (24 persons, 6–9 months).

The implementation of this programme was done through four core institutions—Madras School of Economics, Chennai, Indira Gandhi Institute of Development Research, Mumbai, Institute of Economic Growth, Delhi, and Indian Statistical Institute, Kolkata—as well as through a network of interested institutes. The objectives of the programme were sought to be achieved through a network of four sub-committees that had divided up the work and assigned clear responsibilities, under the overall guidance and supervision of the Expert Committee on Environmental Economics. The programme has contributed significantly to the growth and development of environmental economics in Indian universities and institutes.

1.6 SOME TYPICAL ENVIRONMENTAL PROBLEMS

Newspapers and the electronic media carry several stories almost every day about some environmental problem or the other.[2] The problems that attract the attention of most people include air pollution in metropolitan cities, pollution of rivers and lakes, deforestation, degradation of land, particularly in fragile ecosystems such as mountainous areas and undulating terrain. Kenneth Boulding, an eminent economist, lamenting the problems of degradation and pollution of the environment globally, called the Earth a 'plundered planet' (Box 1.1).

Box 1.1   Kenneth Boulding on Global Environmental Pollution

We live today in a planet that is both 'plundered' and 'polluted'. The process of plundering has not only reduced the utilisable resources but has also polluted the environment. Clean air and clean water can no longer be taken for granted. According to the Living Planet Report 2002, the Living Planet Index, which is an indicator of the state of the world's natural ecosystems, has shown an overall decline of about 37 per cent between 1970 and 2000. This index is basically based on the abundance of forest, freshwater and marine species. Another measure that is used to understand environmental deterioration is the ecological footprint, which compares renewable natural resource consumption with nature's biological productive capacity. According to this study, human consumption of natural resources in 1999 is estimated to have overshot the earth's biological capacity by about 20 per cent. Since the 1980s humanity has been running an ecological deficit with the earth.

Source: ENVISAGE. EMCBTAP-ENVIS: Environmental Economics Node, Vol.1(1), December 2002, Madras School of Economics.

---

[2]A fortnightly magazine, *Down to Earth,* brought out by the Centre for Science and Environment, New Delhi collects, compiles, and disseminates useful information about pollution of the environment. Every issue of the fortnightly is full of case studies of pollution of natural resources and environment such as air, water and land. Besides, a daily e-newsletter, *Green Media,* out by the CMS-ENVIS Centre on Media and Environment and supported by the ENVIS Secretariat, Ministry of Environment and Forests, Government of India also publishes environmental news abstracted from 17 daily newspapers.

Most environmental problems are rooted in the human interference or interaction with Mother Nature and in most cases the main motive of human interference is economic in nature. For example, due to their inability or unwillingness to invest in installing sewerage treatment plants, most municipal corporations find it easier and less expensive to discharge the raw city sewerage in nearby rivers and streams and thereby pollute their waters. A glaring example of this kind of pollution is furnished by the river Ganga. Until not long ago, Ganga water used to be considered, or in fact, was so pure and clean that devout Hindus from all over India would visit Haridwar, Varanasi, Allahabad and other places of pilgrimage along the banks of Ganga to take a holy dip and cleanse their age-old 'sins'. Sadly now the Ganga is so polluted that she needs to cleanse herself and we have a Ganga Action Plan involving hundreds of crores of rupees for cleaning the river. Similar is the case with other rivers and lakes in India. Thus the problem of pollution of Ganga and its solution have an economic component and hence require the knowledge of economics. The success or failure of environmental policies depends on whether they use or ignore the economic aspect of behaviour of individuals, groups of individuals or other decision-making entities.

Until recently, we never questioned the capacity of the environment to provide production inputs and to absorb the waste. But now it is clear that we cannot take the environment for granted and the one-way relationship has to change. We must accept the fact that the environment can no longer meet our ever-increasing demands on it. The signs of environmental stress exerted by our growing demands are seen in the forms of polluted air, degraded lands, depleting groundwater, polluted rivers, streams and lakes, deforestation, climate change, loss of biodiversity and depletion of ozone layer. These problems have heightened the need for treating the environment as a 'scarce' good and for bringing it within the domain of economic analysis. This explains the emergence of environment economics as a nascent sub-discipline of economics.

A sample of some of the contemporary environmental issues and questions that environmental economics can answer is presented in Box 1.2.

Environmental problems are the result of economic expansion that fails to take account of the value of the environment and here the challenge is to build the recognition of environmental scarcity into decision-making. With or without development, rapid population growth may make it more difficult to address many environmental problems.

Box 1.2   Some Typical Environmental Issues and Questions

- **Air pollution:** Why is air polluted? How 'clean' should the air be? What policy measures could reduce air pollution?
- **Water pollution:** Why are rivers, lakes and groundwater aquifers polluted? How 'clean' should rivers be? What policy measures could reduce water pollution? Why do farmers overirrigate their crops from public canals?
- **Land degradation:** Why is land degraded? Which type of land is degraded most and why? Why do farmers not adopt the required conservation measures on their private land? What policy measures could reduce land degradation? What is the optimum level of soil conservation?
- **Deforestation:** Why are forests degraded? Why do people living in or around forests resort to illicit felling of trees and grazing of animals in the forests? What policy measures could promote afforestation of degraded forest lands?
- **Loss of biodiversity:** What is the value of biodiversity conservation? Why do forest dwellers not appreciate the need for biodiversity conservation? What policy measures could promote biodiversity conservation? How should the biodiversity conservation programmes be financed?
- **Climate change:** Why are people not concerned about global warming, acid rain, depletion of ozone layer, droughts and floods? What is the 'right' amount of carbon dioxide in the atmosphere? How can the emissions of greenhouse gases be reduced? Why do nations not cooperate and act collectively to reduce the emissions of carbon dioxide and other greenhouse gases? What policy measures at national and international levels are necessary to improve the global climate?

History is about change not about the *status quo*. The enormous growth in world economy, reflecting both population growth and rising affluence, is taking place on a finite planet. It is no longer today, what it was when human beings evolved four million years ago, when agriculture began 10,000 years ago and when industrial revolution began two centuries ago. One of the consequences of placing ever growing human demands on the natural systems and resources of the finite planet is that sustainable yield thresholds are being crossed in every country.

1.7 A GENERIC APPROACH TO SOLVING ENVIRONMENTAL PROBLEMS

After studying the importance of environmental economics and how it is different from other branches of economics, we would now turn to how it approaches or studies environmental issues. Environmental issues cut across several disciplines and hence require a multidisciplinary approach. Environmental economics can provide valuable insights into the causes of these problems and help identify appropriate strategies for their resolution. It has so happened that only the 'curative aspects (hardware tools covering science and engineering disciplines)' of environment were identified, leaving the 'preventive aspects (covering social disciplines especially economics)' unidentified. There is a strong notion that the study of environmental problems is the subject matter of the study of science or technology and hence treated beyond the scope of economics. It is nevertheless true that any rational decision concerning the utilisation of the environmental resources can be taken only within a framework based on complementary inputs from engineers, scientists and economists. Failure to understand the interdisciplinary linkages of the environment has only resulted in identification of 'curative aspects', leading to neglect of 'preventive aspects'. Various social sciences like economics, sociology and anthropology offer preventive tools for proper environmental identification, planning and management. Economics offers most of the 'cause-effect' attributes of environmental degradation. Whenever economists see externality, environmental activists may see evil wealthy corporations poisoning innocent people and wildlife, violating their rights to clean air and water. It is better to use economics to make incremental improvements in messy public policies than to rally against the imperfections of the public policy process.

Generally, economists would not identify environmental issues like global climate change. They can, however, help environmental policy makers confront the complexities of the issues involved. Developing effective environmental policies requires the policy makers to go through a series of steps as shown in Box 1.3.

1.8 MAIN POINTS

The following are the main points of this chapter:

- By the term, 'environment', we mean the natural environment, which encompasses the entire natural world in which we live, that

---

Box 1.3   Some Steps in a Generic Approach to Solving Environmental Problems

- They must understand economic concepts such as demand, supply, scarcity, value and efficiency and the broader linkages between the economy and the environment;
- They must also understand conflicting philosophical concepts such as equity, fairness, right and justice;
- They must identify and prioritise the most important economic, environmental and philosophical issues to be addressed for solving the environmental problems under consideration;
- They must be familiar with the contents of the economist's 'toolbox' and should have skills and experience in utilising those tools to determine the trade-offs and allocate resources among socially desirable goals;
- They must also be able to measure the value of trade-offs in monetary terms or otherwise;
- They must appreciate the critical role of time because environmental problems (and the policies that address them) can have an impact for years, centuries, even forever; and
- They must know how to manage uncertainty, risk and the unknowable.

Source: Raven et al. (1998: 21–24).

is, air, land, water, forests, seas, animals and all other living and non-living elements of Planet Earth. Without the environment, none of us can survive.
- The environment can no longer satisfy our growing demands and after using and spending resources extravagantly for so long, man has realised that, like economic goods and services, most of the environmental resources and services are also scarce and exhaustible. The challenge of creating and maintaining a sustainable environment is probably the single most pressing issue confronting us today and will remain so in the foreseeable future.
- In the current context of growing pollution, and degradation of the environment worldwide, environmental economics is emerging as an important nascent sub-discipline of economics. It deals with the application of the principles of economics to study and analyse why and how human beings interact with their environment the way they do, how they use and manage the environmental

resources, and what are the impacts of human activities on the environment.

- Newspapers and the electronic media carry several stories almost every day about some environmental problem or the other. The problems that attract the attention of most people include air pollution in metropolitan cities, pollution of rivers and lakes, deforestation, and degradation of land, particularly in fragile ecosystems such as mountainous areas and undulating terrain. Most environmental problems are rooted in the human interference or interaction with Mother Nature and in most cases the main motive of the human interference is economic in nature.

- All environmental problems can be traced to the fundamental economic problem of 'scarcity', that is, we cannot have everything we want because our resources are limited. Environmental problems arise when the use of the environment for one set of functions interferes with, or prevents, the operation of other functions.

- Environmental economics is capable of diagnosing the underlying causes of environmental decay and identifying remedial measures that seek to change the human behaviour vis-à-vis the environment.

- Science and technology have provided technical solutions (curative/'hardware' type) to environmental problems such as eco-friendly or cleaner technologies of production, processing, packaging and so on. But most of the environmental problems have no technical solutions or the technical solutions are very difficult and expensive to implement and hence not socially desirable. In those cases, environmental economics offers 'preventive' or 'software' type solutions through directly addressing the root causes of the problems rather than treating the symptoms. It can help formulate appropriate national and international environment policies to deal with environmental problems in most efficient ways.

1.9 DISCUSSION QUESTIONS

1. What are some of the environmental problems which cannot be addressed by conventional economic analysis and why?
2. Is environmental degradation a necessary consequence of economic growth in the Indian context? Yes/No. If yes, why and if no, why not?
3. Under what conditions could the goals of higher economic growth and better quality of environment be achieved simultaneously?

4. Discuss why technologies alone can't solve environmental problems of air pollution, water pollution, noise pollution and so on.

5. Visit a posh locality and a slum in your town/city, talk to people about environmental problems in their area, observe carefully the state of micro-environment, particularly common spaces, roads, market yards, public toilets and so on and list the environmental problems of both the localities separately and answer the following questions:

   (a) Is there a distinct difference between the overall quality of environment in the two localities? Yes/No. If yes, elaborate the differences.

   (b) What is the perception and attitude of people in the two localities towards environmental problems in their areas:

   Locality I (Posh):_____

   Locality II (Slum):_____

   (c) Is poverty a major factor in explaining the difference in the micro-environment in the two localities?

6. Visit an environment laboratory, or an office of the Central or State Pollution Control Board, talk to the Officer-in-Charge and a few scientists working there and find out the types of environmental problems prevailing in the area of their jurisdiction, the main agents of pollution, and the pollution control measures taken up by the Board concerned and their effectiveness.

2 Environment, Economy and Development

2.1 INTRODUCTION

An economy may be conceptualised as a collection of economic, social, institutional, legal and technological arrangements through which individuals in society seek to increase their material and spiritual well-being. The two elementary functions of an economy are: consumption and production. Consumption is considered the prime pump of an economy. The classical dictum that 'the consumer is sovereign' is based on the consumer power embodied in his demand, which is one of the crucial requirements for the existence of any business enterprise, or for that matter any economic activity including production.

Production is the creation of utilities through the transformation of two or more inputs/resources into one, or more products. The transformation takes place by combining the requisite inputs in various quantities in the production process, which may be biological like production of wheat; or chemical like production of pesticides; or mechanical like manufacturing of tractors or cars.

Any economic system exists within, and is encompassed by the natural environment. The economic system and the environment are interdependent and interact with each other. To be able to diagnose the root causes of environmental problems and identify possible remedies, it is important for the student of environmental economics to understand the nature of the interdependence and interaction between the two systems and their outcomes. This chapter is devoted to explore and discuss the relation and interactions between economy, environment and development. The main objective of the chapter is to enhance the understanding of the reader about the interdependence of environment, economy and development and his ability to trace the root causes of environmental problems.

2.2 ENVIRONMENT AND ECONOMY

Natural environment including natural resources provides several goods, services and amenities to human beings and performs many important functions in the process of economic growth. Two of the important functions are: provision of inputs to production processes and assimilating the wastes generated in the process of production and consumption (Figure 2.1). There are several perspectives on the nature and eventual outcomes of the environment-economy interdependence and interactions. We will now briefly discuss some of the commonly accepted perspectives.

2.2.1 Neo-Malthusian Pessimistic Perspective

The proponents of this school, mostly biologists and ecologists, believe that the carrying capacity of our Planet Earth is limited as the planet is finite, closed, and non-growing. In other words, there is a natural limit to both the critical functions of the environment, that is, the inputs provisioning and waste assimilating capacities of our Planet Earth are both

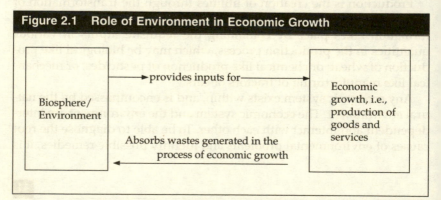

Figure 2.1   Role of Environment in Economic Growth

Biosphere/Environment

provides inputs for ⟶ Economic growth, i.e., production of goods and services

Absorbs wastes generated in the process of economic growth

limited. This means that one cannot go on increasing the production of goods and services using natural resources and dumping the wastes generated in the processes of production into the biosphere forever. There are ecological and natural limits to economic growth and hence it cannot be sustained forever.[1] According to this position, modern industrial society has damaged the environment to the extent that ecological and economic collapse is inevitable. The Club of Rome Report, *The Limits to Growth,* (Meadows et al. 1972), for example, predicted that if the current patterns of population growth and resource consumption continue, the world economic system would collapse by mid-21st century. Similarly, biologist Paul Ehrlich (1968), in his book, *The Population Bomb,* predicted that by the end of the 1970s, we will have a world full of misery and starvation due to overpopulation and extremely high energy prices resulting from dwindling sources of crude oil and natural gas (Lesser et al. 1997: 26). There are many other leading environmentalists including Lester Brown, W. McKibben, Norman Myers and Vandana Shiva, who subscribe to this school, implicitly, or explicitly (McNeely 2005: 3).

2.2.2 Cornucopian Optimistic Perspective

This school comprises mostly technologists, agricultural scientists and economists. They assert that there is no evidence or reason to fear the catastrophic collapse of societies postulated by the scholars subscribing to the Neo-Malthusian school. Thanks to the incentives provided by competitive markets, entrepreneurs are exploring and developing new sources of energy and minerals, and reserves of many commodities have increased due to new discoveries and/or recycling of wastes. Also, research in agricultural sciences has made it feasible now to augment, through appropriate technological and management interventions, the natural flows/harvest of products of nature. For example, fish catch can be increased sustainably through artificial feeding and breeding; crop yields can be increased through application of balanced organic and inorganic fertilisers, biopesticides and scientific soil and water management; and forests can be rejuvenated faster and their natural productivity increased through application of fertilisers and water. Thus, the carrying capacity of our biosphere in terms of population of

---

[1] Sustainable economic growth requires that in the process of economic growth, we maintain our natural resources and environment intact and use or harvest only that much quantity which is regenerated naturally, that is, we live on the 'flows' and keep the 'stock' of natural resources and environment intact.

living beings is, to some extent, amenable to augmentation through technological and managerial interventions.

2.2.3 The Middle Path

Following the teachings of India's great philosophers, scholars and *gurus*, we believe in the middle path between the two extremes represented by biologists and ecologists, and technocrats and economists. This means that, contrary to what growth maniacs and technocrats believe, there are limits to economic growth, and also, contrary to what ecologists assert, the limits are not absolutely rigid; they can be relaxed. We conclude with an optimistic view that, as argued by Simon and Kahn (1984), the 21st century will usher in an era characterised by higher living standards and reduced human impacts on the environment as a result of technological advance and policy innovation. This view is consistent with the principles underlying sustainable development.

2.2.4 Materials Balance Perspective

In this perspective, the real economy in which we live and work is viewed as an open system. Environmental economics draws upon the laws of 'thermodynamics' to understand and explain the relationship between the environment and the economy. The economy-environmental interactions are best portrayed via the material balance model, based on the First and Second Laws of Thermodynamics. The model represents the economy as a material processing and product transformation system. 'Useful' materials from the environment are drawn into the economic system (for example, non-renewable resources such as fossil fuels can be extracted until their stock is exhausted and products from renewable resources like forests and fisheries can be harvested); and then undergo a series of changes in their energy and entropy (that is, usefulness) states. Eventually after a time lag, the non-product output of the system can be partially recycled with residual 'useless' materials (wastes) returned to the environment from various points in the economic process.

The materials that first enter the system are not destroyed by the production and consumption activities; they are, however, dispersed and chemically transformed. In particular, they enter in a state of low entropy (as 'useful' materials) and leave in a state of high entropy (as 'useless' materials such as low temperature heat emissions, exhaust gases, mixed municipal wastes, etc.). At first sight, the entropy concept seems counter-intuitive and it is not used formally or defined rigorously in this discussion. In lay terms, entropy is a certain property of systems which increases in any irreversible process. When entropy increases, the energy in the system becomes less available to do 'useful work'. No material recycling processes therefore, can ever be 100 per cent efficient. Once the materials balance perspective is adopted, it is easy to see the way humans manage their economic impacts on the environment and, in reverse direction, environmental quality impacts on the efficient working of the economy.

2.3 TRACING ENVIRONMENTAL INPUTS INTO THE ECONOMY[2]

As we know the environment provides many inputs for production processes and serves as a sink for dumping the wastes produced in the process of production. We also directly consume many environmental goods and amenities such as air to breathe, water to drink, and wildlife for recreation and hunting. Tracing the flow of environmental inputs into an economy is necessary to determine the ripple effects of different economic and environmental policies and assessing their social desirability. Input-Output (I/O) Table is the most commonly used method of tracing the flow of environmental inputs as also other inputs and outputs into an economic system. A typical I/O table is shown in Table 2.1. It is broken down into different sectors of the economy and shows purchases and sales from one sector to another. For the sake of simplicity, we assume that there are only three sectors, or industries in the economy, each industry purchases some inputs, valued in rupees, from the other two industries, as well as from itself. The purchases are read down the column as X_{1i}, X_{2i}, X_{3i}, where X_{ji}, represents purchases of Industry 'i' from Industry 'j'. Industries also purchase the services of labour and capital to produce goods and services. The total value of the goods and services produced equals the total value of the material inputs, labour, capital, taxes and profit.

The goods and services produced by each industry are purchased directly by consumers and are also sold to other industries which use them as inputs to produce their own set of goods and services. In our

---

[2]For details of environmental input-output analysis see: http://www.Brass.cf.ac.uk/projects/02 measuring_sustainability_Rugby_Six_Nations_Input_Output_Analysis_ENVIO.html.

Table 2.1	An Input-Output Framework of a Hypothetical Three-Sector Economy				
		Outputs			
Sl. No.	Inputs	Agriculture (1)	Manufacturing (2)	Services (3)	Final Demand (4)	Total (5)
1.	Agriculture	X_{11}	X_{12}	X_{13}	Y_1	F_1
2.	Manufacturing	X_{21}	X_{22}	X_{23}	Y_1	F_2
3.	Services	X_{31}	X_{32}	X_{33}	Y_1	F_3
4.	Labour, capital and other value added	C_1	C_1	C_1	D	J
5.	Total	F_1	F_2	F_3	G	T

Source: Adapted from Lesser et al. 1997, p. 29.

hypothetical economy, for example, Industry 1 is Agriculture, Industry 2 is Manufacturing and Industry 3 is Services. Reading down column 1, we see that Industry 1 (Agriculture) purchases X_{11}, inputs from itself, X_{21}, from Industry 2, and X_{31} from Industry 3. Besides, it also purchases labour, capital and other value added inputs worth C_1. F_1, which is the sum of X_{11}, X_{21}, X_{31}, and C_1, equals the total value of production of Industry 1. Sales of Industry 1's output are read across each row of the matrix. It sells output to itself, to the other two industries, and directly to final consumers. Thus, the total sales of Industry 1 are X_{11} to itself, X_{12} to Industry 2, X_{13} to Industry 3, and Y_1 to the final consumers. The total value of the output sold is, by definition, identical to the total value of production. Thus, $\Sigma X_{11} + Y_1 = \Sigma X_{11} + C_1$. By adding up the values from all the three industries, as well as all final demands, we arrive at the total value of output produced in the entire economy, which in Table 2.1 equals T.

We could fit the environment and the policies that affect its quality into the input-output framework as the environment is used both as a source of inputs and as a sink for waste outputs. Environmental policies and laws such as the Water (Preservation and Control of Pollution) Act 1974, as amended in 1978 and 1988, also have economy-wide ripple effects. Using an input-output framework, we can trace the economic and environmental effects of use of environmental resources and environmental policies in an economy, and predict their ultimate impact on the demand for all goods and services produced, including environmental ones.

Table 2.2   An Input-Output Framework of a Three-Sector Economy Incorporating Environmental Goods and Services

Sl. No.	Inputs	Agriculture (1)	Manufacturing (2)	Services (3)	Final Demand (4)	Total (5)	Waste Discharge (6)
			Outputs				
1.	Agriculture	X_{11}	X_{12}	X_{13}	Y_1	F_1	ED_1
2.	Manufacturing	X_{21}	X_{22}	X_{23}	Y_1	F_2	ED_2
3.	Services	X_{31}	X_{32}	X_{33}	Y_1	F_3	ED_3
4.	Labour, capital and other value added inputs	C_1	C_1	C_1	D	J	EDc
5.	Total	F_1	F_2	F_3	G	T	ED
6.	Environmental inputs	EX_1	EX_2	EX_3	EXc	Ex	–

Source: Adapted from Lesser et al. 1997, p. 33.

To trace the impact of use of environmental inputs and disposal of wastes into the environment, we could augment the standard input-output table as shown in Table 2.1, by adding environment to it as a sector, as shown in Table 2.2 in which we added an additional column, Waste discharge, and an additional row, Environmental inputs. Environmental inputs include such natural resources as land, water, air and minerals. Wastes discharged into the environment are out-puts/externalities of all the industries/sectors.

In Table 2.2, EX_1, EX_2 and EX_3 represent the quantities of environmental inputs used to produce goods and services by each of the three industries comprising our hypothetical economy. ED_1, ED_2 and ED_3 represent the quantities of waste products discharged into the environment by each of the three industries. EXc represents the environmental inputs used by consumers such as water, land and fresh air. Similarly, the waste discharged by consumers into the environment are denoted by ED, which include things such as litter, wastewater and pollutants from automobiles. Ex represents the total of all environmental inputs, and EDc the total discharge of wasteproducts. The environmental inputs and outputs are expressed in physical terms. Such inputs and outputs could be valued using appropriate techniques as discussed in Chapter 5 of this book. The input-output framework can also be used to determine the environmental impacts of development policies on various groups/sections of society.

2.4 ENVIRONMENT AND ECONOMIC GROWTH

In simple words, economic growth implies increased per capita availability of goods and services. As we stated in Section 2.2, production of goods and services requires many inputs/resources from Mother Nature, or the biosphere such as land, water, air, solar radiation, trees, animals, minerals, fossil fuels, metals and so on. Besides, in the process of production of goods and services, many wastes—solid, liquid and gaseous—are produced. These wastes are dumped into the biosphere. Thus defined, sustained economic growth requires the use of increasing quantities of environmental goods and services, which is affected by the size of population, and a host of other factors including per capita income. Given the finite capacity of the Earth, it is not possible to sustain economic growth for ever while keeping the quality of the environment intact.

The nature of relation between the quality of environment and economic growth could be explained in terms of several paradigms including the Environmental Kuznets Curve (EKC) hypothesis. We will now briefly describe two of the important paradigms.

2.4.1 The Environmental Kuznets Curve (EKC) Hypothesis

The EKC hypothesis proposes that there is an inverted U-shape relation between quality of environment, as measured by some of the indicators of environmental degradation and per capita income (Figure 2.2). This means that environmental degradation is low initially when the per capita income is low, then it increases with growing per capita income,

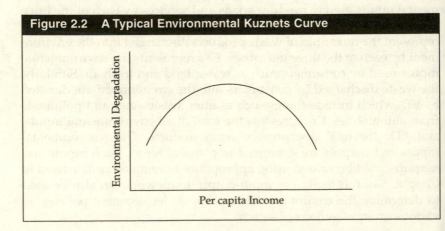

Figure 2.2   A Typical Environmental Kuznets Curve

Environmental Degradation

Per capita Income

and eventually it declines with further increase in per capita income. The EKC is named after Simon Kuznets (1955) who proposed a hypothesis that the relationship between a measure of inequality in the distribution of income and the level of income is depicted by an inverted U-shape curve. The EKC hypothesis has been interpreted by many scholars to imply that economic growth will eventually redress the adverse environmental impacts of early stages of economic growth and that continued growth will lead to further improvements in the quality of the environment. The hypothesis has been criticised by many scholars on both theoretical and empirical grounds (Stern 1998: 173–96). But overall, the general consensus is that it holds for some but not all environmental indicators and that economic growth alone cannot solve all environmental problems. The best fit is for air pollution and a few indicators of water pollution (Barbier, 1997: 357–58).

To sum up, economic growth and natural resource maintenance are related in the following two broad ways:

1. Up to some level of resource base utilisation there is likely to be no trade-off between development and the service of the resource base (complementary relationship).
2. Beyond this level, economic development is likely to involve reduction in one or more of the functions of natural environments—as inputs to economic production, a waste assimilation service and recreation/amenity provision. In this trade-off context, the multifunctionality of natural resources is a critical concept.

In the Indian context, we could say that the EKC hypothesis holds partially in the sense that air pollution and water pollution are both increasing with moderate increase in per capita income in conjunction with growing commercialisation of agriculture, urbanisation and industrialisation. We have not yet reached a stage of economic growth when per capita income is high enough for people to adopt eco-friendly livelihood strategies. Environmental degradation in India is due partly to the abject poverty and partly to wasteful use of natural resources, particularly common pool resources[3] (CPRs) by the rich. The poverty-driven degradation includes: (i) indoor air pollution due to use of biomass as fuel; (ii) water pollution; and (iii) land degradation; and the degradation induced by growing affluence includes: (i) pollution of rivers and lakes due to the discharge of toxic effluents from factories and plants; (ii) vehicular air pollution; and (iii) deforestation and loss of

---

[3]A CPR is defined as a resource which is used in common by an identifiable group of people, irrespective of who owns it.

biodiversity due to commercial logging, and illicit lopping and poaching. These problems are the result of economic expansion that fails to take account of the value of the environment and here the challenge is to build the recognition of environmental scarcity into decision-making processes. With or without development, rapid population growth may make it more difficult to address many environmental problems. There is need for active policy interventions and mass awareness among people to reduce environmental degradation in India.

Adverse environmental consequences of economic growth are not something new; they always were there but today's world is different. Many people in developed countries of the world, having reached high levels of material well-being, are beginning to ask questions like this one: What good is great material wealth if it comes at a great cost of large-scale disruptions of the ecosystem by which we are nourished? More fundamental perhaps is the fact that with contemporary economic, demographic and technological developments around the world, the associated environmental repercussions are becoming much more widespread and lethal. What were once localised environmental impacts, easily rectified, have now become widespread effects that may well turn out to be irreversible.

A view shared by a majority of people is that 'economic' just means flow of money in an economy. But when we talk about money, it is not talking immoral economics; it is not to reduce the importance of the environment. On the contrary, it can be argued that thinking the economic way can help introduce insights into a powerful array of economic tools that can be used to preserve/protect the environment. It is thus obvious that there is no denying the moral case for the environment. For example, we may argue that it is not right to drain the wetlands or burn forests. But the moral argument is only one argument for protecting the environment. We think that the economic argument is often more powerful and especially so when, as is frequently the case, the 'right thing' by nature contradicts other rights such as right to develop economically and the right to have food and shelter.

2.4.2 Ecological and Co-evolutionary Economic Paradigm

According to this paradigm, there is a constant and active interaction of the organism with its environment (Norgard 1984). Organisms (especially humans) do not merely receive a given environment but actively seek alternatives or change what they find. Organisms are not simply the results but are also the causes of their own environments. Economic growth can therefore be viewed as a process of adaptation to a changing environment, while itself being a source of environmental change. From this perspective there are three distinct sources of change: the breakdown of ecological equilibrium (that is, any combination of a method and a rate of resource use which the environment can sustain for long periods); the demands of technical consistency; and the development of new forms of need as the real costs of living are changed. But it is important to note that none of these alone can explain all change. Economic growth is then a process of moving through a succession of ecological niches. Niche occupancy is variable, and a niche may be destroyed by means external to a society's own development process.

Over time the process of economic growth results in an increasing level of environmental exploitation. The available stock of low entropy is diminished by resource extraction and waste generation. Economic production systems become more roundabout and complex as development proceeds. Work done by natural scientists on dissipative structures is relevant to the management of complex systems. Again, it appears that the evolution of such systems is not entirely stochastic, but a subtle mixture of both.

The *co-evolutionary perspective* has been designed to provide a link between ecological and economic analysis. Co-evolution refers to any on-going feedback process between two evolving systems. During co-evolution, energy surpluses are generated within systems, and these are then available for stimulating new interactions between systems. If the interactions prove favourable to society the development process continues. But co-evolutionary development feedback systems frequently shift from the ecosystem to the socio-system, that is, production systems become more roundabout and complex and environmental exploitation increases. Since learning, knowledge and evolution are inter-related, additional co-evolutionary development potential remains untapped. However, the magnitude and extent of this development potential, which will determine how tolerable survival will be, remain uncertain.

The physical limits to growth are manifestations of the increasing complexity of the productive system. Individual subsistence requirements depend on the technology and culture of contemporary society. As complexity in the social system increases so do subsistence requirements. Preferences change because of change in the context in which individuals form their preferences.

2.5 ENVIRONMENT AND DEVELOPMENT

The enormous growth in world economy, reflecting both population growth and rising affluence, is taking place on a finite planet. Consequently, the world is on an economic path that is environmentally unsustainable. This is evident from the following indicators (Singh 1999b):

- falling water tables;
- increasing pollution of air and water;
- increasing degradation of land;
- food shortages;
- shrinking/collapsing fisheries; and
- increasing incidence of natural calamities such as floods and droughts.

It is then no wonder that the quality of the natural environment has become a major focus of public concern, and as expected, people have responded in many ways. Environmental interest-groups and advocates have become vocal at every political level, especially in the countries having democratic systems of governance. Politicians have taken environmental issues into their agendas; some have sought to become environmental statespersons. Environmental laws have burgeoned, becoming a speciality in many law-schools. Thousands of environmental agencies have appeared in the public sector, from local conservation commissions to environmental agencies at the United Nations. At the scientific level, environmental problems have become a focus for chemists, biologists, engineers and many others. And within economics, a new focus of study has emerged: environmental economics and sustainable development. Now, we shall discuss the basic concepts of development, sustainability and sustainable development as they relate to the environment.

2.5.1 Basic Concept of Development

'Development' is a subjective and value-loaded concept and hence there cannot be a consensus regarding its meaning. The term is used differently in diverse contexts. But generally speaking, development could be conceptualised as a set or vector of desirable social objectives or a development index which does not decrease over time (Pearce and Turner 1990: 2–3). Some of the objectives that are usually included in the set are:

- increase in real per capita income (economic growth);
- improvement in distribution of income (equity);
- political and economic freedom; and
- equitable access to resources, education, health-care, employment opportunities and justice.

Whatever the geographic location, culture and historical stage of development of a society, there are at least three basic elements which are considered to constitute the 'true' meaning of rural development (Box 2.1).

The new economic view of development considers reduction or elimination of poverty, inequality and unemployment as an important index of development. Seers (1969) succinctly tackled the basic question of the meaning of development when he wrote:

Box 2.1   Basic Elements of Development

- **Basic necessities of life:** People have certain basic needs without which it would be impossible or very difficult for them to survive. The basic necessities include food, clothes, shelter, basic literacy, primary health care and security of life and property. When anyone or all of them are absent or in critically short supply, we may state that a condition of 'absolute underdevelopment' exists. Provision of the basic necessities of life to everybody is the primary responsibility of all economies, whether they are capitalist, socialist or mixed. In this sense, we may claim that economic growth (increased per capita availability of basic necessities) is a necessary condition for improvement of 'quality of life' of people.
- **Self-respect:** Every person and every nation seeks some sort of self-respect, dignity or honour. Absence or denial of self-respect indicates lack of development.
- **Freedom:** In this context freedom refers to political or ideological freedom, economic freedom and freedom from social servitude. As long as a society is bound by the servitude of men to nature, ignorance, other men, institutions and dogmatic beliefs, it cannot claim to have achieved the goal of 'development'. Servitude in any form reflects a state of underdevelopment.

Source: Singh 1999a: 212–22.

The questions to ask about a country's development are therefore: What has been happening to poverty? What has been happening to unemployment? What has been happening to inequality? If all three of these have declined from high levels, then, beyond doubt, this has been a period of development of the country concerned. If one or two of these central problems have been growing worse, especially if all three have, it would be strange to call the result 'development' even if per capita income doubled (Seers 1969).

While economic growth is an essential component of development, it is not the only one, as development is not a purely economic phenomenon. In an ultimate sense, it must encompass more than the material and financial sides of people's lives. Development is, in fact, a multidimensional phenomenon having economic (material), social, ecological, psychological, philosophical, ethical and spiritual dimensions. The development process involves the reorganisation and reorientation of both economic and social systems. In addition to improvements in the level and distribution of incomes and output, it involves radical changes in institutional, social and administrative structures. Finally, although development is usually defined in a national context, its widespread realisation may necessitate fundamental modifications of the international economic, social and political systems as well. The Vedic prayer, *'sarve sukhinaha bhavantu, sarve bhavantu niramayaha'*, that is, may everybody (in this universe) be happy and healthy, highlights the global and multidimensional nature of development.

At any level of economic development, utilisation of domestically available natural resources constitutes the bedrock of an economy. The quantity and quality of available natural resources along with the intensity and efficiency of their use determine, to a considerable extent, the level and pace of economic development of a nation. Poverty of natural resources does not, however, exclude a high level of economic development as is shown by the examples of Denmark, Switzerland, Israel, Hong Kong and Japan. These countries have compensated for the lack of natural resources by appropriate technologies, institutions and organisations and highly developed human resources. India is relatively well endowed with natural resources but has not been able to develop and utilise them fully and judiciously for the benefit of its people. Hence, the low level of agricultural and rural development in India.

In India, common pool resources play a very important role as a source of food, fuelwood, fodder and many other basic needs of rural people, particularly the poor. India has nearly 100 million ha of common pool land, about 30 million ha of common pool forests and the bulk of its water resources and fisheries are also CPRs. One of the major causes of rural poverty in India is the lack of access of the poor to privately-owned natural resources and natural CPRs. With the growing commercial exploitation of natural CPRs, the rural poor people find it difficult to meet their basic requirements. Depletion of CPRs of land, forests and water has increased the misery and drudgery of the rural poor, particularly women who now have to spend a lot of their energy and time in fetching water, fuelwood and fodder from far away places. Restoration and judicious management of natural CPRs is essential for improving the well-being of the rural poor as also for improving the quality of the environment (Singh 1994a: 16–20). It is a prerequisite for sustainable development. Before we discuss the concept and measures of sustainable development, it would be necessary for us to understand the concept of sustainability and its indicators.

2.5.2 Sustainability: Concept and Indicators

The concept of sustainability basically implies a characteristic of a system, a programme or a resource that will last for ever. The concept first came into prominence in 1980 in the context of the World Conservation Strategy of the International Union for the Conservation of Nature and Natural Resources (IUCN). Thereafter, the World Commission on Environment and Development (the Brundtland Commission) in its 1987 Report, *Our Common Future*, emphasised the key role of agricultural sustainability as the basis of sustainable development (WCED 1987). Currently, in the context of environment, there are two distinct concepts of sustainability in vogue.[4] One, the economist's worldview of sustainability is concerned about the long-term constancy of economic output, income or consumption. Two, the ecologist's and biologist's concept of sustainability relates to long-term preservation of the biosphere, that is, sustenance of human populations and biodiversity conservation in a given geographical area/region, endowed with limited natural resources (Bartelmus 1997: 326–27, FAO 1989: 65). The former, that is, the economic sustainability is production and consumption

---

[4]Besides the economic and environmental dimensions of sustainability, a third dimension of social sustainability has also come into vogue in the recent past. This is in recognition of the fact that man-made capital (economic factors) and natural capital (ecological/environmental factors) cannot explain substantial differences in the level of development achieved by the countries having similar endowments of natural, human and physical capital. The missing link is provided by social capital, that is, relations of trust, reciprocity, cooperation and common norms, rules and sanctions mutually agreed and followed in a community.

oriented and the latter, that is, the ecological sustainability has sustenance of people and biodiversity conservation as its focal points.

Economic sustainability implies the maintenance/constancy of produced capital and natural capital (natural resources and environment) used in the production of goods and services. Ecological sustainability can be defined in terms of compliance with the carrying capacity limit of natural systems. Carrying capacity is usually measured by the number of people a natural system/area/watershed can sustain indefinitely, or for a specified time period, at a particular standard of living. Obviously, carrying capacity depends on the level of desirable standard of living, type of production technologies in use, time horizon of analysis and external trade with other regions/countries. Variations in all these parameters/factors render the concept inapplicable except at the global level which is a utopia (Singh 1999b).

In the context of sustainability, two questions are important : (i) how long will our natural resources last, given current consumption patterns?; and (ii) how should we manage our natural resources and environment so that future generations have access to the same quality of life as present generations? The first question of resource longevity is really one of prediction and accounting; how do technology, taste, population and natural regeneration influence the stock of environmental goods that will be available from one year to the next? Thus, the ethical motives behind sustainability are derived from a concern for the future, and the fear that the current trends in production and consumption are threatening the well-being of future generations.

Questions about how long resources will last have long concerned planners and economists who have worried that the world is running out of agricultural land, fish and other important environmental goods. A variety of indices have been developed to measure the degree to which resources are being consumed sustainably. In their most basic form, these indices simply divide stocks by consumption rates. More elaborate indices take into account the fact that changes in taste or technology may reduce future demand while natural regeneration, especially for biological resources, may increase stocks to keep pace with increasing demand. Generally, most predictions about resource sustainability lack in accuracy. Clearly, a better understanding of trends in demand and technology are necessary before we can say with confidence how environmental quality and goods will fare in a consumption-based world.

The second question of sustainability, 'how should we manage our resources?' requires that we have some management target for the way in which resources are distributed across generations. The concept of

Pareto optimality, useful in the analysis of welfare within a generation, is not applicable when we do not know the tastes, preferences or technologies of future generations. Consumers, particularly the poor, tend to attach higher preference to consumption today than tomorrow. Should we ignore this tendency when thinking of sustainability or should we include society's time preference by discounting the value of future consumption when we decide how to manage for sustainability? What about expected improvements in technology? Could saving too much of our natural and environmental resources make future generations better off at the expense of present generations?

The 'we' in the second question of sustainability, implies that there is some sort of shared vision about the goals of sustainability. However, there is no universal consensus about a single indicator of sustainability. The most commonly used indicator of sustainability of any proposed resource use over time is the maximisation of net present value, as proposed by Neoclassical economists (Grafton et al. 2001: xxvi–xxix).

However, the question, whether sustainability and sustainable development ought to refer to the maintenance of *status quo*, economic growth, redistribution of wealth, the protection of capital stocks or the preservation of natural capital, is still debatable. The answer would vary from society to society and with the stage of economic development within a society. Related to this question are the notions of *weak sustainability* and *strong sustainability*. The former is defined as the maintenance of the value of aggregate stock of capital. It implies that we can substitute human-made capital for natural capital in production and consumption, such that economic growth can be associated with improvements in environmental quality. More rigorously, *weak sustainability* can be defined as follows:

$$K + H + SC + N \geq X^*$$

where K is man-made capital, H is human capital, SC is social capital, N is natural capital and X^* is some pre-determined threshold level of all the forms of capital expressed in monetary terms. This implies that under a policy of weak sustainable development, depletion of the stock of natural capital could be made good by investment in man-made capital. But it is important to note that the substitution of one form of capital for another form is possible only to a certain extent. This means that a certain minimum quantum of each form of capital is essential for development.

By contrast, *strong sustainability* posits that natural and human-made capital are complements and cannot be substituted for each other in either production or consumption. Consequently, economic growth that uses natural resources and generates wastes must increase environmental degradation. A rigorous definition of *strong sustainability is* as follows:

$$K \geq K^*; H \geq H^*; SC \geq SC^*; \text{ and } N \geq N^*$$

This definition implies that each type of capital stock be maintained in its own right above some minimum level. Herman E. Daly (1990) has specified the following three principles for attaining and maintaining strong sustainable development:

1. Renewable resources must be harvested at or below the growth rate for some pre-determined stock of the resource.
2. As non-renewable resources are depleted, renewable substitutes must be developed so as to maintain the flow of goods and services over time.
3. Pollution emissions should be limited to the assimilative capacity of the environment.

The scale of sustainability is also an important factor affecting the success of a policy of sustainability. The scale ranges from local to global and accordingly we could think of local sustainability and global sustainability. The scale determines the type of problems that can be addressed locally, nationally or globally. For example, the problem of global warming or depletion of ozone layer can be addressed effectively only at the global level and not at the local level. The distinction between local sustainability and global sustainability can be related to *weak sustainability* and *strong sustainability*. In most discussions of sustainability, *weak sustainability* and *strong sustainability* are thought of as competing paradigms. However, it is more useful to recognise that both these measures could be valid in different contexts concurrently. For global sustainability, it is essential to maintain stocks of some critical resource, say biodiversity, above a 'safe minimum standard' level for sustainable development, a condition for strong sustainability. But the local economy, while dependent on strong global sustainability, may seek weak local sustainability by depleting its renewable resources, say fisheries, or forest, to maintain its material well-being, without adversely affecting global sustainability.

For many years until recently, maximum sustainable yield (MSY) was considered a good indicator of sustainability. The logic underlying this notion was that for a given stock of renewable resources, there is a level of exploitation, corresponding to the growth of the stock, that is sustainable and does not involve depletion of the stock. Now MSY has been replaced by other approaches, although the term is still being used. It has become institutionalised in a more absolute role than intended by the biologists who originally mooted out this concept.

There is no universally acceptable indicator of sustainability. In view of this, some scholars attempted to explore whether we could have some indicators of loss of sustainability that are easier to compute and more widely acceptable than the indicators of sustainability. Now such indicators are available and widely used (Bartelmus 1997: 325, WRI 1992: xi). Some of those indicators are listed below:

- land degradation;
- depletion of groundwater resources;
- deforestation;
- depletion of conventional sources of energy;
- loss of biodiversity;
- global warming; and
- ozone layer depletion.

All these indicators of loss of sustainability necessitate radical changes in conventional economic planning and policy-making. Generally speaking, in response to such threats to sustainability, two new paradigms are emerging—'economics' and 'sustainable development'. The former focuses on internalisation of environmental costs into conventional micro and macroeconomics and the latter advocates compliance with social and environmental norms in the processes and activities necessary for economic growth. Economics can be seen as an attempt to accommodate externalities in the conventional economic analysis while at the same time incorporating in it the criteria of intergenerational equity defined as long-term maintenance of per capita consumption. This implies a shift from maximisation of Gross Domestic Product (GDP) towards more sustainable growth which can be defined as Environmentally-adjusted Net Domestic Product (ENDP).[5]

The ENDP is consistent with the environmental accounting system as well. For sustainable development, ENDP should be non-decreasing over time. It can be expressed as follows:

$$\text{ENDP} = \Sigma \, \text{EVAi} - \text{E Ch} = \text{ENDP} - \text{EC} = \text{C} + \text{CF} - \text{CC} - \text{EC} + \text{X} - \text{M}$$

This identity defines ENDP as the sum of environmentally adjusted value added of industries (Σ EVAi), minus the environmental costs generated by households (E Ch). The other terms in the identity are Net

Domestic Product (NDP), environmental depletion and degradation costs (EC), final consumption (C), capital formation (CF), fixed capital consumption (CC), export (X) and imports (M).

Several United Nations conferences held recently adopted a number of goals for the 21st century. One of the goals is: 'implementing national strategies for sustainable development by 2005 to ensure that the current loss of environmental resources is reversed globally and nationally by 2015' (World Bank 1998: 10).

Now, we shall discuss the concept of sustainable development and its measures.

2.5.3 Sustainable Development

Related to the concept of sustainability is the notion of sustainable development, which now has become a buzzword globally. The World Commission on Environment and Development (WCED 1987: 43) defined sustainable development as 'development that meets the needs of the present without compromising the ability of future generations to meet their own needs'. This definition emphasises the need for the present generation to safeguard the interest of future generations through maintaining the natural resources capital of this Planet Earth. Thus, the challenge before the present generation is to maintain over time the capacity of economic, environmental and social systems to ensure human well-being in perpetuity.

A working definition of sustainable development is as follows: it involves maximising the net benefits of economic development, subject to maintaining the quality, functions, and services of natural resources and the environment over time. Maintaining the functions, services and quality of the stock of natural resources over time implies, as far as is practicable, acceptance of the following rules:

- utilise renewable resources at rates less than or equal to the natural rate at which they can regenerate; and
- optimise the efficiency with which non-renewable resources are used, subject to substitutability between resources and technological progress.

Another operational definition of sustainable development that takes explicit account of economic, ecological and other non-economic standards and targets is given by Bartelmus (1997: 338) as 'a set of development programmes that meets the targets of human needs satisfaction without violating long-term natural resource capacities and standards of environmental quality and social equity'. In this definition, the emphasis is on the means, that is, programmes and activities that lead to sustainable development and not on the end result. We consider this definition more practicable and useful to policy makers and practitioners who are concerned with the 'what to do' aspect of sustainable development. But it is important in this context to distinguish between the means (programmes) and the end (sustainable development).

There is no universally acceptable measure of sustainable development that captures its multifaceted nature. Choice of measure depends upon the purpose of measurement and availability of the requisite data/information. Commonly used measures of development can be categorised into two classes, namely, measures of level of development and measures of distribution of benefits of development. Of all the measures of level, the Human Development Index (HDI) seems to be the most appropriate indicator of development. Rediscovering the truth that people must be at the centre of all development, the United Nations Development Programme (UNDP) decided to bring out a report on human dimensions of development every year from 1990. The *Human Development Report 1990* was the first such report. The first Human Development Report defined human development as the process of increasing people's options. It stressed that the most critical choices that people should have must include the options to lead a long and healthy life, to be knowledgeable and to find access to the assets, employment and income needed for a decent standard of living. Development thus defined cannot be adequately measured by income alone. The Report therefore proposed a new measure of development, the Human Development Index (UNDP 1990). The HDI is composed of four indicators: life expectancy at birth, adult literacy, combined gross enrolment rate for primary, secondary, and tertiary schools, and Gross Domestic Product (GDP) per capita expressed in Purchasing Power Parity (PPP) in US dollars (PPP US$). The subsequent Human Development Reports have made some refinements in the procedure of defining the component indicators and computing the HDI. The refinements include adjustment of income for differences in purchasing power and disparities in income distribution, combining adult literacy and mean years of schooling into an index of educational attainment, and computing disaggregated HDI for males and females and for different population groups. In addition, HDI has also been supplemented by a human freedom index and indicators of human security for selected countries for which data are available (Singh 1999a: 57–58). The *Human Development Report 2005* takes stock of human development, including progress towards the Millennium Development Goals (MDGs). Looking beyond statistics, it highlights the human costs of missed targets and broken promises. Extreme inequality between countries and within countries is identified as one of the main barriers to human development—and as a powerful brake on accelerated progress towards the MDGs (UNDP 2005).

The HDI is by far the most widely accepted indicator of human development (and lack of development or poverty). Although it does not explicitly take into account the quality of the environment, implicitly this is reflected in the life expectancy component of the HDI. It could better account for the quality of the environment if in the place of GDP per capita PPP US$, it includes environmentally adjusted GDP per capita. We need to qualify the HDI by adding a condition that the value of the index should be non-decreasing over time.

Table 2.3 presents the trend in HDI for selected countries of the world including India and China. As shown in the table, all the countries had registered an increase in the HDI during 1975–2003. India's HDI had increased from 0.412 in 1975 to 0.602 in 2003. India had ranked 135th in terms of HDI in 1993 among 174 countries of the world but its rank improved to 127th in 2003 among 177 nations of the world (UNDP 1996, 2005).

As we stated earlier in this section, improvement in distribution of income is an important element of development. Emphasising the importance of equity in the distribution of gains from development, US President Franklin D. Roosevelt in his Second Inaugural Address in 1937 had stated: 'The test of our progress is not whether we add more to the abundance of those who have much; it is whether we provide enough for those who have little' (UNDP 2005: 5).

Table 2.3 Trend in Human Development Index for Selected Countries of the World, 1975–2003

	Human Development Index						
Year	India	China	Pakistan	Mexico	Japan	Canada	USA
1975	0.412	0.525	0.363	0.689	0.857	0.869	0.867
1980	0.436	0.558	0.386	0.735	0.882	0.886	0.887
1985	0.476	0.594	0.419	0.755	0.895	0.909	0.901
1990	0.513	0.627	0.462	0.764	0.911	0.929	0.916
1995	0.546	0.683	0.492	0.782	0.925	0.934	0.929
2000	0.577	NA	NA	0.809	0.936	NA	0.938
2003	0.602	0.755	0.527	0.814	0.943	0.949	0.944

Source: UNDP (2005: 223–26).

The Lorenz Curve and the Gini Concentration Ratio, the two most popular measures of income distribution, are commonly used for measuring the distribution of benefits from development programmes. Percentage of rural population below poverty line, average life expectancy, literacy rate, infant mortality rare, crude birth rate, crude death rate and per capita real income are some other commonly used indicators of development or lack of it (Singh 1999a: 53–72).

Cases of unsustainable growth patterns and policies that promote such patterns abound in natural resources-dependent countries like India (WRI 1998: 139–40). A lot of data and information is available that underscores the alarming degree to which current patterns of production and consumption are impoverishing and destabilising the natural resources and environment and thereby undermining the prospects of future generations (WRI 1992: xi). Some of the indicators of the non-sustainability of current patterns of production, consumption and economic growth include: growing income inequality, high incidence of poverty and unemployment, degradation of natural resources and the environment and increasing social conflicts.

2.6 MAIN POINTS

The following are the main points made in this chapter:

- An economy may be conceptualised as a collection of economic, social, institutional, legal and technological arrangements through which individuals in society seek to increase their material and spiritual well-being. The two elementary functions of an economy are: consumption and production.
- Natural environment, including natural resources, performs two important functions in the process of economic growth, namely, providing inputs to production processes and assimilating the wastes generated in the process of production and consumption.
- Any economic system exists within and is encompassed by the natural environment. The economic system and the environment are interdependent and interact with each other. To be able to diagnose the root causes of environmental problems and identify possible remedies, it is important for a student of environmental economics to understand the nature of the interdependence and interaction between the two systems and their outcomes.
- For centuries, the environment provided us clean air to breath, clean water to drink and wash, food to eat and so many other

goods and services that we needed, with little or no complaint. Over the past century, however, the situation has undergone a sea-change. The environment can no longer satisfy our growing demands and after using and spending resources extravagantly for so long, man has realised that environment consists of scarce and exhaustible resources.

- Tracing the flow of environmental inputs into an economy is necessary to determine the ripple effects of different economic and environmental policies and assessing their social desirability. Input-Output (I/O) Table is the most commonly used method of tracing the flow of environmental as well as other inputs and outputs into an economic system.

- Sustained economic growth requires the use of increasing quantities of environmental goods and services, which is affected by the size of the population, and a host of other factors including per capita income. Given the finite capacity of Planet Earth, it is not possible to sustain economic growth for ever while keeping the quality of the environment intact.

- The nature of relation between the quality of environment and economic growth could be explained by several paradigms including the Environmental Kuznets Curve (EKC) hypothesis. According to the EKC hypothesis, there is an inverted U-shape relation between quality of environment degradation and per capita income. This means that environmental degradation is low initially when the per capita income is low, then it increases with increase in per capita income, and eventually it declines with further increase in per capita income. The hypothesis holds to some extent in the Indian context.

- The environmental degradation in India is due partly to abject poverty and partly to wasteful use of natural resources, particularly common pool resources. The world is on an economic path that is environmentally unsustainable. This is evident from the increasing degradation and pollution of air, water and land and growing food shortages in many parts of the world. All these indicators of loss of sustainability necessitate radical changes in conventional economic planning and policy-making. Generally speaking, in response to such threats to sustainability, a new paradigm of sustainable development has emerged.

- There is no universally acceptable definition and measure of sustainable development that captures its multifaceted nature. Choice of measure depends upon the purpose of measurement and availability of the requisite data/information. Of all the measures of level, a non-decreasing Human Development Index seems to be the most appropriate indicator of sustainable development.

2.7 DISCUSSION QUESTIONS

1. Think of any economic activity you are familiar with and then answer the following questions:

    (a) What inputs does the economic activity take from the environment?
    (b) Which of the environmental inputs used in the activity are priced and which are not?
    (c) Is the cost of environmental inputs/amenities, which are free, factored in by the economic agent in determining the cost of production of the good(s) produced or services rendered? Yes/No.
    (d) Does the use of environmental inputs/amenities by the economic agent cause any damage to the environment? Yes/No: If yes, describe the nature of damage, and identify the people who suffer from the damage or bear its costs.
    (e) Are there any outputs (byproducts/wastes) of the economic activity that are disposed by the economic agent in the 'environment'? If yes, list them and identify their effects on the environment.
    (f) If the effects of disposal of wastes are negative, for example, air pollution, or water pollution, identify the people who suffer from the pollution.

2. Based on the answers to the questions 1 (a) to (f), discuss why and how the environmental inputs/amenities used in an economic activity should be accounted for in determining the cost of output of the activity.
3. Discuss the relevance of the Kuznets Environmental Curves (KECs) in the Indian context with examples.
4. Why is sustainable development dependent on environmental sustainability?
5. Is it possible to sustain economic growth indefinitely? Yes/No and why or why not?
6. Write a critique of the Human Development Index as a measure of sustainable development.

3

Basic Concepts and Theories: Individual Choices

Like any other discipline, environmental economics also has its own basic concepts, theories and analytical tools, which constitute its foundation. Most of its concepts and theories are drawn from microeconomics, welfare economics and macroeconomics. To appreciate the utility and relevance of environmental economics and to use it in practical life, it is necessary for us to clearly define and understand its basic concepts and theories.

We, as individuals, interact with the environment every day in some way or the other. We inhale oxygen from the environment and release carbon dioxide into it, we eat food directly either obtained from the environment or produced using environmental resources, and we dispose wastes into the environment. In short, we depend on the environment for our survival, growth and development. Our attitude towards the environment and our decisions relating to consumption and provision of environmental goods and services affect the quality of the environment. Hence, it is necessary for us to understand the factors that affect individual behaviour and decisions as they relate to the environment to diagnose the root causes of environmental problems and identify appropriate remedial measures. Demand and supply are the two most important concepts in microeconomics useful in understanding and explaining the behaviour of individuals. The theory of consumer behaviour attempts to explain why an individual demands more or less of a commodity and demands something and not the other. The theory of firm, or the theory of production explains why a producer produces more, or less of a commodity and why and how much he offers to sell in the market.

In this chapter, we first present the main characteristics of environmental goods and services, and then briefly discuss the basic concepts and theories of microeconomics underlying the behaviour of individuals as consumers and producers/providers of environmental goods and services.

3.2 MAIN CHARACTERISTICS OF ENVIRONMENTAL GOODS

To be able to understand the behaviour of their consumers and producers, it is necessary for us to identify the distinguishing characteristics of environmental goods and services. This is done in the following paragraphs.

3.2.1 Pure Public/Collective Goods

Most natural resources and environmental amenities are public goods, ranging from environmental quality and watershed protection to ecological balance and biological diversity. Public goods range in geographical scope from local or regional to national or global. For example, biological diversity is an international public good since it is not possible (or desirable) to exclude other nations from benefiting from its conservation. Therefore, it is unreasonable to expect such a good to be provided in sufficient quantity by an individual country in a free market.

A public good is characterised by jointness in supply, in that to produce the good for one consumer it is necessary to produce it for all consumers. In many cases, no individuals can be excluded from the enjoyment of a public good (for example, national defence) whether they pay for it or not. Since nobody can or should be excluded from the benefits of a public good, consumers would not voluntarily pay for it and hence, no firm would find it profitable to produce such a good, as it is not possible for it to cover its production cost through the market. Thus, the market mechanism would fail to supply a public good, although the good has very high utility and would contribute to social welfare. Thus, a free market will lead to underproduction of public goods.

Environmental goods belong to the entire community and there are no individual rights of ownership. They are consumed simultaneously by a large number of people. Unlike the case of private goods, the consumption of a public good, or use of its services by one person does not diminish its quantity or availability to others. To sum up, there are three main characteristics of public goods: (*i*) non-excludability; (*ii*) non-rivalrous consumption; and (*iii*) indivisibility. Non-excludability means that nobody can be excluded from consuming a public good and no market can exist for it and therefore provision must be made by the government, financed by taxation, for example, defence, roads, street lights, light-houses, eradication of diseases, clean air and water and so on.

A rigorous definition of a pure public/collective good, or a pure non-collective/private good can be given as follows (Singh 1994a: 24):

$$X^1 = a_1 X$$
$$X^2 = a_2 X$$
$$\vdots$$
$$X^n = a_n X$$

where X is the total quantity of the good X and X^1, X^2,... X^n are the quantities of the good consumed by persons 1, 2...n, and a_1, a_2,... a_n are the proportions of the good consumed by persons 1, 2...n. For a pure public good, $a_1 = a_2 = ... = a_n = 1$, and for a pure private good $a_1 = a_2 = ... = a_n = 0$, except for one person (a_i), whose proportion equals 1, i.e., $a_i = 1$.

Examples of environmental goods and services that are pure public/collective goods include solar radiation, biodiversity conservation, ozone layer and air sheds.

3.2.2 Mixed Collective Goods

Some of the environmental goods and services are mixed collective goods. A mixed collective good is one which, like a pure collective good, is used in common by a large number of individuals and from whose use free riders cannot be easily excluded, and whose use, like that of a private good, is subtractable, that is, its use by one of the co-users reduces its quantity available to the other co-users to that extent. Thus, a mixed collective good has one characteristic each in common with pure collective goods and private, or non-collective goods. Examples of environmental goods and services that are mixed public/collective goods include wildlife, marine fish, recreational services of lakes and several watershed services.

3.2.3 Public Bads

Many environmental problems such as water and air pollution may be considered 'public bads' and their correction as a 'public good'. As we will see later in this section, 'public bads' are unintended side effects, or spill-over effects of genuine production, and/or consumption activities, or externalities, which are not factored in computing the cost of production by their producers, and hence they tend to overproduce the 'public bads'.

3.2.4 Externalities

As stated earlier, an externality is defined as an unintended and uncompensated side effect of a human activity. An externality has two important properties, namely, interdependence and lack of compensation. If every person, or activity were independent of any other person, or activity, then there would be no externalities. As all human beings and all activities are interdependent, externalities are present almost everywhere and in every activity: production, consumption, exchange, entertainment and so on. They occur if and when one person's consumption or production depends on the activities, or behaviour of someone else. Someone else could be a person, a group of persons, an organisation or government. The underlying idea is that externalities arise when costs are borne without benefits being received or benefits are received without bearing any costs. An externality could be positive or negative. If an activity of a person causes some unintended benefit to some other person or persons, but he cannot claim any compensation from the beneficiary, then the externality is positive. Conversely, when an activity of a person causes some unintended harm/loss to some other person or persons, and he does not compensate the person(s) affected, then the externality is negative.

An externality is revealed in terms of 'divergence between the private benefits and social benefits, or between private costs and the social costs of a project or an activity'. The concept of externality may be algebraically illustrated by the following production relationship:

Let

$$Y_A = F(X_1, X_2, \ldots, X_n) \tag{1}$$

and

$$X_n = F(Y_B) \tag{2}$$

where:

Y_A = Output of producer A;

Y_B = Output of producer B; and

$X_1, X_2, \ldots, X_n$ are inputs

The existence of an externality may be shown by the following term:

$$\partial Y_A / \partial X_n \neq 0 \tag{3}$$

In simple words, an externality exists when the effect of a marginal change in the output of producer B on the output of producer A is not zero. In a nutshell, externalities arise due to many economic, social, natural and technical reasons and are manifested in many ways.

Almost all natural resources development and environment management projects, including afforestation of degraded lands, soil and water conservation projects, and construction of dams and canal irrigation, have externalities. For example, afforestation of degraded land by an agency, say, a State Forest Department or an NGO, has positive externalities in the form of reduction in soil erosion, increase in groundwater recharge and improvement in microclimate. However, the agency concerned cannot claim any compensation from the beneficiaries. In this case, private benefit to the agency concerned is less than the social benefit to society at large, that is, there is a divergence between the private benefit and the social benefit from the afforestation project. On the other extreme, canal irrigation causes, though unintentionally waterlogging and soil salinity in the canal command area over a period of time. Farmers who suffer the loss of crop production due to these problems cannot claim any compensation from the canal authority. This is an example of a negative externality. Here the private cost to the canal authority is almost nil whereas the social cost to society (farmers in the command area and others) is very high, therefore there is a divergence between the private cost and the social cost. Methods of abatement of externalities are discussed in Chapter 4, Section 4.7 of this book.

3.2.5 Lack of Well-defined Property Rights[1]

In the context of environmental economics, the term, 'property rights' connotes 'a bundle of rights in the use and transfer of environmental resources', and importantly, the right and ability to exclude others from exercising those rights. Examples of these rights include the rights to consume, sell, exchange, lease, bequeath and preserve.

Property rights play an important role in determining the attitude and behaviour of people towards environment, its use and management. It has now been well established that the absence, or the lack of well-defined property rights in environmental resources has led to their overexploitation, degradation, depletion and pollution. Air pollution, pollution of rivers, lakes and other water-bodies, and degradation of common grazing lands are all examples of the problems engendered by the absence or the lack of well-defined property rights.

It may be argued that in an economy with well-defined and transferable property rights, individuals and firms have every incentive to use natural resources as efficiently as possible. Markets and prices emerge from collective economic behaviour, provided exclusion is possible, that is, any individual consuming a good can exclude other individuals from consuming the same good and property rights exist. Environmental pollution is a form of market failure, usually because of the overexploitation of resources held as common property/open access, or not owned at all. The market fails therefore when property rights are inadequately specified or are not controlled by those who can benefit personally by putting the resources to their most highly valued use.

Depending upon the nature and structure of rights in a resource or property, we may classify property into four broad categories: private or exclusive property; state property; common property; and non-exclusive or nobody's property or open access. Exclusive property and non-exclusive property are the two extremes on a continuum of property rights between which lie state property and common property, that is, property jointly owned by more than one individual entity (Figure 3.1). By property regime, we mean a system or set of conventions and rules that govern the use and management of a property. There is nothing inherent in any property or resource that dictates a regime. Any property can be managed as private, state, or common property or not be managed at all, like an open access resource.

[1]This section is largely based on Katar Singh (1997: 131–59).

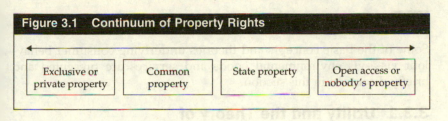

Figure 3.1   Continuum of Property Rights

Corresponding to these four types of property, there are four types of property regimes—private property regime, state property regime, common property regime, and open access regime. Each has its advantages and disadvantages.[2]

In the absence of well-defined property rights, a large proportion of environmental resources and amenities falls in the categories of: (*i*) common pool resources (CPRs), that is, resources that are held and used in common by an identifiable group of people; and (*ii*) open access, that is, resources that are accessible to anybody and everybody without any restriction.

CPRs in India include such diverse things as village panchayat grazing lands, privately-owned fallow lands, privately-owned cultivated lands lying vacant in between two crop seasons, community threshing floors, degraded revenue lands, degraded forest lands, protected and unclassed forests, village forests and woodlots, lands lying alongside railway tracks, roads, water reservoirs, tanks, ponds, lakes, rivers, streams, *nalas*, groundwater basins, marine fisheries, public (state) and community inland fisheries, wildlife and so on. The open access resources include space, airsheds, solar radiation, and high sea fisheries beyond the national Exclusive Economic Zones (EEZ).

In India, most of the environmental resources are *de facto* open access resources or CPRs and hence are prone to degradation, pollution and misappropriation. In a nutshell, most of the CPRs and all open access resources in India are subject to what Garrett Hardin (1968) called 'the Tragedy of the Commons' (Singh 1994a: 5–6 and 12–14). Establishment and effective enforcement of appropriate property rights, wherever possible, could improve the quality, productivity and sustainability of environmental resources and amenities.

[2]For details, see Singh (1994a: 58–70).

3.3 CONSUMPTION AND DEMAND

Some of the basic concepts and theories underlying consumer behaviour vis-à-vis environmental goods and services are presented and briefly discussed in this section.

3.3.1 Utility and the Theory of Consumer Behaviour

The concept of utility is drawn from microeconomics. It is most commonly used in environmental economics to explain and predict the behaviour of consumers of environmental goods and services. By utility, we mean the well-being or satisfaction associated with the consumption of an economic good or service. Utility theory forms the basis of many economic models of consumer behaviour. The utility theory, or the theory of consumer behaviour, could be succinctly stated as : A rational consumer always tries to maximise his utility from consumption of a basket of goods and services subject to his income/budget constraint. A consumer is said to be rational if he is capable of evaluating various alternatives open to him in terms of their relative utility and choosing the one that maximises his total utility.

It is customary for economists to represent the relationship between utility and the quantities of various goods consumed by a consumer in the form of utility function. In its general form, a utility function can be mathematically written as:

$$U = U(X_1, X_2, ..., X_n) \tag{4}$$

where U is the total utility derived by a consumer from consuming a mix of commodities, $X_1, X_2, ..., X_n$. Equation 4 states that an individual's utility is a function of a basket of goods and services that he consumes. If the utility is measurable, it is called cardinal utility and the unit of measurement is called *util*. Cardinal utility is useful in measuring the intensity of preferences and is used in mathematical models of consumer behaviour. However, now economists use another concept of utility called ordinal utility to rank choices or preferences rather than measuring their intensity in terms of cardinal utility.

3.3.2 The Law of Diminishing Marginal Utility

The relationship between utility and the quantity of a good consumed by an individual is governed by a law called the law of diminishing marginal utility. A formal statement of the law is as follows: as a consumer starts consuming a commodity, the utility derived from the consumption of the first few units is high, but eventually it starts declining as more and more units are consumed, and may even become negative (like indigestion or vomiting due to over-consumption). This happens because of biological limits to human consumption; one cannot go on eating more and more apples and derive the same utility from each successive unit. This law is useful in deriving demand schedules of commodities based on their marginal utilities. A demand schedule or curve shows the relationship between quantities of a commodity that would be purchased at various prices, and demand is the quantity of a good or a service demanded at a particular price at a particular time in a particular place. The relationship between demand and price is negative for normal goods and is known as the law of demand which states that as the price of a commodity increases, its quantity demanded decreases.[3] For marketed environmental assets and goods, the law of demand applies.

As we know, for many environmental goods and services there are no markets, and hence no price tags. In those cases the demand is not revealed, but that does not mean that people do not value those goods and services. In fact, some of the environmental goods and amenities like oxygen and water are essential for our survival and hence invaluable. For non-market goods, it is the 'Willingness-to-Pay' (WTP) that can be considered as their price. The willingness of an individual to pay indicates part of one's income that one is willing to give up in order to secure a good or service. WTP is often used to refer to the amount that a consumer would pay for a hypothetical good, service or change in some state of the environment. As shown by the shaded area in Figure 3.2, WTP for a particular quantity of a commodity is the total area lying to the left of a demand curve.

Alternatively, we may also use another term, 'Willingness-to-Accept' (WTA) as a surrogate for price of a non-market good. WTA is the compensation that an individual is willing to accept for giving up the consumption of a good. It is presumed that the compensation is sufficient to return the individual to his original state of economic well-being. In many cases, WTA is considered to be inferior to the WTP as a measure of economic value.

3.3.3 Consumer's Surplus

The concept of consumer's surplus is very useful in environmental economics for evaluating the environmental impacts of a particular project,

---

[3]For details, see Tewari and Singh (1996: 15–16).

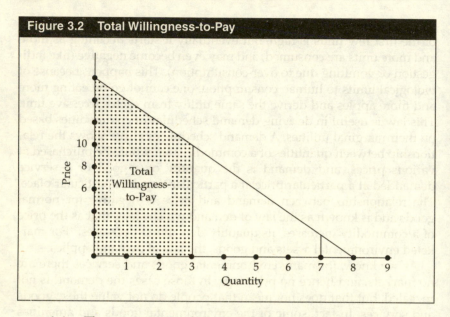

Figure 3.2   Total Willingness-to-Pay

or activity. The concept was first presented in Marshall's Principles in 1890. It was criticised by several contemporaries of Marshall including Walras, Pareto, Nicholson, Knight and Robbins (Hicks 1941). But now the concept is recognised as an important tool of economic analysis. According to Marshall's definition, consumer's surplus is 'the excess of the price which the consumer would be willing to pay rather than go without the thing, over that which he actually does pay'. In other words, it is the maximum amount which the consumer would be willing to pay minus the amount actually paid, provided if the marginal utility of money is constant.

Consumer's surplus can be estimated from the demand schedule/demand function of a commodity. As we know, a demand function shows the quantities of a commodity that would be bought at different prices. If the market price is p_0 and the corresponding market demand is q_0, then those consumers who would be willing to pay more than this market price gain from buying the commodity at the market price p_0 (Figure 3.3).

As shown by the shaded area in Figure 3.3, under certain assumptions, the total consumer's surplus is represented by the area lying to the left of the demand curve and above the line $p = p_0$. The consumer's surplus is hence given by Equation 5 (Tewari and Singh 1996: 317):

$$\int_0^{q_0} f(q)dq - p_0 q_0 \tag{5}$$

Figure 3.3 Computation of Consumer's Surplus

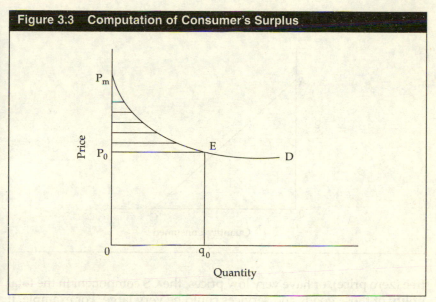

Source: Tewari and Singh (1996: 319).

where the demand function is p = f (q). Alternatively, the same area can be computed by integrating the price axis as well, the consumer's surplus is then given by:

$$\int_{P_0}^{P_m} g(p)dp \tag{6}$$

where the demand function is q = g (p) and P_m is the value of the price when q = 0, that is, the Y-intercept of the demand function. Equations (5) and (6) give the following:

$$\int_{P_0}^{q_0} f(q)dq - P_0 q_0 = \int_{P_0}^{P_m} g(p)dp \tag{7}$$

The concept of consumer's surplus has many uses in welfare economics and environmental economics. Assessment of welfare impacts of any intervention in an economic system is absolutely dependent upon the concepts of consumer's surplus and producer's surplus. The compensation criterion that is commonly used in welfare economics and environmental economics is made operational by the consumer's surplus concept. The concept is also useful in studying the effects of deviations from the optimum level of production or consumption.

The concept is particularly useful in evaluating environmental goods and services. Since many environmental goods and services are

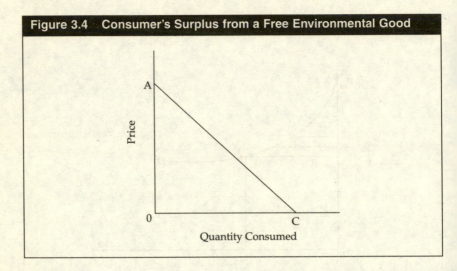

Figure 3.4   Consumer's Surplus from a Free Environmental Good

free (zero price), or have very low prices, the CS component in the total utility of those goods and services could be very large. For example, if an environmental good is free (zero price), the entire area as shown in Figure 3.4, AOC, would be consumer's surplus and would measure the benefit to the individual from consuming the good. If the free environmental goods and services were lost, the loss of welfare in terms of CS would indeed be large (Dixon et al. 1994: 25).

3.4   PRODUCTION AND SUPPLY

In the preceding section, we discussed the theory of consumer behaviour which attempts to explain why an individual demands more or less of a commodity and demands something and not the other. Besides consumers, an economy also consists of producers. Hence, we also need to look at the production and supply of goods and the costs of providing goods. In this section, we shall briefly explore the theory of producer behaviour, or the theory of firm, which seeks to explain why a producer produces and supplies a specific quantity of a product, no more or no less than that, and a certain mix of products.

3.4.1   Supply Analysis

Supply analysis can be graphically demonstrated using the same marginal framework as presented in Section 3.5 of this chapter. The cost of providing one more unit of a good is the marginal cost of that good. As usual, we graphically show the quantity of a good provided on the horizontal axis. The cost of providing one more unit of a good, that is, its marginal cost is drawn on the vertical axis. The relationship between quantity and marginal cost is called the supply function or the marginal cost function. Marginal cost may increase, remain constant, decrease, or even develop an irregular shape known as a backward bending supply curve. The total cost of supplying a good is found by determining the area under the supply curve between zero and the quantity supplied.

According to the theory of firm or production, a rational producer produces that quantity of a product, or that combination of products which will maximise his profit. In pursuit of this goal, a producer will supply a good as long as the price of the good in the market is greater than the marginal cost of production. If the supply curve is upward sloping, then the price will exceed the marginal cost for every unit but the last, and the producer will earn a benefit known as rent or producer's surplus. In Figure 3.5, we demonstrate an upward sloping supply function, price, and the associated producer's surplus that comes from supplying goods up to the point where marginal cost equals price. In the aggregate, there exists a market supply function that reflects the marginal costs of supplying goods when all producers are considered. Some producers may be able to produce goods at low marginal costs and others may produce at higher marginal costs. The former will earn more benefits and thus more rent or producer's surplus.

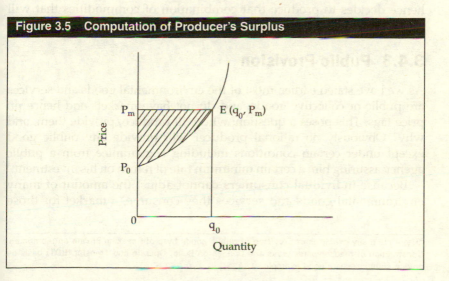

Figure 3.5   Computation of Producer's Surplus

3.4.2 Mother Nature as Producer

In the context of environmental goods such as natural resources of land, water, forests, minerals, and so on, Mother Nature is the producer, that is, she provides those goods at no cost. However, the provision of environmental goods is in certain form, in certain places, and in certain periods of time. Like the production of normal economic goods and services, production of environmental goods and services also involves creation of time, space and form utility, or value addition through use of inputs or resources. For example, most of the fresh rain water is provided only in the monsoon months of June through September in many parts of India, but the distribution of rainfall varies widely from region to region and from year to year. This makes it necessary to harvest the rain water, store it, and deliver it where and when it is needed. All these operations involve real costs and therefore we could say that the water that we get in our homes, factories, or farms is not free but is very much like any other economic commodity having its distinct cost of provision. Similarly, although air is a gift of Mother Nature, but keeping it clean involves costs embodied in air pollution control devices that have to be installed by air polluting firms to minimise the discharge of pollutants from their factories into the atmosphere. This means that the provision of many environmental goods and services involves real resource costs and hence is governed by the conventional theory of production, according to which a rational producer tries to maximise his private profit from production and hence decides to produce that combination of commodities that will yield him the maximum profit.

3.4.3 Public Provision

As we have stated earlier, most of the environmental goods and services are public or collective goods, and do not have markets and hence no price tags. This poses a question: who will produce/provide them, and why? Obviously no rational producer will provide any public good except under certain conditions including a guarantee from a public agency assuring him a certain minimum rate of return on his investment.[4]

Because individual consumers cannot adjust the amount of many environmental goods and services they consume, a market for those

---

[4]There are many examples of provision of public goods by profit seeking private entrepreneurs. Construction of roads/express ways and bridges on Build, Operate and Transfer (BOT) basis by private companies is a good example.

goods and services cannot exist, and when it exists, it does not provide the goods in sufficient quantities. This provides a rationale for many government enterprises established for providing public goods. For the government to provide a public good, it is necessary to know each individual's marginal rate of substitution between the public and private goods, which would determine the optimal level of the public good and (perhaps) each individual's share of the cost. However, because consumers may not reveal their true preferences for fear that they may be taxed on the basis of their willingness to pay, public goods are usually produced or contracted out by public agencies on the basis of collective decisions that are financed from general taxation. Thus, although consumers consume the same amount of the public good, they pay different 'prices', whereas in the case of the private good, consumers pay the same price but consume different quantities of the good.

There is need for a rationing system to control consumption of publicly provided private goods. Three possible rationing devices are: (a) uniform provision; (b) queuing; and (c) user charges. The problem with uniform provision is that everyone gets the same amount regardless of his needs and desires. The problem with queuing is that it requires payment in waiting time and rewards those whose opportunity cost is lowest. User charges are particularly suited to publicly provided goods because users could be charged the marginal cost of providing the good which is often substantial, though not sufficient, to cover the total cost of the public good. User charges result in both improved efficiency of use and partial cost recovery. This is particularly relevant to irrigation water pricing.

However, it must be noted that even when there is a marginal cost associated with each individual using a public good, if the transaction costs of running a price system (that is the cost of collecting user charges) are very high, it may be more efficient for the government to provide the good and finance it from general taxation.

Certain goods are referred to as 'publicly provided private goods' because of the large marginal cost associated with supplying additional individuals. The rationale for the public supply of such goods is their large set-up costs and the high (transaction) costs of running a market for these goods. When private goods are freely provided, they are over-consumed. Since the consumer does not pay for the good, he demands and uses it up to the point where the marginal benefit he receives from the good is zero, although the marginal cost to society is positive and often substantial. The social loss from over-consumption is the difference between the individual's willingness to pay and the marginal cost. A classic example of a publicly provided private good, or a mixed collective good, is irrigation water, whose over-consumption involves a double loss: a direct welfare loss from excessive consumption and an indirect loss from waterlogging resulting from over-consumption.

To the extent that some environmental goods are of a mixed collective type, the conventional theory of firm could be used to determine the optimum level of their production, given a fixed quantity of inputs or factors available for their production. Or alternatively, the least cost combination of inputs could be determined to produce a given quantity of the good. We illustrate the procedure of determining the optimum level of production of a good later in Section 3.5.

3.4.4 Producer's Surplus

Like the concept of consumer's surplus, the concept of producer's surplus is also a very important tool of economic analysis. It is defined as the amount of revenue received by a producer of a good in excess of what is necessary to induce him to provide a specified quantity of the good. It can be estimated from a supply function of a commodity. A supply function represents the quantities of a commodity that would be supplied at different prices. If the market price is P_0 and the corresponding market supply is q_0, then like the consumer's surplus, under certain assumptions the total gain to producers is represented by the area above the supply curve and below the price line $p = P_0$. This is known as producer's surplus. Graphically, it is the area to the left of the product supply curve and below the price line as shown by the shaded area in Figure 3.5. This area is evaluated as shown in Equation 8 (Tewari and Singh 1996: 318):

$$\text{Producer's Surplus (PS)} = p_m q_0 - \int_0^{q_0} f(q)\,dq \tag{8}$$

where $p = f(q)$ is the supply function. We can also compute the producer's surplus by integrating over the price axis as follows:

$$\text{Producer's Surplus (PS)} = \int_{P_0}^{P_m} g(p)\,dp \tag{9}$$

Producer's surplus and consumer's surplus together constitute an important indicator of social well-being. They are useful in evaluating social welfare implications of environmental policies and programmes.

3.5 MARGINAL ANALYSIS

The methodology of marginal analysis was introduced by neoclassical economists in the last quarter of the 19th century to study the relationships between small or incremental changes in demand and supply. Marginal analysis now is an important microeconomics tool most commonly used by the economist for determining the optimum level of consumption and production of a commodity. It draws upon the theory of consumer behaviour and the theory of production, or the theory of producer behaviour.[5] It uses the so-called marginal thinking in the sense that it looks at a change in an economic activity, or in a system in terms of incremental or marginal costs and incremental, or marginal revenue/benefits associated with the change, and then evaluates the net outcome, that is, whether the incremental costs are equal to, or less than, or greater than the incremental revenue/benefits. If the incremental costs are equal to, or less than the incremental revenue/benefits, the contemplated change is economically desirable, otherwise not.

3.5.1 Determining Optimum Level of Consumption

Now we shall show how to determine the optimum level of consumption using marginal analysis and indifference curves as shown in Panel A of Figure 3.6.

Suppose that your utility at a particular time was determined by your level of consumption of just two commodities, X_1 and X_2. A particular level of your utility could be attained from many different combinations of X_1 and X_2. We could write your utility function for a given level of utility U^0 as:

$$U^0 = f(X_1, X_2) \tag{10}$$

where U^0 is constant. Thus, we could think of an infinite number of combinations of X_1 and X_2 that will yield you the same level of utility U^0. The locus of all commodity combinations from which a consumer derives the same level of utility or satisfaction is known as indifference curve and a collection of all indifference curves corresponding to different levels of utility in commodity space is known as indifference map (Figure 3.6[Panel A]). Indifference curves are useful in

---

[5]For details of the theory of consumer behaviour and the theory of production, see any standard text book of microeconomics, including Tewari and Singh (1996).

determining optimum level of consumption as well as in tracing individual demand curves.

As you may recall, the theory of consumer behaviour states that a rational consumer tries to maximise his utility subject to his budget or income constraint. Suppose an individual has a given amount of money income, Y^0, which he wants to spend on the purchase of two commodities, X_1 and X_2. If the prices of X_1 and X_2 are P_1 and P_2 respectively, then the budget, or income constraint can be written as:

$$Y^0 = P_1 X_1 + P_2 X_2 \qquad (11)$$

The individual's objective is to maximise his utility subject to the budget constraint. The combination of X_1 and X_2 that would yield the maximum utility can be determined graphically as well as mathematically. We illustrate the procedure graphically in Figure 3.6.

Figure 3.6 (Panel A) shows different levels of utility of an individual in the form of his indifference map. What we need now to add to the figure is a budget line, which can be obtained by doing the following three operations: (*i*) divide the total income available, Y^0, to the individual for spending on the two commodities in question by the price of X_1, and plot the resultant figure on the horizontal axis (Point A); (*ii*) divide the total income by the price of X_2 and plot the resultant figure on the vertical axis (Point B in Panel B); and (*iii*) connect Points A and B to get the budget line, BA, as shown in Panel B of Figure 3.6. The budget line represents all possible combinations of X_1 and X_2 that can be bought with the given income. Now, we superimpose the budget line from Panel B

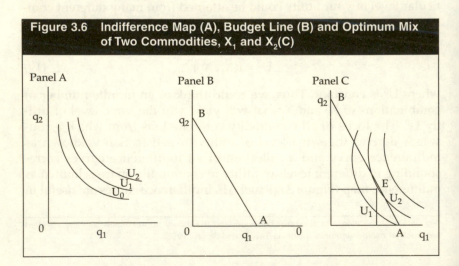

Figure 3.6   Indifference Map (A), Budget Line (B) and Optimum Mix of Two Commodities, X_1 and X_2(C)

of Figure 3.6 on the indifference map in Panel A and locate a point on one of the indifference curves which is tangent to the indifference curve. This is point E in Panel C of Figure 3.6. The utility represented by the indifference curve in question is the maximum possible given the income constraint. The X_1 and X_2 coordinates of this point are the optimum quantities of these two commodities respectively and represent their optimum combination that yields the highest possible utility from the given income. As we stated earlier, the optimum mix of two commodities could also be determined mathematically.[6]

The optimum combination of more than two commodities which can be purchased with a given amount of money is determined by what is known as the Law of Equi-marginal Utility. According to this law, total utility of an individual from the consumption of a basket of goods and services will be maximum when the last rupee spent on each of the commodities yields an equal amount of utility.[7]

3.5.2 Determining Optimum Level of Production

Figure 3.7 illustrates a simple application of the technique of marginal analysis for determining the optimum level of production of a commodity. Here we assume that there is only one output, Y, and only one variable input, X. The optimum level of output, Y*, or alternatively the optimum level of input use, X*, is obtained where the marginal revenue (MR) is equal to the marginal cost (MC). In the figure, this is the point where the MR curve intersects the MC curve.

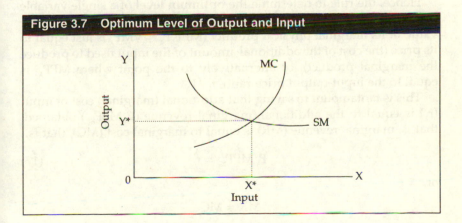

Figure 3.7   Optimum Level of Output and Input

Using elementary calculus, the condition for optimum level of output could also be derived as follows (Tewari and Singh 1996: 102–03):

Given the production function $Y = f(X_1, X_2)$, the market price of a product P_Y and input prices r_1 and r_2, a firm manager will maximise its profits (π):

$$\pi = \text{Total Revenue} - \text{Total Cost}$$

$$\pi = P_Y Y - (r_1 X_1 + r_2 X_2) \tag{12}$$

For maximising π with respect to the use of input X_1, we set the first order conditions as follows:

$$\frac{\partial \pi}{\partial X_1} = P_Y \frac{\partial Y}{\partial X_1} - r_1 = 0 \tag{13}$$

$$P_Y \frac{\partial Y}{\partial X_1} = r_1 \tag{14}$$

$$P_Y MPP_{X_1} = r_1 \quad \text{since } \frac{\partial Y}{\partial X_1} = MPP_{X_1} \tag{15}$$

$$VMP_{X_1} = r_1 \tag{16}$$

where VMP_{X_1}, the value of marginal product of input X_1, is equal to the product of MPP_{X_1} and P_Y.

Equation 15 can also be written as $MPP_{X_1} = r_1 / P_Y$.

Hence, the rule to determine the optimum level of a single variable input used in producing a single product is to use the input until the value of its marginal physical product (MPP P_Y = VMP) is just equal to its price (the cost of the additional amount of the input used to produce the marginal product), or alternatively to the point where MPP_{X_1} is equal to the input-output price ratio, r_1 / P_Y.

This is tantamount to saying that additional (marginal) cost of input (r_1) is equal to the additional/marginal revenue ($P_Y MPP_{X_1}$) obtained, that is, marginal revenue (MR) is equal to marginal cost (MC), that is,

$$P_Y MPP_{X_1} = r_1 \tag{17}$$

or

$$MR = MC$$

The MR = MC is a general optimality condition which is applied to make various production decisions.

In the context of environmental goods and services, the marginal analysis could be used to answer such questions as: whether the installation of a sewerage treatment plant by a municipality would be economically worthwhile, or socially desirable?; whether the treatment of effluents from a paper manufacturing plant would be socially desirable?; and so on. As the benefits from and the costs of most environmental goods and services are spread over a long period of time, the streams of benefits and costs are required to be converted into their present values by a process called discounting to make the two streams comparable.[8] The technique of marginal analysis in those cases is known as Cost Benefit Analysis (CBA), which is briefly discussed later in this chapter.

Here, we would like to point to a limitation of the technique of marginal analysis. As most environmental goods and services are indivisible and hence have to be provided in a certain fixed minimum quantity, the technique cannot be used to determine the most profitable level of provision of those environmental goods.[9]

3.6 MARKETS AND MARKET FAILURE

It is assumed that well functioning or perfectly competitive markets will normally provide efficient mechanisms for allocating resources among uses and overtime in such a way that society attains the maximum possible social welfare. The market functions efficiently when the following fundamental conditions are fulfilled:

- Property rights are clear and secure.
- All scare resources must enter active markets that price them according to supply and demand.
- There are no significant externalities.
- Competition prevails.
- Public goods are minor exceptions.
- Issues of myopia, uncertainty and irreversibility do not arise.

As these conditions are not met in the case of most environmental goods and services, the free market fails to allocate environmental resources and goods efficiently among uses and overtime. It wastes too

---

[8]See Glossary for the definition of discounting.
[9]For determining the optimum level of production of collective goods, or the optimum size of projects designed to provide collective goods, the technique of Cost Benefit Analysis is used. For details, see Chapter 4, Section 4.9 of this book.

many resources today and leaves too little for tomorrow. For instance, for historical and sociocultural reasons, property rights over irrigation systems and water resources in India are ill-defined and insecure. The State (government) makes a deliberate policy decision to provide farmers with irrigation water at a nominal price/fee. In this case, it is not only water, a scarce natural resource of positive opportunity cost which is left unpriced (or zero priced), it is also scarce capital invested in the irrigation systems that is left unpriced. The consequences are many and far-reaching.

- Water is inefficiently and wastefully used without any attempt to conserve it even when scarcity is obvious to the user.
- The state is unable to recover the capital and operation and maintenance costs with the result that watersheds remain unprotected and the irrigation systems are poorly maintained.
- Serious environmental problems such as sedimentation, soil salinisation and waterlogging result from watershed degradation and from over-irrigation, while other potentially irrigable areas receive inadequate water to grow dry season crops.
- Better-off farmers near the irrigation canals/water courses are indirectly subsidised by worse-off farmers who pay taxes but have little access to irrigation water.

3.7 GOVERNMENT INTERVENTION AND PUBLIC POLICY FAILURE

When the external effects are too widely spread, as is usually true in the case of environmental goods and services, the correction of the externality is a public good, in which case, the market does not function effectively and government intervention through public policy measures might be necessary if the externality is worth rectifying. Not all externalities are, however, worth correcting and few, if any, are worth eliminating entirely. The guiding principle should be that the gains in social welfare from correcting an externality should outweigh the costs of the intervention including any distortions in the rest of the economy that such an intervention might introduce.

There are numerous cases of misguided government intervention in a fairly well-functioning market or unsuccessful attempts to mitigate market failures that result in worse outcomes. For government intervention to be justified, it is necessary that the following conditions are met (Panayotou 1992: 339):

- The government intervention outperforms the market or improves its function.
- Benefits from such intervention exceed the costs of planning, implementation and enforcement as well as any indirect and unintended cost of distortions introduced to other sectors of economy by such interventions.

Government interventions are normally through taxation, regulations, private incentives, public projects, macroeconomic management and institutional reforms. But not all government interventions are socially desirable. This is because of the problem of policy failure. Policy failure is defined as a government intervention that distorts a well functioning market, exacerbates an existing market failure, or fails to establish the foundations for the market to function efficiently. Policy success, on the other hand, is the successful mitigation of market failures; success is defined in terms of improvement in the allocation of resources among sectors and over time.

Policy failures include both the failure to intervene when necessary and beneficial, and the failure to refrain from intervention when unnecessary and detrimental. Policy failures are not an exclusive domain of governments. Development assistance agencies may also exacerbate a policy failure.

Project-related policy failures relate to both private and public projects. Like most other countries, India also subsidises the use of irrigation water irrespective of degree of scarcity. Many farmers still think that water is a free and almost unlimited resource. When irrigation water is provided at a much lower price without much attempt to recover its real resource cost, reflecting the scarcity value or opportunity cost of water, it results in over-irrigation with consequent salinisation and waterlogging in some areas and inadequate availability of water in others. Thus, we have low water use efficiency on one hand and failure to achieve any degree of cost recovery on the other, and this combination eventually deprives the canal irrigation system of operation and maintenance funds.

3.8 MAIN POINTS

The following are the main points made in this chapter:

- Like any other discipline, environmental economics also has its own basic concepts, theories and analytical tools, which constitute its foundation. Most of its concepts and theories are drawn from microeconomics, welfare economics and macroeconomics.

- We, as consumers and producers, interact with the environment every day in some way or the other. Our attitude towards environment and our decisions relating to consumption and provision of environmental goods and services affect quality of environment. Hence, it is necessary for us to understand the factors that affect individual behaviour and decisions as they relate to the environment to diagnose the root causes of environmental problems and identify appropriate remedial measures.

- Two of the basic concepts of microeconomics, that is, demand and supply and the theories underlying them are useful in understanding and explaining individual behaviour vis-à-vis the environment. The theory of consumer behaviour attempts to explain why an individual demands more or less of a commodity and demand some thing or the other. The theory of firm, or the theory of production explains why a producer produces more or less of a commodity and why and how much he offers to sell in the market.

- Most natural resources and environmental amenities are public goods, ranging from environmental quality and watershed protection to ecological balance and biological diversity. They are characterised by the existence of externalities, lack of well-defined property rights, and non-existence of markets. The market fails when property rights are inadequately specified or are not controlled by those who can benefit personally by putting the resources to their most highly valued use.

- For valuation of those environmental goods for which there exists no markets, the techniques of Willingness-to-Pay (WTP) and Willingness-to-Accept (WTA) are used.

- Consumer's surplus and producer's surplus are two other important concepts of microeconomics useful in making environmental decisions. They together constitute an important indicator of social well-being. They are useful in evaluating social welfare implications of environmental policies and programmes.

- Marginal analysis is an important microeconomics tool most commonly used by the economist for determining the optimum level of consumption and production of a commodity. In the context of environmental goods and services, marginal analysis could be used to answer such questions as: whether the installation of a sewerage treatment plant by a municipality would be economically worthwhile or socially desirable; whether the treatment of effluents from a paper manufacturing plant would be socially desirable; and so on. However, it cannot be used to determine the most profitable level of provision of indivisible environmental goods.

- When the external effects, or externalities are too widely spread, as is usually true in the case of environmental goods and services, the correction of the externality is a public good, in which case, the market does not function effectively. In such cases, government intervention through public policy measures might be necessary if the externality is worth rectifying.

- Government interventions are normally through taxation, regulations, private incentives, public projects, macroeconomic management and institutional reforms. But not all government interventions are socially desirable. This is because of the problem of policy failure. Policy failure is defined as a government intervention that distorts a well-functioning market, exacerbates an existing market failure, or fails to establish the foundations for the market to function efficiently.

3.9 DISCUSSION QUESTIONS

1. Discuss and illustrate with examples the importance and limitations of the following theories in environment management:

   (a) the theory of consumer behaviour; (b) law of demand; and (c) the theory of the firm or the theory of supply.

2. Explain with examples why individually rational behaviour and attitude towards environment may lead to socially undesirable consequences.

3. In the context of the environment, how would you reconcile the conflict between individual interest and societal interest?

4. Discuss the relevance of the concepts of (a) consumer's surplus; and (b) producer's surplus in the context of environment management, particularly valuation of non-marketable environmental amenities.

5. What are the limitations of the conventional marginal analysis in the context of making decisions relating to the environment?

6. Discuss and illustrate with examples the relevance of property rights in environment management.

7. List all the cases of policy failures in environment management with which you are familiar and identify the remedial measures.

Basic Concepts and Theories: Collective Choices

4.1 INTRODUCTION

In Chapter 3, we presented the basic concepts and theories underlying individual behaviour and choices. Besides individuals—groups of individuals or society as a whole—are also involved in making choices that affect the environment. Therefore, it is equally important for us to understand why and how groups of individuals behave and interact with the environment the way they do. Accordingly, this chapter is devoted to the exposition of those concepts, theories and analytical tools that are most commonly used to explain and predict collective behaviour and choices of individuals vis-à-vis the environment. The main object of the chapter is to enhance the ability of the reader to understand and apply those concepts and theories in the real world context.

4.2 SOCIAL BENEFITS, COSTS AND WELFARE FUNCTION

In this section, we discuss some of the important concepts commonly used in the context of collective choices or decisions pertaining to the environment.

4.2.1 Social Benefits

This refers to the total increase in social welfare from an economic action. In effect, it is the sum of two benefits: (a) the benefit to the agent performing the action (producer's surplus, profit made); and (b) the benefit accruing to the society as a result of action (consumer's surplus). For example, afforestation of wasteland by a farmer yields benefits to the farmer (private benefit) but it also benefits society in the form of recharge of groundwater, reduction of soil erosion and hence reduced siltation of river beds and dams, and better microclimate (external benefits or positive externality).

4.2.2 Social Cost

This comprises the total cost to society of an economic activity. It is the sum of two costs, that is, private costs borne by the agent performing the action, and the external costs or cost to society or the value of externalities. For example, if a paper manufacturing firm is polluting a river, treating environment as a free resource, then it is imposing a cost on society as a whole (external cost or an externality), besides incurring the (internal/private) costs on paper manufacturing.

4.2.3 Social Welfare Function

Neoclassical welfare economics, as developed by Pigou (1920) and Hicks (1939) and others, is concerned with the total welfare of society and it evaluates alternative projects or actions on the basis of changes in social welfare. The following assumptions underlie the neoclassical welfare economics:

- Social welfare is the sum of individual welfare.
- Individual welfare can be measured in terms of prices paid for goods and services.
- Individuals maximise their welfare by choosing that combination of goods and services which yields the largest sum of total utility, given their income constraints.

The concept of social welfare is drawn from welfare economics. It is very useful in environmental economics as a measure of aggregate utility of all individuals in society or social utility of environmental goods and services. Like a production function, Social Welfare Function (SWF) states the relationship between social utility and the factors that affect it. A variety of SWFs have been proposed by economists such as

John Rawl, Nash, Coomb, Bergson, Samuelson and others. Of these, the Bergson-Samuelson social welfare function is the most practical and hence generally used for economic analysis. The Bergson-Samuelson SWF represents the utility levels of all individuals in society. For a two-individual society, this can be written as follows (Tewari and Singh 1996: 230):

$$SWF = W[U^A(X^A, Y^A, \ldots) \, U^B(X^B, Y^B, \ldots)] \qquad (1)$$

where

$\qquad U^A(X^A, Y^A, \ldots)$ is the utility of individual A

$\qquad U^B(X^B, Y^B, \ldots)$ is the utility of Individual B

X, and Y are the two commodities and A *and* B are two individuals.

The above welfare function is directly a function of an individual's utility levels and indirectly a function of consumption baskets of individuals. That is why it is also known as *Individualistic Welfare Function*. The advantage of such a function is that if each individual's utility depends only upon his or her own consumption, then standard economic efficiency rules apply and Pareto efficient allocations and welfare maximisation are intimately related.

The X and Y commodities can be replaced by an income *m* for the sake of a concise and better approximation of an individual's consumption basket, the above function can then be written as:

$$SWF = W[U^A(m^A), U^B(m^B)] \qquad (2)$$

and can be graphically represented by a map of *iso-welfare* or *social community indifference* curves as shown in Figure 4.1. The three important characteristics of iso-welfare curves are discussed below.

First, note the distinction between the society's and the individual's indifference maps: the former is with respect to the utilities of all individuals and the latter is with respect to the commodities in the consumer's basket. As shown in the figure, the utility of Individual A increases while that of Individual B remains constant; resulting in an increase of social welfare from level W_0 to W_1. Hence, a movement from point A to point B is a *Pareto-improvement* in the language of welfare economics. Here, someone's standard is improved without decreasing another person's standard; and this very concept is known as the *Pareto principle*, which is briefly discussed in the next section. Second, given the level of social welfare, say W_0, if the standard of Individual B is improved by moving from A to C, then the standard of Individual A would automatically be worsened. That means the social indifference curves or welfare contours have a negative slope. Third, a trade-off between utilities of Individuals A and B is not possible, given the constant welfare level, say W_0, as society moves along the social welfare contour; this ensures the convexity-to-origin property of social indifference curves.

In passing, it should be noted that the Bergsonian-Samuelson SWF is based upon some basic assumptions, which are as follows: (*i*) the distribution of income is assumed to be given; (*ii*) all individuals are assumed to have identical marginal utility of income; (*iii*) all persons count equally in terms of welfare; and (*iv*) individual utility functions, U^A and U^B, are independent of each other, that is, absence of jealously or altruism.

4.3 PARETO PRINCIPLE OR PARETIAN CRITERION

Pareto principle is one of the several criteria drawn from welfare economics that can be used for comparing welfare effects of alternative states of environmental quality. As per the Paretian criterion, if it is possible to improve the well-being of at least one person in moving from state one to state two without decreasing the well-being of anybody else, then state two is ranked superior to state one by society. In other words, it is desirable to move from state one to state two and this movement is considered as *Pareto improvement*. For example, recall from Figure 4.1 that the movement from point A to B is Pareto improvement. However, when it is not possible to make any Pareto improvement in the existing state, it

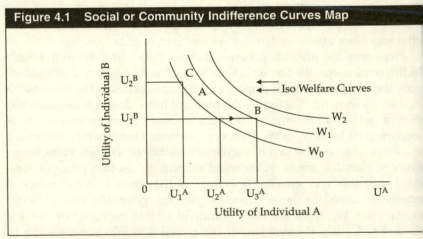

Figure 4.1   Social or Community Indifference Curves Map

Source: Tewari and Singh (1996: 231).

is said that society has attained a *Pareto optimum*. In the Pareto-optimal state of the economy it is not possible to improve the well-being of at least one person without lowering the well-being of someone else.

There are two major weaknesses of the Paretian criterion. First, it cannot be used to choose among alternative income distributions; rather, we can have different Pareto-optimal states of the economy for different levels of income distribution. Thus, it favours a status quo. Second, the Paretian criterion deals only with unambiguous welfare changes. That is, it does not help us in situations where a policy/measure benefits some and harms others. For example, a proposal that taxes be levied on the rich to help the poor cannot be judged on the basis of this criterion. Indeed, any change that benefits some people and harms others falls outside the purview of the Pareto principle. Hence, this evades the question of income distribution. As we know, most policy changes would result in a reduction of someone's utility unless compensation is provided. In view of this, all states of the economy are not comparable using the Paretian criterion. The second criterion known as compensation principle is meant to overcome this limitation.

4.4 COMPENSATION PRINCIPLE OR CRITERION

The compensation principle is also known as the *Kaldor-Hicks compensation criterion* in recognition of their work done during the late 1930s. This principle states that state two is socially preferable to state one if those who gain from such a move can compensate those who lose, that is, if the gainers can bribe the losers to accept state two and yet be better-off in state two. For example, if a proposed change benefits Dave and harms Rita, and if Dave is willing to pay up to Rs 100 to see the change occur while Rita is willing to pay only Rs 50 to avoid the change, the change according to the Kaldor-Hicks criterion is an improvement, even though no money is paid by Dave to Rita. We can explain this criterion using Figure 4.2 in which I is a utility possibility frontier. Suppose the economy is at point Q_1. Then a movement from Q_1 to Q_2, Q_3 or Q_4 or to any point in between Q_2 and Q_4 shows Pareto-improvement since no one is made worse-off and someone is made better-off. However, a movement from Q_1 to Q_5 is not Pareto-improvement as Individual A becomes worse-off after the movement. According to the Paretian criterion, this move is not recommended, but the compensation criterion says that if Individual B can compensate Individual A for the loss, such a move is desirable. That is, Kaldor and Hicks argued that once the economy has reached Q_5, then redistribution of wealth can be carried

Figure 4.2 Kaldor-Hicks Compensation Criterion

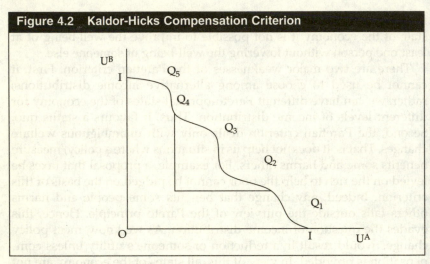

Source: Tewari and Singh (1996: 241).

out so as to move the economy to point Q_3 at which everybody would finally be better-off.

The compensation principle, like the Pareto principle, also suffers from many limitations. For example, it is possible to conceive a situation where gainers can compensate losers in moving from state one to state two and the same is true when moving from state two to state one. Here, the problem is to determine as to which state of the economy is better; this is called *Scitovsky's Reversal Paradox*. The solution is simply obtained by adding one more condition to the Kaldor-Hicks test—and this condition is known as *Scitovsky's Reversal Test*. The reversal test states that if gainers cannot compensate the losers in moving in the reverse direction, that is, from state two to state one, then state two is a preferred position. We can use this test in the case of moving from Q_1 to Q_5. Note that in moving in the reverse direction from Q_5 to Q_1, the gainers cannot compensate the losers and thus Scitovsky's reversal test is passed. The major problem with the compensation principle is that it can, at times, give intransitive rankings of alternative states and as a result the test fails (Just et al. 1982: 38–40).

4.5 HARDIN'S THESIS OF 'THE TRAGEDY OF THE COMMONS'

In his famous 1968 article 'The Tragedy of the Commons', biologist Garret Hardin proposed a hypothesis that seeks to explain why CPRs, or better put, open access resources, are over-exploited, degraded and depleted (Hardin 1968). The logic of the tragedy is purely economic and can be stated as: unregulated access to a CPR creates a decision-making environment in which incremental private benefits to an individual from the increased use of the resource markedly exceed the incremental private costs associated with the increased use. Under these circumstances, each rational consumer or user of a CPR is motivated to consume or use more and more of the resource till the resource is completely destroyed or degraded as a result of collective and uncoordinated use by all the individuals in the community. Thus, individual rationality leads to collective irrationality. The calculus of incremental or marginal private benefits markedly exceeding the incremental private costs follows from the fact that, in the case of a CPR, whereas an individual can appropriate all the benefits resulting from his increased use of the resource, he bears only a small fraction of the incremental costs associated with his increased use; the incremental costs are shared by all the members of the community (Singh 1994a: 12–14). This means that there exists an externality in the use of the CPR in question as evident from the difference between the incremental private cost and the incremental social cost; the former being less than the latter. Thus, the common pool problem is basically one of the existence of externality—a divergence between private cost and social cost of exploitation which eventually leads to either depletion or overcrowding or congestion (Friedman 1971: 855). The problem is a manifestation of either the absence of exclusive private property rights or the breakdown of the structure of property rights (Randall 1975: 734).

Hardin's thesis of 'The Tragedy of the Commons' has since become the dominant paradigm of the exploitation of CPRs resulting from their common ownership. It has formed the basis of numerous policies seeking to privatise or nationalise natural CPRs in many developed and developing countries of the world. Like any other thesis, it also has had its share of criticism and approbation. It is now widely agreed that co-owners of a CPR usually fail to cooperate in using the CPR optimally under the following three conditions:

1. When the perceived private costs of cooperation exceed the perceived private benefits of cooperating.
2. When individuals feel that their own contribution to the collective goal is minuscule and would not be missed if withheld because others will continue contributing, enabling them to easily free ride on the contributions of others.

3. When individuals have no assurance or certainty that other members of the group will make their contributions (or cooperate) and that their lone contribution to the effort would be sufficient to produce the desired outcome.

Furthermore, Hardin makes an implicit assumption that 'commons' are open access. This is not true even in the example of the medieval English grazing pastures that he used to illustrate the logic of his thesis. Even today, the term is generally used to mean common property. This assumption, or rather misnomer, has also attracted much criticism of his thesis.

'The Tragedy of the Commons' in India is evident from the continued and unabated degradation of the CPRs. For example, CPRs of land are degraded due to water erosion, wind erosion, salinity, alkalinity, waterlogging, careless dumping of mine-wastes, removal of topsoil, etc. Community pastures are rendered completely denuded of any vegetative cover due to overgrazing, and community forests due to indiscriminate lopping and illicit felling. Rivers and lakes are polluted by discharge of toxic effluents and sewerage and when dry, their banks and beds are encroached by people.

4.6 PRISONERS' DILEMMA (PD) GAME

The problem of non-cooperation of co-users of a CPR could also be illustrated through the PD game. The classic PD game is analogous to many situations that prevail in the use of environmental resources, particularly CPRs such as communal grazing lands, common pool surface and groundwater resources, marine fisheries and community forests (Singh 1994a: 37–42). The two-person game can easily be extended to a multi-person game played repeatedly if, for Prisoner I, we substitute any CPR user or group of CPR users and similarly, for Prisoner II, all the other CPR users. Such extensions are more plausible than the original two-person game because in real world situations many persons use or share a CPR and face the PD situation repeatedly, that is, day after day, or year after year. In India, CPR users are non-formally divided into caste-based or ethnic groups. These groups pursue conflicting interests and hence they are comparable to players of a game whose outcome is controlled jointly by the players.

The relevance of the classic PD model can be illustrated with reference to the problem of overgrazing of the common village pasture lands. Envision a village in western India with: (1) a population of

50 herdsmen (herders) divided in two caste groups of 25 each where each of them has two animals (cows, buffaloes, goats, sheep, etc.); (2) 10 ha of common grazing land that can sustain at a reasonably good level of productivity, about 50 animals per season; and (3) no formal or informal authority or leader or organisation acceptable to both the groups for arbitration on the matters of grazing. In the absence of any authority or organisation, herd owners do not negotiate towards individual grazing that would lead to socially optimum level of grazing and do not have any grazing norms, rules or regulations—a no-holds-barred situation. Following the structure of the classic PD game, we assume one of the groups is represented by Herder I and the other group is represented by Herder II. There are two strategies open to each herder group: (1) to cooperate with the other group by sending only one animal per member for grazing; and (2) do not cooperate and send any number of animals (more than one) per member for grazing. We show the expected pay-offs of these two strategies in Table 4.1. The first figure in each of the four boxes represents the expected pay-off to Herder I and the second figure to Herder II.

Suppose if, prior to each grazing season, the community of herders is indifferent to the distribution of potential benefits from grazing between Herder I and Herder II, then the pay offs are highest (250) when both the herder groups cooperate, and lowest (150) when they do not cooperate. Now under the given structure of the game, or situation, Herder I asks this question to himself: Given Herder II's decision to cooperate, what is my best strategy? The obvious answer is: I do better by not cooperating because the expected pay-off of Rs 160 from non-cooperation is higher than the expected pay-off of Rs 125 from cooperation. Alternatively, if Herder II decides to not cooperate; still Herder I does better by not cooperating as the expected pay-off of

Table 4.1	Expected Pay-offs from Cooperation and Non-cooperation in Grazing a Common Village Pasture		
			(Rs per season)
		Herder II	
Herder I		*Cooperate*	*Not Cooperate*
	Cooperate	125, 125	40, 160
	Not cooperate	160, 40	75, 75

Rs 75 from non-cooperation is higher than the expected pay-off of Rs 40 from cooperation. Using the same logic, a similar conclusion (non-cooperation) is arrived at by Herder II. Thus, each of the Herder groups finds that it is better off by 'not cooperating' whatever the decision of the other group. So, both the groups home in on (75, 75) which is the second best alternative for them. This means that 'non-cooperation' is the dominant strategy in this game.

The PD game has fascinated many scholars and its analogy used to understand and explain so many complex problems related to the use of CPRs. The outcome of the game is a paradox in that it shows that individually rational strategies lead to collectively irrational strategies and thus poses a challenge to many fundamental concepts in ethics, political philosophy and social sciences (Campbell and Sowden 1985: 3). However, the paradoxical outcome of the PD game is very much contingent, like in other games, on the structure and rules of the game. Structures of many real world situations where CPR problems exist are not similar to the structure of the PD game in that the resource users may be free to communicate with one another and enter into mutually binding contracts, that is, both the structure and the rules of the game can be changed. When this is so, the dilemma or the 'Tragedy of the Commons' can be resolved by cooperative action of the group members. Also, when a situation is repeated again and again, rational resource users could learn from the past sub-optimal decisions and select strategies that yield collectively rational or optimum outcome (Braybrooke 1985; Hardin 1982).

Theoretical, experimental and empirical studies of multi-person repeated games suggest that cooperation can emerge under a wide variety of circumstances and that issues of strategy, ethics and expectations play bigger roles in multi-person games than in two-person games (Magrath 1986: 33). Axelrod (1984) advances several propositions dealing with the emergence of cooperation in iterated prisoners' dilemmas. The most important among them is that the threat of and the willingness and ability to retaliate against defections is vital to the emergence of cooperation. In the hawk-dove game type situations, the 'first come first served' or 'weaker yields to stronger' convention could avoid conflict and produce cooperative behaviour (Hirshleifer 1987: 225–26).

To sum up, we can say that the classic PD game is a good theoretical construct that can be used to explain why people do not cooperate and do not act collectively in using and managing environmental goods and amenities. It also points to the conditions under which people might cooperate and act collectively.

4.7 OLSON'S THEORY OF COLLECTIVE ACTION

Mancur Olson Jr. (1971) has challenged a generally held view that groups of individuals having common interests usually work together to achieve them. He argues that: 'Unless the number of individuals in a group is quite small, or unless there is coercion or some other special device to make individuals act in their common interest, rational, self-interested individuals will not act to achieve their common or group interests' (1971: 2).

Olson considers this situation analogous to one that obtains in a perfectly competitive market situation where profit maximising firms act contrary to their interests as a group by expanding their output till the market price falls and equals their marginal cost and industry's excess profit is eliminated. This happens despite the fact that every firm tries to maximise its profit and has a common interest in a higher price for the industry's product. The logic underlying this phenomenon also explains the behaviour of people towards environmental goods and sevices, particularly CPRs. In the absence of well-defined private property rights and with no ban on the entry of new firms/users, a CPR is over-exploited in the sense that each firm (CPR user) in the industry earns no more than the going rate of return on its investment, and all firms (CPR users) are worse off. This does not, however, mean that each co-user of a CPR is acting against its self-interest. In fact, each of the co-users behaves rationally because if it were to restrict his own output/use of the CPR, anticipating a fall in market price resulting from the increase in industry output, it would lose more than ever, for his price would fall quite as much in any case and he would, in addition, have a smaller output.

Benefits from most CPRs are mixed collective good, much like such activities of a nation state as defence, police protection, etc., which, once produced, are available to all the members of the organisation. Other types of organisations also provide mixed collective goods to their members. For example, labour unions bargain for higher wages and better conditions for their members which, once granted, become a mixed collective good; all workers, members as well as non-members, engaged in similar jobs enjoy the benefits irrespective of whether they have or have not contributed to the collective bargaining. But, given a certain finite wage fund, use of the good (higher wages) is subtractible. Just as a state cannot support itself by voluntary contributions, neither can other large organisations support themselves entirely without coercing their members to pay for the mixed collective goods that they provide for them or without some attraction or incentive that will motivate the members to contribute to the establishment and survival of the organisation. The individual member of a large group, like his counterpart taxpayer in the state or a firm in a perfectly competitive market, is too small an entity to have any significant impact on his organisation by contributing or not contributing to its maintenance, but he can share its benefits even if he has not contributed anything in bringing them about. In other words, free-riding (on the back of those who contribute) is possible in all large organisations.

In general, the larger the group, the less noticeable the actions of its individual members, the higher the transaction costs of bringing them together, higher is the tendency among its members to free ride. This is why large groups frequently fail to provide collective goods for their members. Using two simple tools of economic analysis: graphs and calculus, Olson has shown that certain small groups can provide themselves with collective goods without relying on coercion or any positive inducements apart from the collective good itself. This is because in some small groups each of the members, or at least some of them, will find that his personal gain, from having the collective good, exceeds the total cost of providing some amount of that collective good (1971: 33–34).

This is the essence of Olson's theory of collective choice and action. The theory is useful in explaining why large groups of users of environmental resources do not cooperate with one another to secure socially optimum levels of output from the resources.

More generally, the level of private provision of a collective good that individuals will find profitable can be determined through a simple maximisation exercise. Following Olson (1971: Section D), let the level of output of a collective good be given by T; the size of the group by Sg; cost of providing the good by $c = f(T)$; value or benefit to the group from the collective good by $Vg = Sg.T$; benefit to the ith individual member of the group by Vi; and fraction of the group benefit gained by the ith individual by $F_i = Vi/Vg$.

The net benefit to the ith individual A_i is simply benefit to the individual less cost C, that is,

$$A_i = F_i S_g T - C = Vi - CS_g$$

To maximize A_i, we take the first derivative of A_i with respect to T and set that equal to 0 as follows:

$$dA_i/dT = dF_i S_g.T/dT - dC/dT = dV_i/dT - dC/dT = 0 \qquad (3)$$

or, since $\qquad dV_i/dT = F_i(dV_g/dT),$

we have $\qquad F_i(dV_g/dT) = dC/dT \qquad\qquad$ (4)

In words, for an individual the optimum level of private provision of the collective good will be when his marginal private benefit equals the marginal cost. In contrast, the optimum level of provision for the group would have the marginal cost equated with the marginal group benefit, that is, $dV_g/dT = dC/dT$. This means that normally a rational individual member of a group will not provide a collective good in quantities that are optimal for the group as a whole.

Olson defines three sizes/types of groups, namely, the smallest type group or the 'privileged' group, the intermediate or 'oligopoly sized' group, and the very large or the 'latent' group. For the privileged group, for at least one individual, gains from providing the collective good (V_i) exceed his own private cost (C), that is, $V_i > C$. This means that for at least one of the members of the group it is profitable to provide the collective good entirely at his own private cost and free-riders are privileged by the self-interested provision of the collective good by that individual. In this type of group 'there is a systematic tendency for exploitation of the great by the small' (1971: 29).

At the other extreme, there is a very large 'latent' group for which $V_i < C$ for all i. Large groups are likely to suffer without the collective good because no individual member of the group will have the incentive to provide the good privately. This is why a CPR, jointly used by a large group of people, is often over-exploited and degraded, that is, the group fails to derive the optimum rate of output (collective good) from the CPR. A latent group could, however, be coerced into providing collective goods, in which case it is termed a 'mobilized latent group'. In between the privileged and the latent groups are what Olson calls 'intermediate groups.' Intermediate groups are vaguely defined as ones in which at least two individuals must act together to provide the collective good but will always require some group coordination or organisation for provision.

Olson does not specify the number of individuals that would make up the very small group, but he asserts that the group should be small enough so that 'the individual actions of any one or more members are noticeable to any other individuals in the group'. An important implication of Olson's theory for managing CPRs is that if a group using a CPR is very large and heterogeneous, it should be divided into a number of small and homogeneous subgroups, and each subgroup randomly assigned a portion of the CPR that should be, as far as possible, proportionate to the size of the group. If there are marked variations in the quality of the CPR, the assignments may be rotated every year. This is, however, possible only if the CPR is divisible and if some arrangement exists for dividing and apportioning the CPR among the subgroups.

According to Olson, despite the free-rider problem, voluntary groups can provide collective goods in a wide variety of areas, including education, labour unions and natural resources. Group action can also emerge in such less desirable forms as collusion and oligopolies in which firms or agents collaborate to restrict quantity and maintain high prices.

In an appendix to the 1971 edition of his book, Olson also discusses the possible role of the political entrepreneur in promoting collective action. A political entrepreneur is an individual with a combination of such traits as leadership, the trust of the community or its fear, the ability to discern the motivations of others, and the desire to organise the group for collective action. Olson suggests that the success of the political entrepreneur will be related to his ability to utilise selective incentives to motivate participation in collective action. In our opinion, in the context of CPR management, another important role of the political entrepreneur is to provide requisite assurance to CPR users that expected benefits from collective management would actually accrue to them and that the benefits would be equitably distributed among them.

4.8 METHODS OF ABATEMENT OF EXTERNALITIES

While assessing and mitigating negative impacts of development projects is important, project-level actions are not sufficient to reduce all environmental problems. The underlying causes of many environmental problems are not directly related to the specific projects, but rather stem from policy and market failures. In these cases government action is required to correct these failures through interventions, which may include changes in property rights and other institutions governing resource use; policy instruments such as tax/subsidies, market-based incentives and regulatory measures; and direct public investments. There are two alternative approaches to abatement of externalities, namely, (i) Pigouvian Tax-Subsidy Approach; and (ii) Coasian Property Rights Approach. Now, we briefly discuss these approaches in the following sections.

4.8.1 The Pigouvian Tax-Subsidy Approach

The traditional economic approach to modifying externalities can be ascribed to Pigou (1962), who had argued that taxes and subsidies could be used to encourage economic agents to internalise externalities. In the case of negative externalities, Pigou's solution is that the producer must compensate parties who are affected by negative externalities or be taxed to the extent that the marginal private cost, including the tax, is equal to marginal social cost including the negative externality. The tax should be fixed at exactly the level of marginal external cost. This either induces the one who imposes the externality to: (*a*) eliminate or reduce the externality to acceptable limits (depending on how and to what extent the tax is imposed); or (*b*) compensate the parties adversely affected through the tax proceeds. Conversely, a payment, such as a subsidy, could be made to compensate producers who cause beneficial externalities. The subsidy should be precisely equal to the marginal external benefit so as to reduce the cost of production sufficiently to increase the output to a socially efficient level. The tax-subsidy solution is commonly used in both developing and developed countries of the world. The tax solution of a negative externality (air pollution) is shown in Figure 4.3.

Suppose a chemical fertiliser (for example, urea) producing factory is polluting the air in nearby areas. There are no restrictions on the use of the atmosphere as a sink for discharging the pollutants and on the production of fertiliser. The only way to reduce the pollution is by curtailing the fertiliser production. In Figure 4.3, demand for fertiliser is given by the curve D. The marginal private cost and the marginal social cost of fertiliser production are given by the curves MPC and MSC,

Figure 4.3   Effect of a Negative Externality on Private Production

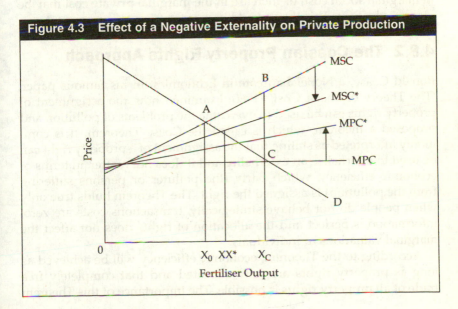

respectively. Without any restrictions on production, the most profitable level of output of fertiliser is Xc. But if the fertiliser producing firm is forced to internalise the externality, that is, the external cost of using the atmosphere as a sink by imposing a tax equal to the amount of external cost, the MPC would shift upward and become MSC. In that case, the most profitable level of fertiliser production will be X_0 which is less than Xc. This means that society will be better off producing less fertiliser than what a private firm will produce. The gain to society is shown by the shaded triangle ABC, which is the amount by which the social cost of producing the excess quantity of fertiliser area ($Xc - X_0$) exceeds the willingness to pay for that quantity of fertiliser.

Now, we could ask this question: Is curtailing of fertiliser production the socially optimum way of reducing pollution? The answer is: perhaps not. Air pollution could be reduced by outfitting the fertiliser plant with special precipitators. In that case, the firm will have to incur additional cost to instal the precipitators and consequently the MPC will increase and will become MPC*, which is less than MSC. However, the new marginal social cost for production of fertiliser, MSC*, will be less than MSC. Now, the socially optimum level of fertiliser production will be X*, which is more than X_0. Thus, society will be better-off if the fertiliser firm reduces the level of air pollution by installing the precipitators than by cutting back the production. To motivate the firm to reduce the pollution, some subsidy equal to, or less than the reduction in marginal social cost, or increase in the marginal private cost may be given to the firm. This then would be a case of *Pareto improvement*.

4.8.2 The Coasian Property Rights Approach

Ronald Coase, a Nobel Laureate in Economics, in his famous paper, 'The Theory of Social Cost' (1960) examined how the assignment of property rights can be used to overcome the problems of pollution and proposed a theorem, which is called the Coase Theorem. It is commonly interpreted as stating that the assignment of a property right can be used to internalise an externality and it does not matter, in terms of economic efficiency, which party (the polluter or persons suffering from the pollution) is assigned the right. The Theorem holds true only when people do not behave strategically, transactions costs are zero, information is perfect and the allocation of rights does not affect the marginal valuations of individuals.

According to the Theorem, economic efficiency will be achieved as long as property rights are fully allocated and that completely free trade of all property rights is possible. The importance of this Theorem is in demonstrating that it does not matter who owns what initially, but only that everything should be owned by someone. Trade will place resources in their highest value occupation eventually.

The Theorem is used to show that a solution to the problem of externalities is the allocation of property rights. For example, if a pesticide manufacturing firm wishes to discharge the toxic effluent from its plant into a river whose water is used by farmers down stream for irrigation, then it is unfair to allow the firm to discharge the effluents into the river as this adversely affects the agricultural production of the farmers downstream. Similarly, it is unfair to prohibit the firm from manufacturing the pesticide as it ignores the firms interests. Social efficiency requires that the firm should be allowed to produce the pesticide only if the social benefit from it is greater than the social cost of it. This efficient outcome can be achieved by giving the firm the right to produce the pesticide but allowing the farmers to bribe it not to produce the pesticide, that is, an option the firm will exercise if the necessary bribe is large enough to compensate it for the loss of profit from pesticide production. Alternatively, the farmers could have the right to enjoy clean unpolluted river water but could allow the firm to produce the pesticide for a fee. It does not matter who has initial prerogative—both arrangements will lead to the pesticide being produced only when the farmers' gains from unpolluted water are sufficiently small in relation to the profit of the firm.

The Coase Theorem is relevant in the context of search of possible alternatives for abatement of externalities. To the extent inadequately defined and insecure property rights are the most important reasons for degradation and depletion of natural resources, creation and assignment of property rights to either the agency that creates the externalities, or the party which is affected by the externalities will internalise the externalities. Therefore, there is need to create and assign secure, tradable and enforceable property rights that will lead to socially optimal use of natural resources through their rational pricing. The property rights will ensure that the cost of degradation/depletion is internal to the user and that the user will use the resource in a socially optimal manner on a sustainable basis. In cases where somebody is polluting a resource belonging to somebody else, the property rights will ensure that the right holder and the user will negotiate a mutually beneficial solution to internalise the externality.

In the real world, things are, however, not as simple as assumed by the Theorem. First, the transaction costs in the case of pollution, or other externalities are very high as the affected people are too many, are unorganised, and are scattered over a large area. Second, measurement of the damage caused by an externality is very difficult in many cases.

Third, assignment of property rights and their enforcement could be technically unfeasible in many cases as in the case of groundwater aquifers, or marine fisheries. To sum up, we could say that creation and assignment of property rights to internalise an externality should be resorted to only when the expected social benefits from it significantly exceed the expected social costs associated with them and when it is physically and socially feasible to do so.

The Coasian solution to an externality is shown in Figure 4.4. In economic terms, a negative externality is a 'bad' good, and a positive externality is a 'good' good, and therefore there is a demand for abatement of a negative externality (avoiding the 'bad') from those who suffer from the externality and there is a supply of abatement from those who create the externality. In Figure 4.4, a negative externality (like air pollution) produced by a firm in the process of producing a commodity is measured on the horizontal axis by movement from left to right from the point of origin 0, and supply of abatement is measured on the same axis by movement from right to the left from point Q^P. The curve MNPB = D represents the Marginal Net Private Benefit to the firm from producing the commodity that creates the externality. This may be considered the producer's demand for the right to produce and hence create the externality or to pollute in the process. The curve MEC = S is the Marginal External Cost imposed by the producer on the affected party.

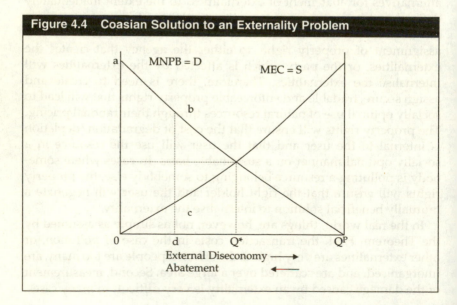

Figure 4.4 Coasian Solution to an Externality Problem

This is equivalent to the amount the affected party would be willing to pay to the polluter to reduce a given level of pollution, or in other words, the curve represents the demand for abatement of the externality. As per the theory of production, the optimum level of externality is Q^*, where MNPB is equal to MES.

If the affected party has the property rights that protects it from the harmful effects of any externality, then the initial level of production of the commodity in question will be zero, with no externality. If, however, there is a possibility of bargaining between the two parties, then some level of production (and externality), say d, would be in the interest of both the parties. For example, increasing the production from zero level to point d will yield a gain to the producer equivalent to the area of abdo, which is greater than the amount of loss to the affected party, ocd. This indicates a win–win situation for both parties through bargaining. The producer will be willing to pay the affected party to produce up to the point at which the net benefits from production are equal to the compensation that must be paid to the affected party. This level of production is attained at point Q^*.

If the producer holds the property rights to produce, the initial level of production will be Q^p, where marginal net benefits fall to zero, that is, marginal private benefits are equal to the marginal private cost. At this level of output, the affected party will be willing to pay the producer to reduce the externality as long as the gains from bargaining are greater for the affected party than the loss to the producer. In this case, bargaining would be desirable up to point Q^*. Thus the bargaining process would lead to the optimal level of externality regardless of which party holds the property rights (Kerr et al. 1997: 168–69).

4.9 OPTIMAL STATIONARY POLICIES FOR RENEWABLE RESOURCES

For environmental assets, particularly renewable natural resources such as forest and fisheries, it is necessary that they are used optimally over a period of time. This is possible if we can determine the socially optimal policy for their exploitation. Dasgupta (1982: 120–33) attempts a formulation and characterisation of optimal stationary policies for renewable natural resources. Following him, we denote by B(Y) the flow of social benefits enjoyed by people when the use/appropriation/harvest rate is Y. In general, the rate at which the regenerative or renewable resource rejuvenates or restores itself in time period, t, is a function, *inter alia*, of natural rejuvenation in the absence of human intervention. Then, the following equation represents an ecological balance in a stable environment:

$$dSt / dt = H(St) \qquad (5)$$

If $H(St) = 0$, the resource is exhaustible as in fossil fuels. But if $H(St) = A$ where A is a positive constant, the resource is renewable and renews itself at the constant rate of A per unit time. In many situations, the natural replenishment rate is a constant percentage of the stock level, that is, $H(St) = ASt$, where A, a positive constant, is the percentage rate of growth.

Now let Yt (≥ 0) denote the harvest/appropriation rate at time t. Then the dynamic equation representing the stock becomes:

$$dSt/dt = H(St) - Yt \qquad (6)$$

Since Yt can be regulated, the dynamic system is a controlled one. If $Yt = H(St)$, then $dSt/dt = 0$. This implies that the stock does not change due to harvesting or appropriation. This is the case where the rate of harvest equals the net replenishment/regeneration rate. If $Yt = H(St)$ for all $t \geq 0$, then we say that Y is a stationary harvest/appropriation policy – 'stationary' because the harvest is constant over time. From Figure 4.5, it is clear that if the threshold (minimum possible) level of the stock, S_l, is less than the optimum level, $\hat{S}$, which is less than the

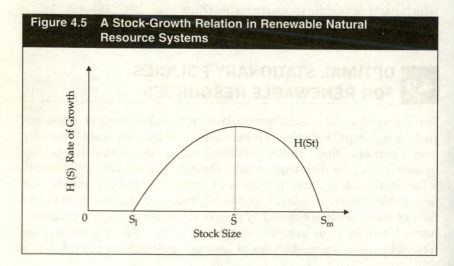

Figure 4.5   A Stock-Growth Relation in Renewable Natural Resource Systems

maximum possible level of the stock, S_m, that is, $S_l < \hat{S} < S_m$, then a stationary harvest policy can be followed, not otherwise. Of the various possible levels of stationary harvest, $H(\hat{S})$ is the maximum and is called the maximum sustainable yield (MSY), which has for long been considered a desirable target but in actuality it almost never is (Dasgupta 1982: 125).

Assuming that social benefit $B(Y)$ is a concave function reflecting non-increasing marginal social benefits, that social rate of discount is a positive constant, r, and that $C(S, Y)$ is the social cost of harvesting Y when S is the stock, we define the net social benefit at time t as follows:

$$N(St, Yt) = B(Yt) - C(St, Yt) \qquad (7)$$

$N(St, Yt)$ is the flow of net social benefit at time t, and $e^{-rt} N(St, Yt)$ is the present discounted value of this flow, assuming that the discounting is done continuously. By adding all present discounted values, we get the following objective function:

$$f^x e^{-rt} N(St, Yt) dt \qquad (8)$$

We know from equation (5) that $dH(S)/dS$ is the marginal productivity of stock which we denote by $H'(S)$. Then, $rH'(S)$ can be regarded as the net social rate of discount that ought to be used in discounting marginal benefits from exploiting the resource in question. The current marginal net social benefit is $Ny(S, Y) \equiv By(Y) - CY(S, Y)$. The marginal cost of increasing current harvest marginally at each future date is: $-\delta C(S, Y) \delta S \equiv -Cs(S, Y)$. Discounted at $r - H'(S)$, the present value of this flow of marginal cost is: $-Cs(S, Y)/[r - H'(S)]$.

For a stationary policy to be judged optimal, the marginal benefit from increasing the current harvest marginally is given in equation (9).

$$Ny(S, Y) \equiv By(Y) - Cy(S, Y) = Cs(S, Y)/[r - H'(S) \qquad (9)$$

Since we are determining a stationary policy, the system must satisfy the following equation:

$$H(S) = Y \qquad (10)$$

An optimal stationary policy must satisfy equations (9) and (10). For the sake of ease in exposition, we assume that equations (9) and (10) have a unique solution which we label as (S*, Y*). For a wide range of plausible cases, optimal stationary policies are really long-run goals. For the immediate future, the right policy would be to allow the existing stock, which may not be optimal except by fluke, to adjust until it attains the long-run target. Dasgupta (1982: 141–47) suggests that this should be done by proceeding as rapidly as possible to a stock size worth maintaining and then staying there forever.

An optimal stationary policy which specifies an optimal level of stock, S*, and an optimal rate of harvest, Y*, has an underlying production function relating labour and capital inputs, natural resource stock, and technology to production of natural resource commodities. A typical natural resource commodity production function may be represented as follows (Howe 1979: 17–19):

$$Y(t) = f[L(t), K(t), S(t), t] \tag{11}$$

where Y(t) is the natural resource commodity or the harvest/output of the natural resource at time t, L(t) and K(t), are the labour and capital inputs respectively used in production of Y, S(t) is natural resource stock and t indicates technology. We know that the output of the resources commodity could be increased by technological improvements or by augmenting the stock, or by intensifying labour and capital inputs. A change in technology may shift the production function upward and thereby may change the optimal stationary policy, *ceteris paribus*. Thus, we may visualise a unique optimal stationary policy associated with every unique resource commodity production function. Based on this relationship technocrats assert that the optimal levels of harvest and stock need not be stationary or constant over time; they could be changed in response to human needs and aspirations. In other words, natural resource systems could be manipulated and managed to produce socially optimum output over time on a sustainable basis. However, with any given technology and at a given point in time, they have a finite capacity to regenerate, or to produce, and beyond this (carrying) capacity nothing can be done to augment the supply. From that state of resource use onwards, adjustments will need to be made on the demand side to bring about an equilibrium of demand and supply.

4.10 SOCIAL COST BENEFIT ANALYSIS (SCBA)

The technique of SCBA is a practical way of assessing the environmental impacts of development projects, or any other governmental or non-governmental interventions in an economy. The technique draws on a variety of disciplines such as welfare economics, public finance, resource economics, public administration and bio-physical sciences.

The SCBA uses economic efficiency as the choice criterion. In general formulation of the SCBA, the aim is to maximise the present value of all benefits less that of all costs subject to specified constraints. The constraints may include a socially desirable pattern of income distribution, level of employment and preservation/improvement of the quality of the environment. This formulation enables us to set out the following questions, the answers to which constitutes the general principles of the SCBA (Prest and Turvey 1965: 686–702): (*i*) which costs and which benefits are to be included?; (*ii*) how are they to be evaluated?; (*iii*) at what interest rate are they to be discounted?; and (*iv*) what are the relevant constraints?

The first task in applying the SCBA to any project is to identify and quantify the full set of impacts, both favourable (advantageous) and unfavourable (harmful), which it is likely to generate. The principles of 'Before and After' and 'With and Without' should be used together to isolate and measure the expected impacts of a project. The net benefit of a project is estimated as follows (Singh 1999a: 329–32):

Net benefit = (expected net benefit to beneficiaries after the project –
        actual net benefit to beneficiaries before the project)

or

Net benefit = (expected net benefit to beneficiaries of the project –
        actual net benefit to non-beneficiaries of the project or
        the control group)

The advantageous or favourable effects of a project are benefits and harmful or unfavourable effects are costs. Benefits and costs are classified as direct or primary and indirect or secondary. Both benefits and costs could be tangible and intangible. Direct benefits consist of gains which accrue to those people who make use of goods and services provided by a project, for example, the value of increased agricultural production from an irrigation project. Indirect benefits are the gains added to the direct benefits as a result of activities 'stemming from' or 'induced by' the project. The 'stemming from' secondary benefits are those that accrue as a result of processing the immediate products of a project. The 'induced by' benefits accrue because expenditure by the producers of the immediate products stimulate other economic activities. Direct costs are the value of goods and services needed for the establishment, maintenance and operation of a project. Direct costs also include associated costs which are incurred by the primary beneficiaries of a project to realise its full benefits. Indirect costs comprise the costs involved in the production of secondary benefits from the project. For example, income from a sugar factory established as a result of an irrigation project constitutes a secondary benefit 'stemming from' and the costs incurred in the production of sugar at the factory are secondary costs. Tangible benefits and costs refer to values of those goods and services that are usually bought and sold at a price, that is, they have markets and price tags. Such benefits and costs may be more appropriately called market benefits and costs.

Intangible benefits are the values of those favourable effects of a project that are not usually bought or sold at a price nor can their value be derived indirectly from secondary benefits. Recreation, scenic beauty and flood control are a few of the examples of intangible benefits of a multi-purpose river valley project. Similarly, intangible costs are values of those harmful effects of a project that are not usually priced in the market, for example, loss of sport fishing and natural forest and wildlife as a result of the construction of a dam. Intangible benefits and costs may be more appropriately called extra-market or non-market benefits and costs. To sum up, total benefits and total costs could be expressed as follows:

Total benefits = Direct (primary) benefits (both tangible and intangible) + Indirect (secondary) benefits (both tangible and intangible)

Total costs = Direct (primary) costs (both tangible and intangible) + Indirect (secondary) costs (both tangible and intangible)

In social appraisal, we are concerned with all direct, indirect, tangible and intangible benefits and costs of a project to the whole society regardless of who in the society receives the benefits and who bears the costs. Some economists, including Ciriacy-Wantrup (1955: 19–20), suggest that all classes of secondary benefits and costs be dropped from consideration if the purpose of analysis is project selection, which is most often the case. This would make the SCBA more straightforward, not only for the professional economist, but also for the layman.

Once a full set of benefits and costs attributable to the project is isolated, the next step in the SCBA is to attach a value or price to each input and output. The price that is attached should represent a value which the society places on the input or the output. If the market system is operating smoothly and is perfectly competitive, observed market prices can be directly applied to most of the inputs and outputs of a project. If the market system is imperfect, or if the market is non-existent, shadow or accounting prices should be used to value the inputs and outputs of public projects. A shadow or accounting price is one which reflects the true value of the output or the input to the society.

Use of shadow prices requires a great deal of extra information as it is unsound to use shadow prices on a piecemeal basis. As soon as some factors are shadow-priced, it is strictly necessary to compute a whole new set of mutually consistent shadow prices. In view of this difficulty, there is a great temptation for project economists to use market prices in social appraisal of projects even where they are inappropriate.

When a project, such as a major irrigation project, causes prices to change, we should consider quantity changes (outputs and inputs) and value them at market prices plus any consumer's surplus or rent on the unit concerned. Changes in surplus on the existing quantity of output are ignored as they represent transfers between consumers of products of the project and owners of the project (Pearce and Nash 1981: 103).

Existence of externalities in natural resources development and management projects causes problems in their social appraisal. A simple rule of thumb to handle externalities is: take into account only those (technological) externalities which alter the physical production possibilities of other producers or dissatisfactions that consumers can get from given resources and ignore those (pecuniary) externalities whose effect is via prices of products or factors, that is, do not consider purely transfer or distributional effects (Prest and Turvey 1965: 688).

Many benefits and costs from natural resources development projects are intangible, that is, they cannot be bought and sold, and cannot be quantified. For example, the scenic effect of a dam and flood control effect of a multi-purpose river valley project are intangible benefits, and loss of natural forest and wildlife due to construction of a dam is an intangible cost. Such benefits and costs are real and reflect true values. It is difficult to handle intangibles in project analysis. Wherever possible, intangibles must be quantified and valued and included in the analysis. If it is not possible to quantify and/or value them, intangibles may be described and listed on the appropriate side, that is, either on the cost side or the benefit side. Other things being equal, a project which has numerous and more valuable intangible benefits should be preferred to the one having no or very few intangible benefits of lower value.

Many natural resources and their products are pure or mixed collective goods. For example, an airshed is a pure collective good and a groundwater aquifer is a mixed collective good. Similarly, water from a public canal is a mixed collective good; once the dam and the water distribution system is built, the marginal cost of supplying water from the given capacity of the dam and canal is zero, that is, many users can share the canal water at no additional cost but its use is subtractable, that is, if one irrigator uses more water, the less is left for the other users to that extent. Following the principle of marginal cost pricing, the optimum price of canal water should be zero so that all users may use it to the fullest possible extent. The project should be financed by taxes either on individual users or on everyone who benefits directly or indirectly from the canal water (Barkley and Seckler 1972: 128–29). In actual practice, however, the principle of marginal cost pricing is not followed anywhere for determining the prices of environmental goods and services. Instead, most natural resources and their products are priced on the basis of average cost or some other concept of cost.

Natural resources development and management projects are subject to greater risks and uncertainty than projects in other sectors. This is so because most natural resources themselves are prone to degradation due to natural processes and calamities, and because their products are biological in nature, they also depend on climatic factors. Besides, given the long gestation of natural resources development projects, there are risks and uncertainties arising from changes over time in prices, technologies and institutions. Risk and uncertainty can be handled by: (*i*) sensitivity analysis; (*ii*) replacing point estimates of outcomes by expected outcomes; (*iii*) shortening the period of analysis; (*iv*) adjustment in the rate of discount by adding to it a risk premium of 1–2 per cent; and (*v*) providing safety allowances, that is, a flat percentage reduction of benefits and increase in costs.

Many public projects to which SCBA is applied are long-lived investments. The outputs of these projects accrue over several years and they require inputs as long as they are producing. Because today's appraisal of the value of inputs and outputs depends on when in the future they will occur, it is important that a consistent mode of accounting for these future effects be determined. The procedure ordinarily used to account for the effect of time on value is called discounting. Discounting is a technique by which one can transform future benefit and cost streams to their present worth. The rate of discount that should be used for computation of present value of future streams of costs and benefits should be the social rate of discount. The social rate of discount is taken to be equal to the marginal productivity (efficiency) of investment. In practice, the government borrowing rate on long-term loans is used as the social rate of discount. Many international funding agencies, including the World Bank, prescribe discount rates to be used in appraisal and evaluation of projects funded by them. However, they may not necessarily reflect the real resource cost of the investment capital and thus could bias the results of the analysis.

There are many relevant constraints that limit the applicability of SCBA. The constraints could be physical, such as the production function which relates the physical inputs and outputs of a project, or legal, such as price controls, or administrative, or distributional, or budgetary. Since the production function constraint directly enters into the calculation of costs and benefits, we need not bother about it. But there may be some other external physical constraints on the choice of design, size and timing of projects which need to be taken into account in making decisions. The income distributional constraint could be taken care of by expressing the choice in terms of maximising the net present value subject to the constraint that share in the net benefit of a particular group should be equal to or greater than a predetermined minimum. It needs hardly to be mentioned that all investment decisions are in fact taken within the framework of a budget constraint.

The most commonly used maxim, where projects involve only costs and benefits expressed in terms of money, is the present value of net benefits. Where no projects are interdependent or mutually exclusive, where starting dates are given, and where no constraints are operative, the choice of projects which maximises the present value of net benefits can be made by following any of these three criteria:

(1) Maximum Net Present Value (NPV): NPV is arrived at by discounting all future net cash flows to their present value equivalent. It is determined by the following formula:

$$NPV = B_0 - C_0 + \frac{B_1 - C_1}{(1+r)^1} + \frac{B_2 - C_2}{(1+r)^2} + \frac{B_n - C_n}{(1+r)^n} \qquad (12)$$

or
$$NPV = \sum_{t=0}^{n} \frac{B_t - C_t}{(1+r)^t} \qquad (13)$$

where B_0, B_1, B_2,..., B_n represent predicted benefits from the project in years 0 (initial year), 1, 2,..., n, C_0, C_1, C_2,..., C_n, are predicted costs for the years, 0, 1, 2,..., n, and r is the social rate of discount.

If one had unlimited funds, it would be desirable to undertake all the projects for which NPV is greater than zero. When the budget is sufficiently limited, as is often the case, not to permit us to undertake all the projects having NPV greater than zero, we rank the projects in order of their NPV and select as many projects as can be undertaken with the given funds.

(2) Benefit-Cost Ratio (BCR): This is another criterion frequently used to select projects. The benefit-cost ratio is defined as follows:

$$BCR = \frac{\text{Present value of benefits}}{\text{Present value of costs}}$$

If the benefit-cost ratio is greater than one, the project is economically worthwhile and may be undertaken. When there are a number of investment alternatives competing for limited funds, we may rank them in descending order according to their BCR and, starting from the top, select as many projects as are feasible.

The BCR is used almost exclusively as a measure of social worth or benefit, that is, for economic analysis and most commonly for land and water resources development projects.

(3) Internal Rate of Return (IRR): The IRR is defined as the rate of discount that just makes the net present value of the cash flow equal zero.

The IRR, in a sense, represents the average earning power of the money used in a project. It happens to be a very useful measure of project worth. The formal selection criterion is to accept all projects having an IRR greater than the opportunity cost of capital. Projects are ranked in order of the value of the IRR. The lowest acceptable IRR is often termed the 'cut off rate' and is normally slightly above the opportunity cost of capital. Project size, where variable, may be optimised by incrementing it until the IRR for the last acceptable increment is equal to the social rate of discount. These rules are, conceptually, identical to the maximum present value criterion. Where public sector investment funds are limited in the initial time period, it is meaningful to select the package of projects that maximises IRR, only if one imposes the constraint that the total investment budget for that time period must be exhausted and no project whose IRR is less than the social rate of discount may be selected.

The IRR criterion has an advantage over the NPV criterion in that it can be calculated on the basis of project data alone; it does not require data on opportunity cost of capital (r) which is critical to the NPV criterion and is often very difficult to estimate. But it has two serious drawbacks. First, there are some projects for which it is not possible to determine IRR uniquely, that is, cases where major items of equipment must be replaced relatively frequently, giving rise to negative net benefits, say every five years, when these replacements are accomplished. All such cases yield multiple solutions for IRR and thus present a problem of choice. Second even when a unique solution is available, it presents problems where some projects are mutually exclusive, for example, two variants of a dam. Suppose variant A yields a higher IRR (20 rather than 15 per cent) and a lower NPV at the market rate of interest of 10 per cent (say Rs 10,000 rather than Rs 20,000). Which of these projects to select? One can say that NPV is a better guide than the IRR. It yields a measure of total gains which the latter does not. Both the methods give the same results so long as the net present value always goes down as the discount rate is increased.

4.11 COST-EFFECTIVENESS ANALYSIS (CEA)

The CEA is an analytical tool that could be used to assess and compare the costs and effectiveness of alternative ways of improving the quality of environment. It seeks to identify the least-cost alternative to achieve a given objective but does not evaluate the economic justification of the project. It involves the following three distinct processes:

1. Identification, quantification and analysis of costs of each alternative project proposal.
2. Estimation and analysis of each alternative's effectiveness.
3. An analysis of the relationship between the costs and effectiveness of each alternative, usually expressed as a ratio.

The cost-effectiveness ratio is calculated by dividing the cost of an alternative by the effectiveness of that alternative which is usually expressed in non-monetary terms. As we know many environmental goods and services such as clean air, natural scenic beauty, flood control and recreation are collective or public goods, which are difficult to quantify and value in monetary terms. In such situations, the CEA is more appropriate than the SCBA. In the CEA, the aim is to minimise the cost of securing a given level of effectiveness in accomplishing the desired outcome. Thus, like the SCBA, the CEA also employs the economic efficiency principle.

As an analytical tool, the CEA has an advantage over the SCBA in that it does not require valuation of benefits or effectiveness which may be difficult, if not impossible, to achieve in many environmental projects. For example, it is very difficult to measure benefits from such projects as flood control, pollution control, preservation of complex ecosystems and outdoor recreational opportunities. Given the social desirability of such projects, CEA is the most suitable technique to use for selection of least-cost alternatives for achieving the project objectives. For example, a flood control project is generally considered socially desirable and worthwhile to undertake as it saves, among other things, invaluable human lives. If we have two alternatives, A and B, costing Rs 100 million and 150 million respectively and expected to save 8,000 and 10,000 lives, respectively, we could employ the CEA. In such case, the cost effectiveness of alternative A will be Rs 100 million/8,000 = Rs 12,500 per life and of alternative B Rs 150 million/10,000 = Rs 15,000 per life. Thus, alternative A will be more cost-effective than alternative B in saving human lives and hence should be chosen. Its major limitation is that it cannot be used to compare alternatives with different goals nor can it help determine whether a project is worthwhile.

Use of the CEA would be appropriate in situations where the following four requirements are met (Reynolds and Gaspari 1985: 13–14):

1. There must be a well-defined objective.
2. Alternative means of achieving that objective must be identified and formulated as project proposals.
3. The alternatives identified must be comparable.
4. The costs and effects of each alternative must be measured.

The results of the CEA depend very much on the assumptions made in estimating costs and outcomes. Before making a categorical recommendation to accept or reject a proposal, the analyst should test whether variations in those assumptions would change the conclusion. One way to do this is to conduct a sensitivity analysis. In this, the analyst identifies the significant assumptions and parameters, varies them, and observes the effect of the variations on the CE ratios. If the sensitivity analysis indicates that the CE ratios are sensitive to changes in certain assumptions/parameters, the analyst should try to collect more data and obtain more reliable estimates of the parameters involved or the decision could be taken on the basis of assumptions that seem to be the most plausible.

4.12 MAIN POINTS

The following are the main points made in this chapter:

- Besides individuals, groups of individuals or society as a whole, are also involved in making choices that affect the environment. Therefore, it is equally important for us to understand why and how groups of individuals behave and interact with the environment the way they do.
- Some of the important concepts commonly used in the context of collective choices, or decisions pertaining to the environment include social benefits, social costs, social welfare function, Pareto principle and compensation principle. These concepts are drawn from welfare economics and can be used for comparing welfare effects of alternative states of environmental quality.

- As per the Pareto principle, if it is possible to improve the well-being of at least one person in moving from state one to state two without decreasing the well-being of anybody else, then state two is ranked superior to state one by society. According to the compensation principle, also known as the *Kaldor-Hicks compensation criterion,* state two is socially preferable to state one if those who gain from such a move can compensate those who lose, that is, if the gainers can bribe the losers to accept state two and yet be better off in state two.

- 'The Tragedy of the Commons' is an important hypothesis proposed by Garret Hardin, a biologist in his famous 1968 article in *Science.* It seeks to explain why commons, or better put, open access, are over-exploited, degraded and depleted. The logic of the tragedy is purely economic—incremental private benefits to an individual from the increased use of the resource markedly exceed the incremental private costs associated with the increased use and this leads to overexploitation of the resource.

- 'The Tragedy of the Commons' arises mainly because of non-cooperation among co-users of a commons. The problem of non-cooperation could also be illustrated through the Prisoners' Dilemma (PD) game. The classic PD game is analogous to many situations that prevail in the use of environmental resources, particularly common pool resources (CPRs) such as communal grazing lands, common pool surface and groundwater resources, marine fisheries, community forests and open access such as marine fisheries and the atmosphere.

- Olson's Theory of Collective Action is an important construct useful in explaining why groups of individuals do not always act in their own interest and how they could be motivated to act collectively. The main argument underlying the theory is: 'Unless the number of individuals in a group is quite small, or unless there is coercion or some other special device to make individuals act in their common interest, rational, self interested individuals will not act to achieve their common or group interests'.

- Given the fact that the use of environmental resources, goods and services is characterised, among other things, by the existence of externalities, it is necessary to abate the externalities to ensure socially desirable production and consumption decisions. There are two alternative approaches to abatement of externalities, namely, (*i*) Pigouvian Tax-Subsidy Approach; and (*ii*) Coasian Property Rights Approach.

- The technique of Social Benefit and Cost Analysis is a practical way of assessing the environmental impacts of development projects or any other governmental or non-governmental interventions in an economy. The technique draws on a variety of disciplines such as welfare economics, public finance, resource economics, public administration and bio-physical sciences.

- The Cost-Effectiveness Analysis is an analytical tool that could be used to assess and compare the costs and effectiveness of alternative ways of improving the quality of environment. It seeks to identify the least-cost alternative to achieve a given objective but does not evaluate the economic justification of the project.

4.13 DISCUSSION QUESTIONS

1. Explain with examples why we need theories of collective choice and action in the context of environment management.
2. What is the relevance of the concept of social welfare function in environment management? Is it possible to estimate a social welfare function empirically? Yes/No. If yes, why, if no, why not?
3. Write a critique of the Mancur Olson's theory of Collective Action, highlighting its strengths and weaknesses, in the context of environment management.
4. Pick up a case of collective action taken against some environmental problem, for example, the *Chipko* movement, or the *Apiko* movement and examine the role of the Olson's theory of collective action and leadership in explaining the emergence and survival of the movement/collective action.
5. What are the strengths and weaknesses of Hardin's thesis 'The Tragedy of the Commons'? Is the common's tragedy inevitable in all circumstances? Yes/No. If yes, why, if no, why not?
6. What is the relevance of the Prisoners' Dilemma (PD) game in the context of environment management?
7. What are the limitations of the Coase Theorem in the contest of abatement of pollution of rivers and lakes in India?

5 Environmental Valuation

INTRODUCTION

By environmental valuation, we mean estimating the economic values of natural resources and environmental assets, goods and services whereas environmental accounting connotes the process and act of recording the values of environmental assets, goods and services in an appropriate set of records/accounts and incorporating those values in the National Accounts. Environmental valuation and accounting can be useful for several purposes such as formulation and appraisal of natural resource development projects (for example, soil conservation, wastelands development and flood control), preparing green national accounts, that is, accounts that incorporate the benefits and costs of natural resources and environmental amenities and services, determining the trade-offs between economic development and quality of environment and the extent of financial liability of firms and households who degrade natural resources and pollute the environment. Estimation of the economic values of natural resources and environmental amenities and services is necessary as there are no markets for most of them and there are externalities involved in their use.

This chapter first examines the meaning of environmental values, and then discusses their types and methods of estimation. The main objective of the chapter is to enhance the knowledge and skills of the reader so as to enable him/her to comprehend and apply the tools and techniques of environmental valuation in real world situations.

5.2 MEANING AND TYPES OF ENVIRONMENTAL VALUES

By the phrase, 'environmental values', we mean the economic values of environmental assets, goods, services and functions. The economic value of a natural/environmental resource as an asset can be defined as the sum of the discounted present values of the flows of all goods and services from the resource over its productive life span. The economic concept of value is based on a premise of neoclassical welfare economics that the purpose of economic activity is to increase the well-being of the individuals who constitute the society and that each individual is the best judge of what is 'good' or 'bad' for him or her. Thus, the basis for estimating economic value of a resource or an environmental amenity is its probable effect on human welfare. However, the anthropocentric focus of economic valuation does not preclude a concern for the survival and well-being of other species. People value other species not only because of their direct utility to them but also because of altruistic or ethical concerns (Freeman III, 1993: 5–6).

The economic value of a natural resource or an environmental good can be expressed as follows:

Total economic value (TEV) = use value (UV) + non-use value (NV)

The UV may be further broken down into direct and indirect use values. The NV comprises bequest value and existence value (Figure 5.1).

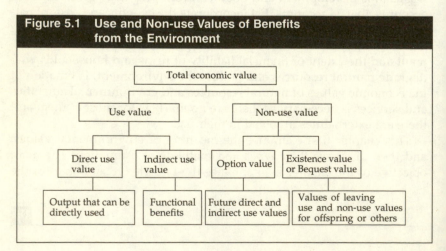

Figure 5.1   Use and Non-use Values of Benefits from the Environment

To illustrate various types of environmental benefits, we use the case of benefits from forests (Box 5.1).

Box 5.1   An Illustrative List of Direct and Indirect Benefits from Forests

Direct benefits associated with consumptive uses
- Commercial/industrial market goods (fuel, timber, pulpwood, poles, fruits, animals, fodder, medicines, etc).
- Indigenous non-market goods and services (fuel, animals, skins, poles, fruits, nuts, etc.).

Non-consumptive uses
- Recreation (jungle, cruises, wildlife, photography, trekking, etc.).
- Science/education (forest studies of various kinds).
- Social, cultural and spiritual values.

Indirect benefits associated with
- Watershed protection (protection of downstream areas).
- Soil protection/fertility (maintenance of soil fertility, especially important in tropical regions).
- Gas exchange and carbon storage (improvement of air quality, reduction of greenhouse gases).
- Habitat and protection of biodiversity and species (potential drug sources, source of germplasm for future domesticated plants and animals).
- Soil productivity on converted forestland (space and soil productivity for agricultural/horticultural crops and livestock).

Option and existence values
- People may value a natural forest or an environmental amenity purely for its existence and without any intention to directly use the resource in future. This includes the intrinsic value of the forest.
- People may value the option to use a forest in the future or merely the option to have it available in the future. Although such values are difficult to measure in economic terms, they should be recognised in valuing the contributions of forests to human welfare.

Note that any of the above values can be considered at different scales, for examples, a catchment, a Forest Management Unit, a region, a nation and even globally.

5.3 MEASURES OF ECONOMIC VALUES

The production of an economic good requires inputs and use of machines or fixed capital. We all know that in the process of production, the machines get worn out. Their useful life is reduced and that for estimation of income earned from this process of production, one must account for the depreciation of the machines, or any other fixed capital used. However, apart from man-made inputs and machines, many economic activities also require natural resources and environmental inputs. We use land, water, air and so on for production of goods and services as well as for direct consumption. As long as environmental resources are available in plenty, they are considered 'free'. But nonetheless, we use them and this changes their quality and quantity available for other uses now and in future. In that sense, those resources have opportunity cost and hence are not 'free' goods.

Environmental degradation associated with economic development and population growth is visible in many places. The changes in the quality of land, air, and water as well as the loss of flora and fauna raise concerns about the cost of such development. Such environmental losses are not justified on any ground; they are indicative of only our carelessness and negligence in using the environment.

It is important to note here that the environmental effects of any economic activity is first conceived/measured in physical units. However, to integrate these effects fully into the national accounts, it is necessary to ascribe a monetary value to them. For example, prior physical measurements of pollution (or emissions) and depletion of a natural resource are always required in order to derive a monetary measurement of the costs associated with them. Such physical measurements also serve effectively in environmental management whether or not they are subsequently used to adjust the national accounts.

There are several methods of valuation of environmental assets, goods, amenities, services and functions. Now, we present and briefly discuss some of the commonly used methods of environmental valuation.

5.3.1 Market Valuation

This is the principal method of valuation used in conventional national accounts. We could use actual or imputed or simulated market prices for valuation of those environmental goods, amenities, services and functions that are marketed. This method has the greatest consistency with conventional accounts. Actual environmental expenditures can have the character of avoidance/prevention or restoration activities whose purpose is to prevent or reduce pollution, or to reduce the net depletion of natural resources. Such activities include planting trees, restocking rivers with fish, plugging leaks in water distribution systems, investing in recycling and developing substitutes such as renewable energy to replace fossil fuels. They are accounted as production cost if incurred as intermediate consumption of goods and services or as depreciation of capital goods used in environmental protection. As final demand categories, they are outlays by households for final consumption, by enterprises for capital formation, and by the government for both. In all these cases, they are valued at the market price at which these goods and services are acquired.

Techniques proposed for the valuation of the natural resource depletion include the present value (of net returns), net price and user cost methods. The maintenance costing is generally applied for measuring the cost of pollution (emissions) from current activities.

Stocks of non-produced tangible assets that are marketed, such as land, can be valued by applying the market prices as observed in market transactions. However, the stocks of many depletable natural assets, like subsoil assets or wild biota, may not have a market price, since they are rarely sold or bought in total. A number of methods to estimate the market value of the stocks of scarce (depletable) natural resources and, by implication, changes in the value of stock have been proposed and applied in practice. We will briefly discuss some of them here.

The basic principle of market valuation of economic assets for which a price cannot be directly observed in the market rests on using the prices of the goods extracted from, or services provided by, these assets for estimating the future sales value, reduced by the exploitation costs. If the exploitation is spread over a lengthy period, the flow of future net returns has to be discounted. In some cases, the reserves of depletable natural assets and exploitation rights are marketed. The market prices will then reflect to a high degree the current value of the expected net returns, since investors would base their decision of buying an asset on relative present values of future net income streams. This assumption will not hold, however, in those countries where concessions to extract the resource are fixed by the government, and frequently done so below market value.

It is also difficult to estimate future returns and costs of natural resource exploitation by industry (agriculture, forestry, mining, construction and so forth) or by the type of natural resource used by different industries. Those estimates would require information on the availability of future stocks (reserves), prices and extraction or harvest costs that are usually available, if at all, only at the microeconomic rather than the sectoral level. In addition, the choice of the discount rate is controversial, with proposed (real) rates ranging widely. In practice, two main valuations are therefore applied, which can be seen as simplifications of the basic principle of present-value calculation. They are the net price method and the user cost allowance.

Net Price Method

The net price valuation neglects future (discounted) losses of net returns from resource depletion. The assumption underlying this simplification is that in long-term equilibrium the net price of the marginal unit extracted will rise at the discount rate neutralising the discount factor. The net price has been applied in various studies. It is defined as the actual market price of the raw material minus its marginal exploitation costs including a 'normal' rate of return of the invested produced capital. The value of a natural resource is then calculated as the product of the quantity of the natural resource stock and the net price. In the case of non-renewable (mineral) resources, this stock comprises only 'proven reserves' which are exploitable under present economic conditions and therefore have a positive net price. The net price method could also be applied to wild biota and water as long as these natural assets are considered economically exploitable assets. The procedure for computing the net price is given in Box 5.2.

Box 5.2   Procedure for Computing the Net Price of a Natural Resource Product

(a) Determine the market prices of different natural resource products based on domestic or export price as applicable. The price should be the average price of each product during the accounting period, that is, the average of the price at the beginning and the price at the end of the period.

(b) Assess the total production cost per unit of resource output and compute the average unit cost during the accounting period, that is, the average of the unit costs at the beginning and at the end.

(c) Assess normal return to the invested capital used in the exploitation of the resource.

(d) Determine the net operating surplus of the industry exploiting the resource.

(e) Calculate the net price as the difference (a) − [(b) + (c)], or as the difference between (d) and (c).

Source: United Nations (2000).

This method of estimation of stock values can also be applied for valuing all *changes* of natural assets during the accounting period. In principle, the net price effective at the time of the resource use should be applied. In practice, the cost of depletion is calculated by multiplying the depleted quantities of the natural assets by the *average* net price between the beginning and end of the accounting period.

User Cost Allowance Method

Another method that approximates the net present value for the depletion of natural resources is the user cost valuation. The idea is to convert a time-bound stream of (net) revenues from the sales of an exhaustible natural resource into a permanent income stream by investing a part of the revenues, namely, the 'user cost allowance', over the lifetime of the resource; only the remaining amount of the revenues should be considered 'true income'. Given a particular net revenue for an accounting period, the calculation of the user cost allowance is straightforward, requiring only two additional parameters, the discount rate and the life span of the resource at the current extraction rate (see for details, United Nations 2000).

The net price and user cost methods differ in their respective objectives of natural capital and income maintenance. The net price method tends to overstate capital consumption, thus representing an upper limit of environmental cost estimates, whereas the user cost allowance assumes full substitutability of natural capital by other production factors; it can thus be considered a lower limit. Both valuation methods have been applied in the Integrated Environmental and Economics Accounting (SEEA) case studies to assess a range of cost estimates.

5.3.2 Maintenance Valuation of Environmental Assets

The market value approach covers only natural assets that have an economic value. They are those assets that are connected with actual or potential market transactions. Market valuation does not cover environmental assets of air, land in the wilderness, waters and species that provide environmental services, nor can market valuation capture environmental functions of 'economic' assets, which are not reflected in their market price. In order to obtain a more comprehensive picture of environmental costs, beyond natural resource depletion, a maintenance cost valuation is introduced in the SEEA as an alternative or addition to market valuation.

Maintenance costs are defined as the costs which one would have had to incur during the accounting period in order to avoid current and future environmental deterioration from the impacts caused during the accounting period. This valuation does not refer to the actual environmental damage generated by this activity, that is to say, its environmental impacts generated during the accounting period and in the future, or in other words, the total environmental capacity loss by current activity. This total capacity loss due to current activities is of illustrative interest but to measure it in routine national accounting is hardly possible.

Maintenance costs are, of course, hypothetical because in reality an actual use of the asset that affected the environment did take place. The rationale behind this approach is based on the following two criteria:

1. The application of a strong sustainability concept which has gained a central role in the discussion of integrated (environmentally sound) development.
2. The extension of the national accounts concept of replacement cost of the consumption of fixed capital, to the use of non-produced natural assets.

The maintenance cost concept reflects a more conservationist view of the environment. It measures the cost that economic agents would incur to meet environmental regulations for maintaining the quality of the environment. Also, the use of maintenance costs for valuing environmental functions is similar to valuing the services of produced capital in the national accounts, based on the consumption (wear and tear) and replacement of fixed capital. As such, they can be deducted from the GDP and gross value added to obtain, after further deduction of conventional capital consumption, the corresponding environmentally adjusted net indicators.

In all cases of permanent environmental degradation and destruction, the value of the maintenance costs depends on the avoidance, prevention or restoration activities chosen. The choice of activities for calculating the imputed maintenance costs of discharging residuals will depend on relative costs and efficiencies, in other words, on the best available technologies. Imputed prevention costs of industries should thus be based on the most efficient methods for preserving environmental assets or meeting environmental standards.

Five types of measures for preventing environmental deterioration or restoring environmental quality by economic activities can be distinguished: (*i*) reduction of, or abstention from, economic activities (value added forgone); (*ii*) substitution of the outcomes of economic activities, that is to say, production of other products or modification of household consumption patterns (incremental costs); (*iii*) substitution of the inputs of economic activities without modifying their outcomes (outputs) by applying new technologies and so forth (incremental costs); (*iv*) activities to prevent environmental deterioration without modifying the activities themselves (for example, end-of-pipe technologies); and (*v*) restoration of the environment, and measures diminishing the environmental impacts of economic activities.

5.3.3 Contingent Valuation Method (CVM)

The CVM may be a modern name for the survey method. Only difference being that the CVM elicits, through appropriately worded questions, how people would respond to hypothetical changes in some environmental service. These questions may be in the form of referendum (yes or no) or a payment card, apart from the direct questioning of the exact amount an individual/household is willing to pay. However, the direct questioning has been criticised as a difficult proposition to elicit the requisite information. The referendum approach includes dichotomous-choice, close-ended, or take-it or leave-it question formats while the payment card format specifies a range of values from which the respondent is asked to mark the highest values he or she would be willing to pay. Another way of eliciting information is through a bidding game procedure, which is somewhat similar to the payment card approach, where the respondent is offered different hypothetical bids until a range is generated. In this, the true willingness to pay is expected to lie between positive and negative responses rather than on a single point. All these approaches are tested for their validity.

The most commonly used hypothetical questions simply ask people what value they place on a specified change in an environmental amenity, or the maximum amount they would be willing to pay to have it occur. The responses, if truthful, are direct expressions of value and would be interpreted as measures of compensating surplus (CS). The term Contingent Valuation Method (CVM) is conventionally used to refer to approaches based on this form of question.

A second major type of hypothetical question asks for a yes or no answer to the question, 'Would you be willing to pay Rs. X...?' Each individual's response reveals only an upper bound (for a no) or a lower bound (for a yes) on the relevant welfare measure. Questions of this sort are often referred to as referendum questions because of the analogy with voting on such things as bond issues. Discrete choice methods can be used to estimate willingness to pay functions or indirect utility functions for data on responses, and on the characteristics of the people surveyed.

The third and fourth major types of hypothetical questions do not reveal monetary measures directly. Rather, they require some form of an analytical model to derive welfare measures from responses to questions. The third approach to questioning is known as Contingent ranking. Respondents are given a set of cards and hypothetical alternatives, each depicting a different situation with respect to some environmental amenity and other characteristics that are presumed to be arguments in the respondent's preference function. Respondents are asked to rank the alternatives in order of preference by placing the cards in that order. These rankings can then be analysed to determine, in effect, the marginal rate of substitution between any other characteristic and the level of the environmental amenity. If one of the other characteristics has a monetary price, then it is possible to compute the respondent's willingness to pay for the good on the basis of the ranking of alternatives.

In the fourth type of hypothetical question—known as Contingent activity questions—individuals can be asked how they would change the level of some activity in response to a change in an environmental amenity. If the activity can be interpreted in the context of some behavioural model, such as an averting behaviour model or a recreation travel cost demand model, the appropriate indirect valuation method can be used to obtain a measure of willingness-to-pay (WTP).

Some issues and problems in hypothetical methods are specific to the particular form of the question being asked. For example, when people are asked how much they would be willing to pay for something, they might say 'zero' because they reject the idea of having to pay for something they consider to be rightfully theirs. Other problems are generic to all methods based on hypothetical questions—for example, problems in scenario specification, sampling and item non-response. The major questions regarding all hypothetical methods concern the validity and reliability of the data, that is, whether the hypothetical nature of the questions asked inevitably leads to some kind of bias or results in so much 'noise' that the data are not useful for drawing inferences.

It is tempting to think of hypothetical methods as being cheap and easy substitutes for the data-hungry indirect methods, with their sophisticated analytical and econometric models. But hypothetical methods have their own difficulties, subtleties and pitfalls. They require more than just going out and asking people questions. Will the answer you get furnish the desired information on the respondent's preferences and values? This question in one form or another has been at the heart of the debate on the merits of CVM and related techniques from the very beginning. And it has provided a major motivation for the recent development and testing of hypothetical methods generally.

The general criticism of CVM is regarding the validity of the insights derived from people's responses to hypothetical situations. How far would the estimates be reliable or accurate? The awareness of the respondent with regard to the suggested environmental amenities, which are often esoteric (for example, polar bear, acid rain and rain forests in arid zones), is crucial for getting reliable estimates from CVM. Lack of knowledge regarding the 'good' or 'bad' in question may result in hypothetical answers as well. Also, contingent valuation is inconsistent with the predominant national accounts application of market prices, since it includes consumer surplus which is appropriate for welfare measurement, but incorrect in recording national accounts transactions. Other methods such as estimating the cost of increased travel, or estimating the change in property values due to environmental deterioration may be more consistent with market values but face problems of distinguishing environmental effects from other effects.

Due to all these reasons, CVM is most controversial among the social sciences research methods. In fact, recent studies even started conducting verbal protocol analysis to understand the psyche of the respondent while answering the CVM questions. In short, CVM is vulnerable to several biases, which are classified into the following five categories: strategic, design, information, hypothetical and operational bias (Lesser et al. 1997: 290–91). *Strategic bias* refers to the problem involved in motivating respondents to reveal their true preference in situations when by not telling the truth they could still obtain benefits. The *design bias* comprises two components: starting point bias and payment vehicle (mode) bias. The *information bias* refers to the problem arising from the amount and quality of information supplied to the respondent. The *hypothetical bias* arises from the fact that the payments, as revealed through WTP, are usually hypothetical. The *operational bias* may occur if the respondent is not familiar with the good or service to be valued. Some of these biases are specific to CVM whereas others are endemic to all survey methods.

In addition to the five types of biases, CVM suffers from one more problem, that is, how to estimate aggregate values based on the individual values expressed through WTP. To go from individual values to aggregate values requires the identification of the relevant population. The ideal population is the one that will benefit from the proposed environmental service or amenity and will pay for it.

In assessing the hypothetical costs of keeping environmental assets intact, maintenance costing focuses on the direct impacts of production. In contrast, contingent and related valuations of the demand/benefit side of environmental services attempt to measure the losses of such services, in other words, environmental damage. Therefore, through CVMs, we attempt to account for the costs borne by economic agents due to environmental degradation. A serious drawback of these methods in the context of national level environmental accounting is the aggregation bias, that is, the problems of applying these valuations accumulate at the national level and distort the estimates of values. In view of this, such valuations do not seem to be applicable in recurrent national accounting. However, they might be useful in experimental studies that focus on selected environmental concerns or regions.

Despite all of its drawbacks, CVM has been extensively used in both developed and developing countries of the world. For example, Singh and Ghatak (1995: 3–8) used this method for pricing of canal irrigation water in Gujarat. A sample of 100 farmers, drawn purposively from two selected villages in Kheda district, were asked as to how much additional price they would be willing to pay if the canal water was made available in adequate quantity and at the time of need. The sample farmers were willing to pay two to three times the existing water rates if the water supplies were adequate and timely.

In a World Bank study, the method was used to assess foregone livelihoods benefits from the proposed Mantadia National Park in Madagascar. The survey respondents were also asked their Willingness-to-Accept (WTA) compensation for loss of access to the forest. Following a pretest, the CVM question was phrased as follows:

> Suppose you are asked to use only the buffer zone, set aside for collecting forest products and for growing crops and are asked not to use the rest of the forests any more. Suppose in order to make up for asking you not to use the forests in the park, you are given X vata of rice every year from now on. Would this make you as content as before when you could use the forest in the national park? If YES, would X vata of rice make you as content? If NO, would Y vata of rice make you as content? (Richards et al. 2003: 207–08).

5.3.4 Avoided Losses or Damage Avoided Method

A typical application of the avoided losses or damage avoided method is for valuing the benefit of avoided flooding damages due to forest management or conservation. When flooding or other damage occurs due to deforestation there are often reports of farming and livestock losses, damage in urban areas, the costs of cleaning it up and sometimes loss of human life. These can be used to estimate the damages that would occur in the without-project (or forest intervention) situation. An example of the use of this method for estimating the cost of sedimentation of a water course in Cameroon is cited in Richards et al. (2003: 203–04).

However, this approach depends on the feasibility of measuring the damage avoided and of being able to attribute the damages to a change in forest cover or condition. There is an ongoing debate about the relationship between deforestation and flooding which casts some doubts on the approach. Moreover, there can be a problem predicting the frequency and severity of flooding.

5.3.5 Replacement Cost and Preventive Expenditure Method

The replacement cost is the cost of replacing an environmental benefit or service that would be lost or damaged in the without-project situation. A possible application would be valuing the carbon retention benefits of a forest that would be lost in the without-project situation. This could be estimated by determining the plantation costs necessary to replace the carbon released on forest clearance.

In some situations it is possible to assess how much people, firms or governments have paid or would be prepared to pay to avoid losses due to environmental damage. The Preventive Expenditure Method is particularly useful for valuing watershed protection benefits such as avoided flooding or sedimentation. In the case of flooding, this method could be used if downstream users are prepared to take such measures as reforestation or building dykes and gulley plugs. In the case of sedimentation of hydroelectric plants, extra equipment would have to be purchased to filter out the silt. Power generation benefits from avoided sedimentation could be estimated by the avoided construction costs (for example, from raising the height of the dam) or the expenditure saved from not having to invest in increased generation elsewhere.

Replacement cost and preventive expenditure are relatively easy to calculate and can be considered as a useful back-up to other valuation methods, but they are considered by some analysts to be unreliable on their own. This is partly because they do not capture the cost of preventing environmental damage, just the cost of lowering it to a tolerable level. The methods also assume that (*a*) the expenditures would actually be incurred, and (*b*) the level of benefits would be the same after the replacement cost and preventive expenditure as before. The latter is particularly doubtful if the replacement cost approach is used to value the ecological or hydrological benefits of a natural forest, since a man-made forest will not result in the same ecosystem.

This method has been used in both developed and developing countries of the world. For example, the replacement cost method was used to value the benefits from soil retention due to a small plantation in Bolivia and the preventive expenditure method was used to estimate flood protection benefits in China (Richards et al. 2003: 123–24 and 205–06).

5.3.6 Travel Cost Method

The travel cost method is often used in research to assess recreational or ecotourism values of a recreation site such as a national park or a hill station. The method could also be used for valuation of water supply and fuelwood. It is based on the recognition that the cost of travelling to a site is a major component of the full cost of a visit. It is also assumed that the amount of money people are prepared to spend to travel to a site, and the opportunity cost (value) of the time involved, can serve as a proxy for their willingness-to-pay (WTP) for the visit. A formal model of an individual's choice of a site for visit is presented in Freeman III (1993: 445–47).

The travel cost method involves estimating the consumer's surplus from a demand curve derived from travel cost and socio-economic data. The usual economic assumption is that as the price of a good goes up, less of it is demanded. Therefore, the number of visits should be inversely related to the travel cost. Information on visitors' travel costs can be used to draw up a demand curve for the resource. The area under the demand curve (the consumer surplus) is used to estimate the WTP for the amenity.

It is necessary to estimate the time and money spent on travel to a particular recreation site. In some cases, the site in question may be the only tourist attraction in the area. In other cases, however, the site in question may be one of many in a popular tourist area, and the travel cost value has to be divided across all these sites. A similar problem arises if the journey to one site is undertaken for multiple purposes. For example, a person travels from the capital city to attend a business meeting in a regional town and then adds on a tourist visit to the nearby attraction. The method has been extensively used in India and other countries. An example of the use of this method for valuation of eco-tourism in Costa Rica is cited in Richards et al. (2003: 202–03).

5.3.7 Tourism Expenditure Approach

A simpler and less precise way of estimating tourism or recreational benefits is to use the tourism expenditure approach. This does not capture any WTP above the actual price paid and hence the estimated value excludes the consumer's surplus. Neither does it establish a relationship between price and demand, and hence it cannot be used to forecast demand at different entry prices, for example. It is however relatively easy to calculate as it assumes that the value of an area for tourism, recreation or scientific tourism can be based on how much people spend to travel and stay in the location.

Calculation of average tourism expenditure requires data on accommodation, food and transport expenditure, as well as any gate and guide fees. This is only possible when there is some control and recording of visitor expenditure. In India, Forest Departments collect these data. A problem with the approach, like the travel cost method, is multiple-purpose trips. Journeys often involve visiting different places or combining work and leisure pursuits, in which case some judgement about how much of the cost should be allocated to a particular recreational or tourism benefit is needed (Richards et al. 2003: 202–03).

5.3.8 Hedonic Pricing Technique

The hedonic price technique is a method for estimating the implicit prices of the attributes that differentiate closely related products in a product category. Generally speaking, if the product class contains enough models with different combinations of attributes, it should be possible to estimate an implicit price relationship that gives the price of any model as a function of the quantities of its various attributes. This relationship is called the hedonic price function. The partial derivative of the hedonic price function with respect to any attribute gives its marginal implicit price (Freeman III 1993: 124). For example, prices of land in a residential area may include premiums for location in a clean and safe area and discounts for dirty and unsafe areas. If they do, it is then possible to estimate the demand for such environmental amenities as clean air from the price differentials revealed in private markets.

Where environmental changes affect producers of market goods, values can also be observed indirectly through examination of changes in product and factor prices and in producers' quasi-rents. Indirect Observed Methods involve a kind of detective work, in which clues about the values individuals place on environmental services are pieced together from the evidence that people leave behind as they respond to prices and other economic signals.

5.3.9 Measures of Non-use Values

As shown in Figure 5.1, there are two types of non-use values, viz., option value and existence value. A brief description of the nature of those values and possible methods of their estimation are described in the following sections. Strictly speaking, these two values are not non-use values in the sense that people impute values to them for their possible use by them or some body else in future. But these values are independent of their present use values.

Option Value (OV)

Weisbrod introduced the concept of option value in 1964 (Freeman III, 1993: 261). Weisbrod argued that an individual who was not sure as to whether he would visit a site such as a national park would be willing to pay a sum over and above his expected consumer's surplus (CS) to guarantee that the site or the national park would be available should he wish to visit it in future.[1] He called this extra sum the option value of the site. If Option Price (OP) is defined as the maximum sum the individual would be willing to pay to preserve an option for future use before his own demand uncertainty is removed, then the excess of OP over the expected consumer surplus can be called OV. It was argued that OV should be measured, if possible, and added to the expected CS in order to obtain the full measure of the value of providing an environmental service or amenity. According to Freeman III (1993: 263–64), OV is the algebraic difference between the expected value of the consumer's surplus and the state-independent willingness-to-pay. Since these two points on the willingness-to-pay curve represent alternative ways of measuring the same welfare change, the difference between their expected values cannot be a separate component of value. Furthermore, OV cannot be measured separately, it can only be calculated if we have enough information about people's preferences to estimate both OP and

---

[1]Although option value is classified as 'non-use value', in fact it represents future use value in the sense that people value an environmental amenity because they may use it in future (Lesser et al. 1997: 271). Thus, the term is used to mean that the environmental amenity in question does not have a present use value.

expected CS. In view of this, Freeman III is of the view that OV should not be considered as possible benefit from environmental protection.

Existence Value (EV)

Existence values arise from preventing the extinction of a species or preventing the complete destruction of a natural resource or an environmental amenity. John V. Krutilla first introduced the concept of EV in mainstream economics literature in 1967 (Freeman III 1993: 143). It would be pertinent to state here that although the source of existence of EV is related to some one's use, it is independent of any use made of the resource by the person holding the EV.

The existence of non-use values is based on the hypothesis that people impute economic values on natural resources and environmental amenities and services independent of their present use of those resources. Based on this hypothesis, we presume that people might be willing to pay for conservation of some environmental services/amenities such as the valley of flowers, endangered species and biodiversity. In the environmental economics literature, resource values that are independent of people's present use of the resource are variously called 'existence', 'intrinsic', 'non-user', and 'non-use' values (Freeman III 1993: 141). These values may arise from various motives such as a desire to bequeath certain natural resource to one's heirs, or future generations or a sense of stewardship, or altruism, or an ethical concern.

5.4 VALUATION OF INTANGIBLE BENEFITS OF THE ENVIRONMENT

Few attempts have been made in India recently to estimate economic value of intangible benefits of forests like ecotourism, recreation, water supply, watershed value, carbon store and biodiversity. An overview of such studies is given in Table 5.1 and some estimates are given in Table 5.2.

A study on the Yamuna Basin by Chopra and Kadekodi (1997) included three districts from Himachal Pradesh (HP), namely, Solan, Shimla and Sirmour, out of the total number of 40 districts from five states from the hill and foothill regions covered by the study. The study estimated the growing stock and biomass depletion and degradation rates in the forests of the Yamuna basin but found 23.18 per cent improvement in quality of forests in HP. It used alternative approaches to work out the value of fuelwood, fodder, tourism and recreation. It covered

Table 5.1	Economic Values of Intangible Benefits of Forests Derived from India Case Studies		
Intangible Benefit	*Annual Value*	*Location*	*Methodology Used*
Recreation/ ecotourism	Rs 427.04 per Indian visitor and Rs 432.04 per foreign visitors (Rs 16,197/ha.)	Keoladeo National Park, Bharatpur	Travel Cost Method
Recreation/ ecotourism	Rs 516/Indian visitor and Rs 495/foreign visitor (Rs 20944/ha)	Keoladeo National Park, Bharatpur	Contingent Valuation Method
Recreation/ ecotourism and other benefits	Rs 90/household per year (Rs 23,300/ha)	Boriwali National Park, Mumbai	Contingent Valuation Method
Ecotourism	Rs 9.5/local (Kerala) visitor Rs 676/ha.	Periyar Tiger Reserve	Contingent Valuation Method and Travel Cost Method
Water supply	Annual rental = Rs 4,745/ha	Almora forests	Indirect Methods
Soil conservation	Cost of soil erosion Rs 21,583/ha	Doon valley	Replacement cost approach
Carbon store	Rs 1,292 billion (total forests) (Rs 20,125/ha)	Indian forests	Species wise forest inventory data
Watershed values (soil conservation)	Rs 2.0 lakh/ha	Lower Siwalik (Yamuna Basin)	Indirect method (reduced cost of alternate technology)

Source: Manoharan 2000.

Table 5.2 Annual Values of Selected Benefits of Forests

Nature of Forest Produce	Nature of Benefits	Value of Annual Flow of Goods and Services per ha (Rs)	
		Minimum	Maximum
Timber	Tangible	2,701	9,270
Non-timber forest products	Tangible	538	2,957
Ecological functions (watershed)	Intangible	624	2.0 lakh
Ecotourism	Intangible	676	20
Carbon store	Intangible	20,125	1.2 lakh

Source: Manoharan 2000.

Kufri Nature Park and estimated consumer's surplus worth Rs 427 per tourist visit to this site. Two watersheds from the state of HP were selected where the sampled households (also from other hilly watersheds) were willing to pay about Rs 454 per household per year for plantation and protection of village forests. Ordinal approach was also used to work out the degree of dependence of rural people for multiple uses of forests—fuelwood and fodder attained higher degree of forest dependence. Further gender differences did not seem to result in differences of perception with respect to value. The study concludes by proposing a Natural Resources Accounting (NRA) system for the forestry sector and suggests an adjustment in National Accounts.

5.5 MAIN POINTS

The following are the main points made in this chapter:

- Environmental valuation involves assigning value tags to environmental assets, goods and services. It can be useful for several purposes such as formulation and appraisal of environmental conservation projects, preparing green national accounts and determining the trade-offs between economic development and quality of environment.
- By the phrase, 'environmental values', we mean the economic values of environmental assets, goods, services and functions. The economic value of a natural/environmental resource as an asset can be defined as the sum of the discounted present value of the flow of all goods and the services from the resource over its productive life span.

- The economic value of a natural resource or an environmental good can be expressed as: Total Economic Value (TEV) = Use Value (UV) + Non-use Value (NV). The UV may be further broken down into direct and indirect use values. The NV comprises bequest value and existence value. Estimation of the economic values of natural resources and environmental assets, amenities and services is necessary as there are no markets for most of them and as there are externalities in their use.

- Estimating economic values of natural resources and environmental amenities and services is a complex and difficult task. Some of the commonly used methods of environmental valuation include market valuation (price) method, maintenance valuation method, contingent valuation method, avoided losses method, travel cost method and hedonic pricing method.

- There are no reliable and universally acceptable methods of valuation of intangible benefits and costs of the environment. If society wishes to optimise the use of its natural resources and environmental endowment, it should compare the social benefits and social costs of any contemplated change in their present use. Only those changes should be made whose expected social benefits substantially exceed the expected social costs.

5.6 DISCUSSION QUESTIONS

1. Explain the difference, with an example, between the concepts of 'economic value' and 'price'. Does the market price of an environmental good always reflect its value? Yes/No and why.

2. Most of environmental goods and amenities such as air and solar radiation, do not have markets and hence no price tags attached to them. Make a list of all such goods and amenities and identify the most appropriate methods of valuation of each one of them, citing real world examples of their use.

3. What are the major conceptual and empirical problems in valuation of intangible/non-marketable environment goods and assets?

4. Compare and contrast the 'net price method' and 'user cost allowance method' of valuation of depletion of natural assets. Which one is more appropriate for valuation of the damage caused by land degradation?

5. Contingent valuation methods (CVM) are now most commonly used for determining the willingness-to-pay (WTP) and

willingness-to-accept (WTA) of current and potential consumers of non-marketed environmental goods. Discuss with examples the strengths and weaknesses of the CVM.

6. It is generally believed that administered prices (prices fixed by public authorities) of environmental goods and services do not reflect the real scarcity value of these goods and hence lead to overexploitation, wastage and degradation of those goods. Pricing of public canal irrigation water is a glaring example of this practice. Discuss the role of environmental economists in minimising the distortionary effects of administered prices of environmental goods.

6 Environmental Accounting

6.1 INTRODUCTION

Environmental accounting connotes the process and act of recording the values of environmental goods, amenities and services in an appropriate set of records/accounts and incorporating those values in the national accounts. It involves identifying and measuring various benefits and costs of the environmental goods and services, putting value tags on them, and recording them in appropriate sets of accounts/statements. It comprises both physical accounts and monetary accounts.

The need to account for the environment and the economy in an integrated way arises because of the crucial role of the environment in economic performance and in promoting human welfare. The natural resource-environment complex provides four kinds of service flows, namely, material inputs; life-supporting outputs and services; recreational opportunities; and space (a sink) for dispersal, disposal and storage of wastes and residues generated in the processes of production, consumption and exchange. Generally speaking, there are trade-offs among these four types of services, that is, increasing the flow of one type of service is likely to reduce the flow of some other type of service.

Conventional national accounts only partly account for the environmental assets, goods, amenities and functions. They include the values of only those environmental goods and services that are marketed; but they do not account for the overall contribution of the environment to human welfare. However, the growing scarcities of natural resources now threaten the sustained productivity of the economy, and economic production and consumption activities may impair environmental quality by overloading natural sinks with wastes and pollutants. By not accounting for the private and social costs of the use of natural resources and the degradation of the environment, conventional accounts may send wrong signals of progress to decision makers who may then set society on a non-sustainable development path.

In view of the above, it is necessary that the costs associated with the degradation and depletion of natural resources be incorporated into the decisions of economic actors at various levels to reverse the tendency to treat these resources as 'free goods' and to pass the costs of degradation to other sections of society or to future generations of the country. For this, at the macro-level, a system of (environmental) accounting is required to assess whether in the course of economic growth we are drawing down or enhancing the natural resource base of production, including all relevant depletable assets. In addition, the environmental costs and benefits associated with various activities, including sectoral policies, should be evaluated to ensure that these factors are duly taken into account in decision making.

In this chapter, we first trace the historical development of national accounts in India, then present the genesis of environmental accounting, and thereafter describe some of the salient features of the Integrated Environmental and Economic Accounting (SEEA). This is followed by an illustration of the current accounting system in the forestry sector. Finally, we discuss how environmental accounting could be integrated with India's national accounts. The main objective of the chapter is to enhance the knowledge and skills of the reader so as to enable him/her to comprehend and apply the tools and techniques of environmental accounting in real world situations.

6.2 HISTORICAL DEVELOPMENT OF NATIONAL ACCOUNTS IN INDIA

National Income Accounts or National Accounts can be defined as a set of systematic statements, which indicate the value of total final output of goods and services produced in various sectors of the economy, together with details of distribution of factor income among different groups and final expenditure of the economy.

In India, prior to the development of the national accounting system, which started in the 1960s, the main focus was on computing the nation's income. Before Independence, several attempts were made to compute the nation's income by individual economists and research workers. But all those efforts were based on macro-level data and involved a number of assumptions for want of requisite data and adequate resources. Notwithstanding the limitations, these studies provided the base for post-Independence work on the subject. Since Independence, due attention is being given to official estimates of national income and related aggregates to ensure that they meet the requirement for planning and policy purposes. Recognising the need for providing estimates of the national income on a regular basis, the Government of India set up, in the year 1949, an expert committee known as 'National Income Committee' under the chairmanship of Professor P.C. Mahalanobis. The main objective was to compute the nation's income and recognise the need to provide the estimates of the nation's income on a regular basis. In 1956, the first official estimates of national income were prepared by CSO and published in the form of a document called 'Estimate of National Income'. These estimates are known as conventional series and this continues till date with modifications in the database and methodology made from time to time in estimating the various aggregates (CSO 1989).

Over the past few decades most countries have come to embrace the notion of sustainable development popularly expressed in the Brundtland Commission Report—*Our Common Future*—as '... development that meets the needs of the present without compromising the ability of the future generation to meet their own needs'. The search for ways to operationalise this notion has focused, in part, on incorporating the role of the environment and natural capital more fully into the System of National Accounts (SNA) through a system of Satellite Accounts for the environment. In India, a System of National Accounts is followed in the form of National Income Accounts or National Income, which helps us to understand in a nutshell, the inter-relation of various transactions and gives us an idea of the working of the economy.

6.3 GENESIS OF ENVIRONMENTAL ACCOUNTING

Growing pressures on the environment and increasing environmental awareness have generated the need to account for the manifold interactions between all sectors of the economy and the environment. Conventional national accounts focus on the measurement of economic performance and growth as reflected in the market activity. For a more comprehensive assessment of the sustainability of growth and development, the scope and coverage of economic accounting need to be broadened to include the use of non-marketed natural assets and losses in income-generation resulting from the depletion and degradation of natural capital. Conventional accounts do not apply the commonly used depreciation adjustment for human-made assets to natural assets. Since sustainable development includes economic and environmental dimensions, it is essential that national accounts reflect the use of natural assets in addition to produced capital consumption.

Following requests made in Agenda 21 of the 1992 United Nations Conference on Environment and Development (Earth Summit) in Rio de Janeiro, the United Nations Statistics Division (UNSD) published in 1993, a Handbook of National Accounting entitled *Integrated Environmental and Economic Accounting* (SEEA). The handbook was based on numerous approaches to environmental accounting, evolved in a series of workshops by the United Nations Environment Programme (UNEP) in collaboration with the World Bank. The SEEA was tested in Canada, Colombia, Ghana, Indonesia, Japan, Mexico, Papua New Guinea, the Philippines, the Republic of Korea, Thailand and the United States of America. Only parts of the SEEA, particularly forest resource accounting, were actually compiled in these studies. The reasons were the lack of data and universally acceptable methods of valuation of several environmental goods and services and their welfare effects.

Given the inadequacies of the conventional system of National Accounts, there is substantial interest in expanding the current national accounting system such that they also include the monetary value of environmental goods, services and functions provided by the environment. More than one hundred studies on green accounting had been conducted in both developed and developing countries of the world.

In the broad field of environmental accounting, forest resource accounting has received the utmost attention. There have been several attempts in the recent past to develop a better system of national accounts. The first attempt was made in 1993, when a system of forest resource accounting (FRA) was developed for the International Tropical Timber Organisation (ITTO) by the International Institute of Environment and Development (IIED) and the United Nations Environment Programme-World Conservation and Monitoring Centre (UNEP-WCMC) and was officially adopted by ITTO member countries. In March 1997, the Committee on Forestry (COFO) of the Food and Agriculture Organization (FAO) granted official recognition and support to FRA. It recommended the FRA as the best means of building National Information Management Capacity in the forestry sector. The FRA is being implemented in several countries including Ecuador, Guyana, Indonesia (one province) and Pakistan and is under consideration for implementation in several other countries. Unfortunately India is not implementing the FRA system as recommended by FAO (IIED Website).

Now we will discuss some of the important features of SEEA.

6.4 SOME SALIENT FEATURES OF SEEA[1]

Conventional systems of national accounts (SNA) address the role of the environment in economic performance in part only. The SEEA supplements the SNA by separately identifying expenditures related to the environment and by incorporating environmental assets and changes therein in the supply, use and asset accounts of the SNA.

The SEEA incorporates environmental concerns mainly by:

1. Segregating and elaborating all environment-related flows and stocks that are already included in the conventional accounts. The objective is to separately present environmental protection expenditures.
2. Expanding the asset accounts beyond economic assets to include environmental assets and changes therein.
3. Introducing impacts on natural (economic and environmental) assets, caused by production and consumption activities of industries, households and government, as environmental costs incurred by these activities.

Environmental protection expenditures have been regarded as part of the costs necessary to compensate for the negative impacts of economic growth. These expenditures correspond to, but do not directly measure, the environmental capacity attained through actual environmental protection measures during the accounting period; they do not measure the actual effects of these measures on the environment. Further expenditures to avoid or mitigate effects on human health and well-being from environmental deterioration can also be considered.

---

[1]This section is largely adapted from UN (2000: 24–40).

But owing to problems of definition and measurement, these expenditures are not assessed in the SEEA.

The distinction between economic and environmental natural assets is at the heart of environmental accounting. Economic assets supply the economy with natural resources or raw materials for use in production and consumption processes. Environmental assets provide environmental services such as waste absorption, habitat, flood and climate control and nutrient flows. Environmental asset accounts include the physical accounts of ecosystems. The monetary valuation of stocks or inventories of ecosystems and their components is not recommended in the SEEA manual because of the controversial valuation techniques required for determining option or existence values for these environmental assets. Physical and monetary emission accounts by media (land, air and water) are calculated and linked to the production accounts. The SEEA considers the depletion and degradation of natural assets as costs to be accounted for in the production accounts. This constitutes a major deviation from the conventional accounts where the depletion and degradation of (economic, non-produced) natural assets are recorded as other changes in volume in the asset accounts.

One should note that these environmental costs are imputed, in the sense, that they are not actually incurred by industries and households. They are, at least in part, so-called social costs that were *caused* by economic agents but were not *borne* by the same agents. Even where those costs were actually accounted for by individual enterprises, as may be the case for the owners of run-down mineral deposits, they would still not be accounted as cost in the conventional national accounts, thus inflating their aggregates of value added income and production. The SEEA corrects this by fully costing environmental depletion and degradation (emissions) and incorporating their value as a change in value of environmental assets in the asset accounts, an approach analogous to the treatment of capital consumption of economic assets.

As satellite accounts, the SEEA has a similar structure to the SNA. The SEEA consists of stocks and flows of environmental goods and services. It provides a set of aggregate indicators to monitor environmental-economic performance at the sectoral and macroeconomic levels, as well as a detailed set of statistics to guide resource managers towards policy decisions that will improve environmental-economic performance in the future. The definition of environmental goods and services in SEEA is much broader than in the SNA. In principle, SEEA attempts to measure total economic value, not just market transactions.

The following objectives can be met through integrated accounting by the SEEA:

1. Assessment of environmental costs: The SEEA expands and complements the SNA with regard to costing: (*i*) the use (depletion) of natural resources in production and final consumption; and (*ii*) the impacts on environmental quality (emissions) resulting from pollution by production and consumption activities;

2. Linkage of physical accounts with monetary environmental accounts and balance sheets: Physical natural resource accounts cover the total stock or reserves of natural resources and changes therein, even if these resources are not (yet) affected by the economic system. Natural resource accounts provide the physical counterpart of the SEEA's monetary stock and flow accounts;

3. Accounting for the maintenance of tangible wealth: The SEEA extends the concept of capital to cover not only human-made capital but also non-produced natural capital. Natural non-produced capital includes renewable resources such as marine resources or tropical forests, non-renewable resources of land, soil and subsoil assets (mineral deposits), and cyclic resources of air and water. Capital formation is correspondingly changed into a broader concept of capital accumulation; and

4. Elaboration and measurement of environmentally adjusted aggregates: The consideration of the costs of depletion of natural resources and environmental degradation from emissions allows the calculation of modified macroeconomic aggregates in different SEEA versions. Indicators thus compiled include, besides the above-mentioned capital accumulation, environmentally adjusted net value added and domestic product.

The SEEA has been designed with a high degree of flexibility without compromising on comprehensiveness and consistency. The purpose is to facilitate choices from a broad range of theoretical approaches for the adaptation of the system to national priorities, environmental concerns and statistical capabilities. This is achieved by means of 'versions' or modules dealing with the above-described objectives of the SEEA through a logical sequence of implementation activities.

The SEEA comprises the following types of accounts : (*a*) Land and Soil Accounts; (*b*) Subsoil Asset Accounts; (*c*) Forest Accounts; (*d*) Fishery and other Biota Accounts; (*e*) Water Accounts; and (*f*) Air Emissions Accounts. We will briefly describe the salient features of the forest resource accounting (FRA) component of SEEA. The major components of SEEA forests accounts are presented in Box 6.1. In addition, SEEA FRA also provides for accounts of the following memorandum items:

Box 6.1   Components of the SEEA Forestry Sector Accounts

1. Forest related asset accounts

(*i*) Wooded land—land area and economic value by main species, natural and cultivated forest land, available for wood supply or not available, etc.

(*ii*) Standing timber—volume and monetary value by main species, natural and cultivated forestland, available for wood supply or not available, etc.

(*iii*) Depletion and depreciation of standing timber.

2. Flow accounts: forest goods and services (volume and economic value)

(*i*) Forestry and logging products
  - Market and non-market production.
  - Non-timber products—Output of edible plants, medicinal plants and wild animals, etc.

(*ii*) Forest services
  - Direct intermediate inputs to other sectors, for example, livestock grazing.
  - Recreation and tourism.
  - Carbon sequestration.
  - Protective services.
    - Biodiversity and habitat conservation.
    - Protective services such as prevention of soil erosion.

(*iii*) Supply and use tables for wood products, forestry and related industries.

(*iv*) Degradation of forests due to forestry and non-forestry activities such as defoliation.

(*v*) Environmental degradation caused by forest related activities, for example, soil erosion from logging, water and air pollution from wood processing industries.

3. Expenditure on forest management and protection

(*i*) Government expenditures.

(*ii*) Private sector expenditures.

(Box 6.1 Contd.)

(Box 6.1 Contd.)

4. Macroeconomic aggregates

(*i*) Value of forest depletion and degradation.

(*ii*) Measures of national wealth, national savings and Net Domestic Product adjusted for forest depletion/accumulation.

Source: Lange 2003: 60.

1. Employment, income and exports from non-timber goods and services.
2. Number of households dependent on non-timber forest products;
3. Rights of forest exploitation.
4. Stumpage fees and other taxes or subsidies for forestry and related industries.
5. Manufactured assets like roads, buildings and equipment for forestry, logging, tourism and other uses of forestry.

These items are important in the Indian context also. In view of this, the SEEA FRA seems to be most appropriate as a basis for developing a new system of FRA for India.

SEEA has the following applications in the context of environment management:

(*i*) identifying environmental priorities;
(*ii*) tracing pressure points;
(*iii*) designing environmental policies;
(*iv*) evaluating policy effects; and
(*v*) international environmental management.

6.5 FOREST RESOURCE ACCOUNTING: A CASE STUDY[2]

In India, there exists some semblance of FRA, which could be called the conventional system of FRA. In this section, we present a case study of

[2]This section is largely based on part of a study sponsored by the International Tropical Timber Organisation (ITTO) and conducted by the Indian Institute of Forest Management, Bhopal, under the leadership of Katar Singh (2005).

the existing (conventional) system of FRA in the State of Madhya Pradesh (MP). We begin with an overview of the procedure of estimating the contribution of the forestry sector to the Gross Domestic Product (GDP) at the national and the state levels.

6.5.1 The Existing Procedure

In the conventional system of FRA at the national level, income from forest resources is aggregated under the head 'Income from Agriculture, Forestry and Fisheries' and the sub-head of 'Forestry and Logging', which includes the income from the following sources: (*i*) industrial wood, (*ii*) fire wood, and (*iii*) minor forest produce (CSO 2002). The GDP from the forestry sector is computed by deducting repair, maintenance and operational costs from the value of the forestry output, and the Net Domestic Product (NDP) is computed by deducting the consumption of fixed capital from the GDP. In short, GDP and NDP from the forestry sector are computed as follows:

- GDP = Value of output – repairs, maintenance and other operational costs
- NDP = GDP – consumption of fixed capital

At the state level, the State Directorates of Economics and Statistics (DoES) prepare estimates of State Domestic Product (SDP). In the state of MP, in the year 1999, many changes were made in respect of both the database and methodology adopted for estimation of the Net State Domestic Product (NSDP), commonly known as State Income.

The present series of SDP uses 1993–94 as the base year. The SDP is defined as the total value, at factor cost, of goods and services produced within the boundaries of the State which are either available for consumption and/or for addition to the wealth of the state (DoES 2003).

In MP, DoES estimates the SDP from the forestry sector by following the production approach for timber and expenditure approach for fuelwood. The estimates are based on the quantity of major and minor forest products supplied by the Management Information and Evaluation Division of the Office of the Principal Chief Conservator of Forests, MP. Data on wholesale prices of the major forest products prevailing at the commercial sale depots of the Forest Department are collected from the Divisional Forest Officers (DFOs) through the District Statistical Officers (DSO) of DoES. For estimating the economic value of output of major and minor forest products, the recorded production is valuated at the producer's price as realised by the Forest Department from the sale of forest produce from its commercial sale depots.

According to reliable sources, considerable quantity of timber and firewood escapes from official recording. In MP, DoES makes an allowance of 10 per cent of the value of recorded production of timber to cover the extent of under-reporting/illegal removal of timber. The production of firewood is assessed using data from the 50th round of National Sample Survey. Similarly, norms for the fuelwood used in industries and in funerals have been revised in the present series of the SDP on the basis of latest data.

Allowance for the value of repairs and maintenance of assets and operational cost is taken to be 10 per cent of the gross value of output from forest products. To estimate the SDP from the forestry sector, operational cost and Financial Service Indirectly Measured (FISIM)[3] are deducted from the gross value of output. Consumption of fixed capital is deducted from SDP to arrive at the NSDP.

6.5.2 Sources of Data and Flow of Information

The DoES collects production data from various forest offices and prices data from the DSOs using a set of prescribed formats. The data sources are as follows:

Production Data

- Production data of timber, fuelwood, industrial wood from the office of the Chief Conservator of Forest (Production), Bhopal.
- Data about production of non-wood forest produce (NWFPs), viz., *tendu* leaves, bamboo, *harra*, *sal* seed, gum, *amla*, etc., from the office of MP Minor Forest Produce Federation.
- Data about production of industrial and commercial bamboo from the MP Forest Development Corporation, Bhopal.

Price Data

District Statistical Offices collect the prices and production data from the offices of DFOs and send it to the DoES. The production data obtained from these sources are aggregated by the DoES under the head, 'Forestry and Logging'. In fact, they first aggregate production according to species and assign them total value. For estimating the

---

[3]FISIM represents charges for services rendered by banks and other financial enterprises to various agencies and individuals working in the forestry sector. It represents an imputed income equivalent to the interest and dividend receipts of banking and financial enterprises net of interest paid to the depositors.

total value, average prices are determined on the basis of the prices data obtained from the DSOs.

6.5.3 Data Collection Formats

The Forest Departments in India have an elaborate system of collection and recording of forest related information at all the levels starting from the beat to the state level. The system was developed and put in place in the late 19th century by the British Government of India. There are several formats prescribed for the purpose of recording information at various levels and for reporting the progress of forestry activities. Several formats for data collection are maintained at the range level. They form the basis for aggregation at the Divisional level. A brief description of the major formats is presented here.

Formats for Estimation of the Volume of Standing Stock

The volume of the standing trees is calculated based on the established Form Factor and site quality, which are included in the Working Plans. There is a table of Form Factors for various girth-classes and site quality. The estimation of volume of standing trees is made for only those coupes which are due for harvesting in the current year. The volume is computed by the following formula:

$$\text{Volume (cmt)} = \text{Number of trees} \times \text{Form Factor}$$

The actual quantity harvested may differ from the estimated volume of standing timber by a factor of 20 per cent on either side.

Formats for Bamboo Enumeration

This set of formats contains nine different forms which together provide for collection of information relating to number of clumps per hectare by clump diametre class, average number of green sound bamboo culms per clump by culm diametre class and age, per hectare density of green (sound and damage) and dry (sound and damage) bamboo and other details.

Formats for Collection of Data on Production of Non-Wood Forest Products (NWFPs)

This set of formats consists of a number of forms, which together provide for recording the details of the NWFPs collectors, quantity collected by them and the amount paid for collection. The formats are filled in every day and consolidation is done weekly during harvesting season.

Formats for Maintaining Records of Nistar[4] Supply

This set of formats consists of 10 different forms as mentioned in *Nistar Patrika*. These forms together provide for maintaining range-wise information regarding the availability of fuelwood stacks, quantity available for distribution as *Nistar*, names of villages eligible for *Nistar* supply and days of sale. The information is also available about the type of produce that would be made available for distribution as *Nistar* such as teak and other poles, bamboo and Nistar and market prices of produce.

6.5.4 Flow of Information

At present, there exists an elaborate system of information for estimating the SDP from the forestry sector and for transferring the information from the state level to the national level. Figure 6.1 shows the flow of accounting information from the lowest level to the highest level in the state of MP. As shown in the figure, there are three parallel channels of flow of information, namely, the Forest Department channel, the Revenue Department channel, and the National Sample Survey Organisation (NSSO) channel. The three channels complement and supplement the functions of one another.

6.5.5 Distortions in the Existing System of FRA

There are several distortions in the existing system of the FRA. They arise mainly due to the failure of the existing system to account for and properly value all the direct and indirect benefits and costs of forests. The distortions have led, among other things, to the gross under-valuation of benefits from forests and hence under-estimation of the contribution of the forestry sector to India's GDP. Now, we will briefly describe and illustrate, with examples, major distortions in the existing system of the FRA.

Unrecorded and Under-valued Tangible Benefits

Benefits in this category include fuelwood and fodder collected by local people and carried as head load, timber, poles and bamboos, harvested by forest dwellers and villagers living in the vicinity of the forests for house construction and making agricultural implements, free livestock

---

[4]*Nistar* is a privilege granted under the Indian Forest Act 1927 to forest dwellers and villagers living within the radius of 5 km from forests. It entitles them to claim certain forest products such as poles, fuelwood and bamboo at concessional rates or free of charge.

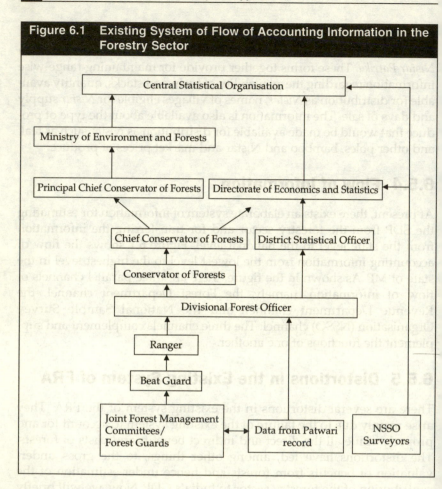

Figure 6.1   Existing System of Flow of Accounting Information in the Forestry Sector

grazing in the forests and various NWFPs collected by people. The Central Statistical Organisation (CSO) has fixed a norm of 10 per cent of the value of recorded production of timber as an estimate of the value of unrecorded production. This is a gross under-estimation of the true economic value of the forest produce. For example, according to an estimate, in India as a whole forest produce worth Rs 197,294 crore was not reported and accounted for properly (MoEF, 1999: 6). This accounts for 71 times the value of the industrial wood for the year 2000–2001, whereas as per the CSO norm, the contribution should be only 10 per cent of the recorded value of timber, or only Rs 277.9 crore in absolute terms. This shows the extent of under-estimation.

Besides, the scope of present day forestry has gone beyond the traditional forest areas. Programmes of social forestry, farm forestry and agro-forestry are being implemented on a massive scale with public participation all over India and they yield huge quantities of timber, firewood, fodder and other benefits. For example, according to the first ever census of trees conducted by the Gujarat State Forest Department in 2004, there were more than 25 crore trees grown in non-forest areas in Gujarat, which together yield nearly 1.49 crore metric tonnes (MT) of timber and 1.75 crore MT of fire-wood annually (Pathak 2004: 3). This gives an idea of the quantity of forest produce contributed by the trees grown in non-forest areas in one of the States of India. For the country as a whole, the quantity of forest produce thus generated would be huge indeed. However, there is no proper recording of the output of timber, fuelwood, pulp-wood, etc., produced from the trees grown in non-forest areas in the country.

Unrecorded and Un-valued Intangible Benefits

Forests provide many intangible benefits to society such as soil formation, carbon sink, recreation, watershed conservation, water yield augmentation, biodiversity conservation, augmentation of oxygen content and so on. These services and benefits are useful to society and hence have intrinsic value to mankind. But in the conventional system of FRA, all these benefit and services are not recorded nor valued.

Recorded but Unaccounted for Benefits/Costs

There are many benefits/uses generated by forests that are recorded but are not accounted for properly. For example, the damages caused due to forest fires are recorded in terms of area burnt (in some cases they are not even recorded) but in all cases the extent of damage in monetary terms is not recorded.

Recorded but Under-valued Benefits

Under the Indian Forest Act 1927, forest dwellers and villagers living within a radius of five km from a forest have been granted *Nistar* rights, that is, they are supplied certain forest products such as poles, fuelwood and bamboo at concessional rates or free of charge. The difference between the market value of such products and the value realised by the Forest Department is tremendous. For example, in the case of the Jhabua Forest Division in MP, the market value of the forest products supplied as *Nistar* in the year 2002–03, was Rs 707,750, whereas the revenue realised by the Forest Department from the *Nistar* was only Rs 325,100.

Failure to Account for the Value of the Standing Stock (Forest Capital)

Standing stock of trees is a natural capital which produces numerous goods and services but whose value is not taken into account in the conventional FRA. However, the potential capacity of the forestland is reflected in the Working Plans in terms of site quality and growing stock. For the Jhabua Forest Division, for example, the volume of the growing stock was estimated to be 10.95 lakh cm, which is worth Rs 328 crore at a conservative price of Rs 3,000 per cm. It needs to be included in the estimates of contribution of forests to the State's/India's natural wealth.

Uncompensated or Inadequately Compensated Land Transfers

In India, a lot of forestland has been transferred to support development in other sectors such as agriculture, irrigation, hydropower, developing urban centres and transportation. Although, the pace of diversion of forest land for non-forest purposes, which was around 150,000 ha/annum between 1950 and 1980, has come down drastically to around 25,000 ha/annum after the promulgation of the Forest Conservation Act 1980, the process of diversion still continues. Such land transfers are made at extremely low prices in the absence of any objective criterion for valuation of forests land. Consequently, the contribution of the forestry sector to India's GDP is under-estimated to the extent of under-valuation of the forestland diverted (MoEF 1999).

Failure to Account for the Value of the Forestland

Forestland has several alternative uses in other sectors such as agriculture, industry, irrigation, mining, etc. In the conventional FRA, the opportunity cost of forestland is not taken into account while computing the NDP. This inflates the contribution of the forestry sector to the NDP but leads to underestimation of the real value of the forest wealth.

Failure to Account for Deforestation and Forest Degradation

As we know there has been a lot of deforestation and forest degradation in India over time. In the current system of FRA, the cost of deforestation and degradation is not considered. This cost is similar to depreciation of man-made assets and therefore should be factored in while computing the contribution of the forestry sector to the GDP.

Failure to Account for Wastage in Harvesting, Storage and Processing

There is substantial wastage that occurs in the processes of harvesting, storage, processing and utilisation of some of the forest products. Some foresters argue that the unmarketable waste should be left in the forests to decay. According to current practice, the value of unsold timber/wood lying in the open forest depots is reduced to half the market value after a period of two years and becomes zero after a period of five years. Financial loss due to this is tremendous which is not reflected in the current system of FRA.

6.5.6 Implications of the Distortions at the National Level

As a result of various distortions in the existing system of FRA, contribution of forestry to India's GDP is grossly under-estimated. For example, it has been estimated that the value of the forests reflected in India's National Accounts represents less than 10 per cent of their real value. The under-valuation of material goods alone from the forests of India is reflected in their estimated (real) value of about US$ 43.8 billion, compared to US$ 2.9 billion recorded as the contribution of the forestry sector to the GNP, which is only about 1.3 per cent of the total GNP of the country (IIFM 2000: 9). The difference between the actual and the recorded contributions will increase further if an imputed value were assigned to the environmental contribution of the forests to society. Similarly, Verma (2000) in a study sponsored by the Himachal Pradesh Forest Department and funded by the Department for International Development (DFID), United Kingdom, estimated the gross economic value of forests in Himachal Pradesh to be a whopping sum of Rs 106,664 crore per annum whereas the revenue as reported by the Himachal Pradesh Planning Board was only Rs 487 crore per annum. Even if we discount the estimates made by Verma heavily, the gap between the actual value of benefits from the forest to society and the revenue accruing to the government is huge indeed. And this gap is only for one of the states of India. For India as a whole, the gap will be mind-boggling. This highlights the need for a better system of FRA, which could facilitate realistic valuation and proper recording of various forest benefits and costs and provide a framework for integrating FRA into the National Accounts.

6.6 INTEGRATION OF ENVIRONMENTAL ACCOUNTS INTO THE SYSTEM OF NATIONAL ACCOUNTS

Integration implies that the economy-environment interactions are fully accounted for in terms of their linkages with one another. However, integrating environmental accounts into the national system of accounts presents some difficulties, which cannot be easily eliminated. In view of this, an alternative approach is to set up what is known as a satellite account for each of the components of environmental accounts. Satellite accounts are defined as being complementary to, but outside the integrated system of national accounts and hence are better referred to as 'complementary' accounts. These accounts throw light on the linkages of the environment with other sectors of the economy. The following adjustments have to be made in the conventional GDP in order to account for the linkages of the forestry sector with other sectors of the economy:

Adjusted Net Domestic = Conventional GDP + Non-market values
Product (NDP)   of forest benefits – Depreciation of
                                 human made capital + Net accumulation
                                 of natural capital.

In general, what we need for integration of environmental accounts into the SNA is the estimation of a set of environmentally adjusted economic aggregates. The expansion of the asset boundary of conventional accounts for the inclusion and valuation of natural assets and asset changes permits the calculation of a range of aggregates. The aggregates can be presented as the sum total of the elements of conventional accounting identities. These accounting identities are maintained in the SEEA in the following manner:

(a) *Supply-Use Identity*:

$$O + M = IC + C +/- CF + X$$

This identity indicates that the supply of goods and services produced (O) and imported (M) equals their use in intermediate (IC) and final consumption (C), capital formation (CF) and export (X).

(b) *Value-Added (Environmentally Adjusted) Identity for Industry* i:

$$EVAi = Oi - ICi - CCi - ECi = NVAi - ECi$$

This identity describes the value added generated by an industry (EVAi) as the difference of output and cost, including fixed capital consumption (CCi) and environmental depletion and degradation costs (ECi) or equivalently as the difference of net value added (NVAi) and environmental costs (ECi).

(c) *Domestic Product Identity (Environmentally Adjusted) for the Whole Economy:*

$$ENDP = \sum EVAi - ECh = ENDP - EC = C + CF - CC - EC + X - M$$

This identity defines the Environmentally Adjusted Net Domestic Product (ENDP) as the sum of environmentally adjusted value added of industries (EVAi) with a further deduction of environmental costs generated by households (ECh). Depending on the types of valuations used and their scope and coverage, alternative indicators, adjusted for natural resource depletion or both depletion and environmental degradation, can be compiled.

The National Environment Policy 2006 (NEP-2006) recommends the following measures for improving the environmental accounting system in the country (GoI 2006):

(*i*) Strengthen the initiatives being taken by the Central Statistical Organisation in the area of natural resource accounting with a view to integrate it in the system of national income accounts.

(*ii*) Develop and promote the use of standardised environmental accounting practices and standards in the preparation of statutory financial statements for large industrial enterprises in order to encourage greater environmental responsibility in investment decision-making, management practices and public scrutiny.

(*iii*) Encourage financial institutions to adopt appraisal practices so that environmental risks are adequately considered in the financing of projects.

(*iv*) Facilitate the integration of environmental values into cost-benefit analysis to encourage more efficient allocation of resources while making public investment and policy decisions.

(*v*) Prepare and implement an action plan on the use of economic instruments for environmental regulation in specified contexts.

6.7 MAIN POINTS

The following are the main points made in this chapter:

- Environmental accounting connotes the process and act of recording the values of environmental assets, goods, services and functions in an appropriate set of records/accounts and incorporating those values in the National Accounts. It comprises both physical accounts and monetary accounts.

- The need to account for the environment and the economy in an integrated way arises because of the crucial role of the environment in economic performance and in promoting human welfare. Conventional national accounts only partly account for the environmental assets, goods, services and functions. This results in the gross under-estimation of the true contribution of the environment to India's GDP.

- In India, a System of National Accounts is followed in the form of National Income Accounts or National Income. But in this system, the costs associated with the degradation and depletion of natural resources are not accounted for, nor are the values of many environmental goods and functions included.

- Given these inadequacies of the conventional system of National Accounts in India, there is need for expanding the scope of the current national accounting system such that they also include the monetary value of environmental assets, goods, services and functions. Globally also, there is substantial interest in developing environmental accounting systems. In the broad field of environmental accounting, forest resource accounting has received the utmost attention.

- Following requests made in Agenda 21 of the 1992 United Nations Conference on Environment and Development (Earth Summit) in Rio de Janeiro, the United Nations Statistics Division (UNSD) published in 1993 a Handbook of National Accounting entitled *Integrated Environmental and Economic Accounting* (SEEA). The Handbook is the most comprehensive and the only internationally accepted document available on the subject.

- The SEEA was tested in many countries but not in India. Only parts of the SEEA, particularly forest resource accounting (FRA), were actually compiled in these studies. The reasons were the lack of data and universally acceptable methods of valuation of several environmental goods and services and their welfare effects.

- In India, there exists some semblance of FRA, which may be called conventional FRA. There is also a system of flow of information from bottom to the top for preparing FRA and National Accounts. But the system has several drawbacks and therefore needs to be improved.

- Adoption of SEEA is one of the several measures that could be used to reform the existing system of national accounts. This would help enhance the degree of accountability, transparency and efficiency in the sector, besides improving decision making.

• The SEEA could be adopted in India without substantial modifications in the existing system of National Accounts. What is required is a set of satellite accounts for each of the components of environmental accounts. The NEP-2006 also recommends the adoption of a system of environmental accounting in India.

6.8 DISCUSSION QUESTIONS

1. How is environmental accounting different from the conventional system of national accounts and why do we need it?
2. How can environmental accounting help prevent or minimise environmental degradation and promote sustainable development?
3. Prepare a project proposal for pilot testing of Forest Resource Accounting (FRA) system as a component of Integrated System of Economic and Environmental Accounting (SEEA) in a forest division.
4. What are the problems and prospects of adoption of environmental accounting in India?
5. Prepare a short note on the rationale of introducing environmental accounting in India.

7 Instruments of Environment Management

7.1 INTRODUCTION

Some form of government intervention is often justified to deal with environmental problems as market forces often fail to realise the socially optimal use and protection of the environment. Existence of externalities is the main cause of market failure in protecting the environment. Externalities result when economic activities have consequences for the environment that are not fully taken into account by their perpetrators. They are generally caused by an absence of, or ill defined, property rights.

Ignorance about the environmental effects of economic activities is another cause of market failure. When producers and consumers are not well informed about the environmental implications of their activities or how best to minimise them, the environmental impacts of their decisions are likely to be aggravated. Moreover, private provision of such information may be less than socially optimal.

Another source of market failure is the 'public good' character of certain environmental goods and services. As we defined it in Chapter 4 of this book, a public good is one which benefits everyone once it is produced, the marginal cost of serving new users is zero and the use of each person is independent of that of everyone else. The nature of public goods means that they can only be provided by a public agency; private (market) provision is rare. The most obvious example of an environmental benefit which has 'public good' characteristics is conservation of biological diversity.

Finally, and perhaps most importantly, there are ethical issues associated with the environment. On their own, some individuals may be willing to run-down environmental assets for personal gain. The community as a whole, however, many consider it a responsibility to preserve the environment for future generations.

In view of the failure of the market and individuals to protect the environment and ensure its socially optimum use as stated above, it is imperative for the government to intervene and manage it wisely in the large interest of society. Fortunately, the need for environmental management now has been recognised in both developed and developing countries of the world and there have been state interventions aimed at preventing the degradation of the environment and improving its quality. There are a variety of instruments that have been used for environmental management. An instrument is defined as something which the environment manager can use to produce a desired effect. It may be an economic quantity such as tax rate or it may be the creation of a new institution such as property rights. An instrument, therefore, is the means by which the objective is pursued. Knowledge about what instruments can be used to improve the quality of the environment is essential for environmental policy makers and managers in order for the environmental management programmes to be effective and successful. This chapter is devoted to a discussion of some instruments which can be used by environmental policy makers and managers to achieve their objectives.

7.2 A CONCEPTUAL FRAMEWORK

Perhaps the most useful framework to illustrate the relationship among policy instruments, target variables and social welfare has been provided by Nobel Laureate Jan Tinbergen (1952: 2). This is illustrated in Figure 7.1.

The important elements of the framework from the policy and management perspectives are W, the Y_i, the Z_j, and the structural relationships that link the Z_j to the Y_i. Each of these elements needs to be further elaborated.

Social Welfare Function (W): Economists call W the social welfare function.[1] It reflects the level of well-being achieved by a society. As

---

[1] A rigourous treatment of social welfare measurement is presented in Freeman III (1993: 3), and a definition of social welfare function is presented in Chapter 4, Section 4.2.3 of this book.

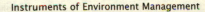

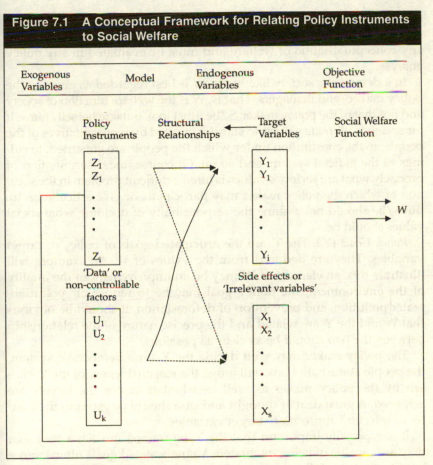

Figure 7.1 A Conceptual Framework for Relating Policy Instruments to Social Welfare

Exogenous Variables	Model	Endogenous Variables	Objective Function
Policy Instruments	Structural Relationships	Target Variables	Social Welfare Function

Z_1
Z_1
.
.
.
Z_i

'Data' or non-controllable factors

U_1
U_2
.
.
.
U_k

Y_1
Y_1
.
.
.
Y_i

Side effects or 'Irrelevant variables'

X_1
X_2
.
.
.
X_s

W

Source: Tinbergen 1952.

such, it represents the aggregate of the satisfaction reached by the individuals composing the society. 'Utility' is 'consumed' ultimately only by individuals and no social or community welfare function exists independent of the well-being achieved by individuals. Since no method has been found to measure utility or well-being, W is entirely psychological and subjective. It is nevertheless a useful concept since it suggests that the end of all policy and planning is the well-being of people. It is necessary to emphasise that W consists of much more than purely economic factors, in fact, even the size and distribution of incomes extant in society are really only the means to superior human ends. W is composed of such final ends as freedom, equality, justice, opportunity, security and quality of the environment. Thus, economic, social, political, cultural and environmental factors must be included in any conceptualisation of welfare and must be evaluated in any policy analysis.

In a democratic society like India, W is best regarded as given to the policy makers and managers. That is, W is the welfare function of socety and not that of the policy maker. S/he must look outside herself/himself for society's ultimate values; to statutes enacted by representatives of the people, to the constitution under which the people are governed, to rulings of the judicial system, and so on. Of course, the determination of precisely what are society's values is often a difficult problem in the solution of which the policy maker may participate, or give articulation to. But s/he should not assume the responsibility of deciding what social values should be.

Policy Goals (Y$_i$): The Y$_i$ are the articulated goals of policy or target variables. They are deduced from the values of W. An example will illustrate this: an element of W may be an improvement in the quality of the environment, the policy goal may be to reduce air pollution, water pollution, and prevention of deforestation. It should be obvious that W and the Y$_i$ are related and the precise nature of the relationship between the two should be as clear as possible.

The policy maker may well decide the Y$_i$. In a democratic system, the people at the ballot box will judge the reasonableness of the Y$_i$ chosen by the policy maker as well as whether or not the targets are achieved. A great deal of thought and care should be given to the matter of selecting appropriate target variables.

It is especially important that the Y$_i$ be framed in such a way that they are capable of being evaluated. Vaguely stated goals often cannot be. Contrast the following goals: (*i*) air pollution in Delhi should be reduced, and (*ii*) average level of pollutants in air in Delhi should be reduced by 20 per cent over the period of one year. The first statement is general and vague, and cannot be easily appraised. The second is specific and quantitative and can be readily evaluated.

Policy Instruments (Z$_j$): The policy instruments available to achieve the target goals are the Z$_j$. For example, to reduce air pollution to the permissible limit (a target to be sought), various policies (Z$_j$) may be utilised. The government may order relocation of air polluting industries, and ban the use of vehicles emitting more carbon monoxide than the permissible limit. Or, a tax reduction may be given to industries which invest in new air pollution control equipment. A great number of policies may be suitable for accomplishment of the target. Policy analysis is largely composed of looking for and evaluating alternative ways to achieve the target goals. The great bulk of science, and most of economics, is concerned with these tasks.

Like any other scientific study, environmental policy analysis should utilise scientific methods. Hypotheses that postulate how a given policy is expected to theoretically influence a given target should be formulated. Experimentation is the process of determining whether or not in fact the policy works in the way expected. Scientists call the set of theoretical hypotheses a model, and this is the analytical bridge between policy instruments and target variables. Models must be tested, however, both for logical consistency and for empirical verification. A set of statistical relationships must be established that reveal the processes of getting from the Z_j to the Y_i and how efficient the processes are. An econometric model may be specified relating the Z_j to the Y_i.

It should be remembered that just as the Y_i are prescribed by the ultimate values of society, so are the Z_j. That is, the Z_j must be evaluated in terms of political and moral acceptability as well as efficiency in reaching the target. Certain kinds of policies, accepted and even encouraged in one class of society, are antithetical in another class. Most democratic or non-totalitarian societies would never permit policies which seriously compromised the rights of individuals.

Non-controllable Factors and Irrelevant Variables (U_k) and (X_s): There are some factors that affect the targets and which cannot be manipulated or affected by policy. In the framework above, these are the U_k. An example might be the weather. Any target of agricultural production would be affected by the quantum and distribution of rainfall or by hailstorms, and till now, man has been largely ineffective in controlling these factors. They must be treated simply as 'non-controllable' in any policy analysis, but nonetheless must always be recognised and accounted for. Finally, some effects of policy do not apply to the targets or do not directly enter the community's welfare function, but should nevertheless be monitored because they are potentially significant. These are the X_s in the above framework and are called the 'side-effects' of policy. A policy to shift the production of energy from steam engines to internal combustion engines will have side-effects that will not be significant for most situations. Internal combustion engines produce a variety of invisible pollutants in the air that are not a problem until they reach certain dangerous threshold levels. These types of side-effects must be watched but may not affect the evaluation of policy until they reach 'problem' proportions, in which case they may be shifted into the category of Y_i.

So much for the policy framework. It is primarily a taxonomic device and should be of value in elucidating what is being sought, the available means of reaching what is being sought, and at what cost. It helps the policy maker to keep things straight.

7.3 AN ACTION SYSTEM FOR ENVIRONMENT MANAGEMENT

In the context of environment management, an action system may be conceived of as consisting of four elements: the environment manager, the objectives, the conditions (physical, technological, economic, social and political), and the means or instruments. Their relationships can be indicated by a simple diagram as shown in Figure 7.2 (Singh 1999a: 142–43).

The environment manager may be an employee of a public sector undertaking, or a private, cooperative, corporate or any other unit.

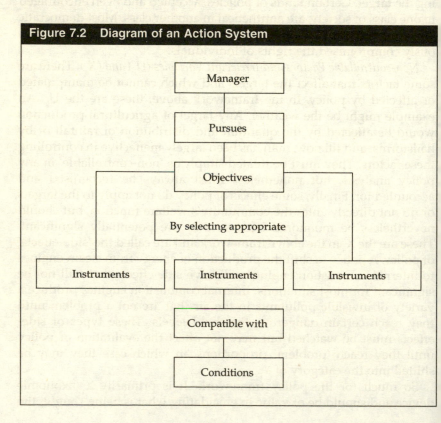

Figure 7.2   Diagram of an Action System

The manager in any given system makes the decisions as to what means should be employed towards a given objective or a set of objectives. The objectives are what the manager wants to accomplish. They need to be clearly defined in operational terms.

The conditions of an action system are all those technical, physical, economic, social, cultural and institutional circumstances that are beyond the control of the manager at least with respect to the particular programme under consideration. The instruments must be adapted to, or compatible with, the conditions under which the programme must operate.

The instruments are the policy measures or programme provisions employed to achieve the objectives. There are often many different instruments that could possibly serve a certain objective. Knowledge of economics is especially useful in making a wise choice in the selection of instruments.

7.4 FORMS OF GOVERNMENT INTERVENTION

Government intervention to offset environmental market failures can take the following five main forms: (*i*) direct control or regulation; (*ii*) safe minimum standards; (*iii*) education and persuasion; (*iv*) economic instruments; and (*v*) changes in the institutional framework such as creation of new or modification of existing institutions. We will now discuss how these interventions or instruments work, and their merits and demerits.

7.4.1 Direct Controls or Regulation

Direct controls are very effective in producing the desired effect. They can take effect very quickly and they can be selective. Because of their quick effect, these instruments are particularly used to deal with short-term environmental problems. The results are graduated and fairly precisely calculable. In general, direct controls are less effective in dealing with long term problems than with short term ones.

Conventionally, direct controls or regulations are given effect through governmental orders or pronouncements by judiciary. In certain cases, laws also are enacted which stipulate that, for instance, you are not allowed to pollute the air above a certain level and if you do, you will be fined or imprisoned or both. This form of intervention has high costs of administration and compliance, is often inflexible and provides little incentive for innovation to reduce environmental degradation. For all these reasons, the use of regulatory instruments in isolation from other measures is unlikely to be the least cost method of achieving environmental objectives in many cases. Control and regulation compares unfavourably with the use of market-based approaches such as taxes and emission charges.

Direct controls have also been used much more to deal with short-term than with long-term or structural problems. Controls do not, as a general rule, modify the underlying market forces which brought about the situation which needed control. Consequently, two things may happen in the long run. First, the market forces which are held back by controls in one sector may break out in another. Second, if it is in the interests of both consumers and producers to evade the controls, then as time goes on, evasion is likely to become more widespread; black markets will spring up and administration will become more expensive.

Despite its weaknesses, control and regulation is still the predominant instrument for addressing environmental problems in most countries, including India. In particular, the use of this instrument is appropriate when some pollution categories, where even small emissions are highly toxic, require a policy instrument where there is no margin for error, and when the necessary institutions such as the courts, and the government have sufficient credibility and adequately trained staff to implement the regulations to a minimum degree of competence.

Finally, there is a cultural dimension. In societies like India's, where there is little respect for the law and where the reflex is to violate the law rather than to obey it, this form of intervention is likely to be less effective, and more expensive than in societies where there is respect for the law.

7.4.2 Safe Minimum Standards (SMSs)

SMSs are used to maintain a safe minimum standard of conservation of renewable critical-zone natural resources like forests, fisheries, groundwater. An SMS of conservation is achieved by avoiding the critical zone, that level of exploitation at which it becomes uneconomical to halt and reverse the depletion (Ciriacy-Wantrup 1968: 253). Since it is impracticable to determine the socially optimum level of use of an environmental resource/amenity in most situations due to non-availability of required information, SMSs could be easily set up which would avoid serious depletion or degradation of the resource in question. In many practical situations, maintenance of SMSs does not require sacrifice of any use; rather, it involves a change in the technology of resource utilisation. These changes may or may not involve any costs. Sometimes the costs are only public in the form of education and/or subsidies.

An important prerequisite to the use of this tool is detailed specification of SMSs for various resources. This job is better done by a team of technical and social scientists and environment managers. According to Ciriacy-Wantrup (1968: 258), 'in soil conservation, a safe minimum standard may be defined as the avoidance of gullies or as a maximum rate of erosion; in forest conservation, as maintenance of a given plant association; in water conservation, a maximum degree of pollution'. For operational purposes, SMSs may be defined in terms of maximum use rates. SMSs when defined in terms of conservation practices could be adapted to suit local conditions, are easy to understand by users and relatively less costly to administer. A drawback of SMSs is that they could be a technical constraint in securing economic efficiency in resource use. Another drawback is that their enforcement in most situations would be problematic and monitoring difficult and expensive.

In India, use of SMSs has so far been limited to the monitoring and control of air and water pollution. Standards have been notified for 26 industries and are enforced by the Central and State Pollution Control Boards. Some 300 water and 106 air quality monitoring stations have been established throughout the country. There are at least five Government of India Acts that have a bearing on environment management. They are the Wildlife Protection Act, 1972, the Water (Preservation and Control of Pollution) Act, 1974 amended in 1978 and 1988, the Forest (Conservation) Act, 1980 amended in 1988, the Air (Prevention and Control of Pollution) Act, 1981 amended in 1988, and the Environment (Protection) Act, 1986.[2] Although, the government has enacted all these laws with good intentions, their enforcement has been very ineffective and lackadaisical. As a consequence, the problems of environmental pollution and degradation continue unabated (Singh 1994a: 86–87).

7.4.3 Education and Persuasion

This instrument seeks to change perceptions and priorities of users of environmental resources and services by internalising environmental awareness and responsibility into individual decision making. Besides education and persuasion, this instrument could also take the form of provision of information and training as well as forms of 'moral

---

[2]For the details of other Acts and rules and regulations, visit the Website of MoEF at: http://www.envfor.nic.in.

suasion' such as social pressure and negotiation. They can complement economic and regulatory instruments and assist in their successful implementation.

Most scholars and practitioners in environment management recognise the need for education as an instrument for averting 'The Tragedy of the Commons'. Most users of environmental resources and services in both developed and developing countries of the world do not use them as they 'should', partly because they are ignorant about the nature and causes of environmental problems and partly because of many economic and institutional factors such as poverty, property rights and tenure. This stands in the way of their adopting socially desirable behaviour. In the short run, education seems to be a logical and simple solution to the extent that environmental problems arise out of ignorance. Education should therefore be used as a means of alleviating ignorance.

In the long run, education also affects environment management in two other ways. First, it influences population growth. With all else equal, people with more education tend to have somewhat smaller families and to that extent population pressure on the environment, and consequently its exploitation and misuse, are reduced. Second, education increases incomes. Many developing countries are trapped in the extreme poverty associated with rapid population growth, illiteracy, unemployment, poor nutrition and hygiene. All these factors tend to have an adverse effect on the environment. Increased incomes therefore help improve the status and management of the environment. In designing education programmes, it is important to keep these questions in mind: who is to be educated, in what subjects, and with what kind of information, by whom, and how? These questions are discussed in the following paragraphs.

When the question of a target group for education in environment management is considered, most people think about users of the environment and policy makers. Admittedly, the knowledge of users of the environment and policy makers is more often than not imperfect in the sense that they do not employ the best information available at the time and place of decision-making. Such imperfections need to be overcome but that is only one aspect of the problem. It is now widely recognised that the environment is degraded and depleted not so much because its users and policy makers do not know any better, as because they are forced by various economic and institutional factors to behave the way they do (Ciriacy-Wantrup 1968: 274). To change these factors and forces in a democracy, it is necessary to educate the politicians and the voting public, and thereby to increase their awareness about the extent and seriousness of the environmental problems and the need for public policy. There are many cases when the education of politicians and the general public has led to desirable changes in rules and regulations affecting the environment. For example, the *Chipko* (Hugging the Trees) movement in the hills of Uttar Pradesh (now the state of Uttarakhand) which aimed at making the people and the politicians living in the area aware of the impending threat to their livelihood and survival from the indiscriminate felling of trees by contractors, forced the then State Government to put a moratorium on felling of green trees for commercial purposes (Bahuguna 1989: 374–77).

As far as education of users of the environment is concerned, we should aim at updating their knowledge about the technologies of resource conservation and utilisation, and helping them in diagnosing the problems correctly and in time before the stage of economic irreversibility is reached. Since resource-use decisions by a group of users are normally made on the basis of the 'best knowledge' available to the group at the time of decision-making, and since better knowledge may be available to other groups elsewhere at the same point in time, it should be possible to improve the existing resource use and conservation decisions by providing to the resource users better knowledge from wherever it is available. Better knowledge may be available from a variety of sources, such as environment research/experiment stations, environment labs, scientists and researchers, extension workers, progressive farmers and other resource users. It will need to be compiled, collated and presented in a form and a language easily understood by the resource users.

As in all other types of education, an attempt should be made to educate and train the users of the environment when they are young, that is, 'catch them young'. Education in environment management should be an integral part of course curricula in all secondary, higher secondary schools and colleges. For training of teachers and undergraduate and post-graduate students, courses in environment management should be included in the curricula of economics, sociology, political science, public administration and agricultural sciences in all colleges and universities. Agricultural colleges and universities seem to be the most suitable places for starting teaching and training programmes in environment management. Periodicals, films, radio and television provide effective media for reaching out to adults (Singh 1994a: 90–92).

Environmental policy makers also need to be educated. They need to be taught about the nature and causes of environmental problems and alternative environment management regimes or systems and tools of environment management that could be used to resolve the problems. There are many cases when lack of knowledge about these aspects of the environment on the part of policy makers has led to the designing of incorrect policies, for example, policies promoting/ permitting indiscreet exploitation of forests for commercial purposes, cultivation of food crops on steep slopes, indiscriminate pumping of groundwater, and unrestricted fishing in coastal areas. Education and training of environmental policy makers should focus on such subjects as the role of the environment in economic development, characteristics of the environmental problems and their underlying causes, and externalities in the use of the environment, and their correction. Short-term training courses and workshops should be designed for this purpose and conducted by the universities and research institutes with requisite expertise in environmental economics and management.

There are many national and international institutions that conduct education and training programmes in the field of environmental economics and management for environment users, managers, policy makers and administrators. For instance, in India, many agricultural universities and the Central Soil and Water Conservation Research and Training Institute, Dehra Dun with its eight regional research centres located in different agro-climatic regions of the country conduct research and training programmes in soil and water management and watershed management: the Forest Research Institute and College, Dehra Dun, and the Indian Institute of Forest Management, Bhopal, in forest management; and the Central Inland Capture Fisheries Research Institute, the Central Marine Fisheries Research Institute and the Central Institute of Fisheries Technology in fisheries management; and several universities in environmental economics.[3] The approach adopted by these institutes and colleges is, however, narrow in scope and technocratic in nature. There is need to reorient their approach to make it more comprehensive, multidisciplinary and people-centred, with greater emphasis on the role of economics, social sciences and management.

The International Crops Research Institute for the Semi-Arid Tropics (ICRISAT) located in Patancheru near Hyderabad in India is engaged in conducting multidisciplinary research in natural resources management in the semi-arid tropics of India and some African countries. Besides, there are many professional associations/societies of environmental economists and ecological economics including the International Society of Ecological Economics, and the Indian Society of Ecological Economics. An International Association for the Study of Common Property is

---

[3]The Madras School of Economics, Chennai has established a Centre of Excellence in Environmental Economics.

engaged in promoting better understanding of common pool resources (CPRs) and improve their management. The Association is a good source for teaching and training materials in CPR management and could be drawn upon by institutions interested in imparting training in this field.

There are many non-governmental organisations (NGOs) in both developing and developed countries of the world that impart education and training in natural resource economics and environment management, conduct and/or sponsor research on environmental problems, and disseminate research and other relevant information about the environment. For example, the Centre for Science and Environment based in New Delhi and the Centre for Environment Education (CEE) based in Ahmedabad are two of the national level reputed NGOs engaged in promoting awareness, education and training in environment protection and management. NGOs are, generally speaking, better oriented to conduct education and training programmes for farmers and other users and should be encouraged and assisted by government agencies to do so if they have the necessary technical expertise and willingness to do the job. NGOs could very well complement and supplement government effort in education and training in environment management.

7.4.4 Economic Instruments

This set of instruments affects the costs and benefits of alternative actions open to economic agents, and thereby influences the behaviour of decision-makers in such a way that alternatives are chosen that lead to an environmentally more desirable situation than in the absence of the instrument. Economic instruments aim to bridge the gap between the private and social costs by internalising all external costs to their sources, namely, the producers and consumers of resource depleting and polluting commodities. Such instruments are often referred to as market-based instruments, as they work by using market signals such as prices, emission charges/taxes, subsidies, interest rates and exchange rate to encourage socially better decisions.

The current near exclusive reliance on instruments of command and control for environmental regulation in India does not permit individual actors to minimise their own costs of compliance. This leads, on one hand, to non-compliance in many cases, and unnecessary diversion of societal resources from other pressing needs, on the other. Economic instruments work by aligning the interests of economic actors with environmental compliance, primarily through application of the 'polluter pays' principle. This may ensure that for any given level of environmental quality desired, the society-wide costs of meeting the standard are minimised. However, in some cases, use of economic instruments may require intensive monitoring, which too may entail significant social costs. On the other hand, use of existing policy instruments, such as the fiscal regime, may significantly reduce or eliminate the need for enhanced institutional capacities to administer the incentive-based instruments. In future, accordingly, a judicious mix of incentives-based and fiat-based regulatory instruments should be considered for each specific regulatory situation.

Compared to regulation, market-based instruments allow greater flexibility in the choice of the means to reduce environmental damage. By doing so, they can be more cost-effective. Economic instruments can also make the costs of environmental protection more transparent and encourage greater innovation in more environment friendly technologies. We will now discuss how most commonly used market-based instruments work and their merits and demerits.

Prices

A combination of institutional failure (absence or failure of secure property rights), market failure (environmental externalities) and policy failure (distortionary subsidies) results in the underpricing of scarce natural resources and environmental assets. As a result, producers and consumers of these products and services do not receive correct signals about the true scarcity value of the resources they consume or the environmental damages they cause. This gap between the private cost of a product (production cost) and the total cost to the environment (including depletion and damage cost) causes incorrect signals. Since the social costs of depletion and damages are not internalised, this results in over-production and over-consumption of products which are resource depleting and environment polluting.

A glaring example of underpricing of a natural resource is the pricing of canal irrigation water in India. Conventionally, water is considered a free gift of nature and a free good. But it costs to harvest, store and deliver water where and when it is needed and in that sense it is not a free good but a scarce economic good. In developing countries, pricing of water on the basis of its scarcity value is neither technically nor socially and politically easy. Yet potential gains justify some form of water pricing in the face of its increasing scarcity. Efficient pricing is at the heart of natural resource management. Almost all resource problems can be traced to discrepancies between private and social valuation of resource commodities and resource stocks; these discrepancies can be bridged through efficient pricing, which reflects the real scarcity value of resources.

The present policy of the Government of India (GoI) seeks to rationalise water pricing to improve efficiency in resource allocation or cost recovery to reduce budget deficits. This could be expected to promote conservation of water resources and reduce environmental costs. Not only could the salinisation and waterlogging be contained, but more importantly the solution of water shortages through demand management could avert the environmental problems of constructing new irrigation systems (supply management).

Prices of environmental goods, inputs and services used in production and consumption could be changed by policy makers to produce socially optimum results. Price changes generally affect the time distribution of use rates. By price changes we mean relative price changes. Effects of price changes depend upon how these changes are distributed over time and how interrelationships between use rates in different intervals through marginal revenues and costs are affected. An increase of product prices which is expected to occur at some future interval and to last indefinitely or to increase with time will induce planning agents to shift rates of use toward the future that will result in conservation. An expected decrease of product prices under corresponding assumptions will result in depletion. As regards production inputs and services, we may say that increases in the prices of conserving inputs and services or decreases in the prices of depleting inputs and services will lead to depletion and vice versa (Ciriacy-Wantrup 1968: 131–33). In general, support of product prices is more likely to bring depletion than conservation. This is because price supports, being dependent on the political fortunes of a government, are not expected to last indefinitely or to increase with time. As a tool of conservation policy, price support is suitable only in those special cases where prices of a *bonafide* conserving input or service or product is supported.

In India, there are many examples where price controls have led to resource depletion. For example, as we stated in the preceding paragraph, low price of canal irrigation water (a depleting input) in conjunction with high support prices of products, such as, sugarcane and paddy has led to over-irrigation and hence wastage of scarce water resources and also to soil degradation as a result of waterlogging and salinity in many areas, particularly in the north-west region. Similarly, low tariff for electricity (a depleting service) has led to the depletion of groundwater resources through excessive pumping in many regions. In many areas, including the coastal regions, extraction of groundwater has already reached the stage of economic irreversibility. Likewise, low prices fixed by the Forest Departments for a long period of time for supply of forest-based raw materials to industries have led to rapid depletion of forests in India. There is, therefore, need for a careful review of the existing pricing policies of environmental goods, inputs and services, and for rationalising their pricing policies. Generally speaking, all resource-depleting practices should be taxed and all resource-augmenting practices subsidised, and prices of both inputs and outputs should reflect as far as possible their real resource costs or opportunity costs (Singh 1994a: 87–88). Economic instruments such as taxes or subsidies for environmentally sound production can be used for full cost pricing of production and consumption.

Taxes

As we have seen in Chapter 4, all environmental problems can be traced to the existence of some form of negative externality. Taxation is the most widely used instrument for eliminating externalities by bridging the gap between social and private costs and social and private benefits, and thereby achieving socially optimal level of use of environmental goods and services, which is also the equilibrium use rate of the resource. As we stated in Chapter 4, it was Pigou (1962), who had argued that taxes and subsidies could be used to encourage economic agents to internalise externalities. The logic of taxation schemes is to raise the private costs of entry and/or use (or equivalently to lower the benefits) to the point where individual action will result in the socially optimum level of production of a good, whose production involves a negative externality (pollution).

Figure 7.3 depicts the typical supply and demand curves for a good X. However, in this case, we have labelled the supply curve S= MC_P because it represents the marginal private costs associated with producing the good. The free market equilibrium output and price are Q_M and P_M respectively. Now suppose that there is a negative externality (pollution) associated with the production of each unit of the good, X, then the MC_P curve would not represent the real costs to society of the good. If each unit of the good produced imposes an externality costing Rs 2 on a third party, then the true marginal social cost will be MC_S. The pollution tax shifts the private marginal cost curve, MC_P, upward by Rs 2 at every point to MC_S in the figure. Q* is the socially optimum level of production of good X and P* is the socially optimum price at the new intersection between the demand curve and MC_S. Thus, by internalising the social costs of pollution, the actual output of the polluting good X is reduced from Q_M to Q* while the price charged to the consumer rises from P_M to P* and the price received by the producer is

Figure 7.3   Effect of a Pollution Tax

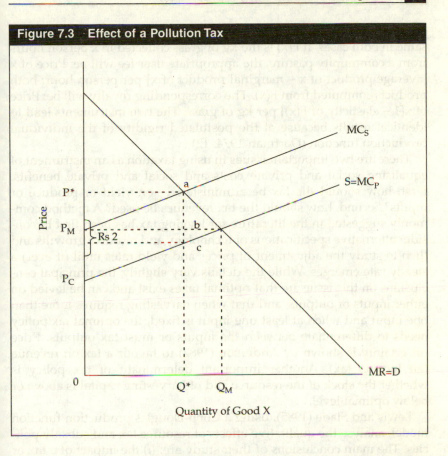

reduced from P_M to P_C. Depending upon the relative elasticities of the demand and supply curves, the burden of the pollution tax is shared by both consumers and producers. In our example, the consumer pays ab and the producer bc of the total tax ac. Thus, the pollution tax affects both producers' behaviour and consumers' behaviour.

It is important in this context to realise that the aggregate effect of a tax could be counter-intentional if there were no restrictions on the number and the size of firms in an industry causing a negative externality, say, water pollution. This is so because, although the contribution of each individual firm to pollution after taxation would be smaller than before taxation, all the firms together are likely to generate more pollution than what can be assimilated by the water body into which the effluents are discharged (Bromley 1991: 62–63).

Tax could be levied in the form of either a user fee/charge or cess/royalty. In the former case, it increases the marginal private cost and in the latter it reduces the marginal private benefits, the result being the same in both cases. If F(x) is the kg of grass collected in x person hours from a community pasture, the appropriate user fee will be: Price of x [average product of x – marginal product of x] per person hour; both products computed from F(x). The corresponding royalty will be: Price of x[1 – elasticity of F(x)] per kg of grass. The two instruments lead to identical results because of the postulated rigidity of the individual production function (Dorfman 1974: 12).

There are two important issues in using taxation as an instrument of equalising social and private costs and social and private benefits. First, how should the tax be administered—on yield or produce or inputs? Second, how should the tax revenues be used? A method commonly suggested in the literature for levying tax has been first to consider alternative specifications of technology and resource growths and then to study the adjustment of prices and yield rates until (if ever) a steady rate emerges. While the details vary slightly, the principal conclusions on this issue are that optimal taxes exist and can be levied on either inputs or outputs, and that when harvesting requires more than one input and when at least one input is fixed, the optimal tax policy needs to differentiate between the inputs or must tax outputs. Price uncertainty is shown by Anderson (1982) to favour a tax on revenue (an income tax). Another important determinant of tax policy is whether the stock of the resource and of harvesting capital is above or below optimal level.

Lewis and Slade (1985), using a Cobb-Douglas production function model, analyse the qualitative effects of resource tax and subsidy policies. The main conclusions of their study are: (*i*) the impact of a tax or subsidy depends on whether it is levied directly on the extracted resource or applied to a processed product which uses the resource as an input; (*ii*) if the resource share in production is low, and if the final product prices are rapidly appreciating over time, a royalty (tax) can lead to a higher extraction rate and a cost subsidy to a lower extraction rate; and (*iii*) taxes and subsidies are both distortionary in the sense that they affect the time paths of production and input use even in cases where the extraction rate is unaffected.

Ciriacy-Wantrup (1968: 13) discusses in detail various aspects of taxation as a tool of conservation policy. His major conclusions are: (*i*) progression in taxation tends towards conservation and regression towards depletion; (*ii*) a high tax on income (from a resource) in conjunction with a lower capital-gains tax may result in conservation; (*iii*) yield taxes are superior to most other taxes in terms of economy and accuracy of assessment and administration but are inferior to net revenue taxes from the standpoint of ability to pay and social justice; and (*iv*) lump-sum taxes are inflexible and generally regressive and may therefore lead to depletion.

Theory is mute on the issue of how the environmental tax revenues should be used. Dasgupta (1982) argues that tax revenues should be returned in the form of some lump-sum payment or via equivalent means, otherwise an optimal tax may not be strictly Pareto-preferred, that is, while the taxing authority gains, the users of the environmental resource in question lose. Hopcraft (quoted in Magrath 1986) suggests that tax revenues can be collected in a community kitty and redistributed among the co-owners of the environmental resource on the basis of ownership shares held by them in the resource. To conclude, we can say that problems with assessment, collection and responsible handling of tax revenue are difficult to resolve in most real-world situations and environment managers need to carefully consider all the issues before taking a final decision regarding the use of taxes as a tool of environment management.

A simple rule of thumb in determining whether to levy a tax or not is to compare estimated loss of revenue/utility to the tax-payer and others who use the resource/resource commodity (consider both loss of the producer's surplus and loss of the consumer's surplus) and estimated gain of revenue to the tax authority. If the gains exceed the loss, then the tax is economically justified. A serious weakness of this instrument is that it is politically very inconvenient to levy a new tax, particularly a direct tax (Singh 1994a: 77–80).

Subsidies

Like taxes, subsidies also are used as an instrument of environment management. They seek to change the behaviour of the users of environmental goods, inputs and services by motivating them to use the environment in a socially desirable way. They could be used in two situations. One, when the private marginal benefit to the user at the socially optimum level of resource use is less than the social benefit, that is, when a positive externality exists. Two, when the marginal social cost of using an environmental resource at the level of private optimum is higher than the marginal private cost, that is, when a negative externality exists. In both the cases, subsidies abate the externalities involved; in the former, by equalising the marginal private benefits and marginal social benefits, and in the latter, by equalising the marginal private costs and marginal social costs. As in the case of taxes, aggregate welfare effects of subsidies could also be counter-intentional (Singh 1994a: 80–81).

In the real world, there are relatively few instances where governments have used subsidies for solving environmental problems. In India, soil conservation subsidies have, for many years, been used to motivate farmers to adopt recommended soil conservation measures on their private lands. For prevention of soil erosion from public lands, many state governments now provide 100 per cent subsidy, that is, all the required soil and water conservation structures are constructed at government cost (Singh 1988). For private lands also, subsidies are available for promoting the adoption of soil and water conservation measures under various watershed development and other programmes. The effect of subsidies on the adoption of an eco-friendly soil conservation measure technology is illustrated in Figure 7.4.

In the figure, the private marginal cost of adoption of an eco-friendly soil conservation measure is shown by the MPC_1 curve and the marginal revenue by the MR curve. The private optimum level of adoption of the measure is at X_e. However, the adoption of the measure has a positive externality in the form of reduced soil erosion and higher recharge of groundwater downstream. But the benefits from these positive externalities are not realised by the adopter. So his marginal revenue remains unchanged. If we provide a subsidy on the use of the measure equivalent to the value of the positive externality, the private marginal cost curve will shift downwards to become MPC_2. At that

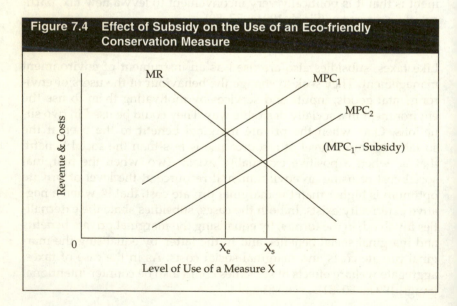

Figure 7.4   Effect of Subsidy on the Use of an Eco-friendly Conservation Measure

level of cost, the equilibrium level of use of the measure will be X_s, which is higher than X_e. Thus, the use of subsidy will provide an incentive to the adopter to use the measure at the socially optimum level.

On the negative side, heavy use of subsidised chemical fertilisers and pesticides also leads to water pollution and poisoning of aquatic life through run-off into the water systems. Furthermore, misappropriation of subsidies by those who administer them has been a serious problem when using this instrument in India and therefore there is need to streamline the existing system of administration of subsidies so as to minimise the chances of misappropriation and leakages. It does not matter that chemical subsidies have been cut to reduce the drain on the budget; their reduction also reduces the drain on the environment. Ideally, however, environmentally destructive inputs (for example, pesticides and chemical fertilisers) should be taxed in proportion to their negative externalities, and environmentally beneficial inputs such as Integrated Pest Management (IPM), organic fertilisers and soil conservation should be subsidised in proportion to their positive externalities.

Reduction of agricultural input subsidies such as fertilisers, pesticides and credit, which is also an integral part of structural adjustment policies, generally has a positive impact on the environment. But in India the use of subsidies in agriculture is highly politically sensitive and there is a strong farmers' lobby against any major reduction in agricultural input subsidies. The political parties in power are also reluctant to use this instrument as the use of both pesticides and chemical fertilisers has helped India increase its crop yield and production on existing land substantially, thereby attaining self-sufficiency in food production. The policy of the Government of India to reduce subsidies on chemical fertilisers is expected to reduce the use of fertilisers through price and substitution effects. The organic manure would become relatively cheaper. This would reduce environmental pollution caused by production of chemical fertilisers by burning fossil fuels and reduce air and water pollution caused by the use of chemical fertilisers, besides reducing soil degradation caused by the excessive use of fertilisers in irrigated areas over a long period of time. The increased use of organic manure would also improve the soil condition.

The subsidy provided on biogas plants in India encourages installation of biogas plants. The use of biogas saves alternative fuels like dung cakes, firewood and kerosene. The use of dung cake as a cooking fuel reduces the availability of organic manure, on one hand, and pollutes the environment by generating carbon dioxide (CO_2), on the other. The use of firewood degrades the environment by causing deforestation and generating CO_2 and is a major source of indoor pollution. Similarly, the use of kerosene as a cooking fuel also pollutes the environment by generating CO_2. The use of biogas for cooking as compared to dung cakes and firewood is also more hygienic. Also, dung as a manure is a cheap soil conditioner containing all essential plant nutrients for plant growth.

The impact of reduction of agricultural credit subsidies is somewhat ambiguous. If credit subsidies are benefiting large farmers engaged in using capital intensive environment polluting technologies for production, the reduction of these subsidies clearly reduces environmental degradation. If, on the other hand, credit subsidies are benefiting small farmers who have inadequate funds for investment in land improvement and soil conservation, any reduction of these subsidies will reduce the level of soil conservation than is currently the case. However, even in the case of the small farmer, there are superior policies to outright credit subsidies, which are in any case fungible and can be used for other purposes. Removal of interest rate ceilings, issue of secure land titles that can be used as collateral, and increased credit availability at competitive rates are better for the farmer, the budget and the environment than credit subsidies, because they optimise the use of both capital and land. Credit subsidies are an incentive to borrow but not an incentive to invest in soil conservation or tree planting if the farmer has no security of land ownership.

The GoI policy also provides for reduction in subsidies (or import duty exemptions) on farm equipment and land clearing machinery, again as part of their objective of reducing budget and trade deficits and eliminating policy-induced distortions. This policy reform has several negative effects on resource use and the quality of the environment because subsidised land clearing machinery: (a) encourages deforestation and the clearing of marginal lands for agriculture; (b) compacts and damages the structure of fragile tropical soils; (c) increases the use of fossil fuels; and (d) distorts the farmer's labour-capital choice in favour of capital and against labour. Aside from the economic inefficiency and misallocation of scarce capital that the latter entails, it also reduces agricultural employment thereby promoting encroachment of forest lands or undue urban migration.

A simple rule of thumb in determining whether to provide a subsidy or not is to compare estimated loss of revenue due to the subsidy and estimated gains to the beneficiaries of the subsidy (consider both gains in the producer's surplus and the consumer's surplus). If the gains exceed the loss, then the subsidy is economically justified. A serious weakness of this instrument is that it is very difficult to withdraw a subsidy once it is granted. Politically, it is highly undesirable for popular governments to withdraw subsidies even when they are no longer justified on economic grounds.

Subsidies are, in principle, fairly flexible and can be used selectively and given to any particular inputs or type of activity or a particular region. The main objective which this instrument can serve is the promotion of use of eco-friendly technologies and methods of production, processing, packaging and marketing in all the sectors of the economy. The instrument can take several forms such as the promotion of use of new eco-friendly technologies by subsidising their prices, and promotion of investment in pollution control devices.

Rate of Interest

The rate of interest is an important macroeconomic parameter with macroeconomic implications for resource allocation because it links the present with the future. The higher the interest rate (or discount rate), the higher the cost of waiting, and therefore, the faster the rate of resource depletion and the lower the investment in resource conservation. However, this effect may be mitigated somewhat by the fact that a higher interest rate means a higher cost of capital, which tends to reduce capital-intensive resource depletion and environmental degradation. Interest rate ceilings and implicit interest rate subsidies for promoted industries have been the main interest rate distortions affecting the agricultural sector and the rural economy in general.

Credit policy has relied on administrative fiats, interest rate ceilings and constrained use of loan proceeds. Yet, there is growing evidence that farmers would prefer more flexible terms and increased credit availability even if they had to pay higher interest rates. The liberalisation of the capital market is critical to land improvements, reforestation investments, resource conservation, agricultural intensification and growth of the rural industry.

Exchange Rate

As most of the resource-based commodities produced in India are internationally traded or tradable (for example, tea, coffee, spices, jute, cotton, fish, rice and rubber) or are substitutes for tradable commodities (for example, natural gas, lignite, hydropower), an overvalued exchange rate would reduce their depletion by reducing their price relative to non-tradable goods (like transport, services, construction). An overvalued exchange rate and export taxes have similar effects in that they discourage exports (and encourage imports) of resource-based commodities, thereby reducing the pressure on the domestic resource base. Increased exports of primary commodities may have an adverse effect on the environment unless the prices of inputs and outputs involved fully reflect the true scarcity of the resources being used and the environmental costs incurred.

Reduction of export duties on certain crops such as horticultural and plantation crops helps diversify the economy away from soil-eroding crops such as rice and sugarcane and towards high value perennial export crops such as fruits, tea, coffee and rubber with positive environmental side-effects. Increased incentives for perennial crops vis-à-vis annual field crops such as cotton and rice can help protect the soil on gentle slopes but are not a substitute for natural forest cover on steep or fragile slopes. India could use tariff reform as an opportunity to favour import or manufacture of environmentally benign technologies and machinery and discriminate against highly polluting technologies.

Minimum Wages

Minimum wage laws (which also encourage capital intensity) reduce labour employment and depress real non-manufacturing wage rates. This, under conditions of labour abundance, leads to (a) increased use of low-cost labour in depleting natural resources, and (b) encroachment of resource sectors by unemployed or underemployed labour.

To sum up, most economists favour the use of economic or market-based instruments, particularly emission taxes, over other instruments, especially control and regulation. This is mainly because of (i) lower cost of compliance and higher economic efficiency; (ii) freedom to private enterprises to decide whether they pay taxes or invest in cleaner production technology; (iii) bureaucratic interference is minimum; (iv) incentives to innovate and to improve environmental performance over time; and (v) pollution taxes could be an important source of revenue to the government.

However, use of market-based instruments, particularly pollution taxes, has several disadvantages. One, political compulsions either not to tax the polluters or impose low taxes, which do not cover the entire external costs. Two, it is very expensive to administer taxes. Three, in developing countries like India, there is a high tendency to evade taxes through unethical practices. And finally, fixing socially optimum tax rates is problematic in view of the difficulties in measurement of the extent of emissions and their valuation.

7.4.5 Changes in the Institutional Framework

The instruments described so far have all been instruments which are used within the existing institutional framework and the changes made in these instruments can be quantified. Changes in the institutional framework for environment management include creation of new institutions or organisations such as creation of private property rights in open access resources, market creation, privatisation of a state property or establishment of pollution control boards and framing new laws and policies. These instruments do not lend themselves easily to quantification and usually require a change in the laws. Since it takes time to change the institutional framework, these changes are usually made with long term rather than short term objectives in mind. But there are occasions on which the institutional framework has been changed in order to facilitate the use of the instruments for short term policy. For example, the nationalisation of 14 leading commercial banks in India in 1969 was a major institutional change aimed at increasing the flow of bank credit to farmers, rural artisans and other rural entrepreneurs.

The establishment of new institutions, or a major change in the institutional framework is usually a fairly major policy step which often meets with more opposition than does the use of an existing instrument. Since changes of this kind usually involve new laws, they have to go through a lengthy procedure of parliamentary approval.

Now we will briefly discuss the uses, merits and demerits of some of the instruments that fall in this category.

Market Creation

This type of instrument helps in internalising environmental damages on the production side because the government creates a market to use the environment as a waste sink or issues pollution permits. These rights can be traded, that is, bought and sold like any other commodity. Tradable pollution permits are good examples of market creation as they allow a company to buy or sell the rights to pollute the environment with an allowable level of pollution. This ensures that a specific level of pollution or emission will be attained at the lowest cost to society.

Individuals or companies using the environment are supposed to pay pollution charges either directly to the government or they would be required to purchase pollution permits. Pricing of the use of environment as a waste sink would internalise the cost of waste into the product prices and therefore, in the long run, reduce the waste per unit of output. This is also an instrument which can ensure that the environment is only affected as far as it can tolerate such impacts. To achieve sustainable use of the environment by charging for polluting it, it is essential to ensure that the environment is used below its self-healing capacity. Otherwise economic activities would still be continued at an unsustainable level, although less than it would be without the pollution changes.

The use of tradable pollution permits is easy to handle from an administrative point of view. After the initial permits are sold, the government is not involved any more. Besides, they are a source of revenue to the government, are flexible, and can be selective, focusing on regional environmental problems. On the negative side, it is difficult to control and monitor the exercise of pollution rights conferred by the permits, as also to find safe minimum standards for environmental pollution that is below the environment's self-healing capacity. Besides, new enterprises might decide to establish a factory in other regions or countries where there are no, or lower limits for pollution, and thereby debar the local population from the benefits of the new investment.

Creation and Assignment of Property Rights

As we stated in Chapter 4, Section 4.8.2, the creation and assignment of a property right can be used to internalise an externality and it does not matter, in terms of economic efficiency, which party (the polluter or persons suffering from the pollution) is assigned the right. Economic efficiency will be achieved as long as property rights are fully allocated and that completely free trade of all property rights is possible. The importance of this instrument is in demonstrating that it does not matter who owns what initially but only that everything should be owned by someone. Trade will place resources in their highest value occupation eventually. In India, this instrument has been used for averting the degradation of common pool lands.[4]

Public Interest Litigations (PILs)

Thanks to the growing judicial activism in India, this instrument is now being used quite frequently for resolving environmental problems. We have numerous examples of cases in which High Courts and the Supreme Court in India, *suo moto*, or in response to PILs have pronounced orders for relocating polluting industries out of cities, using Compressed Natural Gas (CNG) in place of diesel for operating buses and auto rickshaws in several cities including Delhi, and keeping cities clean by institutionalised collection and disposal of garbage by the municipalities/municipal corporations concerned. For illustration, we would like to present a gist of a few of the significant environmental decisions taken by the Supreme Court (SC) of India in 1996 (Box 7.1).

---

[4]See for details, Chapter 8, Section 8.4.3 of this book.

Box 7.1   Examples of Court Orders for Prevention of Pollution

8 July 1996: The Supreme Court (SC) orders closure of 168 Delhi-based industries by 30 November 1996, and directs the Chief Secretary, Delhi government, to fix responsibility on government officials who had been negligent in their duty.

6 August 1996: The SC orders closure of 69 foundries in Howrah, West Bengal, following their failure to install pollution control devices.

28 August 1996: On the basis of a petition from the Vellore Citizens Welfare Forum, the SC imposes fines of Rs 10,000 on each of the 700-odd tanneries in Tamil Nadu, and asks them to pay compensation for polluting the environment; the tanneries are also asked to install pollution treatment plants before December.

6 October 1996: The SC directs another 513 industries out of Delhi for having damaged the health of Delhi's citizens.

9 October 1996: The SC orders closure of 39,000 illegal industrial units operating in residential areas in Delhi.

10 December 1996: The SC bans child labour in hazardous industries.

11 December 1996: The SC orders closure of aquaculture farms within 500 metres of the coast along India's 6,000 km coastline by 31 March 1997; it also passes the directive that employees of the farms be paid six years' compensation in lieu of loss of employment.

17 December 1996: The SC bans all non-forest activity in forest areas without prior approval of the Centre; it also bans the movement of cutting trees and timber from the north-eastern states.

19 December 1996: The SC directs shifting of 550 tanneries located in east Calcutta by 30 September 1997, and the setting up of an environment pollution fund, with each unit depositing Rs 10,000 as fine. This money is to be used for restoring the pollutant-riddled Hooghly river.

30 December 1996: The SC fixes 31 December 1997 as cut-off date for the closure of 292 coke- and coal-based industries within the Taj trapezium in Agra, further directing the stoppage of coal supplies to them from 30 April 1997.

Source: CSE 2001: 161.

Creation of Central and State Pollution Control Boards

In India, we now have a Central Pollution Control Board and State Pollution Control Boards in most of the states. These are all statutory bodies created with the mandate to control and monitor pollution levels. The experience with their functioning has been a mixed bag of successes and failures. Lax enforcement of the prescribed norms or standards and legal hassles have been the major weaknesses of these bodies.

International Treaties and Conventions

There are many 'global commons', that is, parts of the planet that are outside national jurisdiction and that can be managed only through international cooperation and agreements. Although an international environmental management policy still seems a rather distant possibility, there are many historical cases of international cooperation and conventions in this field. We could learn from their experience and try to develop some semblance of an international policy for management of global commons.

The following four major tools have been used in the past to secure international cooperation in environment management: officially sponsored international conferences; treaties (conventions); establishment of permanent international agencies; and international commodity agreements (Ciriacy-Wantrup 1968: 305). Most of the early successful attempts at international regulation of fugitive resources were concerned with individual resources in limited areas. For example, marine fish was the first fugitive resource that was brought under international regulation through a series of regional conferences and conventions. Recently, more ambitious but as yet less successful attempts have been made to cover more resources and wider geographic extent. Examples of some recent international attempts include the United Nations Conference on the Human Environment, 1972, publication of *World Conservation Strategy: Living Resource Conservation for Sustainable Development* (1980) by the International Union for Conservation of Nature and Natural Resources, the United Nations Law of the Sea, 1982, (International) Conference on Common Property Resource Management, 1985, sponsored by the Board on Science and Technology for International Development, National Research Council, USA, the Montreal Convention on Ozone Layer, 1990, the United Nations Conference on Environment and Development, 1992 and the Kyoto Protocol on Carbon Sinks and Emissions Trading, 1997.[5] Besides, many international research institutes, centres and professional

---

[5]For details of selected environmental treaties and conventions, see Grafton et al. 2001, Appendix 7, pp. 339–62.

associations such as the World Resources Institute, the International Institute for Environment and Developments, the International Association for the Study of Common Property, the International Centre for Living Aquatic Resources Management, the International Irrigation Management Institute, and the International Board for Soil Research and Management conduct research on different resource systems and develop innovative resource management practices. In spite of all these attempts, enforcement of existing international regulations and conventions leave much to be desired.

7.5 MAIN POINTS

The following are the main points made in this chapter:

- Given the failure of market to protect the environment and ensure its socially optimum use, it is necessary for the government to intervene with a view to manage it on a sustainable basis.
- A number of policy instruments are now available for environment management. They include direct control and regulation, education and persuasion, economic instruments such as subsidies and emission charges, and changes in the institutional framework such as creation of new or modification of existing institutions, and change in tax rates and interest rates.
- Changes in macroeconomic policies such as monetary, fiscal and foreign exchange policies have more powerful effects on how natural resources are being allocated and used than micro or sectoral policies. For example, other things remaining constant, the higher the costs of inputs of capital and labour used in resource extraction or in polluting industries, relative to the price of outputs, the lower the rate of resource depletion and the amount of pollution.
- Identification of appropriate instruments and determination of their optimum levels are better done by public policy analysts than anyone else using a quantitative framework that relates the instruments to the objectives of the environment policy.
- Choice of appropriate instruments needs to be made carefully keeping in view the prevailing socio-economic and political environment. In many cases, instruments are not properly selected and their levels are not consistent with the objectives they seek to achieve. This results in wastage of valuable public resources and unnecessary delays in achieving the objectives.

- A simple rule of thumb in determining whether or not to use a policy instrument is to compare its expected social benefits and social costs. If the former exceeds the latter, the contemplated use of the instrument is socially desirable and hence must be implemented.
- It is also important to note that no instrument, howsoever good it may appear on paper, is meaningful unless it is enforced fully or is executed faithfully. In India, enforcement of all policy measures in general, and natural resources and environment management policy measures in particular, has always been problematical and far from satisfactory.
- There are many 'global commons', which are over-exploited, degraded and polluted. They are part of the planet that are outside national jurisdiction and that can be managed only through international cooperation and agreements. Although there are many historical cases of international cooperation and conventions in this field, there is need for more effective enforcement of international laws, treaties and conventions.
- For effective implementation of the various instruments outlined in this chapter, strong political will and good leadership at all levels, appropriate organisational structures, dynamic and well-informed bureaucrats committed to the cause of environment management, professional environment managers, and above all, well-informed, enlightened and environment-conscious citizens are all essential. In their absence, effective enforcement will be difficult and lackadaisical. In a nutshell, enforcement of chosen policy instruments deserves the highest priority at present in India and perhaps also in all other countries of the world.

7.6 DISCUSSION QUESTIONS

1. Discuss and illustrate with examples the merits and demerits of direct regulation/controls and taxes and subsidies as instruments of controlling air pollution.
2. In India, we now have the technologies available for reducing air pollution and water pollution but still both the types of pollution have been increasing over time. Explain why.
3. In India, we have so many laws and rules for preventing environmental pollution but they are by and large ineffective. Explain why and how they can be made effective. For details of the Acts and Rules, visit the Website of the Ministry of Environment and Forestry (MoEF), Government of India at http://www.envfor.nic.in

4. Can the creation of property rights as advocated by R.H. Coase in open access solve the problem of their degradation? Yes/No. If yes, why and if not, why?

5. What are the pros and cons of use of the 'polluter pays' principle for controlling environmental pollution in India?

6. In India there are many communities who on their own voluntarily protect the environment, especially the wild life and certain tree species. This is the most *cost-effective* and *self-sustaining* means of biodiversity conservation. What are the limitations of this alternative?

7. Write a critique of education as an instrument of environment protection.

8. Write a critique of public interest litigations as an instrument of environment management.

9. Many environmental problems have global dimensions, for example, depletion of ozone layer and acid rain and there are several international laws, conventions and protocols to mitigate them. What are their limitations in mitigating global climatic changes.

8 Land and Environment

8.1 INTRODUCTION

Land is one natural resource that affects and is affected by the environment. For example, land in steep hill slopes, devoid of vegetation is prone to soil erosion, which is a major source of silting of river beds and dams/water reservoirs, reducing the water carrying capacity of rivers and storage capacity of reservoirs. This results in deterioration of quality of water and flash floods, which cause tremendous loss of life and property and degrade the environment. On the other hand, natural environmental hazards such as earthquakes, landslides, droughts and cloud bursts adversely affect the quality of land and water. Given this role and importance of land in the context of the environment, it is imperative for students of environmental economics to understand the nature and extent of land-related problems that affect the environment, the economic logic underlying those problems and the alternatives available to remedy them.

In this chapter, we will first describe the nature and extent of land degradation in India, then examine the economic logic of land degradation, and finally explore various alternatives for restoration of degraded lands thereby improving the quality of environment as well as productivity of land. The purpose of this chapter is to enhance the knowledge and skills of the reader to identify and analyse the problems of land degradation from both causal and curative perspectives.

8.2 THE NATURE AND EXTENT OF LAND DEGRADATION

A certain level of land degradation is an inevitable consequence of natural processes and human activity. Any exploitation and use of non-renewable resources inevitably results in their partial or total depletion, as well as the degradation of the landscape and generation of waste. Agricultural extensification leads to deforestation, cultivation of marginal lands and soil erosion while agricultural intensification leads to pesticide and fertiliser run-off(s), waterlogging and soil salinity. When identifying alternatives for mitigating the problems of land degradation, we should aim at minimising it, or at least restricting it to a level consistent with society's objectives, rather than trying to prevent or eliminate it altogether.

There are some problems engendered by land degradation that are common to all countries regardless of the type of economic system and levels of development prevailing there. For example, the underlying causes of land degradation, as we will discuss in the next section, are fundamentally similar in all countries. Yet, its manifestations, dimensions and implications differ depending on the history, geography and level of development, among others. Even in the same country, land degradation evolves over time with population growth, migration, urbanisation, industrialisation, structural change and economic growth. India is no exception to this.

It is estimated that in India in 1994, about 188 million ha of land, which is 57 per cent of the country's total geographical area of about 329 million ha, was degraded. Of the 188 million ha of degraded land, about 149 million ha was affected by water erosion, 13.5 million ha by wind erosion, about 14 million ha by chemical deterioration and 11.6 million ha by waterlogging (Sehgal and Abrol 1994). A recent survey by the National Bureau of Soil Survey and Land Use Planning revealed that 66 per cent of India's total geographical area (around 192 m ha) was at varying stages of degradation (quoted in Haque 1997).

Land degradation can result from both the intrinsic attributes such as location, environment and chemical and physical properties of the soil as well as from man-made circumstances. It has significant impacts on crop productivity and the environment. Joshi and Jha (1991) in a study of four villages in Uttar Pradesh found that a 50 per cent decline in crop yields over a period of eight years was due to salinisation and waterlogging caused by the irrigation system.

The wastelands can broadly be divided into two categories according to ownership—privately owned wastelands (about 35 million ha) and government owned wastelands (about 49 million ha). The government owned wastelands also include the village common (grazing) lands and other open access lands, which are owned by the Revenue Department or the Forest Department or by other government agencies such as the Indian Railways and the National Highways Authority of India.

A characteristic feature of land resources in India is the preponderance of common pool lands, that is, the lands which are used in common by identifiable groups of people. These lands, irrespective of their legal ownership are accessible to local people without any restrictions and are used without any rules and regulations. In this sense, they may be called Open Access Resources (OAR). All OAR suffer from what Hardin (1968) called, albeit erroneously, 'The Tragedy of the Commons'. The problem should correctly be termed 'the tragedy of the open access'. Most OAR are degraded, eroded, denuded of vegetation, encroached and polluted.

In India, the western and central states of Gujarat, Madhya Pradesh (including Chhattisgarh), Maharashtra and Rajasthan have relatively large tracts of wastelands (Table 8.1). It can be seen from the table that the extent of wasteland in each of these states as a proportion of the total reporting area varies from nearly 18 per cent to 29 per cent. This means that these

Table 8.1 Estimates of Wasteland in Selected Western and Central States of India by Category

('000 ha)

Type of Wasteland	Gujarat	Madhya Pradesh	Maharashtra	Rajasthan
1. Guillied &/or Ravinous Land	736.97	7,924.40	1,548.07	4,473.59
2. Upland with or without Scrub	12,228.20	31,920.88	20,359.55	16,753.92
3. WaterLogged & Marshy Land	164.94	49.96	296.12	1.29
4. Land affected by Salinity/Alkalinity-Coastal/Inland	3,028.99	162.81	78.50	2,279.11
5. Underutilised Degraded Notified Forest Land	2,776.16	17,527.87	10,168.75	10,815.64
6. Shifting Cultivation Area	0.00	0.00	0.00	0.00
7. Degraded Land under Plantation Crops	31.84	914.43	687.43	100.39
8. Degraded Pastures/ Grazing Land	209.75	145.19	1,349.40	9,243.82
9. Mining Industrial Wastelands	9.79	118.95	6.37	64.00

(Table 8.1 Contd.)

(Table 8.1 Contd.)

				('000 ha)
Type of Wasteland	Gujarat	Madhya Pradesh	Maharashtra	Rajasthan
10. Sands-Desertic Coastal	76.09	24.57	50.61	13,303.64
11. Steep Slopping Area	323.92	180.49	1,389.57	182.28
12. Barren Rocky/Stony Waste/ Sheet Rocky Area	1,402.48	2,600.11	2,388.84	3,190.23
13. Snow Covered and or Glacial Area	0.00	0.00	0.00	0.00
14. Total wasteland	20,989.13	61,569.66	38,323.21	60,407.91
15. Total reporting area	118,878.00	337,871.00	208,893.39	205,869.00
16. Wasteland as %of total reporting area	17.66	18.22	18.35	29.34

Source: The National Wastelands Identification Project (NWIP), NAEB Home Page http://envfor.nic.in/naeb/naeb.html.

states suffer most from land degradation and its economic and environmental consequences.

8.3 THE ECONOMIC LOGIC OF LAND DEGRADATION

Given their open access nature, wastelands are bound to be degraded/ overexploited and given their finite extent, their use is subtractable/ competitive, that is, if one of the co-users uses more of a piece of wasteland, the less is left to that extent for the other co-users. In resource economics, this phenomenon is known as interdependence of the underlying appropriation/production functions or existence of externalities in appropriation/production. An externality is defined as an unintended and uncompensated side effect of an activity.

When an externality is present, the competitive equilibrium use of the resource (open access) is socially inefficient (Dasgupta 1982: 19–23; Singh 1994a: 26–31). We illustrate this with an example of a village grazing land, which is, *de facto,* an open access resource for the villagers. We presume that there are N identical village households owning together 100 animals and interested in grazing their animals in the village grazing land, which has a carrying capacity of only 50 animals. Under the above-mentioned assumptions, each rational (profit maximising) animal owner will try to graze all the animals owned by him/her. In doing so, s/he would reduce the quantity of forage grass available to the other animal owners. This shows that there exists the problem of a negative externality which causes the grass stock of the grazing land to fall down, which in turn leads to the increased cost of stall-feeding the animals to compensate for the reduced quantity available from the pasture and hence a loss of net revenue to all the animal owners. Every rational animal owner behaves in the same manner. The consequence of this rational behaviour on the part of individual animal owners is disastrous for all of them as a group or community in the sense that the grazing land is overexploited and every animal owner's revenue goes down. Why this happens can be explained in terms of divergence between the private marginal cost and the social marginal cost of grazing, that is, the existence of an externality. Each animal owner considers only his (private) costs of grazing and not the cost of overgrazing (an externality), which he is inflicting on the other animal owners. This results in the private marginal cost of grazing being less than the social marginal cost of grazing and therefore the competitive equilibrium level of grazing being higher than the socially optimal level of exploitation. This is illustrated in Figure 8.1.

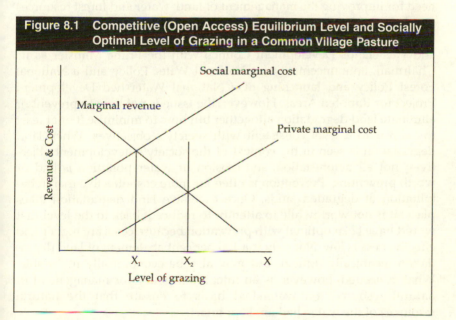

Figure 8.1   Competitive (Open Access) Equilibrium Level and Socially Optimal Level of Grazing in a Common Village Pasture

As shown in the figure, the competitive equilibrium level of grazing is attained when the level of grazing is X_2 where the private marginal cost is equal to the marginal revenue and the socially optimum level of grazing is X_1, where the social marginal cost is equal to the marginal revenue. Thus, the open access equilibrium is attained at a higher level of grazing and hence a higher level of exploitation than the socially optimum level of exploitation, that is, $X_2 > X_1$.

To avert the tragedy of the common village grazing land, it is necessary to change its status from an open access to a cooperative property of its co-users. This could be done by organising the co-users in some form of formal or non-formal organisation and vesting in their organisation the usufructuary rights to the grazing land on a long-term lease basis.

8.4 ALTERNATIVES FOR RESTORATION OF DEGRADED LANDS AND IMPROVING THE ENVIRONMENT

The Central and the State governments in India have now realised the need for improving the management of land, water and forest resources and have initiated a number of measures to achieve this. Some of the important measures include the establishment of a National Land Use and Wastelands Development Council with the Prime Minister as its Chairman, announcement of a National Water Policy and a National Forest Policy and launching of a National Watershed Development Project for Rain-fed Areas. However, the issue is not how to prevent or eliminate land degradation altogether but how to minimise it or at least to keep it to a level consistent with society's objectives. When land degradation is seen in the context of the society's development objectives, not all deforestation, soil erosion or water pollution is bad or worth preventing. Prevention is often far more cost-effective than rehabilitation of degraded lands. Once excessive land degradation takes place, it is not worthwhile to attempt to reduce it back to the level that would have been optimal with prevention because costs are higher and effectiveness is low. Not only is a 100 per cent abatement of land degradation technically difficult but may also be economically not viable. What is needed, however, is an integrated policy for management of natural resources on watershed basis to ensure that the natural resources of the watershed are kept intact.

Now we will discuss a few practicable approaches to minimise land degradation keeping in view the developmental objectives of India's policies and programmes.

8.4.1 The Watershed Approach

A watershed may be defined as an area from where rainwater is drained through a common outlet into a water body such as a river, a rivulet, a tank or a lake. The watershed has a clear conceptual identity in hydrology, physical geography and other natural sciences. The use of this term in social sciences is of rather recent origin. The term is often used synonymously with two other words, namely, basin and catchment. Basically, a watershed is a hydrologic unit which, in view of the interdependence of its natural and human resources, is ideally suited for natural resource planning and management (Singh 1994a: 166).

In the watershed approach, a watershed is used as the basic unit for planning and management of land, water and other resources of the watershed. The approach is holistic, multidisciplinary and is a practicable approximation of the systems approach. It enables the planners and managers to consider together various physical, biological, sociocultural, economic and institutional factors operating within a watershed and its surrounding environment and formulate a comprehensive and integrated watershed development plan to achieve specific social objectives.

In a watershed, natural and human resources are all interdependent and interact with one another. This gives rise to the problem of externalities. For example, pumping of groundwater in a watershed affects the aquifer that is a common pool resource to which all those who live in the watershed have a legitimate claim. If one of the co-users pumps more water, to that extent, less is left for use by the others in the watershed. Optimum use of groundwater in a watershed, therefore, requires the cooperation or participation of all the people living and using groundwater in the watershed. Similarly, soil and water conservation in a watershed requires the participation of all the land owners having land in the watershed in the form of adoption of recommended soil and water conservation measures. In a nutshell, all uses of all natural resources irrespective of whether they are owned privately or publicly are interdependent and require cooperation of all the resource users for internalising/minimising the externalities involved. This is best achieved when planning and management of natural resources, especially common pool resources, is done on watershed basis and the resources are managed by their users who are organised into some sort of formal association such as watershed users' association.

In a typical watershed development project, the following activities are included:

1. Soil and water conservation measures and land development in both arable and non-arable lands.
2. Introduction of improved crop production practices in dry lands.
3. Initiation of dry land horticulture in marginal lands and introduction of silvi-pastoral and agro-horticultural systems.
4. Afforestation of wastelands.
5. Support of existing supplementary enterprises like animal husbandry, dairying, sericulture, pisciculture, etc.

In India, the watershed approach was first adopted on a significant scale in 1974 when the Government of India (GoI) enforced its implementation under the Centrally-sponsored 'Scheme of Soil Conservation in the Catchments of River Valley Projects' (Bali 1988). In 1982, the GoI, under the auspices of the Indian Council of Agricultural Research (ICAR), sanctioned 46 model watershed projects to be implemented in the dry land areas of the country. These projects were implemented by the State governments through their Agriculture Departments and technical backup provided by the All India Coordinated Research Project for Dryland Agriculture (AICRPDA), the Central Research Institute for Dryland Agriculture (CRIDA) and the Central Soil and Water Conservation Research and Training Institute. The CRIDA and AICRPDA scientists were responsible for monitoring 30 of these model watershed projects.

In July 1986, the Union Ministry of Agriculture and Rural Development launched the National Watershed Development Project for Rain-fed Areas (NWDPRA) as a Centrally-sponsored scheme. It covered 99 districts in 16 states in the country. The criteria for selection of districts were: (*i*) the annual rainfall should be 500–1,125 mm; and (*ii*) the irrigated area should be less than 30 per cent of the cultivated area. The project had been taken up on watershed basis. The main objective of the project was to optimally utilise the available rainwater and minimise the risk of crop failure. The project was financed by the Government of India to the extent of 100 per cent. It was a major thrust programme of Department of Agriculture and Cooperation in the Eighth Plan and was intended to be extended to all the blocks in the country where the arable area under assured irrigation is less than 30 per cent (GoI, n.d.: Foreword and Preface). Besides the ICAR projects and NWDPRA, there are many other watershed development projects currently underway in different states of India. They are funded by both governmental agencies and non-governmental organisations including foreign donors.

In India, the Government of Karnataka (GoK) has taken quite a few pioneering steps in the development and management of dryland watersheds. A project in Integrated Watershed Development was launched in a selected watershed, Kabbalnala, in Bangalore district in 1983 with financial aid from the World Bank. It became widely popular in India for its innovative approach. Consequently, in 1984, the GoK decided to replicate the Kabbalnala model of watershed development in all the 19 districts of the state. For this purpose, the GoK created, by an administrative fiat, an ingenious three-tier organisation structure with a state-level Watershed Development Council, divisional-level Dry Land Development Boards (DLDB), and project-level Watershed Development Teams and launched, in 1984–85, a District Watershed Development Programme (DWDP) in the state. The main objective of DWDP was to enhance and stabilise the productivity of both arable and non-arable lands. The DWDP covered one purposively selected watershed in each of the 19 districts in the state. The programme is rated as highly successful (Singh 1991).

There are many success stories of watershed development projects in India, confirming the suitability of watershed approach to dry land development. This approach, besides resulting in increased crop yields and incomes, also creates positive environmental impacts such as reduced soil erosion and consequent reduction in siltation of river beds and reservoirs and increased recharge of groundwater (Singh 1995b). We present here a case study of a watershed project.

A Case Study of Mendhwan Watershed, Ahmednagar District, Maharashtra[1]

This ex-post evaluation study was conducted in the Mendhwan Watershed in the months of April–May 1999. The Mendhwan watershed falls in the water-scarce zone in Sangamner *taluk* of Ahmednagar district in Maharashtra. The zone has an annual normal rainfall of only 400 mm. In the pre-project stage, the watershed had vast chunks of degraded lands and used to face extreme scarcity of even drinking water. Large-scale seasonal migration of labour in search of employment was prevalent in the area. Sheep rearing based on seasonal migration of herds in search of grazing areas was the major source of occupation. This watershed was included under the National Bank for

[1]This case study has been adapted from Vimal Kishor (2000: 54–56).

Agriculture and Rural Development–Indo-German Watershed Development (NABARD–IGWDP) Programme in 1992 and the project was completed in 1996. After two years of completion of the project, an ex-post evaluation study was conducted by NABARD to assess the impact of the programme on the economic, social and environmental benefits accrued to the watershed community and also to identify constraints at the farmer level, community level and at the level of NGO.

Some of the highlights of the case study are as follows:

Increase in Area Under Cultivation

The project interventions resulted in an average increase of 23 per cent in the area under cultivation per family in the watershed. The increase in the cultivated land was made possible by bringing fallow lands under cultivation.

Increase in Irrigation

The net irrigated area increased by 29 per cent in the post-development period as compared to the pre-development period. The increase in the land under irrigation was observed on the lands of the majority of the farmers, irrespective of the location of their cultivated land in upper, middle and lower reaches of the watershed. The gross irrigated areas as a percentage of the gross sown area increased from 10.33 per cent to 38.56 per cent, an increase of 28.23 percentage points.

Impact on Groundwater Resources

The number of wells in the sample farms had gone up from 41 to 64 and the number of wells, which used to become dry in summer months declined from 54 per cent to 14 per cent. The average depth of water in the wells increased from 4.2 feet in the pre-development period to 8.8 feet in the post-development period. The direct impact of all these developments was reflected in the irrigation intensity, which increased from 106 per cent to 128 per cent due to the watershed development interventions.

Cropping Intensity

The cropping intensity, which was 115 per cent in the pre-development stage, increased to 133 per cent in the post-development stage, registering an increase of 18 percentage points.

Changes in Cropping Pattern

The project had a significant impact on diversification of the cropping pattern. This was evident from the increase in the total number of crops grown, which increased from seven during the pre-development stage to 18 in the post-development stage. Diversification of cropping pattern resulted in introduction of several high value commercial crops such as onion, which accounted for 4.3 per cent of the cropped area in the post-development stage, a crop which was non-existent in the watershed in the pre-development stage. Dry land horticultural crops like *sapota*, guava and *ber* were also introduced on a significant scale in the watershed.

Yield of Crops

The average yield of *bajra*, which is the main crop grown in dry lands in the watershed, increased significantly and was comparable with the average yield of irrigated *bajra*. This was made possible due to the improved moisture regime in the watershed. Similarly, significant increases in the yield rates of all other crops were also observed in the post-development stage.

Impact on Income from Cultivation

The gross value of produce per hectare of cultivated area in the post-development stage increased to the level of Rs 5,743 as compared to Rs 2,673 in the pre-development stage, registering an increase of over 100 per cent due to the project interventions. The average net income generated from per hectare of gross cropped area of the sample farmers was Rs 4,739 in post-development stage as compared to Rs 2,089 in the pre-development stage.

Impact on Allied Activities

Next to farming, dairy activity picked up in a substantial measure. The net income from dairy activity increased from Rs 538 in the pre-development stage to Rs 3,935 per household in the post-development stage. The practice of stall-feeding of dairy animals replaced the earlier activity of sheep rearing based on grazing. This was due to the increase in the assured fodder supply in the watershed and the restriction imposed on free grazing on common lands.

Employment

Due to availability of employment opportunities within the watershed, the seasonal migration was drastically reduced. Employment in the farm sector increased substantially and the project work also provided ample employment to the landless. The incremental labour employment per hectare of gross cropped area was 18 man days per annum. The study revealed that the relative shares of different occupations within the watershed had undergone a significant change with new sources of income like dairy and retail trade gaining importance and income from wages and sheep rearing declining. Income from the service sector increased from 8.73 per cent to 10.5 per cent and that from business activities increased from almost nil to 10.91 per cent.

Sustainability of the Village Watershed Committee (VWC)

The Government of Maharashtra made the VWC a partner in harvesting the benefits of the forestland on a 50:50 basis. The income derived from the forestland by the VWC was estimated at Rs 158 per hectare per annum.

Impact on Social Sector

The higher and more stable farm income made possible by watershed development had induced several positive impacts on education, housing and health-care. The enrolment of children in primary as well as secondary standards had gone up, while number of drop-outs from the school had reduced substantially. There was an improvement in the ratio of girls to boys in school enrolment as also participation of elders in the non-formal education programme. The increase in number of *pucca* houses was spectacular.

Rate of Return on Investment

The Financial Internal Rate of Return (FIRR) without including the cost of management provided under the project directly to the NGO was estimated at 31.5 per cent. The FIRR with the cost of management included was 27 per cent. The Economic Rate of Return (ERR) was 35.0 per cent.

On the whole, we could conclude that the watershed project was a grand success. There are many success stories of watershed development projects undertaken in various parts of India (Singh 1995b). An important lesson from the experience with those success stories is that the watershed development approach holds the highest potential as instrument of restoring degraded land, water and forest resources of India and thereby increasing income, employment and improving the quality of environment (Singh 1990).

8.4.2 Afforestation of Wastelands

Afforestation of degraded lands seems to be the most cost-effective and environment-friendly alternative for their restoration. A review of 21 studies on the economics of afforestation undertaken in the last two decades in India showed that wastelands afforestation projects in India were financially feasible even when non-market benefits of afforestation projects such as reduction in soil erosion, increased recharge of groundwater aquifers, moderation of microclimate and improvement in the micro environment are not taken into consideration (Balooni and Singh 2003). Further, it was also found that the Financial Internal Rate of Return (FIRR) from the afforestation projects was more than the prevailing interest rate on the long-term loans for forestry projects in India. This means that afforestation projects are financially viable and bankable, besides being eco-friendly.

Afforestation activities generate substantial employment opportunities as 70–80 per cent of the expenditure incurred on plantations is incurred on wages paid to labourers. In view of this, the Government of India (GoI) is encouraging, through various programmes, the afforestation of wastelands to generate employment opportunities in rural India. This is substantiated by the fact that GoI provides funds under several of its rural development schemes for afforestation.

Besides, at the macroeconomic level, afforestation projects provide a number of backward and forward linkages to various sub-sectors of India's economy. New afforestation projects might further enhance these linkages. For example, the recent spurt in plantations of poplar tree species in the state of Haryana in northern India has led to the emergence of the poplar-based veneer industry in the region; veneers are used for production of plywood and different types of composite woods.

In India, the western and central states of Gujarat, Madhya Pradesh (including Chhattisgarh), Maharashtra and Rajasthan offer a higher scope for tree plantation on such lands than most other states. This is because these states have a relatively high proportion of their total geographical area classified as degraded/wastelands as shown in Table 8.1.

It seems to us that afforestation of wastelands is going to emerge as a big enterprise in the coming years in India to meet the rapidly increasing demand of raw material for wood-based industries. This is mainly because the supply of wood from the government-owned forests has been declining over recent years owing to the forest conservation oriented strategies adopted by the government. The new Indian Forest Policy, 1988 stipulates, *inter alia*, that the wood-based industry should collaborate with farmers to grow trees on their private lands or to establish their own captive plantations; in the past the wood-based industry in India was provided wood at subsidised rates from government-owned forests. On the other hand, the government is promoting farm forestry and community forestry programmes on private and community lands respectively to meet the wood and fuelwood needs of the rural poor. Thus, in view of the increasing importance of tree plantation on wastelands and their contribution to the Indian economy, there is need for stepping up the pace and scale of afforestation programmes in the country.

These are the following three major models of afforestation of wastelands that have been adopted in India:

1. The State Forest Department (SFD) Model
2. The Non-Governmental Organisations (NGOs) Model
3. The Tree Growers' Cooperative Societies (TGCS) Model

The SFD Model

The State Forest Departments (SFDs) in India are the most important and resourceful of all the organisations engaged in tree plantation on wastelands. The SFDs launched social forestry programmes in the late 1970s and the early 1980s with the objectives of arresting and reversing the depletion of India's forest resources and to meet the biomass needs of the rural poor. The programmes laid special emphasis on community participation. They got a big boost in the early 1980s when several international development and financing agencies started co-financing (with SFDs) social forestry projects in India. Consequently, during the decade of 1980–90, some 14 externally aided social forestry projects were underway in as many states of India. The funding agencies included the World Bank, the Food and Agriculture Organization (FAO), the United States Agency for International Development (USAID), the Canadian International Development Agency (CIDA), the Swedish International Development Agency (SIDA), the Overseas Development Administration (ODA) and the Danish International Development Agency (DANIDA).

Typically, under the SFD model, the following four types of activities are taken up:

1. Reforestation and rehabilitation of degraded forestlands.
2. Strip plantation on roadsides, along canal banks and railway lines.
3. Community forestry on village and state-owned land.
4. Farm forestry.

As we stated earlier in this chapter, the village common lands in India suffer from what Hardin (1968) called 'The Tragedy of the Commons'. Government intervention through afforestation of wastelands by the SFDs has been extensively tried in India as one of the instruments of averting the 'tragedy' of the common grazing/wastelands lands. We present in Box 8.1 a case study of a village wood lot established on village common land in a village in Gujarat state by the Gujarat SFD.

Box 8.1   A Case Study of Aslali Village Woodlot (VW) in Ahmedabad District

Aslali was one of the earliest few village panchayats (VP) selected under the VW scheme by the Gujarat State Forest Department. The village is located in Dascroi taluka of Ahmedabad district about 14 km south of Ahmedabad city. It had 125 ha of community grazing land of which about 10 per cent had been encroached and privatised by villagers. The Aslali VP agreed to provide 13 ha of its *gauchar* (common grazing land) for plantation initially. The first plantation was raised in the year 1974–75 in 13 ha of land. The trees were harvested in 1985–86.

The total cost incurred by both the SFD and the VP on the woodlot over the 12-year period was Rs 47,646 or Rs 3,665 per ha. The total benefits to the VP and villagers from the woodlot over the 12-year period amounted to Rs 119,850 or Rs 9,219 per ha. The present value of net benefits from the woodlot over the 12-year period was Rs 200,957 or Rs 15,458 per ha. The annuity of this sum at the 15 per cent discount rate was Rs 37,076 per year. The benefit cost ratio at the 15 per cent discount rate was 1.73 and the internal rate of return (IRR) was 28.71 per cent. This shows that the woodlot was financially viable. Besides, the woodlot also improved the quality of land and microclimate in the village.

Source: Singh (1994: 247–63).

Quite a few studies have been conducted to evaluate the performance of social forestry schemes of the SFDs in India including village wood lots. Generally speaking, the following are the major findings and conclusions of most of the evaluation studies of the SFD model (Singh 2001):

1. The approach has been physical target-oriented with very little emphasis on community participation and sociological aspects.
2. Forest Department officials have been reluctant to hand over the management of woodlots and other community plantations to village panchayats and forest protection committees, even where such organisations are functional.
3. Employment has been the main and most tangible benefit to the people.
4. The objective of meeting the biomass needs of the rural poor has remained, by and large, unfulfilled.
5. Of all the components of social forestry, farm forestry has been the most popular with big farmers emerging as main beneficiaries.
6. The response of villagers to community forestry has been poor, due partly to small and uncertain benefits and partly to the lack of mechanisms for equitable distribution of benefits.
7. Although they are called social forestry projects, beneficiaries view them as government projects as everything is done by the SFDs with very little people's participation.

The NGO Model

In India, over the last one decade or so, there has been a tremendous growth in the number of NGOs involved in social forestry projects. It is estimated that at least 500 NGOs are engaged in this activity in the country. The Gujarat State Forest Department is one of the pioneers in India in involving NGOs in social forestry projects. At present, some 54 NGOs in the State are directly or indirectly implementing various social forestry projects. We present in Box 8.2 a case study of a tribal village in Dahod district (erstwhile part of Panchmahals district) of the state where an NGO, Sadguru Water and Development Foundation, hereafter termed as Sadguru, has done exemplary work in tribal development through a water-centric approach.

The TGCS Model

TGCS are of a relatively recent origin in India. The Fadval Tree Growers' Cooperative Society, organised in the mid-1970s in Surat district of Gujarat state, is probably the first such society established in

---

Box 8.2 **A Case Study of Transformation of Wasteland in Village Shankerpura through Tree Plantation**

Shankerpura is a small village of some 250 tribal households in Dahod district of Gujarat. The total population of the village is about 2,000 and the geographical area about 588 ha. In 1976, Sadguru commissioned a community Lift Irrigation (LI) scheme in the village. Now, all the families have access to irrigation from the lift scheme as well as from their private wells fitted with pump sets. The village had a lot of wasteland lying barren for decades. Tree plantation was found to be the most profitable use of this land. So Sadguru launched a massive programme of tree plantation on both village common lands as well as marginal lands privately owned by villagers. Besides, an intensive watershed development scheme funded by both the Government of Gujarat and Sadguru was also implemented in the village.

As a consequence of all these activities, the village has been completely transformed from a treeless, semi-arid backward one to an agriculturally advanced green oasis over a period of only about 20 years. Tree plantation was a highly profitable activity for farmers in the village with every household owning, on an average, 4,700 trees. The average benefit annuity was Rs 42,815 per ha and the benefit-cost ratio at 15 per cent discount rate of 4.93. Construction of new houses, increased employment and higher rate of literacy were the other major impacts.

Source: Singh (2001).

India. A bold initiative was taken by the National Dairy Development Board (NDDB) in 1986 to organise TGCS under a pilot project in selected states of India. For this purpose, a national-level cooperative organisation, the National Tree Growers' Cooperative Federation (NTGCF) was established with its headquarters at Anand. It was a co-operative institution registered under the Multi-State Cooperative Societies Act. The NTGCF initially selected the five Indian states of Andhra Pradesh, Gujarat, Karnataka, Orissa and Rajasthan for organising TGCS. Later on, two more states, namely, Madhya Pradesh and Uttarakhand, were included in the project. In February 2001, a new organisation called the Foundation for Ecological Security (FES) was created and with effect from April 2001, the responsibility for implementing the TGCS project of NTGCF was transferred to it. The FES is an autonomous NGO registered under the Societies Registration Act XXI of 1860. It has a broader mandate than NTGCF in the sense that it seeks to work with and facilitate the promotion of a wide range of democratic village/people's institutions, besides, of course, TGCS. Its mission is ecological restoration and conservation of land and water resources in the eco-fragile zones of India (FES 2002).

The main objective of TGCS is to enable villagers to grow trees and grasses of suitable species on their own marginal agricultural lands and village degraded revenue lands to meet the local needs of fuelwood, fodder and small wood. The ultimate goal is to improve the socio-economic condition of the members and the quality of local environment. Any 11 or more adult persons belonging to different families can form a TGCS by making an application to the District Registrar of Cooperative Societies. A TGCS is registered under the Cooperative Societies Act. Any person is entitled to be a member of a TGCS if s/he is residing within the area of its operation, and has completed 18 years of age.

By the end of March 2005, NTGCF/FES had organised 973 village institutions[2] including 540 TGCS in 21 districts spread across seven states (FES 2005: 9). As of March 2002, the TGCS had altogether 105,598 members and had planted 21,771 ha of government-owned wasteland and village panchayat grazing land. Nearly 14.2 million trees had been planted on common as well as private lands. The average expenditure incurred on tree plantations varied from as low as Rs 3,901 per ha in Orissa to as high as Rs 25,293 per ha in Uttarakhand depending on the location and physical characteristics of the land. The overall average expenditure for all the seven states taken together was Rs 7,258 per ha (FES 2002: 22 and Table 2). The total expenditure incurred on tree plantation by the TGCS and other village institutions in India as of March 2002 was Rs 158 million.

Initially, NTGCF used to provide a loan of Rs 458,000 to each TGCS established under its auspices for the initial period of five years for planting trees on 40 ha of village wastelands. The NTGCF, in turn, received funds and grants from many national and international agencies including the Canadian International Development Agency and Swedish International Development Authority.

We present in Box 8.3 a case study of the Vatra TGCS in Kheda district of Gujarat. It is too early to assess the performance and sustainability of the TGCS that have been established under the auspices of

---

[2]The village institutions comprise TGCS (540), Van Panchayats (64), Village Committees on Gramya Jungle Lands (40), Grazing Land Development Committees (41), Village Forest Committees (167), Panchayati Raj Institutions (49) and Village Committees (72).

Box 8.3 The Vatra Tree Growers' Cooperative Society:
A Case Study

Vatra is a medium-sized village in Kheda district of Gujarat. In 1996, it had a total human population of about 3,965 distributed in 566 households. Of the total population, about 63 per cent were farmers, 22 per cent landless labourers and the remaining 15 per cent were engaged in other non-farm activities. The total geographical area of the village is about 722 ha of which, in 1987, about 522 ha (72 per cent) was arable (cultivable) and about 142 ha was *gauchar*, i.e., village common grazing land. A TGCS was organised in the village by a Spearhead Team of the National Tree Growers' Cooperative Federation (NTGCF) and formally registered on 20 July 1987 under the Multi-State Cooperative Societies Act 1984. The TGCS had 560 members of whom 311 (56 per cent) were landless, 190 (34 per cent) marginal farmers having less than 1 ha land, and the remaining 59 (10 per cent) were small farmers having 1–2 ha land. The TGCS got 40 ha of degraded land from the Revenue Department of the Government of Gujarat on lease for 15 years for tree plantation. The TGCS planted some 121,745 saplings of 21 different tree species on 40 ha land over the period, 1987–92. The survival rate was about 89 per cent.

The total employment generated over the period, 1987–92, was 11,464 person days of which women accounted for 61 per cent. The average cost of tree plantation was Rs 9,359 per ha at the 1995–96 prices and the projected net present value of benefits to the members at 15 per cent discount rate and the 1995–96 prices over the 16-year period, 1987–88 to 2002–03 was Rs 162,240 per ha. The benefit-cost ratio at the 15 per cent discount rate was 5.35 and the Financial Internal Rate of Return was 61.95 (Balooni 1997: 240). Thus, the tree plantation was economically and financially viable. In addition, the TGCS restored the productivity of the degraded land on a sustainable basis, improved the microclimate and empowered its members through education, training and participation in the management of its affairs (Saxena 1996: 57).

Source: Adapted from Saxena (1996) and Balooni (1997: 190–204).

the NTGCF/FES. But on the basis of data on actual costs and intermediate benefits and estimates of final harvest, we found that a typical TGCS can be financially viable over a period of 15 years or so. Singh and Balooni (1997) estimated the average cost of tree plantation for a sample of three TGCS in Kheda district of Gujarat to be Rs 13,523 per ha at the 1995–96 prices over a period of five years. The costs included the cost of plantation of trees and after-care; cost of land development and soil and water conservation; and overhead costs of the TGCS. The costs incurred in earlier years (before 1992–93) were compounded at the rate of 10 per cent to express them at the 1995–96 prices. The benefit-cost ratio at the 15 per cent discount rate varied from 4.46 to 5.35 over a period of 16 years on the basis of projected benefits (Balooni 1997). The survival rate of the saplings planted in the three sample TGCS in Kheda district of Gujarat varied from 47 per cent to 89 per cent, depending upon the type of land and climatic conditions.

In most of the situations obtaining in India, the TGCS seems to be the most appropriate form of organisation for promoting social forestry as it is member-centred and its primary goal is to serve its members while having a high degree of social responsibility. If the poor people including the landless interested in social forestry are organised in TGCS, they could have access to institutional finance, technical advice and training, managerial support, production inputs, and national and international markets. TGCS can bargain better than individual tree growers with those to whom they sell their produce and from whom they buy their production inputs.

Recently, the Ministry of Environment and Forests, Government of India issued fresh operational guidelines for the formulation of *National Afforestation Programme* for the 10th Five Year Plan (2002–07). These guidelines seek to promote a participatory approach to development of forests for the Government of India sponsored afforestation schemes. Afforestation schemes operational during the 9th Plan have been merged under the new National Afforestation Programme so as to 'avoid multiplicity of schemes with similar objectives' and to ensure 'uniformity in funding pattern and implementation mechanism'.

Another significant landmark in the history of afforestation of wastelands is the Government of India-sponsored 'Greening India Programme', which proposes to cover 43 million ha of degraded forest and non-forest lands under the watershed approach in a 10-years time-frame. This includes regeneration of 15 million ha of degraded forests under JFM. The government has proposed to set up Green India Authority and Green India Fund to undertake this programme. The implementation of this programme requires Rs 4,800 crore annually against the current availability of Rs 1,615 crore through the Government of India's budgetary resources (Balooni and Singh 2003). Given the limitation of budgetary resources for forestry activities, the government will have to seek funding from other sources. One such source is 'institutional finance', which has not yet been fully tapped for forestry activities in India.

8.4.3 Creating Private Property Rights in Common Lands

According to Hardin (1968), and many other scholars, one of the ways of averting 'The Tragedy of the Commons' is their privatisation, that is, creating and enforcing private property rights in the commons. In India, there are many success stories of privatisation of common lands. One of them is the privatisation of public lands (state property) and village common (waste) lands in West Bengal under the Land Patta Scheme launched in 1977. The basic objective of the scheme was to improve the socio-economic status of the poor landless households and marginal farmers through provision of land on lease and other basic necessities such as fuelwood, fodder, timber and minor forest produce. Under the scheme, common pool wastelands were allotted to the target group on long-term lease by the Land Settlement Department. Another significant landmark in the process of privatisation of lands in the state was the launching of a special programme called 'Operation Barga' in 1979. The main objective of this programme was conferring legal rights in the land, which was being cultivated by *bargadars* (share croppers) for many years. The distribution of *patta* lands got an impetus in 1984 when the Government of West Bengal integrated the Land Patta scheme with its social forestry scheme. The patta holders (lessees) planted trees, mainly eucalyptus, on the *patta* lands. They were given saplings and fertilisers at subsidised rates by the State Forest Department, besides provision of technical information and training in planting trees. This resulted in not only best possible use of these wastelands but also improved the microclimate and averted the tragedy of those lands (Singh 1994a: 149–63). To conclude, we could say that privatisation of common wastelands in India following the West Bengal model could become an important instrument of restoring them, making them more productive and improving the environment.

8.5 MAIN POINTS

The following are the main points made in this chapter:

- Land is one of the natural resources that affects and is affected by the environment. India has vast tracts of wastelands, which have been lying barren for ages for a variety of reasons. These lands pose a serious threat to the environment. But if restored and used judiciously, these lands could contribute significantly to improving both the quality of environment and the well-being of millions of rural poor, who mainly depend on them for their livelihood.

- Most of such lands are owned by government and village panchayats and are *de facto* open access resources. Given their open access nature, wastelands are bound to be degraded/overexploited. Restoration of those lands is urgently needed to generate income and employment opportunities and to improve the quality of the environment.

- A certain level of land degradation is an inevitable consequence of natural processes and human activity. Any exploitation and use of non-renewable resources inevitably results in their partial or total depletion, as well as the degradation of the landscape and the generation of waste. Agricultural extensification leads to deforestation, cultivation of marginal lands, and soil erosion while agricultural intensification leads to pesticide and fertiliser run-off(s), waterlogging and soil salinity.

- Watershed approach to wasteland development has been tried successfully in many areas in India. This approach, besides resulting in increased crop yields and incomes, also creates positive environmental impacts such as reduced soil erosion and consequent reduction in siltation of river beds and reservoirs and increased recharge of groundwater. This approach also facilitates the internalisation of externalities within a watershed.

- Tree plantation on common pool wastelands is economically viable and environment friendly. There is, therefore, need for exploring alternative ways of afforestation of such lands.

- One of the institutional alternatives for afforestation of wastelands, which has been successfully tried in several states of India, is Tree Growers Cooperatives and other types of people's organisations. Besides, as many NGOs have also done a good job of motivating villagers to plant trees on their marginal lands and village common lands, they should also be involved in tree plantation programmes.

- Creation of property rights in common pool wastelands and assigning them to individuals or their organisations is also an important alternative for averting the tragedy of the wastelands.

- What is needed is a comprehensive national policy for management of wastelands in India. This would facilitate the using of India's wastelands for socially desirable purposes and help improve the microclimate, besides creating lots of employment opportunities and producing raw materials for wood-based industries.

8.6 DISCUSSION QUESTIONS

1. Enumerate the problems of pollution of land in India caused by human activities and discuss why people pollute the land.

2. As you enter any Indian city including Delhi, Mumbai and Kolkata, travelling by train, you see lots of shanties/*jhuggies*, and huts built on the railway land on both the sides of the track and the people living there throwing garbage, defeacating and urinating and thereby polluting the land. What is the root cause of this problem and how can it be solved?

3. Go to a nearby village and look around, observe carefully and talk to a few villagers. Thereafter, describe the kind of land degradation which you may have observed in the close vicinity of the village. Who has caused this and why? How can this problem be resolved?

4. In India, around 100 million ha of land are wastelands of various types. Most of those lands are common pool lands, and are highly degraded. They suffer from 'the tragedy of the commons'. Discuss various alternatives for averting the tragedy and their effectiveness. Could the privatisation of those lands solve the problem? Yes/No, and why?

5. Can the problem of soil salinity caused by over-irrigation be solved by rational pricing of irrigation water? Yes/No, and why or why not?

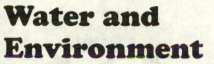

9 Water and Environment

9.1 INTRODUCTION

Water is a finite but renewable natural resource and like other natural resources, it is an integral part of the environment. It is essential for survival of all living beings on this planet and so also for socio-economic development of households, communities and nations all over the world. It is also necessary to maintain and enhance biodiversity and quality of the environment (Figure 9.1). In a nutshell, water has multifaceted roles as a consumption good, as a production good and as an environmental good or amenity. It is well known and documented that all ancient civilisations evolved and flourished around water-bodies. Irrigation had made it feasible then, as it does now, to produce adequate foodstuffs without which it would not have been possible for those civilisations to develop and flourish. In future, irrigated farming will have to play an even greater role in meeting the food and fibre requirements of growing population, especially in Asia where it is estimated to contribute around 60 per cent of the total value of crop production nowadays (Wolf and Hubener 1999: 84–85).

Water is required for several purposes such as drinking, bathing, washing, agricultural production, industrial production, generation of hydro-power, abatement of pollution, navigation, recreation and maintenance of ecosystems. Water is a critical input for agricultural production

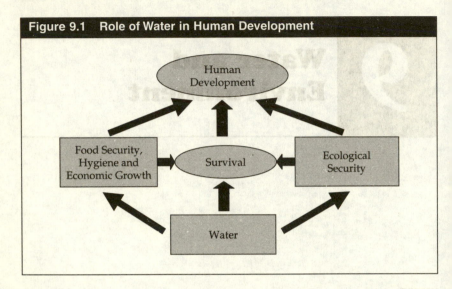

Figure 9.1 Role of Water in Human Development

and activities allied to agriculture in India. With its net irrigated area of about 55 million ha, and gross irrigated area of about 75 million ha in 2000–2001, India ranks first in the world in terms of irrigated area. The irrigated area accounted for about 39 per cent of the net area sown in 2000–2001 in the country. The contribution of irrigated area to the country's total agricultural output is about 55 per cent.

Water resources of India are under great biotic and abiotic pressure. Most of the rivers, lakes, tanks and ponds are polluted and the groundwater aquifers are being over-exploited in most of the arid and semi-arid regions and are on the verge of complete exhaustion/depletion. Besides, in many areas the groundwater aquifers have been polluted/contaminated. Droughts and floods also have been a bane of India's economy since time immemorial. All these factors together have adversely affected the quality of the environment. In this chapter, we present the current status of water resources in India, examine the nature, extent and root causes of water-related environmental problems, and finally suggest how those problems could be addressed, using the tools and techniques of environmental economics.

9.2 CURRENT STATUS OF WATER RESOURCES

We will now examine the current status of water resources in India in terms of their availability and requirement.

9.2.1 Availability of Water

India, as a whole, is reasonably well endowed with fresh water resources. It receives nearly 3,800 billion cubic metres (BCM) of fresh water annually through rainfall and snowfall. Most of the rainfall is concentrated in 100 to 120 days during the period June through September. Besides, there are also wide variations in the annual rainfall from region to region—100 mm in parts of western Rajasthan to as high as 11,000 mm in Cherrapunji in the eastern part of Meghalaya. Thus, the distribution and availability of water is not uniform over space. Similarly, there are wide year-to-year fluctuations in the rainfall in the country.

It is estimated that out of the total quantity of rainwater received annually, 700 BCM seeps into the ground and 500 BCM is lost due to evaporation and transpiration. Of the total quantum of seepage, nearly 432 BCM is replenishable groundwater through recharging of underground aquifers, of which 396 BCM can be annually extracted economically. The surface run-off to the ocean is estimated at 1,900 BCM, which is approximately half of the total annual rainfall received. This leaves nearly 690 BCM as the fresh utilisable surface water, which together with the extractable groundwater of nearly 396 BCM, makes the utilisable water resources of the order of 1,086 BCM. So far, of the total utilisable water resources, nearly 600 BCM have been put to use in the country (GoI 1999: 14–15).

It is estimated that India accounts for about 4 per cent of the world's fresh water resources. This, when seen against India's share of 2.50 per cent in the total land area of the world, seems more than adequate. However, when we consider the fact that India accounts for about 16 per cent of the world's human population and 15 per cent of the world's animal population, the picture changes from optimistic to pessimistic. The picture is bleak when we consider the declining trend in per capita availability of freshwater. The per capita renewable freshwater availability in the country at present is estimated to be only 1,086 cubic metres (CM) per annum. It has been declining over time and will continue to do so in future as well. While this is the picture at the aggregate national level, there are significant regional and temporal variations in water availability caused by spatial and year-to-year fluctuations in the annual rainfall that India receives. This causes the problems of regional and seasonal scarcity and surpluses. There are regions where the average per capita freshwater availability is far below 500 CM per annum. Below this level of availability, water becomes a constraint to life. Droughts and floods have been a recurrent phenomena in many parts of the country for ages. They further aggravate the regional and seasonal scarcity of water. Droughts and floods result in enormous economic loss to the nation and sufferings to the millions of affected people.

Since river basins are the natural hydrologic units, the estimate of water resources has to be made basin-wise. For this purpose, the entire country is now divided into 24 river basins. Annual mean flow in a river basin is reckoned as the water resource of the basin. The total water resource of the country is estimated now at nearly 1,953 km^3 (Table 9.1). The water resource of the *Ganga-Brahmaputra-Meghna* basin is estimated as 1,200 km^3 which is 60 per cent of the country's total water flows while the basin accounts for about 33 per cent of the country's geographical area. Water resources of the west flowing rivers south of Tapi are estimated to be 200 km^3, which is 11 per cent of the total water resources, whereas the basin occupies only about 3 per cent of the geographical area of the country. The remaining 64 per cent of the area has only 553 km^3 of water resources.

According to the Central Water Commission (CWC), the utilisable flow[1] from conventional schemes of water resources development is estimated to be 690.31 km^3 (GoI 1999).

With the total utilisable water resource potential of 1,086 BCM, and the total population of 100 crore (1 billion), the average amount of utilisable freshwater available in India at present is 1,086 CM per capita per annum. This is likely to go down further with the increase in population, and growth of urbanisation, industrialisation and commercialisation of agriculture in the future. The average quantity of water used in India at present is about 650 CM per capita per annum. According to the National Commission for Integrated Water Resources Development, the projected water use per capita per year in the year 2050 would be 725 to 750 CM.

Groundwater is an important source of water in many areas of India. For its use and development, only annual replenishable component of groundwater is considered. The total replenishable groundwater is estimated as 432 km^3. Out of this, 396 km^3 is estimated as utilisable—71 km^3 (15 per cent) for domestic, industrial and other uses and 325 km^3 (90 per cent of the balance) for irrigation. Nearly 50 per cent of irrigation in the country is by groundwater. Groundwater also occurs in the aquifer zones below the zone of water level fluctuation, called static groundwater. The Central Ground Water Board

---

[1] The utilisable flow from a basin can be taken as the quantum of water that can be withdrawn from its place of natural occurrence.

Table 9.1   Average Annual Flow of Utilisable Surface Water
Resources of India by Basin

Sl. No.	River Basin	Water Resources	Utilisable Surface Water
		(Billion Cubic Metres)	
1.	Indus	73.31	46
2.	Ganga-Brahmaputra-Meghna	–	–
2a.	Ganga sub-basin	525.02	250
2b.	Brahmaputra sub-basin	629.85	24
2c.	Meghna-Barak sub-basin	48.36	–
3.	Sabarkantha	12.37	6.81
4.	Brahmati-Baitarani	28.48	18.3
5.	Mahanandi	66.88	49.99
6.	Godavari	110.54	76.3
7.	Krishna	69.81	58
8.	Pennar	6.32	6.86
9.	Cauvery	21.36	19
10.	Tapi	14.88	14.5
11.	Narmada	45.64	34.5
12.	Mahi	11.02	3.1
13.	Sabarmati	3.81	1.93
14.	West Flowing rivers of Kachchh & Saurashtra	15.1	14.98
15.	West Flowing rivers of South of Tapi	200.94	36.21
16.	East Flowing rivers between Mahanandi & Godavari	17.68	–
17.	East flowing rivers between Godavari & Krishna	1.81	13.11*
18.	East flowing rivers between Krishna & Pennar	3.63	–
19.	East following rivers between Pennar & Cauvery	9.98	16.73**
20.	East flowing rivers south of Cauvery	6.78	–
21.	Rivers draining into Bangladesh	8.57	NA
22.	Rivers flowing into Myanmar	22.73	NA
	All	1,952.87	690.32

Source: National Commission for Integrated Water Resources Development Plan (NCIWRD)
(GoI 1999: 32).
Notes: *The estimate represents the combined water resources of basins listed at serial numbers 16–18.
**The estimate represents the combined water resources of basins listed at serial numbers 19–20.

(CGWB) has recently made preliminary estimates of static ground-water available in the country.

9.2.2 Water Requirement

Estimates of water requirements have been made by the National Commission for Integrated Water Resources Development (NCIWRD) for the years, 2010, 2025 and 2050 at the all-India level. Several assumptions were made to arrive at the figure of the total water requirement for the country as a whole. While estimating the demand of different sectors, aspects of management and technology were given due consideration. Also, international and Indian norms and standards were taken into account. As we know, the requirement of food production would mainly depend upon the country's population, per capita income and changes in dietary habits. After examining the latest trends and the views expressed by different demographers, the higher and lower limits of India's population in the year 2050 corresponding to those estimated by Visaria and Visaria (Standard) and United Nations (low variant) were 181 million and 1,346 million respectively. Long-term estimates for food demand extending up to the year 2050 were made through a special study based on three scenarios of economic growth rate.

With the goal of achieving food self-sufficiency at the national level, the demand estimates were converted into the domestic supplies, the latter being a factor of arable area and yield per hectare. Keeping in view the past trend and incremental changes in land use, cropping pattern, irrigation conditions, suitable assumptions were made for estimation of water requirement for irrigation. Water requirement for irrigation has been estimated between 628 km^3 (Low Demand Scenario) and 807 km^3 (High Demand Scenario) for the year 2050.

Keeping in view the existing national average of water supply and various norms, the NCIWRDP has suggested the final goal of providing 220 litres per capita per day (lpcd) for the urban areas and 150 lpcd for the rural areas in a phased manner. The total water requirement for domestic use for rural and urban areas was estimated at 111 km^3 and 90 km^3 in two population scenarios for the year 2050.

On account of serious dearth of information on the present use of water by industries and uncertainty about the future growth and composition of manufacturing activities, it is extremely difficult to estimate future water requirement of industries. However, despite these limitations, the NCIWRDP has estimated the water requirement for industrial development at 81 km^3 for the year 2050. Water requirement for the energy/power sector has been estimated for high and low demand scenarios as 70 km^3 and 63 km^3 respectively for the year 2050.

The requirement of flow for navigation in water channels is mostly expected to be met by seasonal flows in various river systems or canals. However, taking into account the actual releases downstream of the Farakka Barrage, as an example, the requirement of water for navigation for the year 2050 has been projected as 15 km^3.

Table 9.2	Projected Total Water Requirement of India for the Years, 2010, 2025 and 2050	
		(Billion Cubic Metres)
Year	*Low Demand Scenario*	*High Demand Scenario*
2010	694	710
2025	784	850
2050	973	1,180

Source: GoI (1999: iii).

Requirement of water for abatement of pollution and managing the quality of water in rivers and other water-bodies has been assumed as 20 km³ for the year 2050 in the absence of reliable and adequate data. The evaporation losses from reservoirs have been estimated as 76 km³.

To sum up, the NCIWRDP has estimated the total water requirement of the country to be 694 to 710, 784 to 850 and 973 to 1,180 km³ by the years, 2010, 2025 and 2050, respectively depending on the low demand and high demand scenarios (Table 9.2). Irrigation would continue to have the highest water requirement, between 628–807 km³ (or about 68 per cent of the total water requirement), followed by domestic use, including drinking and bovine needs, estimated at about 90–111 km³ (or about 10 per cent of total water requirement) in the year 2050. The projected water use per capita per year in the year 2050 would be about 725–750 m³ as compared to about 650 km³ at present.

9.3 SOME WATER-RELATED PROBLEMS

Now we will discuss some serious water-related environmental problems of India.

9.3.1 Growing Gap Between Availability and Requirement

The country's total water requirement would barely match the utilisable water resources in the year 2050 and the gap between the water requirement and availability will widen over time. The most serious challenge of the 21st century for India will be how to meet the deficit or demand-supply gap, especially the regional and seasonal deficits. In view of this, it is of paramount importance that we aim at reducing water requirement to the low demand scenario. While there appears to be no need to take an alarmist view, three major considerations have to be kept in the forefront while formulating an integrated water policy. First, that the balance between the requirement and availability can be struck only if utmost efficiency is achieved in water use, particularly in the agricultural sector. Second, average availability at the national level does not imply that all the country's basins are capable of meeting their full requirement from internal resources. Third, the issue of equity in the access to water, between regions and between sections of population assumes greater importance in what is foreseen as a fragile balance between the aggregate availability and aggregate requirement of water.

9.3.2 Lack of Well-Defined Property Rights in Water

There are no explicit statements or laws in India, which clearly recognise and define property rights in either surface water or groundwater. The public ownership of surface water is implied, however, in government appropriation and regulation of surface water through irrigation projects. It is also implied in the Northern India Canal and Drainage Act of 1873. Where surface water is not appropriated/used by the state, riparian rights prevail, that is, farmers owning land contiguous to the source of water, stream, pond or lake, have the first claim to water.

Groundwater has never been declared to be publicly owned nor has public ownership been implied through the operation of state/public tube wells. The system of groundwater rights prevailing in India can be best characterised as a version of the English doctrine of absolute right. Under that doctrine, a farmer has an unrestricted right to exploit groundwater underlying his piece of land. In India, customarily, the ownership of groundwater rests with the owner of overlying land. Thus, *de jure*, property rights in groundwater are not clearly defined but, *de facto*, it is accessible to all those who own the overlying land. In view of this, groundwater can be considered as a common pool resource (CPR), that is, a resource that is used in common by an identifiable group of people. Therefore, it is not surprising that groundwater, being a CPR, is overexploited, depleted, polluted and misappropriated. In particular, groundwater has in fact become an overexploited open access in most arid and semi-arid regions and is on the verge of complete exhaustion/depletion. Besides, in many areas the groundwater aquifers have been polluted/contaminated. For example, in coastal areas in Saurashtra (Gujarat), the vacuum created through over pumping of groundwater has been filled in by intrusion of seawater, causing the problem of salinity ingress. Consequently, groundwater has become unfit for irrigation as well as human consumption. In a nutshell, it suffers from what Hardin (1968) called 'The Tragedy of the Commons'. In my opinion, for efficient and equitable water management, it is necessary to vest the ownership rights in the State and usufruct rights in water users' associations (WUAs).

In India, as per the India Easement Act of 1882, ownership of groundwater is tied to ownership of land, that is, groundwater is treated as an easement of land ownership. All landowners have the right to extract the groundwater that lies under their land. Technically, they can use it only for 'socially acceptable' purposes and not in a way that causes harm, *albeit* unintended, to other co-owners of the aquifer. But in practice there are no real restrictions on the type or level of use. As long as water remains underground, all co-owners own it, *de jure*, but once it is pumped to the surface it belongs to the owner of the lifting device and the plot to which it is applied. The owner can transport the water to other locations, including neighbouring plots and can also sell it to others.

Property rights to groundwater are complicated by the fact that more than one user can tap the same aquifer. Aquifers can range in size from a few to tens of thousands of hectares, and in India even small aquifers are likely to lie under land belonging to a large number of farmers. In view of this, groundwater thus cannot meet the requirements necessary for complete private property.

9.3.3 Irrational Pricing of Water

Virtually all countries, regardless of the degree of scarcity of water, subsidise water for irrigation and domestic uses and in many cases, they supply it free of charge. Since time immemorial, India has been experiencing the problems of water scarcity, droughts and floods concurrently. Yet these problems remain unresolved, despite the fact that we now have the technologies and resources available to solve them. Most people, including farmers, continue to think of water as a free, virtually unlimited resource whereas the facts increasingly suggest otherwise.

Agricultural sector in India accounts for over 85 per cent of the total water used for various purposes in the country. But the water use efficiency in agriculture is very low—about 40 per cent in the case of surface irrigation and about 60 per cent in the case of groundwater irrigation. Part of the reason for the low efficiency is the highly subsidised price of irrigation water that does not cover even the operation and maintenance (O&M) costs. Besides, the failure to achieve any degree of cost recovery deprives the system of funds for repair and maintenance of the system.

Subsidised irrigation water charges encourage excessive application of water to crops and leads to low investment in the maintenance of irrigation infrastructure, resulting in high seepage and conveyance losses. Several on-farm studies have shown that an increase of 20–30 per cent in water use efficiency is possible if water saving micro irrigation technologies such as drips and sprinklers were used. But under the prevailing flat (fixed) rate system of canal water pricing, farmers do not have any incentives to use the water saving irrigation technologies. So the main issue involved is how to motivate the farmers to use water saving irrigation technologies so as to increase water use efficiency and save water for other, more valuable, uses. Rationalising the existing water prices so that they reflect the real resource cost of supply seems to be one of the possible alternatives to do that. Theoretically speaking, price as an instrument of public policy changes the attitude and behaviour of consumers and motivates them to act in socially desirable ways.

9.3.4 Depletion and Degradation of Water Resources

A certain level of degradation of water resources is an inevitable consequence of human activity. For example, any exploitation of groundwater aquifers beyond the rate of natural and artificial recharges will result in their partial or total depletion, as well as degradation through contamination. Industrialisation leads to increased generation of water pollution through disposal of hazardous wastes into water-bodies. Agricultural intensification leads to pesticide and fertiliser run-off(s), waterlogging, and soil salinity.

The question is not how to prevent or eliminate degradation of water resources altogether but how to minimise it or at least to keep it to a level consistent with society's objectives. When depletion and degradation of water resources are seen in the context of society's development objectives, not all depletion or pollution of water resources is bad or worth preventing. As long as all costs involved, including those arising from diminished quantity, deteriorated quality and lost diversity of forests have been accounted for; as long as both the productivity and the sustainability of the alternative uses have been considered with a due margin of error; and, as long as any side effects or externalities associated with water use have been internalised and paid for, degradation of water resources should not be something we would like to prevent.

Pollution of surface water resources, particularly lakes, rivers and tanks/ponds and degradation of quality of groundwater have assumed worrisome proportions in India. Surface water is hardly fit for drinking. The river Ganga, which is worshipped by devout Hindus as 'Mother Ganga' is no exception; it is highly polluted at several places.[2] Similarly, groundwater in many arid and semi-arid areas has been depleted due to over-extraction and degraded due to leaching of fertilisers and pesticides residues from cultivated fields. Consequently, the incidence of water-borne diseases has increased significantly in recent years.

The Centre for Science and Environment, New Delhi, through its fortnightly magazine, *Down to Earth*, is rendering a yeoman service to society by collecting, compiling and publishing information about pollution of the environment. Every issue of the fortnightly is full of case-studies of pollution of natural resources and environment such as air, water and land. In its special issue, 'Survival Primer' (15 September 2000), brought out on the occasion of completion of 200 issues of the publication of the fortnightly, it carried stories of pollution of the environment, particularly pollution of Damodar river, pollution of Lake Kolleru in Andhra Pradesh, pollution of river Yamuna, air pollution and degradation of India's rangelands. The space available here does not permit us to even present a summary of the stories published. However the sum and substance of the stories is that India's natural resources and environment have been subjected to all kinds of misuse, misappropriation, wastage and degradation, rendering the quality of the environment unfit for healthy and safe living. The extent of degradation of India's water resources has reached a stage when immediate intervention by governmental and non-governmental agencies through appropriate measures has become absolutely essential. It seems to us that the social benefits from such interventions will be markedly higher than their social costs.

9.3.5 Existence of Negative Externalities

There are several negative externalities associated with the use of water. A glaring example of a negative externality associated with water use is the damage that an upstream rice farmer's use of pesticides causes to a downstream fish farmer who uses the same water

---

[2]According to a Green Media report dated 25 January 2006, over three lakh sadhus who had assembled in Allahabad for Magh Mela which started on 14 January 2006, had launched an agitation complaining against the high-level of pollution in the river Ganga in Allahabad, and demanding government intervention to prevent the pollution and keep the Ganga waters clean.

source. Society as a whole (not only the fish farmer) would be better off if less of this negative externality is produced, but again there is no market (or other) incentive for the upstream farmer to take the down-stream farmers' interest into account. The government may respond to this problem by banning the use of pesticides altogether. This however may reduce social welfare if the loss from rice production outweighs the gain from fish production (and if no other environmental effects are involved). The ideal solution would be for pesticide use to be reduced exactly to the level where the combined value of rice and fish is max-imised. The level is obtained where the marginal benefit from pesticide use equals its marginal cost, where this cost is understood to include both, the production costs of the pesticide and its environmental cost (effect of fish production). There are two ways in which this could happen: (a) the price of pesticide that the rice farmer pays includes a surcharge above production cost to account for the pesticide's environ-mental cost, or (b) if the same decision-maker owns both the rice farm and the fish farm.

Another example of existence of a negative externality in water use is furnished by canal irrigation water. Excessive use of canal irrigation causes, unintentionally though, waterlogging and soil salinity in the canal command area over a period of time. The farmers who suffer the loss of crop production due to these problems cannot claim any com-pensation from the canal authority. This is an example of a negative externality. Here the private cost to the canal authority is almost nil whereas the social cost to society (farmers in the command area and others) is very high, that is, there is divergence between the private cost and social cost. Similarly, extraction of groundwater by a farmer has a negative externality for all other farmers sharing the aquifer.

Will a free market produce either of these outcomes? The answer is no, except under very special circumstances. Environmental costs are outside the domain of markets because these costs arise from a techno-logical rather than a market interdependence between economic activ-ities. It is a fundamental premise for an efficiently functioning market that economic units interact only through their effect on prices; tech-nological interdependence is ruled out.

The next step in the process of reforms in irrigation water pricing should be volumetric pricing of water. This requires regular monitor-ing of water delivery (duration of water delivery) at the field and flow measurements. Introduction of such modes of pricing has to go along with creating appropriate institutional structures at various levels. Technological innovations in the design and construction of irrigation systems would be the cornerstone of the entire exercise of bringing in such reforms in the pricing policies. Pricing of water should be done in such a way that the volumetric prices reflect the economic value of water.

The existing flat rate system of pricing of electricity does not provide any incentives to the farmers to use groundwater efficiently. On the other hand, due to interruptions in the power supply, farmers do not have absolute control over water in their wells. For instance, power failure is very common in the rural areas. The quality of power supply is also very poor. The time of power supply in the farm sector changes once in every fortnight. The farmers have to water their crops when the power supply is available and often excessively. As a result, crop watering is not timely and optimum. In spite of the fact that the implicit cost of irrigation (per unit area) using an electric motor is much lower as compared to diesel pumps, the electric well commands yield much lower yield rates and net economic returns as compared to diesel well commands. This means that control over watering will have greater bearing on the net returns from irrigation than the cost of irrigation. The differential yield obtained due to timely and adequate watering in the case of diesel well irrigation is sufficient to offset the increased energy cost that the diesel well owners have to incur for energy.

The introduction of variable unit pricing system, if implemented properly with adequate institutional arrangements in place to provide good quality power supply and monitor the use of electricity by the individual farmers, will create disincentives for overuse of energy and water. Thus, farmers will not only use water efficiently, but also invest in improving the efficiency of electric motors and pumps. But given the wide regional variations in the energy requirements for pumping a unit volume of water across regions, a blanket unit rate will not be socially acceptable to the farmers in regions where pumping depths are very large.

9.3.6 Inequity in Access to Water

Allocation of water from public reservoirs between irrigation and urban use is highly inequitable, and is in favour of the latter (IRMA-UNICEF 2000). This is further compounded by rising income levels in urban areas. However, the scope for augmenting the existing water supplies through local sources is limited in cities. As a result, water from irrigation reservoirs increasingly gets reallocated to meet growing urban demands. This leads to conflicts between irrigators and urban water users. Cornering of rural water resources by urban dwellers and industries has already resulted in many a conflict in the country in general and in industrially developed states in particular. Besides, this has also resulted in increased water pollution from industrial effluents, which has emerged as a significant source of conflict between rural communities and industries in the recent past. Though stringent pollution control norms exist, they are not enforced by the concerned agency. Indiscriminate pollution of water-bodies used for irrigation and drinking purposes has already led to public interest litigations in the Gujarat High Court from several areas, namely, Matar taluka of Kheda district due to pollution of Khari River, Jetpur town in Rajkot due to pollution in Bhadar River, Vapi due to pollution of Damanganga River, and Sarigam near Ankleshwar due to pollution of Amla Khadi stream (IRMA-UNICEF 2000).

As absolute scarcity of water increases, access to water, both surface and groundwater, becomes highly inequitable. This leads to conflicts. The right to use water from the rivers is often politically contested. The influential groups manage to get political patronage to build small dams for cornering water from rivers for irrigation and other purposes in their localities. Often dams are built in the upper catchment of existing reservoirs, without considering the quantum of total dependable run-off in the basin. This results in the over-appropriation of available water and increasing reallocation of the available water from existing users to new users.

A classical example of this phenomenon is the Sabarmati river basin wherein the increasing demand for irrigation water from farmers and politicians from different parts of the basin has led to the construction of a large number of irrigation reservoirs in different tributaries and over-appropriation of the basin's surface water flows. This has caused 'drying up' of areas that were previously 'wet', and 'wetting' of areas that were previously 'dry'. This has led to several environmental problems and conflicts among farmers.

In canal command areas, distribution of water is highly inequitable, both by design and default. First, the hydraulic systems are designed and built in such a way that in the case of a shortfall in the release of water, the share of water allocated for release in the tail-end portions of the command gets reduced. Second, farmers in the head-end portions, including those who are not beneficiaries of the scheme, engage in the pilferage of water. In the process, the head-enders in the canal network receive more than their fair entitlement at the cost of the tail-enders. Even in the water abundant irrigation schemes, the tail-end farmers are deprived of water. Such inequities lead to conflicts among the farmers in canal commands, besides the problems of waterlogging and soil salinity in the head reaches of the canal commands.

9.3.7 Droughts and Floods

Natural and man-made disasters have been a bane of India's economy since time immemorial. In ancient Indian literature, there are references to natural disasters such as prolonged droughts, flash floods, hail-storms, landslides, cyclones and forest fires. All those disasters were generally attributed to planetary factors and evil spirits (Kanwar 2001: 3). According to Kautilya's *Arthashastra*, disaster management was a prime duty of the state. The state used to provide relief when the distress conditions became acute (Sharma 2003: 3). According to the Indian Famine Commission (1888), droughts were the root cause of the devastating famines of the nineteenth century in India. In a nutshell, we could say that India was then and still is vulnerable to almost every type of natural disaster. About 60 per cent of the landmass in India is vulnerable to earthquakes; over 40 million hectares (ha) are prone to floods;[3] about 8 per cent of the total area is prone to cyclones; and about 68 per cent of the total area is susceptible to droughts. The 8,000 km long coastline is prone to severe cyclonic formations. About 55 per cent of the total area lies in Seismic Zones III–V and is vulnerable to earthquakes. Sub-Himalayan regions and Western Ghats are vulnerable to landslides (GoI 2004a: 32; Kanwar 2001: 7).

It is an irony that in many parts of India, we have droughts and in many others, we have floods occurring almost every year.[4] Yet, this kind of risk is not even recognised in India's policies and plans, not to speak of absence of any national policy for disaster management. It is a sad commentary that despite several programmes launched by the Government of India (GoI) from time to time for minimising their adverse impacts, every year natural disasters such as droughts, floods and cyclones continue to haunt millions of people living in disaster-prone areas of India and there is no national policy on disaster management.

Floods and droughts have several adverse economic and environmental impacts. For example, in Orissa, soon after the Super Cyclone of 2001, the entire sea coast was adversely affected by high sea tides, flooding the cropped area and depositing salts on good fertile soil. Floods cause increased erosion of soils and siltation of river beds and

---

[3]India is one of the most flood prone countries in the world and accounts for one fifth of the global death count due to floods. Over 30 million people are displaced annually due to the floods.

[4]Over the last 125 years or so, droughts of moderate to severe nature have occurred in India in at least 40 years. Thus, on an average, India suffers from droughts once in every three years (Singh and Ballabh forthcoming).

reservoirs, reducing their capacity to store water, and thereby increasing the incidence of flash floods. Among the major ecological effects of droughts are decreased scrub growth, increased desertification, reduction in forest area and wet land and loss of mangroves. Among the ecological changes, the desertification cycle is of utmost concern. The impact of droughts and floods cannot be assessed on the basis of the economic loss alone. Many of the social and the ecological/environmental damages caused by them are irreversible, and their impacts remain for years together.

9.3.8 Waterlogging and Salinity

Waterlogging and salinity are two serious problems in many of the canal command areas in India. The National Commission on Agriculture (GoI 1976: 180) defines an area to be waterlogged when the water table rises to an extent that the soil pores in the root zone of crops become saturated resulting in restriction of the normal circulation of air, decline in the level of oxygen and increase in the level of carbon dioxide. According to the Central Ground Water Board (CGWB), the areas where groundwater table occurs within 2 m of land surface are considered waterlogged, and areas where depth of water table is within 2–3 m of land surface are considered potential areas for development of a similar problem (GoI 1991; Shishodia 1994).

According to an estimate made by a Working Group constituted by the Government of India in 1991, an area of about 2.46 million ha in 42 different commands in 15 states is affected by the problem of waterlogging and salinity in the irrigated canal commands in India (GoI 1991). Among the states, Bihar is worst-affected by the waterlogging problem followed by UP, AP and Haryana. Incidentally these are the states where canals have been the major source of irrigation.

Waterlogging and salinity occur due to various causes, either man-made or natural. These causes are complex, involving both environmental factors and the design and operation of canal systems. In the majority of cases, it is due to excess recharge to groundwater contributed from surface irrigation structures. It is caused by surface over-irrigation, which is due mainly to underpricing of canal irrigation water. Both waterlogging and salinity lead to land degradation and consequent decline in land productivity and value. The critical depth of water level which is considered to be harmful depends on the type of crop, soil, the quality of water and the period for which the water table remains in the root zone. Therefore, it may vary from area to area and crop to crop.

There is an urgent need to seriously view this problem and take remedial measures in order to make the land fit for agricultural production and improve the environment.

The following reclamation measures are advocated for reclamation of waterlogged areas:

- Propagation of efficient irrigation management methods and application of optimum quantities of irrigation water to prevent excessive soil wetting, for example, use of sprinklers and drip irrigation method. Flood irrigation should be avoided as far as possible.
- Minimisation of seepage losses from irrigation and field canal networks through proper lining and conjunctive use of ground and surface water to control the rise of groundwater level.
- Provision of an adequate and efficient drainage system, surface as well as sub-surface.

9.4 ALTERNATIVES FOR ADDRESSING WATER-RELATED PROBLEMS AND IMPROVING THE ENVIRONMENT

Now we will discuss some alternative approaches/strategies for mitigating water-related problems and improving the environment.

9.4.1 Drought Proofing

In the post-Independence era, the Drought Prone Areas Programme (DPAP) was the earliest area development programme launched by the Central Government in 1973–74 to tackle the special problems faced by those fragile areas which were constantly affected by severe drought conditions. These areas are characterised by large human and cattle population which continuously exert heavy pressure on the already fragile natural resources base for food, fodder and fuel. The major problems are: continuous depletion of vegetative cover, increase in soil erosion and fall in groundwater levels due to continuous exploitation without any effort to recharge the underground aquifers. Though the programme has had some positive impact in terms of creating durable public assets, its overall impact in effectively containing the adverse effects of drought was found to be not very encouraging (GoI 2002: 114–17). Thus, DPAP has not been able to achieve its primary goal of drought proofing.

India now has the requisite technology, manpower and material resources available for solving this problem. Gujarat provides several examples of the successful experiences of NGOs and government agencies of the range of technologies that are available for water harvesting and artificial recharge of groundwater in different geological settings. NGOs such as N.M. Sadguru Water and Development Foundation, Dahod, Shri Vivekananda Research and Training Institute (SVRTI), Mandvi, Kachchh and Aga Khan Rural Support Programme (India) have implemented several water management activities including artificial recharging of groundwater using small water harvesting structures. The most common water harvesting structures that have been adopted in NGO and government-sponsored projects in Gujarat are check dams, percolation tanks, recharge tube wells and underground dykes.

The Sadguru Water and Development Foundation based in Dahod, Gujarat, has done pioneering work in designing and building cost-effective small check dams in its project area comprising over 600 semi-arid villages in three western Indian states of Gujarat, Madhya Pradesh and Rajasthan (Singh and Gupta 1998). This strategy is people-centred and community-based and seems to be appropriate for replication in other drought prone areas in India. The financial resources required could be mobilised from the ongoing programmes.

SVRTI had built recharge structures in several villages of coastal Kachchh in which watershed has been used as the basic unit for planning the recharge work. The recharge structures they used are check dams (built in series along the river course), percolation tanks, recharge tube wells in conjunction with check dams or percolation tanks, and sub-surface dykes in conjunction with recharge tube wells. SVRTI's experience shows that groundwater depletion can be arrested and groundwater quality improved, especially reducing the Total Dissolved Solids (TDS) and salinity of groundwater, by harnessing local run-off and recharging the aquifers. Their experience further shows that in areas where groundwater levels are deep, recharge tube wells, built in conjunction with check dams will be most effective. In villages that are affected by serious depletion problems and sea-water intrusion, and where SVRTI had built artificial recharge structures, the groundwater levels had risen significantly, increasing the well yields. The salinity of the groundwater was also found to have reduced making it suitable for irrigation.

The successful experience of SVRTI and several other non-governmental organisations had inspired the State Government to take up local water conservation and artificial recharge projects on a significant scale, especially in the water scarce regions of Saurashtra, Kachchh and North Gujarat. In Saurashtra and Kachchh region, more than 50 per cent of the rainwater during monsoon flows into the sea as run-off in good rainfall years. Even the evaporation of the surface water resources stored in the various dams is more than 20 per cent. The geomorphological conditions in this region are suitable for the construction of check dams for storing water underground. Thus, not only is the water saved, which is otherwise lost in run-off, but also the loss of water through evaporation is prevented.

In view of this, the Government of Gujarat launched the 'Sardar Patel Participatory Water Conservation Project' to conserve and harvest water resources in the State. The government has decided to earmark sufficient funds from the Budgetary Provision and taken up these community-oriented works on a large scale with the active participation of local people. Under this Project, water conservation and water harvesting activities such as construction of check dams, and percolation tanks were taken up in the scarcity-hit districts of Saurashtra, North Gujarat and Kachchh regions. While 60 per cent of the cost was borne by the Government, the remaining 40 per cent cost comes through contributions from the beneficiaries.

Deficient rainfall together with the overuse of the groundwater in many semi-arid and hard rock areas has led to the lowering down of the water table. This implies that groundwater extraction in those areas exceeds the natural recharge rate. This has not only increased the cost of water extraction from tube wells but has also resulted in the drying up of shallow wells in the areas. In view of this, there is dire need of recharging groundwater aquifers and improvement in the on-farm water management as a means of drought proofing. The extraction of groundwater needs to be regulated by the communities concerned, or water users' associations, wherever they exist. Here again, several innovative methods have been tried by NGOs in Saurashtra and North Gujarat regions of Gujarat. They are cost effective and simple to construct and maintain. They are also suitable for replication in other water scarce areas in India.

Watershed management approach has been found to be the most appropriate strategy for optimum and sustainable use of land, water and other resources in rain-fed farming areas. There are many success stories including those of Sukhomajri, Ralegan Siddhi and PIDOW (project in Gulbarga), that document how the adoption of the watershed approach led to overall development of the watershed and restoration of its natural capital in semi-arid areas of India (Singh 1995b). Improved watershed development technologies are now available with various research institutes in most states in India. Modern techniques are also available for early warning and monitoring of droughts. Some of the techniques are vegetation index map, remote sensing and Geographic Information System (Singh 2000: 20–22). What is needed is an organisation structure for compiling, collating, screening and releasing new technologies found suitable for adoption by farmers.

9.4.2 Flood Proofing

As we stated earlier in this chapter, many regions in India (over 40 million ha of land) are highly prone to floods. Although India had formulated its first Flood Policy as far back as 1954, even to date floods continue to cause havoc every year; we have failed to achieve any semblance of flood proofing. What is needed urgently is a long-term policy and a plan for flood proofing. The policy should be backed by a floodplain management act as recommended by the Central Water Commission (Subbiah 2004: 206). The plan should comprise, among other things, flood risk zoning, prepared by using satellite-based remote sensing, mapping of river configuration and flood control works, estimates of the area likely to be affected by floods, expected duration of floods, the measures required for control of floods and their cost implications. Some of the important flood management measures adopted in India so far include: (*i*) dams/reservoirs; (*ii*) embankments; (*iii*) drainage channels; (*iv*) raising flood level of flood-prone villages; (*v*) flood forecasting; and (*vi*) flood relief and rehabilitation. However, we still have to go a long way before any substantial progress in resolving the problem is made.

The only solution to the problem of floods in Bihar is to allow a smooth passage to the floodwater and removing, as far as possible, all the impediments to such a passage and allow the rivers to perform their normal functioning. Embankments obstruct the flow and the proposed dams will do even worse. Almost all the Government Reports recognise this basic fact but when it comes to doing something on the ground, only obstructions are created. The Bihar Government minces no words in ridiculing the embankments but the same Government does not mind building the embankments on the Bhutahi Balan.

The farmers, too, will support such moves of improving drainage as they always maintain that earlier the water used to come and go and they used to welcome the floods. Now, water only comes, but it takes a very long time to go.

9.4.3 Use of Water Saving Micro Irrigation Technologies

As we know a lion's share of the water in India is used for irrigation. Therefore, improving the efficiency of water use in irrigation would be the key to managing the demand of water to match with the available supplies in future. The existing irrigation practices are, by and large, traditional. In the case of canal irrigation, the irrigation practice followed is flooding. In this method of irrigation, a large portion of the water applied is lost in run-off from the fields. A significant portion of the water percolates down the soil to join the groundwater table and is not available to crops. A good portion of the water is lost in evaporation from the soil surface. The depth of water application is highly uneven with a high depth of the water column in the head reaches and very low depth of the water column in the tail reach. Thus, the amount of water available to the crop is much less than what is applied and the overall efficiency (here we refer to the physical efficiency) of water use in canal irrigation is very low at about 40 per cent in the flooding method of irrigation. Poor field efficiencies also lead to poor crop yields, apart from wastage of water.

In the case of well irrigation, the conventional practices followed are slightly modified versions of flood irrigation such as 'small border irrigation' and 'furrow irrigation'. In *border irrigation*, a significant portion of the water applied to the field is lost in deep percolation. Run-off losses are found to be negligible. But, evaporation losses are high and distribution efficiencies low. Distribution efficiency depends on the length of the border used, discharge rate of water, soil type, field slope and the roughness of the soil surface. Distribution and evaporation losses are found to be much less in furrow irrigation in comparison to small border, as the wetted area is less. But, on an average, water use efficiency in the case of groundwater irrigation is 60 per cent, which is higher than in surface water irrigation.

Given the low physical efficiency of water use in the traditional irrigation practices such as small border irrigation and furrow irrigation, and given the fact that irrigation water is scarce in many regions of the country, it is imperative to increase the physical efficiency of water use, and thereby economic efficiency through use of appropriate irrigation technologies. Drip irrigation is one such technology. By using drip, the net saving in irrigation water can be as high as 40–50 per cent for most of the crops.[5] Research has also shown that adoption of the drip system results not only in water saving and increase in yield rates, but also reduction in input costs. This is achieved by reduction in the level of fertiliser consumption and labour inputs needed for irrigation and weeding.

---

[5] The research on water use efficiency impact of drip systems on Brinjal crop has shown that the amount of water applied can be reduced by 50 per cent of the amount used in traditional method, while at the same time the yield rates increase by 10 per cent.

However, under the current system of pricing of electricity for groundwater pumping and water from canals, there are no incentives for farmers to abandon the conventional method of irrigation, which involves heavy wastage of water. Also, farmers do not perceive the significant impact that drip technology can have on the crop yields. Therefore, promotion of this technology has to be complemented by use of market-based instruments such as appropriate pricing of irrigation water and electricity and establishment of property rights in water.

The adoption of conventional water saving irrigation technologies has been very low in the past in India, even in water scarce states like Gujarat. One major reason for this is the lack of disincentive for using water with low levels of efficiency. In the case of groundwater, there is no marginal cost of extraction of water where electric motor is used for pumping,[6] while the cost of saving water using these technologies is very high. In the case of diesel pumps, the cost of extraction per unit volume of water works out to be much less than the cost of saving per unit volume of water using efficient technologies. Another reason is the large capital investment requirement. The cost of installing a conventional drip systems in an area of one hectare works out to be Rs 50,000 with a 50 per cent government subsidy for crops such as sugarcane, vegetables and cotton. The conventional sprinkler systems, which are also eligible for government subsidy, fall in the same price range. They are also difficult to operate and maintain. Over and above, they are not divisible to fit small plots and as a result not attractive to small holders.

Micro-tube drip technology requires very low capital investments and is easy to operate and maintain. Both farmers with very small landholdings and large holdings can use this technology to irrigate vegetables such as brinjal, cluster bean, tomato, chillies and row crops such as cotton, castor and horticultural crops. Custom-made micro-tube drip systems can be used for large plots and can be connected to the outlet pipe of wells. The advantage of the micro-drip system is that it can operate at very low pressures unlike conventional drip systems in which minimum pressure needs to be maintained for the dripper to function.

Farmers not owning land and irrigation sources can also use this technology for irrigating small plots of vegetables in their backyard. It has been found that the use of the micro-tube drip system in cotton crop could result in up to 50 per cent saving in water use as compared

---

[6]This is due to the current pricing policy of the Gujarat Electricity Board where a flat rate charge is levied on horsepower of motor irrespective of the duration of use. So the marginal cost of pumping water is zero.

to the conventional flooding method of irrigation, while increasing the yield by 20–30 per cent.

Micro-sprinklers are the low cost versions of the sprinkler technology. As a micro-sprinkler uses linear low density polyethylene pipes, it is cheaper as compared to conventional sprinklers. The overhead sprinklers (with two sprinkler heads) can run on a 0.5 HP motor and can irrigate up to 1 acre in 8–10 shiftings of the sprinkler heads. Therefore, the energy requirement for running the system is very low.

9.4.4 Rationalisation of Pricing of Water and Reform of Water Markets

In India, water markets exist in many agriculturally advanced areas such as Punjab, Haryana, many parts of Uttar Pradesh and Bihar, central and north Gujarat and West Bengal. However, in most cases, the water markets are informal, unregulated and have several imperfections. In those areas, the market prices do not reflect real resource cost of water (in terms of supply) and its real use value (in terms of demand). Consequently, they fail to use and allocate the water efficiently from a societal perspective (Shah 1993: 44–71). Besides, there is a lot of government intervention in such markets in the form of subsidies, administered prices, rationing, quotas and so on. All these result in wastage, misuse and unsustainable use of water. For example, the overall technical (physical) efficiency of water use is as low as 40 per cent for canal irrigation. Part of the reason for the low efficiency is the highly subsidised price of irrigation water that encourages excessive application of water to crops and the poor investments in the maintenance of irrigation infrastructure that result in excessive seepage losses in conveyance. Though the overall physical efficiency of water use is better) in groundwater irrigation (about 60 per cent) due to lower conveyance losses, the flat rate pricing of electricity for groundwater pumping—with a zero resultant marginal cost of extraction leads to overuse of water.

To promote sustainable use of water, it is necessary to do away with all kinds of distortions in the existing markets in a phased manner. Proper pricing of water in India would mean elimination of, or reduction in subsidies for water, which is a highly politically sensitive issue. But it is true that failure to price water at its full resource cost in both rural and urban areas has encouraged its wastage, misuse and pollution. To some extent, and in the short run, direct regulations can restrict the behaviour of water users wasting it, misusing it, overexploiting it and causing pollution. But in the long run, pricing policies such as pricing of water at a level that covers at least the variable costs of supplying it and direct pollution taxes based on the principle of 'the polluter pays' and tradable emission permits may be more efficient and effective. Differential pricing of water according to the principles of 'ability to pay' and 'utility from use' based on its volumetric measurement, although difficult propositions to sell and implement, seem to be the most appropriate solutions to resolve the problems of water scarcity, wastage and misuse of water and water pollution.

The current canal irrigation rates in India are very low relative to the incremental gross value of output from irrigation of crops as also to the actual cost of supply of canal water. In Kakrapar, Gujarat, irrigation command, for example, the percentage contribution of irrigation water charge to the gross income from canal irrigated crops varied from 1.96 per cent to 6.15 per cent for land irrigability classes I to IV. In the case of cotton, it varied from 1.1 per cent to 6.91 per cent and in the case of paddy from 1.15 to 5.86 per cent (IRMA-UNICEF 2000). Therefore, *prima facie*, there is a case for enhancing the rates of canal water. However, the question is to what extent or to what level irrigation water rates can be raised so as to improve the financial working of the irrigation schemes without adversely impacting on the economic viability of farming.

It costs many times more for well owners in canal commands to irrigate one hectare of land as compared to canal irrigators (Gajja and Prasad 1998). At the same time, they get as much net return as the farmers who depend on canal irrigation. This is because they get much higher yields as compared to farmers who use canal water. In the case of canal irrigation, the poor quality of irrigation—unreliable and inadequate—leads to poor yield rates. The differential productivity achieved in diesel—well irrigated fields offset the increased cost of irrigation that water buyers and diesel well owners have to incur.

These observations lead us to the conclusion that the rates for canal water can be increased to substantially higher levels, if the Irrigation Departments could increase the quality of irrigation in terms of adequacy and timeliness. To begin with, irrigation water can continue to be charged using the crop area as the basis. But, the water charge per unit area of a particular crop can be fixed on the basis of the crop delta, which means that the crops that have higher water requirement will be charged more than crops that have low delta. For instance, summer paddy, which has a delta of 1,200 mm, has to be charged 4–5 times more than mustard that has a delta of only 240–300 mm for every single hectare of irrigation. This can create incentives for farmers to adopt the crops that are comparatively more efficient from the point of view of water use. Such a pricing structure would also mean that in different regions, the water charge per unit area of the same crop could potentially vary. However, such a pricing structure could also result in water wastage. The reason being that the price a farmer has to pay is only dependent on the type of crop and the area. However, this would be a better alternative than the existing one.

The next step in the process of reforms in irrigation water pricing should be volumetric pricing of water. This requires regular monitoring of water delivery (duration of water delivery) at the field and flow measurements. Introduction of such modes of pricing has to go along with creating appropriate institutional structures at various levels. Technological innovations in the design and construction of irrigation systems would be the corner stone of the entire exercise of bringing in such reforms in the pricing policies. Pricing of water should be done in such a way that the volumetric prices reflect the economic value of water.

The existing flat rate system of pricing of electricity does not provide any incentives to the farmers to use groundwater efficiently. On the other hand, due to interruptions in the power supply, farmers do not have absolute control over water in their wells. For instance, power failure is very common in the rural areas. The quality of power supply is also very poor. The time of power supply in the farm sector changes once every fortnight. The farmers have to water their crops when the power supply is available and often excessively. As a result, crop watering is not timely and optimum. In spite of the fact that the implicit cost of irrigation (per unit area) using the electric motor is much lower compared to diesel pumps, the electric well commands have much lower yield rates and net economic returns as compared to diesel well commands. This means that control over watering will have greater bearing on the net returns from irrigation than the cost of irrigation. The differential yield obtained due to timely and adequate watering in the case of diesel well irrigation is sufficient to offset the increased energy cost that the diesel well owners have to incur for energy.

The introduction of the variable unit pricing system, if implemented properly with adequate institutional arrangements in place to provide good quality power supply and to monitor the use of electricity by individual farmers, will create disincentives for overuse of energy and water. Thus, farmers will not only use water efficiently, but also invest in improving the efficiency of electric motors and pumps. But given the wide regional variations in the energy requirements for pumping a unit volume of water across regions, a flat unit rate will not be socially acceptable to the farmers in regions where pumping depths are very large.

There is plenty of evidence now available in India to show that water users in both rural and urban areas are willing to pay much more for dependable, safe, timely and adequate water supplies and sanitation services. For example, in a sample survey of 100 farmers conducted in two purposively selected villages in Kheda district of Gujarat, it was found that the sample farmers were willing to pay 150 to 300 per cent of the prevailing tariff for timely and adequate supply of irrigation water (Singh and Ghatak 1995: 6–7). Similarly, studies conducted in urban areas show that consumers are willing to pay much higher water tariff if the supplies are regular and adequate and the quality of water supplied is good.

9.4.5 Abatement of Externalities in the Use of Water

As we discussed in Chapter 4, Section 4.8, there are two alternative approaches to abatement of externalities in the use of water, namely, (a) Pigouvian Tax-Subsidy Approach; and (b) Coasian Property Rights Approach. We briefly discuss them below in the context of water.

The Pigouvian Tax-Subsidy Approach

In the case of groundwater, an externality arises due to a combination of institutional failure (absence of secure property rights), market failure (environmental externalities) and policy failure (distortionary subsidies). This is reflected in the gap between the private cost of extraction of water and the total cost to society, including depletion and damage cost. Since the social cost for depletion and damages is not internalised by the water extractor, this results in underpricing and hence overexploitation of groundwater. The pricing of water on the basis of its scarcity value is neither technically nor politically easy to introduce in developing societies, including India, in which water has traditionally been regarded as God given and, therefore, a free good. Yet potential gains justify some form of water pricing in the face of increasing scarcity. Efficient pricing is at the heart of natural resource management. Almost all resource problems can be traced to discrepancies between private and social valuation of resource commodities and resource stocks. In the case of irrigation water, the private cost of both is positive and rising.

The Pigouvian tax-subsidy approach aims at bridging the gap between the private and social costs by internalising all external costs to their sources, namely, the water extractor in this case. Pigou proposed two economic instruments, namely, tax and subsidy to internalise the externalities. Both the instruments seek to affect costs and benefits of economic agents, with a view to influence their behaviour in a way that is favourable to society.

Taxes or subsidies for environmentally sound production can be used for full cost pricing of production and consumption. For example, current prices of canal irrigation water do not reflect the social costs of water. The effects of canal irrigation on soil and human health (through water-borne diseases) are not considered at all. Fiscal instruments, therefore, try to bridge the gap between the private and social cost of production and consumption. Ideally, the taxes or subsidies should be equal to the marginal environmental damage caused by a certain activity. If this were the case, it would adjust the price of a good exactly by the amount of reduction in social welfare caused by the externalities associated with such a product (see for more details, Chapter 4, Section 4.8).

Coasian Property Rights Approach

As stated in Chapter 4, Section 4.8, the Coase Theorem is relevant in the context of search of possible alternatives for abatement of externalities. According to the Theorem, creation and assignment of property rights to either the agency that creates the externalities, or the party which is affected by the externalities will internalise the externalities. Inadequately defined and insecure property rights are the most important reasons for overexploitation and depletion of water resources. Therefore, there is need to create and assign secure, tradable and enforceable property rights that will lead to socially optimal use of water resources through their rational pricing. The property rights will ensure that the cost of degradation/depletion is internal to the user and that the user will use the resource in a socially optimal manner on a sustainable basis. In cases where somebody is polluting a water body belonging to somebody else, the property rights will ensure that the right holder and the user will negotiate a mutually beneficial solution to internalise the externality.

Assigning property rights in surface water to the private sector can be a useful instrument to tackle the problem of soil salinity/alkalinity and waterlogging. Private sector here includes not only the corporate sector, but also the consultancy and contracting firms, Water Users' Associations (WUAs), Non-Governmental Organisations (NGOs) and the general public. WUAs can play a major role in managing the problems of irrigation-induced land degradation and exploiting full potential of irrigation. In any scheme of things/plan, farmers—both as individuals and in groups—have a central role to play either as the main or as supportive actors. A well-organised and effectively running network of WUAs with capacity and experience in functions like water distribution, water charge collection, and system maintenance and monitoring can be a facilitating factor both for private investment in irrigation as well as for private involvement in management. In order to elicit the form of farmers' participation appropriate for irrigation privatisation, it is critical to move from mere 'participation' to 'organisation' and eventually 'turn-over' of the irrigation system itself to WUAs farmers' management.

Advantages: In short, the assignment of secure, tradable and enforceable property rights would have the following advantages:

- Transaction costs are very low.
- Assignment of property rights internalises the externalities for ever and no further intervention is necessary.
- Administrative costs are low after property rights are assigned.
- They adjust automatically to changing circumstances.
- Market distortions are very low as compared to those introduced by changes in prices.

In reality, however, things are not so simple because we have to contend with transaction costs and incomplete information and the assignment of property rights should not be expected to solve all environmental problems. For example, the assignment of property rights is not feasible if there are a lot of users of a specific environmental commodity, such as air, atmosphere or water, since exclusion of other users is technically not possible. Assigning and enforcing property rights in surface water resources is very difficult. Even if property rights were established, it would be difficult for the affected parties to reach agreements on how to internalise the costs because the associated transaction costs might exceed the potential benefits of working an agreement. This is especially so if a major effort is needed simply to obtain sufficient information about the costs of the externality and benefits of removing them. Some of the economic gains achieved by fixing water prices that reflect the real resource cost of water, or establishing water markets will be offset by transaction costs that include efforts to measure water deliveries, collect revenue from water sales, record market transactions and protect water rights. The transaction costs of implementing water rights and pricing programmes may be particularly high in the developing countries where large-scale irrigation projects deliver water to many small farmers. Public agencies can reduce private transaction costs by collecting and sharing of information about water markets and providing an efficient and secure procedure for transferring water rights.

The administrative costs of water pricing, allocation and marketing programmes can be substantial, particularly in countries where improvements in delivery channels, measuring devices and operational procedures are required to enable better control and measurement of water deliveries. Capacity building of water-related institutions such as WUAs may also be required to support volumetric water pricing and trading of water rights or allotments. However, administrative costs may be reduced by choosing the appropriate level at which to implement innovative programmes and by adopting technologies that support programme goals. For example, it seems feasible to introduce volumetric 'water wholesaling' in which a public agency sells water to a WUA at some point in the delivery system where volumetric measurement is feasible. The WUA is then responsible for recovering water costs from individual members. Measurement capability might be extended to lower levels of the delivery system by designing and installing new metering devices that provide volumetric measurement at a reasonable cost.

Limitations: In short, there are the following constraints/limitations in assigning property rights:

- It is a politically sensitive issue, since it can be used to achieve political objectives (for example, reward political supporters).
- It is difficult to distribute property rights. As they carry a lot of value (rents from future activities), water rights should not be given away free. However selling them in an open market would exclude poor people from buying them and therefore would have undesirable social consequences.

To sum up, we could say that in most cases, a combination of both, the tax-subsidy and property rights approaches, will be needed to resolve the problems of externalities. But the most important thing to remember is that the cost of externality abatement should not exceed the benefits from abatement. For identifying and measuring externalities, we need expertise in natural resource economics and welfare economics.

9.4.6 Creating a Congenial Policy, Legal and Institutional Framework

Water resource development and management is now in the State List (List II) of Schedule VII of the Constitution of India.[7] This means that water is a State subject and that only the State Governments have the Constitutional power to enact legislation and frame rules and regulations for development and management of the country's water resources. But given the importance of water as a critical natural resource for country, the Union Ministry of Water Resources lays down policies and programmes for the development and regulation of the country's water resources. There is an enabling provision under Entry 56 of the Union List (List I) in the Constitution of India, by which the Government of India can take over the regulation and control of any or all of the inter-state rivers and river valleys in the larger national interest, if required. This provision has not been invoked so far. But now, in view of the increasing number of inter-state disputes over sharing of inter-state river waters, this provision needs to be invoked in the larger national interest.[8] There is also a growing consensus among scholars and civil society organisations about the need for transfer of water to the Concurrent List (List III).

To sum up, we could say that water is both a State subject and a Central subject as most of the country's rivers are inter-state (Iyer 2003: 22). Consequently, both the Central and the State governments are responsible for framing policies and programmes for water resources development, use and management. In fact, now we have in India a National Water Policy 2002 and several State Water Policies co-existing. The first National Water Policy (NWP) of India was adopted in September 1987. It stresses, among other things, that

> Water is a prime natural resource, a basic human need and a precious national asset. Planning and development of water resources need to be governed by national perspectives.

It recommends an integrated and multidisciplinary approach to planning, formulation and implementation of projects in such a way as

---

[7] Entry 17 in the State List has a bearing on the matter but it is subject to the provisions of Entry 56 of the Union List (List I).

[8] It would be pertinent to state here that Article 262 of the Constitution of India provides for adjudication of disputes relating to waters of inter-state rivers and the Inter-State Water Dispute Act 1956, was enacted under Article 262 to operationalise that provision.

to be able to meet the demands of water from various sectors and to free the country, as far as possible, from the scourge of recurring floods and droughts. A new National Water Policy was announced in 2002 (GoI 2002a). This policy supersedes the 1987 Policy but it also echoes similar concerns.

The NWP 1987 and NWP 2002 do not clearly specify their goals, nor any operational guidelines as to how various provisions made in the Policy documents would be actualised. In view of this, we could say that the Policy framework is ineffective. In our opinion, its main goal should be to attain water security for all and for ever through restoring, developing, conserving, utilising and managing the surface water and groundwater resources of the country in a socially optimum and eco-logically sound and sustainable way. Besides, the policy should have a legal back-up and operational guidelines to achieve its objectives. Also, the government must accept the access to water for survival as a basic human right and include it in the set of development goals and use it as an entry point for development work. A minimum of 40 litres of water per capita per day is required for meeting personal consumption, hygiene and sanitation requirements (WSSCC 1999).

The goal of 'water security for all and for ever' implies efficiency, equity and sustainability as the guiding principles of water resources management. The sustainability principle requires that water resources be used in such a way that the stock is not depleted beyond the socially and ecologically desirable level and is available for meeting the legiti-mate requirements of present and future generations. To the extent, sustainability subsumes the socially optimum rate of resource use in perpetuity, it takes care of the goal of economic efficiency as well. But maximisation of economic efficiency in the short run may conflict with the goal of sustainability; however the latter is superior to the former as a goal of the strategy.

A responsible strategy should also provide for equitable distribution of benefits and equitable sharing of costs of water development proj-ects among their users. Many development projects have failed in the past because they ignored equity considerations in their design and implementation and did not legitimise the local use rights. Availability of benefits and their equitable distribution should be guaranteed through appropriate legal provisions. Similarly, cost-sharing arrange-ments should also be worked out and put in place to reduce or elimi-nate the problems of free riding and shirking by water users.

At present there is no water law in India to back up the National Water Policy. Consequently, the Policy is not effective in realising its objectives. There have been several attempts in the past by many of the state governments to enact laws to regulate the extraction of ground-water. Only eight state governments in India have so far enacted groundwater laws following the advice of the Government of India. But the acts are limited in their scope and apply only to certain speci-fied areas.

Thus, at present, there is virtually no legal control of government over surface water resources and regulation of groundwater use is done through restrictions on the flow of institutional credit from banks as per the guidelines issued by the National Bank for Agriculture and Rural Development (NABARD). The restrictions are in the form of minimum spacing requirements between tube wells financed by banks. Such restrictions are not very effective because of their lax monitoring by the banks and because rich farmers resort to borrowing from non-institutional sources and thereby bypass these restrictions.

What is needed to effectively manage India's water resources is an appropriate legal framework that clearly specifies the rights and respon-sibilities of various stakeholders in water. A central legislation drafted on the pattern of the water laws of South Africa and China but modified to suit India's conditions would provide an appropriate legal framework.

An ideal water legislation should provide for the following:

- A unified organisation structure to formulate strategies, plans and programmes for water resources development in the country.
- Use of the river basin or region as a basic unit for overall planning for water resources development and management.
- Provision for granting usufruct rights to Water Users' Associations.
- Fixation of water prices taking into account its real resource cost and ability of water users to pay.
- Encouragement and support by the State to various non-governmental organisations including WUAs for developing and utilising water resources.
- Regulation of extraction of water in identified areas where groundwater is on the verge of depletion.

9.5 MAIN POINTS

The following are the main points made in this chapter:

- Water is a finite but renewable natural resource and like other natural resources, it is an integral part of the environment. It is essential for survival of all living beings on this planet and so also for socio-economic development of households, communities and nations all over the world. It is also necessary to maintain and enhance biodiversity and quality of environment.

- The country's total water requirement would barely match the utilisable water resources in the year 2050 and the gap between the water requirement and availability will widen over time. The most serious challenge of the 21st century for India will be how to meet the deficit or demand-supply gap, especially the regional and seasonal deficits.

- The present water scarcity and crisis in many areas of India is caused by increased overexploitation and pollution of both surface and groundwater, lack of rational pricing of water, lack of well-defined property rights in water backed up by law, and the shortcomings in the National Water Policy.

- Floods and droughts have been a bane of India's economy since time immemorial. It is an irony that in many parts of India, we have droughts and in many others, we have floods occurring almost concurrently every year. Yet, this kind of risk is not even recognised in India's policies and plans, not to speak of absence of any comprehensive national policy for their mitigation.

- The main instruments for mitigation of environmental problems related to water include creation of property rights and assigning them to water users' associations, rationalising of water prices, drought and flood proofing, use of water saving micro irrigation facilities, and internalising of externalities in the use of water.

- An ideal water law should provide, *inter alia*, for formulating policies, and strategies for regulating and governing the use of water, fixing water rates taking into account the scarcity value of water and revising them from time to time, creating appropriate organisations of water users at the national and state levels, vesting usufruct rights in them and helping them with technical information, funds and legal advice.

- There is need for a pragmatic national water policy backed up by an appropriate water law. The main goal of the policy should be to ensure water security for all and for ever. This implies that the objectives of the policy should be to ensure sustainability, efficiency and equity in the use and management of the country's water resources through the use of appropriate instruments including rationalising water price and promoting the use of water saving irrigation technologies.

9.6 DISCUSSION QUESTIONS

1. Pollution of common pool sources of water particularly rivers, *nallahas*, lakes and tanks/ponds is a serious problem today in India. Make a list of all human activities that contribute to water pollution and identify policy instruments that could be used to reduce the pollution of water-bodies.

2. Visit a nearby village and talk to a few knowledgeable villagers, *Sarpanch* of the Gram Panchayat and village level officials. List all the diseases that are caused by polluted water in the village and estimate the cost of the treatment of those diseases for the village. Ask the affected people whether they would be willing to pay the equivalent of the cost they incurred on the treatment to the village panchayat for controlling water pollution in the village. Prepare a short note on your findings.

3. Can we implement a programme based on the 'polluter pays' principle to control water pollution in our country? Yes/No. If yes, how and if no, why not?

4. In India, there is a lot of wastage of water in all sectors – agriculture, domestic uses and industry. A major factor responsible for it is underpricing of water. Can pricing of water at its real resource cost reduce the wastage of water? Yes/No. If yes, how and if no, why not?

5. Some social activists argue that 'water is a free gift of mother nature' and hence should not be priced, particularly for domestic uses. Do you agree with this argument? Yes/No. If yes, why and if no, why not?

6. Write a critique of the National Water Policy 2002 with special reference to its role in mitigating the problems of degradation of water resources and ensuring efficient use of water.

10 Forests and Environment

Forests are natural renewable resources and have been an integral part of India's economy and culture since time immemorial. They are held in high esteem. The ancient religious, political and literary writings are a testimony to the fact that people were considered an integral part of nature, not superior to it. It is difficult to put together the historical forest management practices before the British Raj in India, given the diversity in culture, forest types and administrative set-ups in different parts of the country; forests were managed by erstwhile princely states under different land tenure systems. But it is well known that many of the forests in India were managed under a set of conventions, rules and regulations evolved by the communities from time to time. Even today, some of these so-called self-initiated forest protection groups with different nomenclature have survived or have been reinvented in response to the need of the hour to conserve the community forests. On the other hand, recorded information on forest management of those areas held directly by the British administration is available. It is widely agreed that scientific management of forests started with the appointment of Dietrich Brandis, a German botanist, as Inspector General of Forest in India in 1867 (Khanna 2004). It was also around the time that the process of the shift in the management of forests from communities to the State started. The shift was facilitated and legitimatised by the Forest Acts of 1865 and 1878. Degradation of forests and deforestation started after the forest dwellers and communities living in the vicinity of forests realised that the forest no longer belonged to them but to the State. The process went on unabated and led to wide spread deforestation and degradation through out the course of the 20th century and is still going on, *albeit*, at a lesser pace.

In this chapter, we will first examine the role of forests in India's economy, and then diagnose the nature and extent of the problems of deforestation and degradation of forests. This is followed by presentation of a conceptual framework for optimum level of exploitation of forests, and identification of some practicable alternatives for mitigating the problems identified and ensuring sustainable harvest and management of India's forests.

10.2 THE ROLE OF FORESTS IN INDIA'S ECONOMY

Forests occupy an important place in India's economy in terms of their contribution to the Gross Domestic Product (GDP), employment and livelihoods of poor people. Table 10.1 presents the estimates of contribution of forests to India's GDP for the period, 1993–94 to 2002–03. As shown in the table, in 2002–03, forests contributed to India's GDP Rs 27,013 crore

Table 10.1 Contribution of Forestry and Logging to the Gross Domestic Product (GDP) at Current Prices and 1993–94 Prices in India

	Current Prices			1993–94 Prices		
Year	Total GDP (Rs Crore)	Contribution of Forestry (Rs Crore)	%	Total GDP (Rs Crore)	Contribution of Forestry (Rs Crore)	%
1993–94	781,345	11,454	1.5	781,345	11,454	1.5
1995–96	1,073,271	13,390	1.2	899,563	11,701	1.3
1996–97	1,243,546	14,493	1.2	970,083	11,865	1.2
1997–98	1,390,148	16,249	1.2	1,016,595	12,114	1.2
1998–99	1,598,127	17,840	1.1	1,082,748	12,301	1.1
1999–2000	1,761,838	19,555	1.1	1,148,368	12,753	1.1
2000–01	1,902,998	22,422	1.2	1,198,592	13,064	1.1
2001–02	2,090,957	24,341	1.2	1,267,833	13,244	1.0
2002–03	2,249,493	27,013	1.2	1,318,321	13,573	1.0

Source: CSO 2004.

| Table 10.2 | Contribution of Forestry and Logging to the Net Domestic Product (NDP) at Current Prices and 1993–94 Prices in India |

	Current Prices			1993–94 Prices		
Year	Total GDP (Rs Crore)	Contribution of Forestry (Rs Crore)	%	Total NDP (Rs Crore)	Contribution of Forestry (Rs Crore)	%
1993–94	697,992	11,166	1.6	697,992	11,166	1.6
1995–96	955,345	12,999	1.4	800,411	11,392	1.4
1996–97	1,107,043	14,042	1.3	862,808	11,546	1.3
1997–98	1,238,151	15,736	1.3	901,735	11,785	1.3
1998–99	1,430,061	17,260	1.2	960,555	11,960	1.2
1999–2000	1,579,497	18,919	1.2	1,019,297	12,400	1.2
2000–01	1,705,103	21,762	1.3	1,062,492	12,702	1.2
2001–02	1,873,203	23,629	1.3	1,125,286	12,870	1.1
2002–03	2,014,450	26,267	1.3	1,168,224	13,194	1.1

Source: CSO 2004.

at the current prices, which was 1.2 per cent of the GDP. The contribution of forests to India's GDP has varied from 1.0 to 1.5 per cent over the nine year period from 1993–94 to 2002–03. The contribution of the forestry sector to India's Net Domestic Product (NDP) also varied from 1.1 to 1.6 per cent at both current prices and the 1993–94 prices (Tables 10.2).

In India, forests meet nearly 40 per cent of the energy needs of the country of which more than 80 per cent is utilised in the rural areas, and about 30 per cent of fodder needs of the cattle population. Forest products also play a very important role in rural and tribal economy as many of the Non-Wood Forest Products (NWFP) provide sustenance to the rural poor. For landless families and marginal farmers, forest related activities often represent the primary source of income.

It is estimated that about 270 million tonnes of fuelwood, 280 million tonnes of fodder, over 12 million m^3 of timber and countless NWFP are removed from forests annually. At a conservative level of pricing (Rs 500 per tonne of fuel/fodder) the value of these commodities will approximately aggregate to over Rs 300,000 million per annum (MoEF 1999).

Besides the direct tangible economic benefits mentioned above, forests confer a number of benefits which are not directly visible to the human eye and yet they have a great influence in affecting the quality of life. These benefits are as follows:

- Amelioration of climate
- Conservation of moisture

- Conservation of soil
- Flood control
- Beautification of human environment
- Enhancement of diversity of agro-forestry systems
- Control of environmental pollution
- Carbon sequestration

We will now briefly discuss these intangible benefits of forests.

Amelioration of Climate

Forests exercise a great influence in amelioration of climate by their influence on temperature, rainfall, humidity and wind. Forest cover makes temperature, of both air and soil, more equable than it is in the open. This is due to the fact that forest cover acts as a screen and prevents the sun's rays from heating the air and soil inside the forests to the extent as it does in the open. On the other hand, large-scale deforestation results in deteriorating climate. The influence of forests in increasing the total rainfall of a place has been disputed but there is no doubt that forests exercise considerable influence in increasing the number of rainy days over limited areas. As forests keep on drawing water from inside the earth and transpiring it in the atmosphere, they have a favourable effect on humidity. A strip of trees and shrubs reduces wind velocity considerably and reduces the destructive impact of the wind on forests.

Conservation of Moisture

Forests affect not only the distribution of rainfall over a period of time but also its proper utilisation, because they control its excessive run-off and force most of it to percolate into the soil, from where it could be extracted when needed. Thus, forests (every tree, shrubs and tuft of grass) in the catchments (and this holds true even elsewhere) act like dams to store water and release it gradually. These natural dams are far more effective than engineering dams constructed in the river valleys because the latter allow rain water to damage the soil and then store it, thereby affecting their own life seriously.

Conservation of Soil

It is estimated that about 6,000 million tonnes of topsoil in India is washed away every year. Considering that the most valuable layer of cultivable soil is the top 18 cm, this represents a loss of 6 million acres of cultivable land every year. This soil loss results in annual loss of nearly Rs 15,000 million in terms of cost of food crops and nutrients. Furthermore, the value of indirect benefits conferred by a 50 year old tree is as high as Rs 15.7 lakh, of which Rs 2.5 lakh is on account of control of soil erosion and enhancement of soil fertility.

Flood Control

Forests control floods to a great extent and this is of great importance in view of the fact that every year they cause a loss of about 300 crore rupees by way of damage to crops, animals and public and private property and to the river channels themselves. This is an underestimate as it does not include the recurring loss to forest and agricultural crops as a result of soil washed away by floods and or otherwise deteriorated by deposition of detritus. It also does not include the damage by floods caused by cloud burst as happened in Morbi (Gujarat) in 1979 and Shimla (Himachal Pradesh) in 2003.

Beautification of Human Environment

Small forests dotted here and there are a great source of recreation to the local people. Though material wealth is necessary for prosperity of a nation, its healthy development depends upon a beautiful environment. A landscape without trees is drab, dreary and desolate and it has a depressing influence on the minds of people. On the other hand, a landscape with trees, climbers, shrubs produces a soothing effect on them because of their beautiful green foliage, colourful flowers and above all sweet chirping of beautifully coloured birds hopping from branch to branch.

Enhancement of Diversity of Agro-Forestry Systems

Even small forests interspersed in cultivated areas create diversity in the agro-ecosystem, and help in the establishment of natural food chains resulting in the biological control of insects and other paste.

Control of Environmental Pollution

As a result of the population explosion and the tremendous increase in industrialisation, pollution of the environment is now increasing at such a high rate that it is likely to cause serious health hazards to human beings very soon. For instance, oxides of sulphur are reported to be major contributors of lung diseases such as asthma and bronchitis. A direct correlation is reported to be existing between air pollution and 80 per cent incidence of cancer. While in the developed countries, pollution of environment is being reduced by cleaning the pollutants at source by costly technological devices, it is not possible to adopt them in India because of prohibitive cost and, therefore, biological control of environmental pollution is the only answer.

Carbon Sequestration

One of the important roles of a forest on a global level is to act as a carbon sink. Trees act as carbon sinks when they absorb CO_2 from the atmosphere and build up the same in the form of wood. Forests are estimated to store carbon—about 20 to 100 times more per hectare than pastures or croplands. New tree plantations and agro-forestry systems have potential to sequester and conserve up to 10 Gt of carbon annually in the terrestrial biosphere, while at the same time continuing to provide needed goods and services for people. Globally, estimates of carbon emission resulting from tropical deforestation range from 1–2 Gt only on an annual basis.

Attempts have been made in several instances recently to quantitatively define carbon sequestration benefits of tree plantations and to evaluate them to provide broad guidelines and indicators of carbon offset projects. The potential carbon storage ranges of forest management and agro-forestry practices by major latitudinal biomes over a 50-year period are shown in Table 10.3. The median cost efficiency across all management practices as determined from establishment costs over a 50-year period is about US$ 5/tC (US$ 5 per tonne of carbon) with an adequate range of US$ 19/tC (Chandrasekharan 1996).

Hardwood contains about 48 per cent carbon in the form of cellulose and wood, and it is estimated that 2.2 tonnes of wood is required to sequester one tonne of carbon. On the other hand, while the wood is burnt, the reverse process takes place in which the atmospheric oxygen

Table 10.3 Potential Carbon Storage Ranges of Forest Management and Agro-Forestry Practices by Major Latitudinal Biomes on a 50-year Period

Type of Forest	Forestation (tC/ha)	Silviculture (tC/ha)
Boreal	15–40	3–10
Temperate	30–180	10–45
Tropical	30–130	14–70

Source: Chandrasekharan (1996).

is used and CO_2 is released into the atmosphere. Hence, forests act both as a source as well as a sink of carbon, depending upon the manner and purpose for which they are raised and managed. The growth rate and the carbon sequestration potential of forests decline as the plant matures. In a matured forest, growth rate is largely offset by wood decay. Matured and climax forests are neither sources nor sinks of atmospheric carbon and forests that experience a net loss of biomass volume through mortality due to disease or fire become net carbon emitters (Kyrklund 1990).

10.3 DEFORESTATION AND DEGRADATION OF FORESTS AND THEIR ENVIRONMENTAL CONSEQUENCES

In India, millions of rural people depend on the forests for their livelihood. In view of this, sustainability of the flow of forest products is essential for sustaining their livelihoods. But, over the last three decades or so, forests resources have been under great biotic and abiotic pressures. They have been subject to overexploitation, degradation and encroachment (Singh 1994a: 226). Besides substantial chunks of forest land are being diverted to non-forestry uses. Further, only 59 per cent of the actual forest cover in the country is classified as dense. Consequently, forest area, productivity and production have declined and their sustainability is threatened. The low productivity of forests in India in terms of volume of growing stock is evident from the fact that the volume of growing stock in India in the year 2000 was 43 m³ per ha as compared to 119 m³ in Malasiya and 100 m³ in Nepal (FAO 2001). All this poses a threat to the survival of millions of poor people, especially tribals, who mainly depend on forests for their livelihood.

The recorded forest area as per legal documents for the years 1997, 1999 and 2001 is shown in Table 10.4. As shown in the table, most forest

Table 10.4	Trend in Area Under Different Categories of Forests in India				
	Forest Area (sq km)				% of Geographical Area Under Forest Cover
Year	Reserve Forest	Protected Forest	Unclassified	Total	
1997	416,516	223,309	125,385	765,210	23.28
1999	416,547	223,321	125,385	765,253	23.28
2001	423,311	217,245	127,881	768,463	23.38

Source: FSI 1997, 1999, 2001.

areas (over 90 per cent) are under public/government ownership and managed by the State Forest Departments (SFDs). Some forest areas such as the Civil and Soyam Forests in Uttarakhand and customarily owned forest lands in the north-eastern States are outside the SFD control. As one could see from the table, there has been a marginal increase in the area under reserved forests over the period, 1997–2001 whereas the area under protected forests has marginally declined. On the whole, the total area under forests in India has gone up marginally.

According to an assessment made by the Forest Survey of India (FSI), India had 23.38 per cent of its geographical area under forests in the year 2001. But only 12.68 per cent of it can be considered to be reasonably well stocked. Also, the extent of forest cover as well as the percentage share of forest land in the total geographical area vary widely from state to state. For example, according to the 1997 FSI Assessment, Arunachal Pradesh had 82 per cent (68,602 sq km) of its geographical area under forests, whereas Haryana had only 1.4 per cent (604 sq. km). The entire north-eastern region, which accounts for 8 per cent of the total land area of India, had 26 per cent of the country's forests. Some 50 per cent of the country's total forest land is concentrated in the five states of Madhya Pradesh, Chhattisgarh, Arunachal Pradesh, Orissa and Maharashtra.

There are several reasons for the degradation and depletion of forest resources in India. First, deforestation on a large scale started during the Second World War for commercial purposes under the 'Grow More Food' campaign launched in India after Independence for agricultural production purposes. This was followed by transfers of forest land for development projects and waves of encroachments and land assignments by the State governments under social welfare programmes. Deforestation reached a peak in the 1970s with an average annual deforestation rate of 0.339 million ha. It came down significantly in the 1980s. The recent reduction in deforestation is partly because of growing public concern, especially by environmentalists, over the encroachment and transfers of forest land for non-forest uses.

Second, there has been an increase in the demand for diversion of forestland for non-forestry purposes in India. For example as of 31 October 2002, there were as many as 8,015 proposals approved by the Ministry of Environment and Forest (MoEF), Government of India (GoI) and nearly 5.76 lakh ha of forest land had been diverted for non-forestry uses.

Of this, 2.28 lakh ha of forest land was diverted in Madhya Pradesh and 15,929 ha in Chhattisgarh (www.indiastat.com). The rate of deforestation in India during the last 50 to 60 years has been considerably

Table 10.5	Diversion of Forest Land for Non-Forest Uses in India Since the Enforcement of the Forest Conservation Act 1980		
Year	Forest Land Diverted (ha)	Year	Forest Land Diverted (ha)
1980	Nil	1990*	138,551.38
1981	2,672.04	1991	625.21
1982	3,246.54	1992	5,686.94
1983	5,702.01	1993	11,785.64
1984	7,837.59	1994	13,527.69
1985	10,608.07	1995	46,158.52
1986	11,963.11	1996	8,764.79
1987	72,780.05	1997	16,313.20
1988	18,765.35	1998	12,630.00
1989	20,365.05		

Source: GoI (2000).
Notes: *1990 data includes:
    (i) 1.83 lakh ha for regularisation of encroachments in Madhya Pradesh.
    (ii) 0.12 lakh ha for field firing range of Indian Army in Sagar.

higher than in the last 10 years or so. It is reported that the rate of diversion of forest land in the country dropped from 1.43 lakh ha per annum to mere 15,000 ha per annum after the enactment of the Forest Conservation Act 1980 (Khanna 2004: 23, and Table 10.5).

Third, there has been forest policy failure in the sense that the past as well as present forest policy has not been congenial to promoting sustainable use and management of forest resources. In the pre-Independence era, the forest policy followed by the British administration head commercial interests at it core. It had the main objective of serving agricultural interests, which was the major source of revenue. These motives are explicitly documented in the National Forest Policy of 1894, the first formal forest policy in India. This policy stipulated that forests which are the reservoirs of valuable timbers should be managed on commercial lines as a source of revenue to the States and wherever an effective demand for culturable land exists, which can only be supplied from forest area, the land should ordinarily be relinquished without hesitation. According to this policy, the sole object with which the forests were administered during the British administration was state interest.

Meeting of people's needs from the forests was not a priority consideration of the British administration. People's requirements were to be met from the third class of forests—'minor forests' that yielded only inferior timber, fuelwood or fodder, and the fourth class of forests—'pastures and grazing grounds' that too with certain restrictions. In general, the policy dictated 'the constitution and preservation of a forest involve, in greater or less degree, the regulation of rights and the restriction of privileges of user in the forest area which may have previously been enjoyed by the inhabitants of its immediate neighbourhood' and further suggested that the cardinal principle to be observed is that the rights and privileges of individuals must be limited. To conclude, we could say that people's interests were subservient to the state's commercial interests in the forests during the colonial rule.

After Independence, the GoI came out with its first post-Independence National Forest Policy in 1952. This was an attempt to revise the National Forest Policy of 1894. This policy was framed at the time when post-war reconstruction schemes, including industrial expansion, river valley projects and development of communications were underway and there was heavy demand for the produce of forests. This policy proposed the classification of forests into protection forests, national forests, village forests and tree lands (Government of India 1952). However, this policy statement could never be implemented. One of the reasons for this ineffectiveness was that this policy was issued as a resolution by the government but was not adopted by the State Legislatures (GoI 1976).

Misdirected policies to curb deforestation in India on the other hand led to the introduction of laws against cutting and marketing of trees from both the public and private lands. This had a counter-intentional effect in the sense that farmers reduced the number of trees they planted on their private lands fearing that they would not be able to sell trees. This, coupled with the increasing demand for wood, which fetched a good price, increased the pressure on government forests, relatively with open access, to meet the increased demand for wood. This misdirected policy has resulted in the depletion of forests in the country. Singh (1994) has identified three reasons for the deforestation and degradation of forests in India. They are: defective forest policy, faulty implementation of the policy and poverty.

However, the National Forest Policy, 1988, the second forest policy after India's Independence, has some redeeming features. It is both conservation and production oriented. The basic objective of this policy is the maintenance of environmental stability through preservation of forests as a natural heritage with people's participation. It also emphasises the need for increasing substantially the forest/tree cover and the productivity of forests in the country to meet essential national needs. However, it is too early to assess its impact on the status of forest conservation and productivity.

Another reason for the existing state of affairs is the lack of an appropriate governance and management system in the forestry sector.

Besides, there is gross under-valuation of forest benefits in computing the contribution of the forestry sector to India's Gross Domestic Product (GDP). This has led to gross under-estimation of the true contribution of forests to the GDP of India and the consequent inadequate budgetary allocation of funds to the sector. Forest Resource Accounting (FRA) is one of the several measures that could be used to reform the existing governance system through a better Management Information System (MIS), leading to a higher degree of efficiency, accountability and transparency. Any system of governance requires a good MIS, which could furnish adequate, reliable and timely information as a basis for making various policies and operating decisions.

Last but not the least, under the new World Trade Regime ushered in by the World Trade Oganization (WTO) in 1995, the World Bank and the IMF are advocating that the free market is the key to economic growth of developing countries. They are forcing developing countries, including India, to adopt Structural Adjustment Programmes (SAPs) and integrate their national economies into the world economy by removing all barriers to the free flow of goods and capital across their borders. The end result of such policies will be environmental degradation and depletion of natural resources both of which will reduce the real wealth of the society and impair the future productive potential of the economy. This is exactly what is happening now in most developing countries of the world. The trade in tropical timber, for example, is one factor underlying tropical deforestation. Need for foreign exchange encourages many developing countries to cut timber faster than forests can be regenerated. This over-cutting not only depletes the resource that underpins the world timber trade but also causes the loss of forest-based livelihoods, increases soil erosion and downstream flooding, and accelerates the loss of species and genetic resources. International trade patterns can also encourage the unsustainable development policies and practices that have steadily degraded the crop-lands and range-lands in the dry-lands of Asia and Africa.

10.4 SOCIALLY OPTIMAL LEVEL OF EXPLOITATION OF FORESTS

When identifying alternatives for mitigating the problems of degradation and depletion of forest resources, we should aim at minimising them or at least restricting them to a level consistent with society's objectives, rather than trying to prevent or eliminate them altogether. When forest degradation is seen in the context of the society's development objectives, not all deforestation is bad or worth preventing. Some deforestation is necessary and beneficial when the forest land is put to a superior use which may be agricultural, industrial or residential. As long as all costs involved, including those arising from diminished quantity, deteriorated quality and lost diversity of forests have been accounted for; as long as both the productivity and the sustainability of the alternative uses have been considered with a due margin of error; and as long as any side effects of the forest conversion have been internalised and paid for, deforestation should not be something we would like to prevent. However, the main problem in the Indian context is that due to their mismanagement and several other factors, most of the forest lands have very low vegetative cover and are, for all practical purposes, wastelands with little current benefits and enormous current and future costs. It is unfortunate when such wasteful forest destruction is lumped together with socially optimal forest conversion into a single deforestation figure.

Considering the importance of forests in India, and India's need for a higher level of economic development, it would be desirable to determine the socially optimal level of exploitation of forests. This would help reconcile, to some extent, the conflicting goals of forest conservation and security of livelihood of the poor forest dwellers, who depend on forest resources for their survival and facilitate the formulation of effective policies to deal with the problem of forest degradation. In Figure 10.1, we show graphically how the optimal level of forest exploitation can be determined.

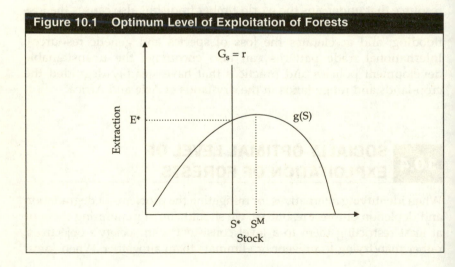

Figure 10.1 Optimum Level of Exploitation of Forests

In the figure, the curved line g(S) represents the growth rate of a natural stock of trees. This also represents the amount, at each level of the stock, that can be harvested without depleting the stock. Therefore, S^M is the level of the stock at which the 'maximum sustainable yield' (MSY) can be harvested. But MSY is not the socially optimum level of exploitation except in rare cases (Dasgupta 1982: 186–87).

It can be shown mathematically that the socially optimum exploitation policy that maximises the net present value of the stock will deplete the stock until the growth rate or the slope of the curve g(S) is equal to the rate of discount, r. In the figure, this stock level is S^*.[1] However, for a slow-growing resource like a tropical rain forest, there may be no level of the stock at which this condition is met. In this case, depletion is the optimal policy.

This analysis may not account for the non-timber benefits from sustainable resource use, and almost certainly will not consider the indirect benefits provided by a forest to nearby agricultural land, such as hydrological regulation and the protection of the land from excessive water run-off. Likewise, global values of the biodiversity contained in the forest and its role in local and global climate regulation are not accounted for in this analysis. More efficient resource use can be achieved if these benefits are internalised.

10.5 ALTERNATIVES FOR MITIGATING THE PROBLEMS OF DEGRADATION AND DEPLETION OF FOREST RESOURCES

In this section, we examine some socially desirable and economically viable alternatives for minimising the problems of forest degradation and depletion and ensuring their sustainable use and management.

10.5.1 Rectify the Policy and Market Failures

India is one of the few countries in the world that has had a forest policy since 1894. After Independence, in recognition of the importance of forests in the national economy and to ensure the best possible use of land, a new forest policy was enunciated in May 1952. The new policy

---

[1]For mathematical proof, see Lesser et al. (1997: 488–95). A more rigorous procedure for determination of socially optimum exploitation policy for a renewable resource such as forests and fisheries is presented in Chapter 11, Section 11.4 of this book.

provided, *inter alia*, that the area under forests should be at least one-third of the total geographical area and that the forest areas should not be brought under cultivation of crops indiscriminately. The National Commission on Agriculture (1976) recommended a further revision of the 1952 Forest Policy. The forest policy was revised in 1988. The main plank of the revised Forest Policy of 1988 is protection, conservation and development of forests. The revised Forest Policy has several implications for various sectors of the economy like energy, industry and agriculture. Development projects now are carefully examined to ensure that ecological balance is not destroyed. This is done through assessment of their impacts on ecosystems.

However in the past, India's forest policy has not been congenial to promoting sustainable use and management of forest resources. The current policy also needs to be overhauled if the link between scarcity of forest resources and their prices is to be re-established. Now that we are facing a growing scarcity of forest resources, forest product prices should be rising to slow down deforestation and accelerate reforestation. At present, not only are many of the forest products and services not priced at all, but even timber which is an internationally tradable commodity is priced below its true scarcity value due to implicit and explicit subsidies and institutional failures. Forest concessions are typically inadequate to provide incentives for conservation and replanting. Failure to value non-timber goods and services results in excessive deforestation, conflicts with local communities, loss of economic value and environmental damage. Promotion of local processing of timber often leads to inefficient plywood mills, excess capacity, wastage of valuable tropical timber and loss of government revenues. Replanting subsidies often end up subsidising the conversion of a valuable natural forest to inferior mono-species plantations with the associated loss of the value of both tropical hardwoods and biological diversity.

There is also need to adopt a better system of Forest Resource Accounting (FRA). As we stated in Chapter 6, the existing FRA system has several drawbacks. For example, there is no accounting of the free collection of fuelwood, grass and other NWFPs, benefits from free grazing of animals in forests and a whole set of intangible benefits such as soil and water conservation, maintenance of productivity of adjoining lands, biodiversity conservation, moderation of micro-climate, carbon sequestration, release of oxygen, recreation and so on. This leads to gross under-estimation of the contribution of the forestry sector to India's GDP. In view of this, there is need to adopt the new system of FRA as recommended by FAO.

10.5.2 Improve the Governance and Management

The term 'governance' is commonly used to connote a formal or an institutionalised system or structure vested with the supreme power and authority required for smooth functioning, monitoring and control of an entity, which could be an organisation or an administrative unit, or a sector of economy of a state or a nation. In the context of the forestry sector, it comprises the existing organisation structure of forest departments in the country at both the national and state levels, forest laws, policies, rules and regulations, processes and inter-relationships through which people who have stakes in the sector articulate their interests, aspirations and concerns, exercise their legal rights, meet their obligations and mediate their differences.

The present system of overall governance in India comprises at the national level: (*a*) the Constitution of India; (*b*) the Legislature; (*c*) the Executive; and (*d*) the Judiciary; besides a host of several other Constitutional bodies and authorities, civil society organisations and many other Non-Governmental Organisations (NGOs). Governance in the forestry sector is part of the India's general governance system. It was set up in the mid-19th century and is in that sense, a legacy of the then British Government of India. The system is not congenial to promoting sustainable management of forests. After Independence, some cosmetic changes have been made in the system but the basic structure remains the same. The forestry sector now is in the Concurrent List (List III) of the Constitution of India. This means that both the Government of India, through the Ministry of Environment and Forests and the State Governments through their Ministries of Forests and Departments of Forests have the powers and responsibility to govern and manage the country's forests in the larger interest of society. Besides, a host of other organisations such as Joint Forest Management Committees, and Forest Protection Committees are also involved in forest management.

An ideal system of forest governance is characterised by efficiency, accountability, transparency, decentralised, democratic and participatory decision making and sustainability. In the context of the forestry sector, it should facilitate the realisation of the goals of sustainable use and management of forest resources and improvement in the quality of life of people dependent on the forests. Under India's existing governance system, forests are overexploited, depleted, and degraded and the goals set for the sector remain by and large unrealised. This indicates the need for overhauling the existing system of governance.

Despite the Government intention to promote participatory forest management as expressed in the new Forest Policy of 1988 and various

Resolutions on JFM adopted by the Central and the State governments, the attitude of most of FD personnel, especially at the Range and the Division levels, continue to be anti-people; at the most they pay lip service to the new paradigm of JFM. There is need for change in their attitude. This could be possible only if they are required by their senior officers to involve local people in forest management and their performance is judged, among other criteria, by the extent of involvement of local people in forest management. At present there is no incentive for them to promote JFM, nor any disincentive for not involving local people in forest management.[2]

Training in behavioural sciences, refresher courses, change in the existing system of performance appraisal and introduction of a Forest Resource Accounting (FRA) system are some of the several measures that could be used to reform the existing governance system through a better Management Information System (MIS), leading to higher degree of efficiency, accountability and transparency. Any system of governance requires a good MIS, which could furnish adequate, reliable and timely information as a basis for making various policies and operating decisions.

10.5.3 Internalise the Externalities or Spillover Effects

A major factor that drives a wedge between private and social valuation of environmental resources and leads to inefficient pricing is the presence of external costs or spillover effects known as externalities. As we defined it earlier, an externality is an effort of one firm's or individual's actions on other firms or individuals who are not party to those actions. Externalities might be positive or negative. An example of a positive externality in the forestry sector is the benefit that upstream forest owners provide to downstream farmers in the form of a steady water supply made possible by a forested watershed. It is to the society's (and the farmers') benefit that more such positive externalities

---

[2]This is based on Katar Singh's personal experience as Co-coordinator of a project on Participatory Micro Planning and Implementation in GIR Protected Area, Gujarat (1997–99), sponsored by the Gujarat State Forest Department and funded by the Global Environment Fund/World Bank, New Delhi. Despite the clear mandate of the project to involve local people in preparing eco-development plans, the FD personnel concerned were reluctant to do so as it was a time-consuming job, requiring patience, pro-people attitude, and other behavioural skills that they did not possess and also because they were under pressure to prepare the plans in a short period of time so they could use the budget allocated for the financial year. There was no incentive for them to involve local people in the planning process; in fact there was a disincentive in the sense that those personnel assigned to the project had this additional job, besides their routine chores.

are provided, but since forest owners receive no payment for their watershed service they have no incentive to provide more of this service by logging less and planting more. The result is that more logging and less planting than is socially optimal takes place. Looked at from another angle, logging has negative externalities (or spillover effects) on downstream activities such as farming, irrigation, transport and industry, in the form of flooding, sedimentation and irregular water supply. These are real costs to downstream activities and to society as a whole, but not to upstream loggers or shifting cultivators who have no cause or incentive to consider them as they do not affect the profitability of logging or shifting cultivation. In fact, taking such costs into account voluntarily amounts to a conscious decision to lower one's profit and price oneself out of the market. Unless every logger and every shifting cultivator takes such external costs into account, those who do are certain to lose to competitors who do not. This is exactly why government intervention is necessary to establish and enforce similar standards and incentives or disincentive for all competitors.

As we discussed in Chapter 4, Section 4.8, tax-subsidy is one market-based instrument that could be used to internalise the externalities. Creating and enforcing well-defined property rights wherever feasible is another alternative. However, a simple rule of thumb while considering the use of any of these instruments is that the expected social benefits from the use of the instruments must substantially exceed the expected social cost of using the instrument. In addition, economic viability and social and political feasibility of the instrument under consideration should also be carefully assessed before any final decision to use the instrument is taken.

10.5.4 Promote Participatory Management of Forests

Participatory approach to forest management at the grassroot level through community-based institutions has been tried in India since the 1970s and is considered, by and large, successful and an ideal forest management model in the present world forestry scenario. The principle of participatory forest management, popularly known as Joint Forest Management (JFM) in India is based on the principle of co-management and a 'give and take' relationship between the two major stakeholders, the village communities and the Forest Department (FD), mediated in most cases by an NGO. It is a total departure from the earlier forest policies practised in India, whereby the FDs managed the forests with the main objective of generation of maximum revenue for the State and by excluding village communities from the management process. However, the 'management change' with people-oriented forest policies is not a new phenomenon that has cropped up suddenly. It is an outcome of several circumstances like the inability of the Forest Departments to prevent the rampant and increasing degradation and decline of forest cover over time in the country, and the policy failure to factor in the history of forestry use patterns by local communities and their age-old symbiotic relationship with forests.

From people's perspective, the National Forest Policy of 1952 laid down that 'it would be the duty of the forester to awaken the interest of the people in the development, extension and establishment of tree lands wherever possible, and to make them tree-minded'. This was a general statement without any concrete strategies spelt out for its achievement, just like other policy proposals such as balanced and complementary land-use, bringing 60 per cent of the total geographical area of India under forests in the mountainous tracts and 20 per cent in the plains. To be precise, this policy did not provide an inkling about people's participation in co-management of forests. In fact, the government continued with erstwhile British forest policies even after Independence.

It is true that people living in and around forests are, to a large extent, responsible for degradation of forests and that it is not possible for the FD armed with strict forest protection laws to protect a large extent of forests from a large number of people, given the small number of FD personnel in the country. This means that the FDs can effectively protect forests in India only if people's participation is solicited in forest management. Conversely, the village communities as forest users should also shoulder the responsibility for protection and management of their forests along with the FD. Under such an arrangement the local community could harvest various forest produce from their forest in a sustainable manner and with the sense of ownership. Ideally this forest management model should have been in place long back, keeping in view the continued significance of forests in the village economy. Perhaps the government's pre-occupation with the development model focusing on agriculture and industry after Independence overlooked such a management perspective.

The efforts to encourage adoption of participatory forest management of forests in India were underway even before the adoption of the National Forest Policy of 1988 as illustrated by the case of Arabari experiment in West Bengal (see Box 10.1 and Singh 1994a: 274–87). However, it picked up the necessary momentum to formally institutionalise participatory forest management after people's participation was

Box 10.1 Arabari Experiment in JFM

Arabari Forest Range is located in Midnapur district in the state of West Bengal. In the early 1970s, a group of the West Bengal FD personnel under the leadership of the then Divisional Forest Officer, A.K. Banerjee, were concerned about the progressively increasing degradation of forests in the division and elsewhere in the state and the country. After a great deal of reflection and analysis, they realised the importance of people's participation in regeneration of degraded Sal (*Shorea robusta*) forests in the range. This innovative forest rejuvenation strategy was first pilot-tested as an experiment and later on replicated on a large scale, first in West Bengal and later on in other parts of country. The West Bengal Forest Department issued the first government order in 1989 to involve village communities in forest protection with a provision to grant the participating villagers 25 per cent of the net revenue from timber harvest from the protected forest. This successful experiment led to the development of a new forest management strategy known as 'Joint Forest Management' (JFM). The village communities involved in the management of government forests in their vicinity under the JFM are called forest protection committees. This is the first recorded case of co-management of forests by FD and village communities in India.

Source: Singh (1994: 274–80).

envisaged in the new forest policy of 1988. In this direction, the first policy directive was a JFM circular issued by the Central government for the *Involvement of Village Communities and Voluntary Agencies in Regeneration of Degraded Forests* (Circular No. 6.2 1/89-F.P., dated 1 June 1990, Ministry of Environment and Forests, Government of India). This circular gave a background and modalities for the implementation of JFM by the state FDs with the involvement of village communities. It also envisaged the participation of voluntary organisations/non-governmental organisations with proven track record in JFM to facilitate participation by village communities in development and protection of forests with an emphasis on regeneration of degraded forests. Further, the Circular highlighted such management concerns as ownership or lease rights over such forests, membership of village forest committees (also known as forest protection committees or joint forest management committees), usufruct rights of beneficiaries, and management and supervision of afforestation and protection activities. This circular also suggested other dos and don'ts for the village forest committees and voluntary agencies/NGOs and implications thereof, however, in a broader sense only.

Consequently, the State Governments passed their own resolutions on JFM. These resolutions varied from state to state depending on the socio-economic and political scenario as well as cultural characteristics of each state. Nevertheless, the basic principle of community/people's participation as envisaged in the National Forest Policy of 1988 and the JFM Circular underlie all these State resolutions. By now, 27 State Governments have issued their own JFM orders for implementing the JFM programme. The first JFM Circular by the Government of India has been followed by other government orders and notifications from time and time, as and when required to support its policy to facilitate the JFM in the country. Accordingly, many States have come up with revised JFM orders. For example, the State of Orissa's latest JFM resolution is the fifth since the first order was issued in 1988.

In this context, it is also important to highlight that the 73rd Amendment in the Indian Constitution has also facilitated the implementation of JFM in the country. This amendment empowers village *Panchayats* to undertake village level planning for all developmental activities including forestry, irrigation and agriculture sectors.

At present, there are 63,618 forest protection committees (joint forest management committees) in India spread over 27 states managing about 14.09 million ha of forests. This means that 22 per cent of total forest cover of 63.73 million ha in India is being managed under the JFM. Besides, there are also a large number of Self-Initiated Forest Protection Groups (SIFPGs) managing forests in India on the principle of participatory forest management. Thousands of SIFPGs, established by village communities with 'strong economic dependence on forests and where often a tradition of community resource management is still surviving', in the states of Orissa, Bihar, Gujarat, Rajasthan, Karnataka, Madhya Pradesh and Andhra Pradesh are protecting large areas of the state forests.

While discussing the development of participatory forest management initiatives, it is important to take note of the active involvement of NGOs in promoting participatory forest management at the grassroots level. In most of the cases, the NGOs are facilitating the village communities as well as the FDs in formation of JFM Committees. In many a case, NGOs have developed their own participatory forest management models on policy directives of the government on JFM.

During the inception of the participatory forest management in India, the FD was sceptical about the involvement of NGOs. NGOs faced non-cooperation from the FDs for assisting village communities in undertaking community forestry programmes. The conflicts between the FDs and NGOs was indicative of the FD's reluctance to share with the people their power and authority. Over the last decade, however, the state of affairs has changed in favour of NGOs, which may be mainly attributed to the 'change in the mind set' of the FD personnel towards forest management. Now substantial rural development funds earmarked by the Government of India are routed through NGOs for the participatory forest management programmes. Besides, pressure from external aid agencies on FD to involve NGOs in JFM programme and to restructure the FD accordingly, as a condition for aid to India, has also resulted in overcoming the problem.

10.6 MAIN POINTS

The following are the main points made in this chapter:

- Forests are natural renewable resources and have always been an integral part of India's economy and culture. They are held in high esteem. The ancient religious, political and literary writings are a testimony to the fact that people were considered an integral part of nature not superior to it.
- Forests contribute to the well-being of human beings in several direct and indirect ways. In view of this, sustainability of the flow of forest products is essential for sustaining their livelihoods. Sadly, due to several reasons including increasing biotic and abiotic pressure, and policy and market failures, forest in India are overexploited, degraded and depleted. This poses a threat to the survival of millions of poor people, especially tribals, who mainly depend on forests for their livelihood, and also to the quality of the environment.
- Considering the importance of forests in India, and India's need for a higher level of economic development, it would be desirable to determine the socially optimal level of exploitation of forests and follow that in practice. This would help reconcile, to some extent, the conflicting goals of forest conservation and security of livelihood of the poor forest dwellers, who depend on forest resources for their survival and facilitate the formulation of effective policies to deal with the problem of forest degradation.
- There are several instruments that could be and should be used to restore the degraded forests and promote their sustainable use and management. They include both market-based instruments such as taxes and subsidies, and non-market-based measures such as reforms in forest policy, laws, governance and management.

- The existing Forest Resource Accounting (FRA) system has several drawbacks, leading to gross under-estimation of the forestry sector's contribution to India's GDP. In view of this, there is need to adopt a better system of FRA as recommended by the Committee on Forestry (COFO) of the Food and Agriculture Organization (FAO) in 1997.
- Governance in the forestry sector is a legacy of the then British Government of India. After the Independence, some changes have been made in the system but the basic structure remains the same. It is not congenial to promoting sustainable development and management of forests and hence it needs to be reformed. An ideal system of governance should facilitate the realisation of twin goals of ecosystem restoration and sustainable improvement in the quality of life of people dependent on the forests.
- Participatory approach to forest management at the grassroots level through community-based institutions has been tried in India since the 1970s and is considered, by and large, successful and an ideal forest management model in the present world forestry scenario. The principle of participatory forest management, popularly known as Joint Forest Management (JFM) has now been accepted as part of Forest Policy in India.

10.7 DISCUSSION QUESTIONS

1. List all the tangible and intangible goods and services provided by forests that help improve our environment.
2. Identify all human activities that have caused depletion and degradation of forests.
3. Why do the people dependent on forest for their livelihood resort to destroying their own source of livelihood?
4. Why do tribal people in some areas of India voluntarily protect their forests from commercial exploitation whereas their counterparts in some other areas do not?
5. It is argued by many economists that most of the benefits from forest protection and conservation accrue to people living far away from forests whereas the people living in the vicinity of forests have to bear most of the costs in the form of foregone opportunities to collect fuelwood, fodder and NWFP. Make a case for rational sharing of costs and benefits from forest protection and conservation.
6. What policy instruments would you recommend for reconciling the conflicting goals of forest conservation and sustainable livelihoods of people dependent on forests?

11 Fisheries and Environment

Fisheries and Environment

11.1 INTRODUCTION

India is the third largest producer of fish and second largest producer of inland fish in the world. Fish production in the country has registered tremendous growth over the last two decades or so, ranging from 5.5 per cent to 5.8 per cent per annum, which is much higher than that for the agricultural sector as a whole. Fish production can be increased significantly if judicious development, conservation and harvesting of marine and inland fishery resources of the country by way of adopting suitable scientific technologies and conservational measures were adopted.

The fisheries sector occupies an important place in the socio-economic development of India. It is a source of cheap and nutritious food and is an important foreign exchange earner.[1] Besides, it is considered a major source of livelihood for 11 million people in the country, engaged fully, partially, or in subsidiary activities pertaining to the sector. It is estimated that the fisheries sector alone can provide one million jobs in the next five years.

---

[1] In 2004–05, the value of fish and fish products exported from India was Rs 6,188 crore (http://indiabudget.nic.in).

The performance of the fisheries sector has been good and consistent. The total fish production in India was only 0.75 million tonnes in 1950–51. It increased to 2.44 million tonnes in 1980–81, 3.84 million tonnes in 1990–91 and to about 6.30 million tonnes in 2004–05 (Table 11.1). However, like other common pool resources, the fisheries in India also suffer from what Hardin (1968) called 'The Tragedy of the Commons'. Being part of the environment, they affect it and are affected by it.

In this chapter, we examine the current status of the fisheries sector in India, identify the main environment-related problems of the fisheries and their causes, and then present a theoretical model for determining the optimal level of harvesting of marine fishes. Thereafter, we suggest some instruments of addressing the problems of fisheries and managing them on a sustainable basis. Finally, we present a critique of India's Marine Fishing Policy 2004 in the light of the basic elements of an ideal public policy. The main objective of the chapter is to enhance the understanding of the student about the fisheries sector of India's economy and the nature and root causes of the problems of overexploitation and degradation of fisheries, and equip him/her with the skills and tools of environmental economics necessary for addressing those problems and analysing the policy problems in the sector.

Table 11.1	Fish Production in India for Selected Years, 1950–51 to 2004–05		
			(Lakh Tonnes)
Year	Marine	Inland	Total
1950–51	5.34	2.18	7.52
1960–61	8.80	2.80	11.60
1970–71	10.86	6.70	17.56
1980–81	15.55	8.87	24.42
1990–91	23.00	15.36	38.36
2000–2001	28.11	28.45	56.56
2001–02	28.30	31.26	59.56
2002–03	29.90	32.10	62.00
2003–04	30.00	34.00	64.00
2004–05	28.00	35.00	63.00

Source: Department of Animal Husbandry and Dairying, Ministry of Agriculture, New Delhi (http://agricoop.nic.in/statatglance2004/AtGlance.pdf) and Economic Survey 2005–06 (http://indiabudget.nic.in).

11.2 THE TYPES AND EXTENT OF FISHERY RESOURCES

The fisheries sector of India comprises two sub-sectors, namely, marine fisheries and inland fisheries, including freshwater and brackish water aquaculture. In this section, we briefly describe the salient features of both the sub-sectors including their importance in India's economy.

11.2.1 Marine Fisheries

The geographic base of Indian marine fisheries has an 8,118 km long coastline, 2.02 million sq km of Exclusive Economic Zone (EEZ) including 0.5 million sq km of continental shelf, and 3,937 fishing villages. There are 1,896 traditional fish landing centres, 33 minor fishing harbours and six major fishing harbours which serve as bases for about 208,000 traditional non-motorised craft, 55,000 small scale beach-landing craft fitted with outboard motors, 51,250 mechanised craft (mainly bottom trawlers and purse-seiners) and 180 deep sea fishing vessels. The post-harvest infrastructure consists of freezing plants, canning plants, ice making plants, fishmeal plants, cold storage and peeling sheds which together cater to a sizeable labour force of one million people engaged in fishing and another 0.8 million in post-harvest operations. A large number of scientists, technocrats and other categories of personnel are involved in research, education, technology development and administration in marine fisheries. The estimated first sale value of the marine fish landings in the year 2000 was Rs 10,200 crore. There is a lucrative and organised seafood export trade with the value of the export being about Rs 6,200 crore (GoI 2004c).

The marine fishery resources of the country's EEZ are estimated to be 3.93 million metric tonnes as per the latest update of 2000. These resources are distributed in inshore (58 per cent), off-shore (35 per cent) and deep sea (7 per cent) waters. The major share of the resources is demersal (2.02 million tonnes) followed by 1.67 million tonnes of pelagic and 0.24 million tonnes of oceanic resources (ibid.). The marine fisheries sector has vast potential for further development. Against an estimated fishery potential of 3.93 million metric tonnes from the sector, only 2.8 million metric tonnes are presently tapped. Fishing efforts are largely confined to the inshore waters through traditional artisanal and mechanised fishing vessels. About 90 per cent of the present production from the marine sector is from within the depth range of up to 50 to 70 metres and the remaining 10 per cent from the depths extending up to 200 metres. It is estimated that about 93 per cent of the total marine fish production is contributed by artisanal, mechanised and motorised vessels and the remaining 7 per cent is contributed by deep sea fishing fleets, which confine their operations mainly to the shrimp grounds in the upper East Coast.

11.2.2 Inland Fisheries

India is one of the 20 countries in the world known for rich inland fisheries resources. With approximately 1 million tonnes of annual fish production contributed by inland capture fisheries, India is the second highest (next only to China) in the world in terms of inland fish production (FAO 2003). However, the production per km^2 is less than 0.5 tonne per hectare as against 4.7 tonnes in Bangladesh.

Inland fisheries can be classified broadly into three categories: (i) inland capture fisheries such as rivers, lakes and reservoirs, and floodplains, with limited access rights and no access restrictions; (ii) culture-based fisheries which utilise natural productivity of the aquatic ecosystem for fish production such as community tanks and ponds, reservoirs with leased-in rights wherein stocking is carried out and harvesting is done collectively or individually with access to only members of the community/cooperative or private contractor; and (iii) aquaculture ponds owned and operated by individual fish producers with full private ownership rights. In general, the open/large water-bodies are more suitable for culture-based fisheries and the closed/small water-bodies for aquaculture. The total expanse of wetlands of our country is estimated at 58.29 million hectare (m ha) excluding the 0.19 million km long riverine stretches and canals. The resources amenable to culture-based fisheries are: reservoirs (3.15 m ha), floodplain lakes (0.12 m ha), deepwater paddy fish (3.48 m ha) and estuarine wetlands and lagoons (0.2 m ha); and the resources amenable to aquaculture are freshwater (2.36 m ha) and brackish water (1.2 m ha) (Katiha 2006: 19). However, it is estimated that only about 20 per cent of the fresh water area and 14 per cent of brackish water area have been utilised so far and thus a vast potential exists for enhancing fish production.

The trend in growth of inland fish production in India showed major contribution of capture fisheries till the mid-1980s, but afterwards it has reversed in favour of aquaculture. In order to increase fish production from community water-bodies the state and central governments have supported the growth of culture-based fisheries and fish farming through various technological, institutional and financial measures during the last five decades. As a result, the share of production from aquaculture and culture-based fisheries increased remarkably. Aquaculture has emerged as a fast-growing enterprise and a viable alternative to the declining open natural water fisheries. Now, it contributes over 80 per cent of the total inland fish production in the country. The average productivity of the inland water-bodies is very low, around 50 kg per hectare.

Freshwater aquaculture has registered tremendous growth in the past two decades, but there still exists immense scope for further expansion and increase in productivity. This is evidenced by the fact that so far only one-third of the available area (0.85 m ha) could be brought under scientific aquaculture and the average fish yield is only one-third of that achieved in farm trials.

To augment production through aquaculture and to sustain and increase the exports, the Government of India promotes the following activities:

- Micro and macro level survey to identify suitable sites for fish farming.
- Preparation of site specific project reports.
- Technical advice on various aspects of farming.
- Training of farmers and entrepreneurs in fish farming.
- Arranging visits of farmers from one state to other states for learning different aspects of fish farming.
- Conducting workshops/seminars/symposia/farmers' meets for the benefit of farmers and entrepreneurs.
- Promoting eco-friendly aquaculture.

11.3   THE PROBLEMS OF FISHERIES AND THEIR UNDERLYING CAUSES

Given their open access nature, marine fisheries are bound to be over-exploited (Berkes 1986; Cruz 1986; Gordon 1954) and eventually suffer from what Hardin (1968) called 'The Tragedy of the Commons'.[2] The underlying reason for the tragedy is best summed up in the conservative dictum that 'everybody's property is nobody's property' (Gordon 1954: 135). The logic of the tragedy is purely economic and can be stated as follows: unregulated access to marine fisheries creates a decision-making environment in which incremental private benefits to an

---

[2]See for details, Chapter 4, Section 4.5 'Hardins's Thesis of "The Tragedy of the Commons"'.

individual fisherman from the increased capture markedly exceed the incremental private costs associated with the increased capture. Under these circumstances, each rational fisherman is motivated to capture more and more of the fish till the harvestable fish stock is completely exhausted as a result of collective and uncoordinated actions of all the fishermen in the community. The tendency for this kind of opportunistic behaviour is further strengthened when fishermen have no assurance or certainty that the other members of the fishing community will abstain from over-fishing or cooperate with them, and that their lone contribution to the effort (by abstaining from over-fishing) would be sufficient to produce the desired outcome.

Another main cause of over-fishing is the poverty of fishermen. In the absence of any other alternative source of livelihood, fishermen are compelled to indulge in over-fishing, knowing fully well that this is irrational for the fishermen community and this level of catch is not sustainable.

Over-fishing is a serious problem in the coastal areas of India, particularly Kerala. The problem of declining yield is now evident in many inshore waters that were previously high yielding, supporting large numbers of traditional fishermen. Although the real causes of this phenomenon are difficult to identify, generally new fishing technology characterised by mechanised trawlers is blamed for this. The technologies which are available to fisherfolk today are much more powerful. Fishing hauls which once took days to recover now take a few minutes. Traditional trawlers used long steel lines and stout nets which were either dragged mid-water or across the dark ocean floor eased on the way by rollers and drums. Today they have been replaced by bigger and faster ships with thinner but stronger lines and wider drums. The maws of the trawls can be enormous, often hundreds of feet wide. What was earlier military technology is now being applied for hunting fish. Radars are used to navigate boats through dense fog, sonars are used to hunt deep shoals and navigation satellites direct the boats into rich localities. This has resulted in the depletion of life from many continental shelf regions and shallow seas, and now the nets are plunging still deeper. By studying old military maps which reveal the hidden features of the deep seas, fisherfolk are able to pinpoint the rich fertile zones for their purpose.

With the increase in the number of mechanised trawlers in the late 1970s in Kerala, the total catch of marine fish declined significantly, with the mechanised sector capturing a lion's share in the declining catches. An analysis of the catches revealed that many demersal species had declined, indicating over-fishing by the trawlers. The trawlers had also damaged the natural habitat of fish like corals and small reefs, leading to the depletion of fish stock in coastal waters (Singh 1994b: 91).

Besides, many small scale artisanal fishermen have been left worse off; they could not afford to invest so much money in modern fishing craft and gear and hence were compelled to join the rank of casual labourers. Balakrishnan et al. (1992) examined the perceptions of a sample of fishermen in two coastal areas of Kerala regarding the impact of new technology on various aspects of their lives. With regard to the change in volume of catch, all the respondents from Vizhinjam (Trivandrum) felt that instead of the expected increase, there had been a decline in catch. At Moothakkara (Quilon), the response was a little different in the sense that only 75 per cent of the respondents felt that it was decreasing; 20 per cent of the respondents felt that their catches had increased. About 85 per cent of the respondents from Vizhinjam and 100 per cent from Moothakkara observed that fish availability in the inshore areas had substantially reduced in recent times leading to decrease in both individual catch and the total catch. In other words, the perception of the respondents with regard to changes or increases in catch have, by and large, been negative. But it would be fair to say that the mechanisation of fishing has definitely led to higher catch per unit of fishing effort and reduction of physical effort and drudgery in day-to-day fishing operations. The new technology has also provided the artisanal fishermen access to the outer seas. Although they do not travel great distances on a regular basis, it has made possible for them to move rapidly and harvest shoals at greater distances and with greater speed.

As we discussed in Chapter 9, Section 9.3, India is highly prone to floods and droughts. These natural disasters have several adverse impacts on the environment in general and on fisheries in particular. For example, in Orissa, soon after the Super Cyclone of 2001, the entire sea coast was adversely affected by high sea tides, flooding the cropped area and depositing salts on good fertile soil. The flood increased erosion of soil and siltation of river beds and reservoirs, reducing their capacity to store water and, thereby, increasing the incidence of flash floods. Among the major ecological effects of droughts are decreased scrub growth, increased desertification, reduction in forest area and wet land and loss of fisheries and mangroves. More recently, the tsunami adversely affected marine fisheries in coastal areas of Kerala, Tamil Nadu and Karnataka. Due to the bottom of the sea coming up very close to the sea surface during the course of the tsunami, most of the fish perished, and those which survived, migrated to other areas.

The main challenges facing the inland fisheries sub-sector in India are the lack of any scientific assessment of fishery resources and their potential in terms of fish production, low productivity, lack of eco-friendly modern technologies for harvest and post-harvest operations, pollution of fisheries leading to fall in fish production and inadequate infrastructure facilities for processing and marketing.

11.4 DETERMINING OPTIMUM LEVEL OF HARVESTING OF MARINE FISH

Marine fisheries management on a sustainable basis requires the information about the socially optimum level of harvesting of fish. This is essentially a renewable resource management problem, whose solution is illustrated in Figure 11.1. The upside-down, U-shaped curve represents the natural growth rate of the marine fish, $G(Q)$, which is a function of the size of the resource stock (a fishery). If the resource stock is either too low, Q_L, or too high, Q_M, the growth rate is zero. In contrast, population level, Q^*, leads to a maximum sustainable growth rate, as this is the maximum harvest level (that is, $q = G(Q^*)$) that can be sustained indefinitely without depleting the population (Barbier et al. 1994: 140–41).

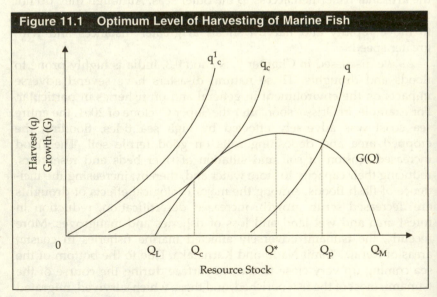

Figure 11.1 Optimum Level of Harvesting of Marine Fish

Source: Barbier et al. (1994: 140).

In Figure 11.1, harvesting of the fish, which is a renewable resource, from a common pool fishery is represented by the upward sloping curve q. We presume that fishing in the fishery is properly regulated by the fishermen community through their own organisation, say, a fishermen cooperative. Note that at stock level Q_p, where the harvesting rate just equals the growth rate of the resource ($q = G(Q_p)$), the population is at a stationary state level. Given the relationship between the harvesting rate and the resource stock as shown, this stationary state must be stable in the long run. For example, if the initial resource stock is less than the stationary state level, that is, $Q_o < Q_p$ then the natural growth rate will exceed the harvesting rate. This means that the population will grow until it reaches the stationary state level, Q_p where growth is just offset by harvesting. On the other hand, if $Q_o > Q_p$, harvesting will exceed the natural growth. The population will therefore decline until, once again, the stationary state level, Q_p attained. So, no matter what the initial resource stocks are, given the rate of harvesting represented by curve q, the population will eventually settle down to the long run equilibrium represented by Q_p.

Now, we relax the assumption that the fishery is properly regulated and examine its impact on the rate of harvesting. This is consistent with what happens in the real world. A frequent problem that occurs in marine fisheries is the breakdown of common property rules, thus creating a situation of open access resource use. When this occurs, users of the resource tend to harvest more for a given stock level as they will now ignore any user and externality cost. Thus, curve q_c now represents the new harvesting rate. The new stationary state level would now be Q_c but this is not always sustainable in the long run. As the diagram shows, if the resource is initially greater than this level ($Q_o > Q_c$), then harvesting exceeds natural growth and the stock will decline to Q_c in the long run equilibrium. If the initial stock is much lower, ($Q_o < Q_c$), the harvesting will still exceed natural growth. As a result, the resource will not increase to Q_c in the long run but will instead decline towards zero. Hence, an open access resource may be exhausted to extinction if the initial stocks of that resource are too low (Dasgupta 1982: 128–33).

A second problem occurs in fisheries management when the value of the harvested resource increases or technological change lowers the per unit harvesting costs. Under these conditions, users will be able to harvest even more for a given stock level. In Figure 11.1, this is represented by curve q^1_c which has shifted even further to the left. As a consequence, harvesting always exceeds the natural growth rate, irrespective of the initial stock level and the resource will eventually be exhausted.

11.5 INSTRUMENTS OF MANAGING FISHERIES

Like other biological systems, fisheries also are amenable to management. It is possible for human beings to intervene in their natural reproduction and food cycles, both in seas as well as in other water-bodies and thereby increase and sustain their harvest at a socially desirable level in perpetuity. In other words, technically, it is possible to manage marine fisheries on sustainable yield basis. A simple principle of management of marine fisheries on sustainable yield basis is to catch only that much which is naturally reproduced (flow) keeping the resource (stock) intact, that is, live on the interest (flow) and keep the capital (stock) intact. Unfortunately this simple principle is violated more often than not everywhere. This happens mainly due to lack of exclusive property rights and appropriate local institutions and organisations that could propagate fish and regulate fishing for sustained yield.

We will now briefly discuss some of the potent instruments that could be used to regulate over-fishing and manage marine fisheries on a sustainable basis.

11.5.1 Creating Property Rights Including Sea Tenure

The problem of over-fishing and consequent resource depletion in all common pool fisheries can be solved by creating property rights/sea tenure. This instrument seems to hold high promise as a means of managing the marine fisheries for sustained yield as well as improving the socio-economic well-being of marine fishermen. By sea tenure, we mean territorial use rights in fisheries (TURFs) granted to local fishermen. In recent years, there has been a lot of interest in TURFs as an instrument of averting the tragedy of open access marine fisheries. Provision of Extended Economic Zone (EEZ) under the UN Law of Sea 1972 which is a form of TURF is an example of the concern of the international community with creating and enforcing property rights in marine fisheries (Christy Jr. 1982).

Sea tenure can be conferred upon an individual, a private company, a group of individuals such as a cooperative or a governmental organisation. Generally, individuals can make decisions quickly and more easily than groups of individuals. Transaction costs in group decision-making are higher and the process is more time consuming than in individual decision-making. However, from the equity point of view, communal/cooperative sea tenure is more desirable than any other form of ownership (Christy Jr. 1982: 4). A real world example of the use of this instrument is from Japan, where fishery cooperatives are granted sea tenure and, therefore, they are able to undertake both propagation and regulation activities in sea waters under their jurisdiction. In Japan there are some 2,100 local (primary) fishery cooperatives with a total membership of 5,30,000. The local cooperatives are affiliated to Prefectural (regional) level cooperatives which, in turn, are federated into a national level federation.

Fishery cooperatives in Japan perform the following functions: (1) guidance and instructions to member fishermen; (2) marketing; (3) credit; (4) supply of fuel and other inputs; (5) insurance; and (6) administration of fishing rights systems. Of these functions, administration of 'fishing rights systems' is the most important. Legally there are three different fishing rights (FR): set-net FR; demarcated FR; and common water FR. The *set-net FR* is, of course, for set-net fishing. The *demarcated FR* is meant for sea farming and collection of shellfish and seaweeds in a marked portion of the water. The *common water FR* is for fishing in coastal waters, usually just in front of a community where fishermen live. Because of these FR systems, no one can fish in the waters covered under the 'rights' unless he is a member of the fishery cooperative concerned. This explains the extremely high membership rate (virtually 100 per cent) of fishery cooperatives in Japan.

Murakami (nd) documents the operations and management of two model fishery cooperative societies in Japan—Notsuke in Hokkaido and Aji in Shikoku. Both the cooperatives have successfully promoted the restoration and propagation of fish stock and regulated the harvesting of fish involving all of their members. Notsuke Fishery Cooperative is known for producing salmon, scallop and a kind of prawn. It is one of the best fishery cooperatives in Hokkaido with 270 members, a marketing turnover of 10.7 billion Yen and deposits of 10.6 billion Yen. Its most conspicuous feature is its successful performance of fish propagation; it releases into its waters 50 million salmon fries every year. All the members participate in making annual fishing plans with proper goals on the basis of the existing stock estimated by their own research. The plans include such things as 'restrictions on fishing methods', 'obligation to join the propagation scheme', and 'rules on individual fishing pursuits', etc. As a result of all these management practices, production of fish has gone up from 3,632 mt in 1983 to 15,879 mt in 1991.

The Aji Fishery Cooperative has 290 members and annual production from boat fishing is worth 1.25 billion Yen and from fish culture worth 2.05 billion Yen. The waters in its jurisdiction used to be known for their abundant and diversified fish stocks. However, of late, waste water from factories and residential areas released into the sea has polluted the fishery and thereby reduced the fish stock and fish catch and consequently, income from fishing. To mitigate the hardships of their fellow fishermen, 130 trawler owning members of the cooperative set up the 'Trawlers' Section' of the cooperative and sought the restoration of depleted fish stocks, higher efficiency in fishing and improvement in the well-being of member fishermen through cooperative endeavours. The Section put into action a number of unique and effective practices such as a five-day work week, restriction on working hours per day, prohibition of catching younger fish, and positive participation in the propagation scheme. Severe penalties, such as suspension of fishing or confiscation of the whole catch are imposed for violation of the rules.

Adoption of these practices and rules has led to an improvement in the health of the member fishermen, reduction in accidents at sea, reduction in operating expenses and higher member participation in propagation programmes (Singh 1993).

In India too a similar policy is needed. Cooperative sea tenure offers opportunities for local control over fishing, possibilities of improvement in the socio-economic conditions of small scale poor fishermen and equitable distribution of benefits from marine fisheries. It is important to realise in this context that enforcement of sea tenure is problematic for a number of reasons, such as, difficulties in demarcating and defending boundaries, the migratory nature of certain species of fish and problems in monitoring fishing activities. However, the introduction of artificial reefs in Valiathura village in Trivandrum district and consequent restriction of access of outsiders to fishing in waters around the reefs shows that it is possible to create and protect property rights in marine fisheries (Vivekanandan 1991).

11.5.2 Organising Fishermen Cooperatives

Fisheries being a state subject, most of the state governments favour cooperative governance structures or small fisherman groups to manage the common pool water-bodies. Similar is the case for culture-based fisheries, especially small reservoirs and flood plain wetlands, having multiple uses and ownership. Consequently, the number of fishermen's cooperatives in India had gone up to 13,884[3] by 2000–01 and the total

---

[3]The performance of the fishery cooperatives in general has not been good; only 18 per cent of them made profits in the year, 2000–2001 and 1,586 of them were dormant for various reasons (http://www.ncui.net).

membership to 21.66 lakh. The government participation in the share
capital of the fishery cooperatives in the country accounted for about
29 per cent in 2000–2001.[4] The membership of inland fishery cooperatives accounted for about 72 per cent of the total membership and the
remaining 28 per cent by the marine fishery cooperatives.

Fishermen cooperatives seem to hold high promise an institutional
measure to improve the well being of poor fishermen and regulate the
harvesting of fish.[5] In India, Kerala is well known for its rich marine fish
resources, especially prawns and oil sardines. It has a coastline of 590 km
and a continental shelf area of about 36,000 sq km. It ranks second in
terms of total inland and marine fish production and first in terms of
marine fish production in India. Kerala thus occupies a place of prime
importance in the marine fisheries sector of India's economy. The
Government of Kerala (GoK) has taken a number of pioneering measures, including the establishment of marine fishermen's cooperatives to
improve the well-being of fishermen.

There are two apex organisations in Kerala at the state level—
Kerala State Cooperative Federation for Fisheries Development Ltd.
(MATSYAFED) and the South Indian Federation of Fishermen Societies
(SIFFS)—that are engaged in organising and assisting fishermen's
co-operatives in the state. MATSYAFED has a clear mandate of coop-
erativization of traditional fishermen and spearheading of development programmes for them. It has a three-tier structure with Primary
Fishermen's Cooperative Societies (PFCS) at the village level, district
level offices, and the state level federation. The main activities of the
MATSYAFED include organisation of the PFCS, procurement of fishing
equipment and inputs, establishment and operation of manufacturing
facilities such as net factory and ice plants, implementation of fisheries
development programmes through the PFCS and development of
infrastructural facilities.

The SIFFS promotes organisation of fishermen's cooperative societies in Kerala and Tamil Nadu. The SIFFS is a non-governmental
organisation (NGO) registered under the Travancore-Cochin Literary,
Scientific and Charitable Societies Act XII of 1955. The main objectives
of SIFFS are to: organise fishermen into cooperative societies, facilitate
the marketing of fish collected by its member-societies, assist member
societies with funds in the form of loans and grants, establish and run
manufacturing units for fishing craft and gear, processing units for fish

[4]This information is derived from the Website of the National Cooperative Union of India:
http://www.ncui.net.
[5]For success stories of fishery cooperatives, see Singh (1994b) and Singh and Ballabh (1996:
11–15).

and fish products, and undertake export, import and other activities in the interest of its member-societies. The area of operation of the SIFFS extends to the whole of Kerala, Tamil Nadu, Andhra Pradesh and Karnataka. The SIFFS serves as an apex organisation in the three-tier cooperative structure with District Fisheries Federations at the middle (district) level and primary fishermen's cooperative societies at the village level.

In Kerala, although neither MATSYAFED nor SIFFS has any mandate to promote the management of marine fishery resources on a sustainable yield basis but they could very well undertake this responsibility and regulate the harvesting of fish through formulation and enforcement of mutually agreed rules, as has been done in Japan. Similarly, at the national level, there is no awareness about the need to manage the marine fisheries on a sustainable basis.

11.5.3 Regulation of Marine Fish Catch

The GoK has, however, been concerned about the growing depletion of marine fisheries in the State. It has taken a number of pioneering steps to regulate the exploitation of marine fisheries through legislation. The Kerala Marine Fishing Regulation Act 1980, provides for regulation and prohibition of use of fishing craft in contravention of any orders issued under Section 4 of the Act, and licensing and registration of fishing vessels (GoK 1983: 49). The main objectives of the Act are to protect the interest of artisanal fishermen, to conserve fish and regulate fishing on scientific lines, and to maintain law and order in the sea. However, the implementation of the legal provisions has been lax, thanks to the economic and political clout of the trawler owners. There is need to enforce various provisions of the Act more effectively and this cannot be done unless there is a strong political will to do so at the state level.

The GoK had also appointed three expert committees, namely, D. Babu Pal Committee in 1981, A.G. Kalawar Committee in 1984 and N. Balakrishnan Nair Committee in 1988, to study the problem, review the steps taken by it and advise it about conservation and management of the marine fisheries. These Committees have made important recommendations for the management of marine fisheries in the State. For example, the Kalawar Committee has suggested a number of measures for conservation and management of marine fisheries. They include, bringing down the number of trawlers to 1,145, motorised craft to 2,690, and non-motorised craft to 20,000 and imposing a ban on purse seining (Nair 1989: 3–4). Due to various reasons, including vested interests, these measures have not been effectively implemented. There is, therefore, need to implement them forcefully.

11.5.4 Regulation of Exports of Fish

In the wake of the new world trade regime ushered in by the World Trade Organization (WTO) in 1995, international trade is going to be liberalised and freed from various kinds of regulations. India, being a member of WTO, is bound to abide by the new rules of international trade. International trade in fish affects the environment both directly and indirectly. By inducing export demand, it provides incentives to fish producers through increased prices to increase their production. Fish producers have responded by using mechanised boats and trawlers and fishing nets of better quality to increase their production. This has reduced the productivity of marine fisheries and degraded the quality of the environment. It is a bit too early to assess the impact of liberalised international trade in fish on the environment in India. However, the evidence available to us proves that the export-led increase in the catch of fish had an adverse effect on the environment. Foreign exchange earnings from exports encouraged many entrepreneurs and private companies to use large mechanised trawlers to harvest fish at a rate faster than that at which fish can be regenerated. This over-fishing has not only accelerated the loss of species and genetic resources, but has also caused the loss of livelihoods of those poor artisanal fisherfolk who exclusively depend on fishing. In addition, the trawlers have destroyed the natural habitat of the fish, that is, corals and reefs, and fumes from the engines of the trawlers and motor boats have polluted the sea water. Both these side-effects of mechanisation of fishing have led to depletion of fish stock and hence production (Singh 1994c: 89–102).

11.5.5 Appropriate Legal Framework

The first national policy for managing (marine) fisheries was announced by the Government of India in 2004. This was a good step as an enabling legal framework is a prerequisite for proper management and control of the fisheries sector, as at present the subject of fisheries is in the state list. Under Article 21 of the Indian Constitution, management and control of coastal fisheries is vested with the maritime states and union territories. At the same time the Union Government carries out management and control of the fishing activities beyond territorial limits in the EEZ.

The 2004 Policy provides for reviewing the existing legal framework for regulating the fishing operations. It also envisages the introduction of additional legal instruments in such areas as operation of Indian flag vessels in the EEZ, introduction of new fishing units, ensuring conservation of marine resources, especially in limited access fisheries, and fishery harbour management.

In view of increase in the incidence of straying by small-mechanised boats into each other's territorial waters and consequent confiscation of the fishing craft and arrest of the crew, a mutually agreeable system is proposed to be brought in place with friendly neighbouring countries to have a lasting solution to the problem. Besides, it is also proposed to endorse international laws and conventions in the marine fisheries sector and to harmonise national laws with the international ones wherever necessary, with active participation of the regional fisheries management bodies and greater cooperation amongst countries in the region.

11.5.6 International Treaties and Conventions

Marine fish is a fugitive resource, that is, the marine fishes migrate from place to place without respecting territorial boundaries of nations. In view of this, regulation of harvesting of marine fish requires international measures. Most of the early successful attempts at international regulation of fugitive resources were concerned with individual resources in limited areas. For example, marine fish was the first fugitive resource that was brought under international regulation through a series of regional conferences and conventions. Some of the important international treaties and conventions relating to the marine fisheries are listed below (Grafton et al. 2001: 346–49):

1. International Convention for the Regulation of Whaling (International Whaling Convention), 1946.
2. Convention on Fishing and Conservation of the Living Resources of the High Seas, 1958.
3. Convention on the High Seas, 1958.
4. United Nations Convention on the Law of the Sea, 1982.
5. Agreement relating to the Implementation of Part XI of the 1982 United Nations Convention on the Law of the Sea, 1994.
6. Agreement for the Implementation of the Provisions of the 1982 United Nations Convention on the Law of the Sea relating to the Conservation and Management of Straddling Fish Stocks and Highly Migratory Fish Stocks, 1995.

11.6 POLICIES AND PROGRAMMES FOR FISHERY DEVELOPMENT

Until the first national policy for managing (marine) fisheries was announced in 2004, there was no national fisheries policy in India. However, the Government of India (GoI) had sought to increase fish production in the country through several research and development programmes. More specifically, the GoI had established several fisheries research institutes under the aegis of the Indian Council of Agricultural Research (ICAR) to undertake research for development of a composite fish culture and induced breeding technologies and to promote their adoption. Besides, it also launched a national level programme, Fish Farmer Development Agency (FFDA) in 1976 with initial assistance from the World Bank to promote aquaculture in the country. The FFDA provided technical, financial and extension support to fish farmers for taking up culture fishery in common pool village ponds and tanks. As of 1999–2000, the total number of FFDAs established in India was 422 and they had brought within their fold over half the area covered under aquaculture in the country. Consequently, the national average fish yield in the FFDA-supported ponds had increased from 50 kg/ha per year in 1974–75 to about 2,135 kg/ha in 1994–95, and this increasing trend in the yield continues to date (Katiha 2006: 19). In addition to the GoI, the State Fisheries Departments also promote inland culture fishery through granting leases to poor fishermen to take up culture fishery in public/common pool village water-bodies and provision of subsidies.

The Ministry of Agriculture (GoI) has also paid due attention in the past decade to the development of deep-sea fisheries in the country. The declaration of Exclusive Economic Zones in 1976 facilitated the exploration, exploitation and utilisation of marine living resources in the sea around India extending to 200 nautical miles, thereby giving the nation immense opportunities and challenges to harvest the resources and to manage them on sound scientific basis. The past three decades have witnessed rapid initiatives by government and private agencies in the marine fisheries sector of the country. On realisation that most of the deep sea fishery resources beyond the conventional fishing limit and fishing capability of the indigenous craft can be gainfully exploited only if the upgraded and sophisticated vessels of adequate size and capabilities were inducted into the fishery, the GoI facilitated the mobilisation of capital and expertise indigenously to address this issue in the 1981 Charter Policy.

After the expiry of five years of operation of this policy, the Government revised it to rectify the deficiencies noticed during its operation to make it more beneficial to the country. Accordingly, a revised 1986 Charter Policy was pronounced. This Charter Policy envisaged acquisition of vessels by Indian companies either through import/construction in India or through joint ventures. As a result of the Charter Policy, 97 companies were permitted to operate 311 foreign fishing vessels. Besides augmenting the marine fish production in the country, the policy also facilitated greater inflow of foreign exchange through export of fish caught by these vessels. All these vessels were operating on 100 per cent Export Oriented Units (EOU) basis. The conditions for acquisition of vessels of adequate type and number by the Indian companies who chartered vessels helped the growth of Indian deep sea fishing fleet within a short span of time.

Having laid the foundation for the Indian deep sea fishing industry, the Government went ahead to broad-base the initiatives through the Deep Sea Fishing Policy 1991. This policy envisaged to promote joint ventures, test fishing and leasing, besides allowing the vessels chartered under the 1986 Policy to operate till the validity of their permits lasted. From the beginning of 1994, the Deep Sea Fishing Policy was criticised by various fishermen groups, Members of Parliament, Members of Legislative Assemblies, mechanised fishing vessel owners, fish processors and other stakeholders. The fishermen groups also resorted to agitation stating that their operational area is being encroached upon by the larger vessels operating under charter, joint ventures and lease arrangements. In response to those criticisms and agitations, the GoI appointed a committee to review the deep-sea fishing policy. The committee submitted its report in 1996. The Government, with minor modifications, accepted all the 21 recommendations of this committee. Consequently, the Government rescinded all the earlier policies on deep-sea fishing. It was also decided that the fishing policies of the government should be revised from time to time. Subsequently, the Government of India constituted a few other committees in order to gather inputs on the availability of the fishing craft, status of marine fishing resources, issues relating to the various stakeholder groups and so on and announced its first Marine Fishing Policy in 2004 (GoI 2004c).

The 2004 Policy seeks to address the concerns of traditional and coastal fishermen together with those of the other stakeholders in the deep-sea sector, so as to achieve harmonised development of marine fishery both in the territorial and extra-territorial waters of the country. The rationale of the Policy is enshrined in the National Agriculture Policy promulgated by the GoI in 2000.

The policy objectives are: (*i*) to augment marine fish production of the country up to the sustainable level in a responsible manner so as to boost the export of sea-food from the country and also to increase per capita fish protein intake of the masses; (*ii*) to ensure socio-economic security of the artisanal fishermen whose livelihood solely depends on this vocation; and (*iii*) to ensure sustainable development of marine fisheries with due concern for ecological integrity and biodiversity.

Some of the salient features of the 2004 Policy, relevant to fishery resources management and environmental conservation, are as follows.

11.6.1 Resource Management

In view of the overexploitation of living resources within 50-metre-deep zone, the Policy stipulates the adoption of a stringent fishery management system. In particular, it provides for the following measures:

1. A review of the Marine Fishing Regulation Acts (MFRAs) of coastal states and the Union Territories of India to ensure that they have adequate provisions for management of resources and fishing operations. If necessary, a fresh model bill on coastal fisheries development and management could also be proposed.

2. All existing boat-building yards shall be registered and construction of any new fishing units will be permitted only after obtaining a license. Standards for fishing vessel construction and registration, and for training, certifications and keeping watch over fishing vessel personnel, would be fixed and enforced through a new legislation.

3. There will be 'closed season' mandate promulgated in both the coasts, the duration of which would be decided by a designated authority. Such closed seasons shall be uniform for neighbouring states unless the geographic or climatic conditions warrant deviations. This would be supplemented by a strict ban on all types of destructive methods of fishing and regulation of mesh sizes in different parts of the fishing gear. The designated authority would be competent to declare any method as destructive after it is convinced of the same based on facts and data. Penalties would be fixed for violations of mesh regulations.

4. The designated authority would, if necessary, decide the quota for different classes of fishing vessels in any region.

5. Catching of juveniles and non-targeted species and discarding less preferred species once they are caught would be strictly prohibited through legislation.

6. Posting of observers on commercial fishing vessels and enforcing monitoring control and surveillance system (MCS) would be ensured.

7. A resource enhancement programme will be taken up on priority. This would include setting up of multi-species hatcheries for producing seed as required for sea ranching. Designating certain areas as marine sanctuaries and regulating capture of brood stock from these locations would be implemented. Besides, open sea cage culture would be promoted to rear or fatten commercially important species of fish.

11.6.2 Environmental Concerns

Since they are the final destination for most of the wastes—solid, liquid, radioactive or otherwise, seas are getting more and more polluted over time. This adversely affects the health and productivity of living resources. Such adverse environmental effects of human activities on oceans need to be minimised. Besides, health hazards due to consumption of fish harvested from contaminated water is also becoming a matter of great concern in many parts of the world. The agencies responsible for legislation relating to environmental pollution will be urged to implement them more stringently so that the impact of pollution on fisheries can be minimised.

The fishermen, as the main stakeholder of the marine environment, have to be sensitised about the growing land-based pollution. They also need to be educated about eco-friendly fishing practices, which would cause the least disturbance to the marine ecosystem including mangroves. Consumers also need to be protected from the deleterious effects of consuming fish contaminated with heavy metals and other hazardous chemicals discharged from industrial establishments. The 2004 Policy, therefore, lays stress on the following aspects:

1. In order to minimise the impact on coastal waters of industrial effluents, the Central and State Pollution Control Boards will need to work in harmony and consider enacting suitable legislation for all industrial establishments discharging effluents into the sea. Such regulations should provide for mandatory inclusion of the Hazard Analysis and Critical Control Points (HACCP) in effluent discharge systems.

2. Coastal area protection by planting mangroves with a view to producing nurseries for shrimp and fish would be introduced

as a participatory programme with the active involvement of coastal people, particularly in the fishing community.

3. The Coastal Regulation Zone notification would review the present zonation of areas keeping in view the topography of each region and ensure that any human activity in the high tide limit (HTL), which may cause degradation of the coastal environment, is not permitted.

4. The Policy provides, among other things, for India's participation in the Regional Fisheries Management Bodies (RFM) to ensure greater cooperation amongst the neighbouring countries in the region.

11.6.3 Infrastructure Development

Development of infrastructure for marine fisheries is of vital importance and requires an integrated approach. The Policy provides for creation of such facilities as jetties, landing centres, and provision for fuel, water, ice, and repair of vessels and gear. For this purpose, a master-plan for development of infrastructure for the next 10 years would be drawn up. Besides, alternatives to the present system of financing of the infrastructure projects by the Centre and the State, with cost sharing through 'Build-Operate-Own' and 'Build-Operate-Transfer' systems would be explored.

Areas such as use of Information Technology, strengthening of database in marine fisheries, Human Resource Development, and eco-labelling of marine products would also be paid needed attention.

The 2004 Policy has, however, a few drawbacks. For example, it does not clearly state any long-term vision for the fisheries sector. Similarly, it does not specify any particular organisation structure or management system for implementing the policy and monitoring its progress, nor has it a coherent vision of genuine decentralised governance and grassroots empowerment. Also, no specific instruments have been identified for achieving the objectives of the Policy. Last, but not the least, there is no mention of gender in the entire policy document. This is despite the fact that fisherwomen play an active and important role in grading, processing and marketing of fish locally.

Notwithstanding these drawbacks, we could say that the Marine Fishing Policy 2004 is a good step in the direction of regulating overfishing and marine fishery resources management. However, the policy needs to be implemented faithfully, using appropriate instruments and involving all major stakeholders, particularly fishermen and fisherwomen through their representatives and organisations.

11.7   MAIN POINTS

The following are the main points made in this chapter:

- The fishing sector occupies an important place in India's economy as a source of cheap but nutritious food, means of livelihood for millions of the poor, particularly fishermen and fisherwomen, and an important source of foreign exchange.
- Over-fishing is a serious problem in the coastal areas of India. The problem of declining yield is now evident in many inshore waters also which were previously high yielding and supporting large numbers of traditional fishermen. Although the real causes of this phenomenon are difficult to identify, generally new fishing technology, characterised by mechanised trawlers, is blamed for this.
- In India, there is need to regulate and coordinate fishing operations through creating and granting sea tenure to local fishermen's organisations preferably their cooperatives. The cooperatives can then frame mutually agreed rules of access and exploitation. The rules so framed will need to be legitimised through a legislative act and will also require a new policy frame for their implementation.
- Creation of cooperative sea tenure offers opportunities for local control over marine fisheries and improvement in the socio-economic conditions of poor fishermen. It may also create new problems of boundary determination and transboundary stock management. For solving such problems, inter-village authorities that have sufficient legal powers to enforce sea tenures of constituent villages may be constituted in fishing areas.
- International trade in fish and fish products needs to be regulated to minimise its adverse effects on fish stocks and quality of fish habitats.
- The Marine Fishing Policy 2004 is a good step in the direction of regulating over-fishing and marine fishery resources management. However, the policy needs to be implemented faithfully using appropriate instruments and involving all major stakeholders, particularly fishermen and their organisations.

11.8   DISCUSSION QUESTIONS

1. Fish are natural renewable resource in the sense that they breed and reproduce themselves naturally in water-bodies including

oceans. Most of the open access fisheries in India are overexploited and degraded. Identify and discuss the reasons for their overexploitation and policy instruments to address the issues involved.

2. What should be the guiding principle for sustaining the catch/yield of fish in perpetuity?

3. Discuss why the level of Maximum Sustainable Yield (MSY) is not necessarily the socially optimum level of harvesting of fish. Show your logic graphically.

4. What policy instruments would you recommend for ensuring the socially optimum level of harvest of open access fisheries and why?

5. How does international trade in fish affect the environment? Who benefits from the trade and who bears the cost?

6. Critically evaluate the Marine Fishing Policy 2004 in the light of the attributes of an ideal public policy? Can this policy ensure ecofriendly and sustainable harvest of both inland and marine fishes? Yes/No, and why?

7. Evaluate the pros and cons of creating cooperative property rights/sea tenure in marine fisheries in India.

12 Biodiversity Conservation and Environment

12.1 INTRODUCTION

The term, 'biodiversity' or 'biological diversity' refers to the total variation in all forms of life on earth or within a given area or ecosystem, typically expressed as the total number of species found within the area of interest or the genetic diversity within a species. The concept of biodiversity came into vogue relatively recently, having been introduced in 1980 (Lovejoy 1980). There are three main types of biodiversity, namely, genetic diversity, species diversity and ecosystem diversity. Genetic diversity refers to total genetic information contained in all the animal, plant and micro-organism species on earth. Species diversity refers to the number of species within a system or a given area. Species is defined as populations within which breeding can take place. Ecosystem diversity means the number of habitats, biotic communities, ecological processes in the biosphere, as well as, the extent to which ecosystems vary. Species are organised into ecosystems such as the Thar desert ecosystem in India. Here species are adapted to live in hot and dry conditions. Among all ecosystems, tropical rainforests contain the maximum number of species per unit area.

An ecosystem consists of plants, animals and micro-organisms which live in biological communities and interact with each other, with the physical and chemical environment, with adjacent ecosystems and with the atmosphere. They are complex systems that exhibit a diversity of structural and functional characteristics, which affect both their sustainability and their relationship with their users. Well-functioning ecosystems are a prerequisite for economic and other human activities.

There are no reliable estimates of the extent of biodiversity available worldwide. Estimates vary from 2 million to 100 million species with the best estimate of somewhere near 10 million. Only 1.4 million have actually been named so far. As one of the world's oldest and largest agricultural countries, India has an impressive diversity of crop species and varieties. It is rated as one of the 12 mega diversity countries in the world accounting for 60–70 per cent of the world's biodiversity. Areas on the planet with exceptionally high biodiversity are known as biodiversity hotspots. India has two of the world's 25 biodiversity hotspots, namely, Western Ghats and Eastern Himalayas (Source: www.conservation.org). It has 6 per cent of the world's flowering plant species, 14 per cent of the world's birds, one-third of the world's identified plant species, numbering over 45,000 and about 81,000 identified species of animals (World Bank 1996: 1). A biodiversity profile of India is presented in Table 12.1.

At least 166 species of crop plants and 320 species of wild relatives of cultivated crops originate in the subcontinent. About 90 per cent of all

Table 12.1   A Profile of India's Biodiversity

Particular	Number	Area
1. Wetlands of National Importance	1,193	3,904,543 ha
2. Mangroves	15	482,000 ha
3. Coral Reef Area	06	2,321 sq km
4. World Heritage Sites	26	–
5. Grassland Types	05	12 million ha
6. Deserts (Hot)	–	278,330 ha
7. Cold Deserts	–	10,990 ha
8. Botanical Gardens	33	–
9. Natural Breeding Centres	24	–
10. Plant Species	45,523	–
11. Animal Species	86,905	–
12. Mammal Species	397	–
13. Reptile Species	460	–
14. Amphibian Species	240	–
15. Pisces Species	2,546	–
16. Bird Species	1,232	–
17. Invertebrate Species	76,455	–

Source: Kotwal et al. (2005).

medicines in India come from plant species, many of which are harvested in the wild. Medicinal plants and other non-timber forest products are particularly important as a source of income and sustenance for the poor tribal population. Biodiversity depends to a large extent upon the type and status of natural ecosystems, which are important, not only for agriculture, but also for sustainable development. As seen in Chapter 2, the World Commission on Environment and Development defined sustainable development as 'development that meets the needs of the present without compromising the ability of future generations to meet their own needs.' This definition, although a bit loose, emphasises the need for the present generation to safeguard the interest of future generations by maintaining the natural resources capital of this planet (WCED 1987: 43).

In this chapter, we will first briefly discuss the main functions performed, and services provided by, ecosystems and the biodiversity subsumed therein, then identify benefits from biodiversity conservation and briefly discuss methods of their valuation, and thereafter, diagnose the causes of loss of biodiversity and its environmental and other consequences in India. This is followed by identification and discussion of some of the practicable instruments of biodiversity conservation, and an overview of India's biodiversity conservation policy and programmes.

12.2 THE FUNCTIONS OF ECOSYSTEMS AND BIODIVERSITY

Biodiversity and the ecosystems in which it is contained, represent the foundation of all life, including human life. In addition to the direct and measurable services that biodiversity affords, it also provides a life support system comprising services necessary for existence of human life. It is from wild plants that humans originally bred food crops and it is from there that new genes are constantly being found for crop improvement.

Ecosystems, whether natural or managed, are required to capture the sun's energy and the food and raw materials on which we depend. Biodiversity, in turn, is required to maintain the productivity and stability of these ecosystems. Part of this process is the hydrological cycle whereby water evaporates, falls as rain, and is absorbed and used in photosynthesis as well as for direct human consumption. Well functioning ecosystems regulate this cycle and help avoid the extremes of floods and droughts.

Another part of the natural productive process is the production and maintenance of the fertile soils. Micro-organisms within ecosystems are responsible for making the soils fertile by breaking down waste, both natural and man-made, into nutrients, which maintain soil productivity. Likewise, the loss of protection provided by ecosystems usually results in the loss of fertile soils. Ecosystems themselves can be responsible for recycling; trees can capture airborne dirt that washes back down to the ground as productive soil.

Another life support service provided by ecosystems and its constituent biodiversity is climate regulation, both on a local and a global scale. As noted, ecosystems are necessary for regulation of the hydrological cycle. On a global scale, they are necessary to maintain the composition of the world's atmosphere and therefore its system of climate regulation. The mitigation of global warming is the best known example of this service.

Diversity of species and environments is essential to long-term productivity and sustainability. Its preservation is a form of investment for the future or insurance against future uncertainties. Its diminution constitutes environmental degradation even if its loss as a factor of production or a source of consumption has been fully compensated via substitution for an equally productive asset.[1] In conclusion, when we speak of environmental degradation, we should keep in mind four dimensions that is, quantity, quality and diversity, and their interdependence.

Solar energy is the driving force of ecosystems, enabling the cyclic use of materials and compounds required for system organisation and maintenance. Ecosystems capture solar energy through photosynthesis by plants. Biodiversity increases the productivity of ecosystems by utilising more of the possible pathways for energy flow and nutrient cycling. Besides, it also provides the ecosystem with the resilience to respond to unpredictable natural or man-made disasters. The species that keep the system resilient in the sense of absorbing perturbation are those that are important in the release and reorganisation phases. They can be thought of as a form of ecosystem 'insurance' (Barbier et al. 1994). Resilience is the capacity to absorb perturbations and is dependent on flexibility and adaptation. Ecological resilience is fostered by use levels, which maintain enough surpluses to allow response and adaptation

[1]Expanding the supply of one resource or an attribute of the environment at the expense of another (known as substitution) may be beneficial up to a point, but as any given resource is driven to depletion or extinction, diversity is lost, and with it an option and an element of the quality of life.

to changing environmental conditions. It requires stewardship practices that successfully promote social behaviour over individual behaviour. To achieve resource stewardship, decisions must be made over a longer time horizon than the one used by individuals acting alone, and regulations must be monitored and enforced.

12.3 IDENTIFICATION AND VALUATION OF BENEFITS FROM BIODIVERSITY CONSERVATION

Identification and economic valuation of benefits from biodiversity conservation are the most intractable and controversial issues in environmental and ecological economics. Some of the benefits from biodiversity conservation can be measured by the use of travel-cost and contingent valuation methods. However, it is generally believed that benefits from biodiversity conservation far exceed the costs.

The total economic value of biodiversity consists of the same components as are included in other areas of economic valuation. These values include use values (direct and indirect), non-use values, option values, bequest values and existence values.

In this context, we would like to emphasise the fact that it is often very difficult to separate the value of biodiversity from the value of the habitat that supports it and which is supported by it. For instance, many ecosystem services such as soil protection and the regulation of water run-off depend on the existence of certain types of ecosystems such as forests, and not on any particular species. However, a loss of species diversity may put the ecosystem, and therefore the service, at risk. Likewise, it is often possible to put an economic value on a particular species but again it is difficult to consider this value in isolation from that of the habitat which supports it, and therefore from the rest of the species and populations necessary for the maintenance of the habitat. In view of these complementarities and interdependence of various components of an ecosystem, and the consequent difficulties in isolating and measuring the value of any one of the components of the ecosystem, we consider the value of all inter-related components as the value of biodiversity.

Direct use values derive from direct use of, or contact with, a biological resource or ecosystem. The most obvious example of the economic value of biological resources in all societies is the use of wild and domesticated plants and animals in production and consumption.

The world's food production is now based on a remarkably small number of species—54 per cent of the developing world's calorific consumption is accounted for by wheat, maize and rice. Despite this, genetic diversity in agricultural crops has significant economic value. In traditional agricultural systems, a high genetic variability among crop plants creates greater stability in the face of climatic, disease and pest risks. In those systems, crop yields are lower on an average, and so also the variability of yields. For societies that rely directly on the land for food, this 'insurance' service provided by genetic diversity is extremely important. As the use of more genetically uniform improved varieties increases, the value of genetic resources will increase, since these varieties have a limited life and need periodic influxes of genetic material to remain viable. In view of this, there is need to preserve, *in situ* and *ex situ*, all the genetic materials that we have on this Planet Earth for the sake of present and future generations.

Use values of habitats that support biodiversity are an important aspect of the benefits of preserving biodiversity. These include, in the case of forests, the value of the timber and non-wood forest products (NWFPs) that can be sustainably harvested. They also include such benefits as the provision of shelter and grazing of domesticated animals in forests.

Another significant direct use value of biodiversity is the value of medicines directly or indirectly derived from wild species. Up to 80 per cent of people in developing countries use traditional remedies for their primary health care, most of which is derived from plants. Moreover, many synthetic drugs sold in developed countries are also derived from plants.

Non-consumptive direct use values of diverse habitats and species can be an important component of the value of biodiversity preservation. These include the use of the reserve of diverse species for scientific research and the value generated by tourism. Tourists are, generally speaking, attracted more towards visiting national parks and wildlife sanctuaries and other natural habitats, which have higher degree of biodiversity than those which have only a few species. Similarly, certain charismatic species such as tigers and Asiatic lions attract visitors and generate revenues. The tourism revenues are positively affected by the diversity of species that can be seen on a visit and the variety of habitats and landscapes that can be visited. The tourism revenues can be measured directly, using the travel cost method.

Indirect use values of biological resources and ecosystems derive from the role of these resources in supporting economic activity, or in supporting other biological resources which yield direct use value.

This relates to the ecological functions performed by ecosystems, such as the regulation of water run-off and the storage of carbon by forests. It can also relate to the services provided by species and biodiversity in sustaining the ecosystems that provide direct values.

Option value is the value placed on preserving an asset which, while not used at present, may be used in the future. In the case of biodiversity, this could refer to the value the potential researchers place on preserving ecosystems as a store-house of genes of hitherto undiscovered plant and animal species that might be useful in the future. Similarly, potential tourists might like to preserve certain habitats and landscapes that they might wish to visit in the future. If ecosystems are destroyed, causing the loss of species whose identity and potential use are unknown, then potential benefits from the ecosystems are lost for ever. Therefore, the option of capturing this potential value can be secured by preserving ecosystems, and thereby conserving biodiversity.

Similarly, biodiversity conservation has bequest values and existence values. Most people place value on preserving natural resources, including biodiversity, with a view to pass them on to future generations for their possible use. Besides, people also place value on knowing that a particular species or ecosystem exists. For example, many people in India value the existence of tigers, Asiatic lions, elephants and a variety of medicinal plants, herbs and shrubs, and in deference to their desire, the Government of India has established several National Parks, wildlife sanctuaries, tiger reserves and biosphere reserves in the country. This is despite the fact that those people may never use those species directly or indirectly, or may never visit those habitats.

12.4 CAUSES OF LOSS OF BIODIVERSITY AND ITS CONSEQUENCES

The existing level of biodiversity in the world has developed over the last about 5 billion years since life on earth began. It developed initially through the process of mutation and expansion of species into previously unoccupied niches. By the end of the first 4 billion years, only very simple multi-cellular organisms had evolved. The development and speciation of complex organisms occurred in the relatively short space of 100 million years. Since then, speciation and extinction have occurred at similar rates, so that evolution has been characterised in the Darwinian tradition as the 'survival of the fittest'. To this extent, extinction can be seen in a positive light, since inferior species make way, given limited resources, for their more advanced successors.

However, the role of humans in the extinction of species has meant that the natural process is distorted, and that this view of extinction is no longer necessarily valid.

Natural resources, including environment and biodiversity in India, have been under great biotic pressure for decades now. India's high levels of human and domestic animal populations, their high density and rapid growth, high rate of urbanisation and industrialisation, commercialisation of agriculture, high incidence of poverty and high level of illiteracy have all contributed to degradation of natural resources and environment, and loss of biodiversity. Many plant and animal species are on the brink of extinction. It is high time that India adopted a responsible national policy of natural resources management and biodiversity conservation, which is in tandem with its economic and social development policies.

We will now discuss some causes of loss of biodiversity and its consequences.

12.4.1 Degradation of Habitats

The prime reason for the loss of biodiversity is the destruction and degradation of habitats. Related to these are the over-harvesting of species and ecosystems and the introduction of exotic species into ecosystems. The biological heritage of the Planet Earth is increasingly at risk. It is estimated that one-quarter of the species are in danger of extinction; and 5,000 to 150,000 species are lost annually due to destruction of biomass and habitat by destructive agriculture, deforestation, pollution and other destructive fishing and grazing practices (Bartelmus 1997: 325). Almost 20 per cent of the world's vertebrates are in danger of extinction, at least in part, because of invasive species. Perhaps the best known example of this phenomenon is the introduction of the Nile Perch into Lake Victoria, resulting in the loss of at least 200 fish species in the lake.

12.4.2 Pollution

Pollution is another factor contributing to species loss in an ecosystem. It increases the load on ecosystem beyond its assimilating capacity, leading to increased stress and eventually to the reduction or loss of populations inhabiting the ecosystem. For instance, discharge of toxic effluents in water-bodies in many parts of India, in combination with other forms of pollution, has virtually eliminated fish in most of the affected water-bodies. Similarly, the use of fertilisers and plant protection chemicals in agriculture has led to pollution of water-bodies, particularly rivers, through leaching of toxic residues. While the beneficial role of fertilisers and other chemicals in increasing food production is indisputable, they leach into rivers and lakes causing vast increases in algae, a reduction in oxygen (eutrophication) and consequently the loss of other species.

12.4.3 Socio-Economic Factors

Although, loss of habitat, over-harvesting and pollution are immediate causes of loss of biodiversity in most of the cases, the underlying causes of these actions are several socio-economic factors such as population pressure, poverty, unemployment, ignorance and lack of incentives for using natural resources and biodiversity on a sustainable basis in the larger interest of society. So long as the human and animal population was within the carrying capacity of locally available natural resources and the local environment, there was no environmental degradation and no loss of biodiversity due to human actions. But as the population increased and local economies got integrated with external economies through trade, the process of degradation of natural resources and loss of biodiversity started. Further, the fact that many communities who depend directly on natural resources for their livelihood are very poor, ignorant, and have no alternative employment opportunities means that they are compelled by their circumstances to overexploit and degrade the natural resources accessible to them. Illicit felling of trees from forests, hunting, encroachment of forest land and poaching are some of the activities resorted to by the communities, partly driven by their basic needs and partly by greed. This might happen even if it is to the longer-term detriment of the communities' own well being.

Another important economic reason for the loss of biodiversity is the fact that biodiversity conservation has a high opportunity cost, especially in developing countries. For instance, in the case of forests, the opportunity cost is the value that could be derived by clear-cutting the timber and using the forest land for agricultural purposes, or as a site for a hydropower project. Likewise, the opportunity cost of conservation of a marine ecosystem is the value that could be derived from depleting the entire fish stock to extinction. In view of this, while formulating biodiversity conservation projects, one must ensure that the intended benefits to the local communities from the project substantially exceed the costs to them. Otherwise, no biodiversity conservation projects should be taken up. In other words, one must weigh the costs and benefits of biodiversity conservation from local communities' perspective.

12.4.5 Biodiversity as a Public Good

As we stated in Chapter 3, Section 3.2.1, most of the natural resources and the environmental goods and services, including biodiversity conservation, are public goods. As a matter of fact, biological diversity is a global pubic good of open access type since it is not possible (or desirable) to exclude other nations from benefiting from its conservation once it is provided by some one. Therefore, it is unreasonable to expect that such a good would be provided in sufficient quantity by an individual country in a free market, even if the good has very high utility and would contribute to social welfare. Thus, a free market will lead to under-provision of biodiversity conservation. Further, given the externalities involved in the conservation of biodiversity, in the sense that the social marginal benefits from its conservation are higher than the private marginal benefits on one hand, and the marginal social costs from its loss are higher than the marginal private costs, on the other, it is bound to be overexploited and is subject to what Hardin (1968) called 'the tragedy of the commons'. In view of this, public intervention through appropriate measures is essential for biodiversity conservation.

12.4.6 Introduction of High Yielding Varieties of Crops

One of the major reasons of the loss of biodiversity is the fact that beginning from the mid-1960s, there has been widespread adoption of high yielding varieties of crops of a few of the major food grains crops such as rice and wheat in India. Besides, high yielding exotic breeds of cows have also been adopted in certain regions of India, replacing low yielding non-descript indigenous breeds. This has led to increasing uniformity within species and varieties of crops and breeds of animals and the consequent reduction in their viability and the services that they provide. The clearest example of this is the loss in variability of crop plants as shown in Table 12.2. We should not overlook the fact that intensification of animal agriculture, which depends on a narrow range of improved high yielding genotypes, can be a cause of extinction of as high as 30 per cent of all livestock breeds (ILRI 2000). Also, the greatest

Table 12.2	Increasing Genetic Uniformity in Crop Varieties in Selected Countries of the World	
Crop	*Country*	*Number of Varieties*
Rice	Sri Lanka	From 2,000 varieties in 1959 to 5 major varieties today
Rice	India	From 30,000 varieties to 75 per cent of production from fewer than 10 varieties
Wheat	USA	50 per cent of the crop in 9 varieties
Potato	USA	75 per cent of the crop in 4 varieties

Source: World Conservation Monitoring Centre 'Valuing Biodiversity' in World Conservation Monitoring Centre, Global Biological Diversity, Chapman and Hall, London.

threat is in developing countries to indigenous breeds that are poorly characterised.

One of the negative effects of lower genetic diversity in a species is that a larger proportion of a planted crop is susceptible to the same diseases. This means that although uniform varieties may produce higher yields on average, they are more likely than a genetically diverse crop to fail altogether. A recent study by Prakash and Pearce (1998) measures the effect of genetic uniformity and biodiversity loss on the stability of agricultural systems. This consists of comparing the variability of harvest yields before and after the Green Revolution in India. They show that while average yields have increased, their variability has also increased since the Green Revolution, implying that the reduction in biodiversity has decreased the stability of the system.

Scientific knowledge of ecosystem structure is far from complete. This results, to a certain extent, from the immense complexity of the interdependence of species and ecosystems. Therefore, it is very difficult to predict the effect that removing or changing the level of a population of one species will have on the rest of the species in a community, or on the viability of the ecosystem.

Some species are known as 'keystone species'. These are species whose removal would have a profound effect on the structure of an ecosystem. An animal that is the only large predator in an ecosystem is likely to be a keystone species. If such a species is lost or depleted, then this will have a more significant effect than the depletion of another species in the ecosystem. However, different species in an ecosystem can be keystone species under different states of nature. Thus, there are latent relationships that cannot be observed under the current state of nature. This constitutes an inevitable source of uncertainty.

12.4.7 Unregulated International Trade

In the opinion of the World Bank and the IMF, a free market is the key to economic growth of developing countries. In a world where the ecological limits to growth have already reached, growth-oriented free market-based policies serve primarily to intensify competition for the finite stock of natural resources. Economic growth in such a situation is a zero sum game; there cannot be too much of it somewhere without too little of it being elsewhere. If markets are not regulated, such competition leads to concentration of control of resources in the hands of those who have economic and political power and consequent widening of disparities between the rich and poor. The end result of such policies will be environmental degradation and depletion of natural resources, both of which will reduce the real wealth of the society and impair the future productive potential of the economy. This is exactly what is happening now in most developing countries, including India, that have been forced to adopt Structural Adjustment Programmes (SAPs) and integrate their national economies into the world economy by removing all barriers to the free flow of goods and capital across their borders.

The trade in tropical timber, for example, is one factor underlying tropical deforestation. Need for foreign exchange encourages many developing countries to cut timber faster than forests can be regenerated. This over-cutting not only depletes the resource that underpins the world timber trade, but also causes the loss of forest-based livelihoods, increases soil erosion and downstream flooding, and accelerates the loss of species and genetic resources. International trade patterns can also encourage the unsustainable development policies and practices that have steadily degraded the crop-lands and range-lands in the dry-lands of Asia and Africa.

Daly (1973) argues that in a free trade regime, a country that internalises the costs of using natural resources, including environment, into its prices will be at a disadvantage vis-à-vis a country that does not, since its prices will be higher. Therefore, there will be no incentives for any country to internalise environmental costs and thereby attain sustainable development in an open trading system.

12.5 DETERMINING LOCALLY AND GLOBALLY OPTIMUM LEVELS OF BIODIVERSITY CONSERVATION

In view of the fact that biodiversity conservation is both a local and a global public good, it is also true that there exists a local demand and a global demand for its benefits and that global benefits from it are substantially higher than the benefits to local communities. We could think of there being a local market for biodiversity conservation with the supply approximated by the opportunity cost of and the demand represented by the benefits from biodiversity conservation. The locally optimum level of biodiversity conservation could then be determined by the interaction of demand and supply as depicted in Figure 12.1.

In the figure, on the horizontal axis, we measure the extent of ecosystem or biodiversity conservation and on the vertical axis the estimated costs and benefits from biodiversity conservation. E^T represents the entire amount of land available in a particular ecosystem under consideration. The supply of biodiversity is represented by the opportunity cost of the land to be put under conservation. The local demand is represented by the social benefits or direct and indirect use values of biodiversity conservation expected to accrue to the local community. The locally optimum level of biodiversity conservation is attained where the supply and demand curves intersect each other, that is, at the level denoted by E^*. This is the level where the marginal social (opportunity) cost is equal to the marginal social benefits from biodiversity conservation from the perspective of local communities.

Figure 12.1   Locally Optimum Level of Biodiversity Conservation

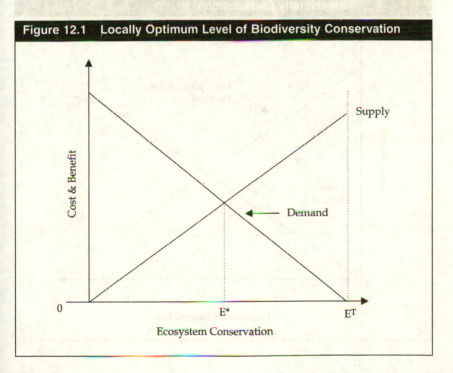

Given the fact that global benefits from biodiversity conservation are higher than the benefits to local communities, it follows that the global demand for biodiversity conservation will be higher than the local demand and consequently the globally optimum level of biodiversity conservation will be higher than the locally (nationally) optimum level as shown in Figure 12.2.

In the figure, E_L^*, represents the locally optimum level of biodiversity conservation. At this level the local demand and supply curves intersect each other. The globally optimum level of biodiversity conservation is represented by E_G^*, where the local plus global demand curve intersects the supply curve.

However, we would like to sound a caveat here, that in actual practice, it is very difficulty to precisely estimate the local demand and global demand for various direct and indirect benefits of biodiversity conservation. In view of this, the determination of locally and globally optimum levels of biodiversity conservation is also very difficult.

Figure 12.2   Locally and Globally Optimum Levels of Biodiversity Conservation

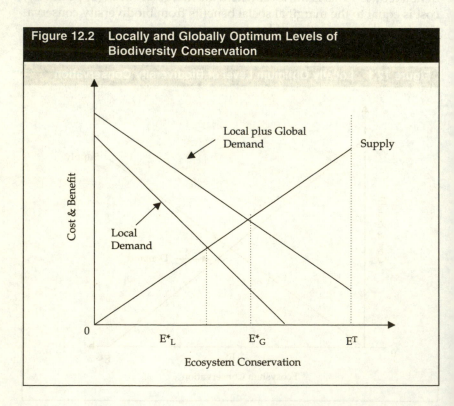

12.6 INSTRUMENTS OF BIODIVERSITY CONSERVATION

In this section, we discuss some of the instruments that could be used to reduce biodiversity loss at the local level.[2]

12.6.1 Creation and Assignment of Property Rights

In Section 12.3, we have stated that biodiversity, being a public good and an open access, is bound to be overexploited and is subject to what Hardin (1968) called 'The Tragedy of the Commons'. The problem of excessive biodiversity loss can be described as a problem of environmental externalities. This is a problem familiar in environmental economics, and the solution to such problems involves the creation and assignment of property rights.[3] In the case of pollution externalities, the assignment of property rights over the atmosphere may mean that a firm must pay local people compensation for polluting the air. Likewise, in the case of biodiversity conservation, assigning property rights to communities who use natural resources would ensure that any development of the resource would compensate the local communities for the loss due to biodiversity conservation. Thus, the (previously) external costs of development of natural resources would be internalised.

Domestic policies to preserve biodiversity ought to attempt to ensure that a locally efficient level of preservation is achieved. This means establishing a 'level playing field' between preservation of natural ecosystems and alternative land uses. In particular, this means removing the subsidies and other incentives, which encourage the short-term depletion of natural resource stocks. It also means accounting for the effects of poorly defined property rights, especially where this means that the benefits local communities derive from direct use of natural resources are not accounted for in decisions as to whether to conserve or develop land.

This policy might involve providing local communities with land tenure and access to credit, markets and the technology necessary for them to manage forest lands sustainably and profitably. The problem of population pressure on natural resources might also be relieved by investing in non-land based employment.

---

[2]In Chapter 7 of this book, a detailed account of instruments of environment management is presented. Those instruments are also applicable in the context of biodiversity conservation.
[3]This instrument is discussed in detail in Chapter 4, Section 4.8.2 and in Chapter 7.

12.6.2 Internalising the Benefits from Ecotourism

The benefits from ecotourism could be internalised to the local community, rather than accruing solely to urban entrepreneurs, who mostly own tourist resorts near national parks and wildlife sanctuaries. This would give local communities a stake in the preservation of natural habitats, compensate them for the negative externalities suffered by them in the form of crop damage and loss of animal and human lives caused by wild animals from the national parks and wildlife sanctuaries,[4] and reduce the problem of encroachment. This can be done partly by providing employment to local people as tour guides and partly by allocating part of the revenues from ecotourism to local employment projects. Local entrepreneurs may also be encouraged and financially supported through low-cost loans to build and operate low-cost tourist lodges equipped with modern amenities in villages in the vicinity of national parks and wildlife sanctuaries.

12.6.3 Environmental Bonds

The use of natural resources can be made more conservation friendly by the use of environmental bonds. These are payments made by developers, in advance of development, such as logging and mining, to cover potential damages. This means that they have an incentive to minimise the damage due to their development activities, and to carry out restoration of the landscape. Moreover, funds are then available to carry out the restoration if developers fail to comply. Environmental bonds have been used as a condition for granting logging concessions in many countries of Asia. However, in India, this instrument has not been used so far, but should be used in future.

Similarly, as we know from Chapter 10, many indirect benefits of forest ecosystems such as watershed protection and hydrological regulation accrue mainly to farmers and residents downstream from the forest ecosystem. The fact that these benefits are external to the process of forest preservation means that it is under-funded. Local populations

---

[4]In a study funded by the FAO, New Delhi, and sponsored by the Wildlife Institute of India, Dehradun, titled, 'Planning and Funding Eco-development Projects in and Around Protected Areas in India', Katar Singh found, during the course of conducting field studies in neighbouring villages, that the villagers had suffered heavy losses due to the damage caused to their crops by wild animals, particularly wild boars, monkeys and elephants, from the nearby national parks and wildlife sanctuaries. The villagers also complained that whereas they bear all the costs of biodiversity conservation, no benefits accrue to them; most of the benefits from ecotourism go to the outsiders, who own restaurants and tourists lodges (Singh 1995a).

have no incentive to account for these benefits in their use of the forest. Therefore, a system of charges for water use could be used to internalise these benefits to the communities who help protect and conserve the forest.

12.6.4 Education

Education is one of the instruments that could be used for biodiversity conservation and maintaining the ecosystems intact in the process of economic growth. This instrument seeks to change perceptions and priorities of users of ecosystems and their services by internalising ecosystem awareness and responsibility into individual and group decision-making. Besides education and persuasion, this instrument could also take the form of provision of information and training as well as forms of 'moral suasion' such as social pressure and negotiation. They can complement economic and regulatory instruments and assist in their successful implementation.[5]

Education for ecosystem management requires a multidisciplinary approach involving several disciplines such as ecology, economics, sociology, political science, public administration, natural sciences, engineering and technology, and agricultural sciences This kind of approach helps individuals and groups to understand the basic concepts of ecosystem, environment, biodiversity and sustainable development and the factors affecting the environment and to broaden their perspective. The ultimate aim of such education and understanding is to enable the users of the biodiversity to act responsibly to conserve it and create awareness and concern about the interdependence of social, political, economic and ecological issues. Environmental education is a continuous life-long learning process considering the environment in totality at micro as well as macro levels.

Most scholars and practitioners in environment management recognise the need for education as an instrument for averting what Hardin (1968) called 'the tragedy of the commons'. As most of the components of an ecosystem are common pool resources (CPRs), or open access, they are prone to overexploitation, degradation and depletion (Singh 1994a: 11–16). Most users of ecosystem services, in both developed and developing countries of the world, do not use them as they 'should', partly because they are ignorant about the nature and causes of environmental problems and partly because of many economic and institutional

---

[5]For details of this instrument, see Chapter 7, Section 7.4.3 of this book.

factors such as poverty, property rights and tenure. This stands in the way of their adopting socially desirable behaviour. In the short run, education seems to be a logical and simple solution to the extent that environmental problems arise out of ignorance. Education should therefore be used as a means of alleviating ignorance.

In the long run, education also affects biodiversity conservation in two other ways. First, it influences population growth. With all else equal, people with more education tend to have somewhat smaller families and to that extent population pressure on the environment, and consequently its exploitation and misuse, are reduced. Second, education increases incomes. India, as also many other developing countries, is trapped in poverty associated with rapid population growth, illiteracy, unemployment, poor nutrition and hygiene. All these factors tend to have an adverse effect on the ecosystems and the environment. Increased incomes therefore help improve the status and management of the environment. In designing education programmes, it is important to keep these questions in mind: who is to be educated, in what subjects, and with what kind of information, by whom, and how?[6]

Education in ecosystem maintenance and biodiversity conservation should be an integral part of course curricula in all secondary, higher secondary schools and colleges. The Union Ministry of Environment and Forests is currently implementing, in 16 states of India, a project to green the text books of languages, science and social sciences for standards six, seven and eight. The project is supported by the World Bank, and the Centre for Science and Environment is a consultant to the project. Besides, quite a few universities, institutes and colleges in India have already started offering courses in environment and environmental economics at both undergraduate and postgraduate levels. These programmes are financially supported by the University Grants Commission and the Union Ministry of Human Resources Development.

12.6.5 Involvement of Indigenous and Local Communities

The indigenous communities represent a fund of knowledge. They have a major role in management of natural resources and biodiversity conservation by fine-tuning them to suit diverse local contexts. Their participation should be sought by governmental and non-governmental

---

[6]These questions are discussed in Chapter 7, section 7.4.3 of this book.

organisations (NGOs) in designing and implementing biodiversity conservation and ecosystem management projects. The Convention on Biological Diversity (CBD) in its Article 8j makes a plea that each nation signatory to the CBD should, *inter alia*, respect, preserve, and maintain knowledge, innovations and practices of indigenous and local communities, relevant for the conservation and sustainable use of biological diversity, and promote their widespread adoption with their involvement (Sengupta 2005: 61). However, in this context, we would like to emphasise the need for an appropriate mix of traditional and modern knowledge of biodiversity conservation. Indigenous knowledge should complement rather than be a substitute for modern knowledge in the implementation of biodiversity conservation projects.

12.6.6 Organisation of Local Biodiversity Users

Local people's participation in planning, implementation and monitoring of biodiversity conservation projects is essential for sustainable development. For this to happen, it is essential that the local people are organised into formal or non-formal groups, conscientised about the need for biodiversity conservation, empowered through education and training and motivated and guided, preferably by local NGOs. There are many factors that affect people's participation in collective action of the type required for biodiversity conservation. But the most important among them is that the expected private benefits from participation must markedly exceed the expected private costs, and that the expected benefits must be assured and equitably distributed among participants in proportion to contribution in the form of labour, cash or both. Singh (1991) identifies various factors that affect people's participation in natural resource management. They include project design, characteristics of the resource, characteristics of local people, type and orientation of project personnel, and institutional arrangements and incentives for people's participation. The National Forest Policy of 1988 and the Resolution of 1 June 1990 of the Government of India, Ministry of Environment and Forests, provide for people's participation in the protection and development of forests. Following the GoI Resolution, many state governments have issued similar Resolutions/Orders facilitating the participation of local people in what has come to be known as Joint Forest Management (JFM).[7]

---

[7]See for details, Chapter 10 of this book.

12.6.7 National and International Laws, Rules, Regulations and Conventions

The loss of biodiversity is a matter of crucial concern, both at the national as well as global levels. There have been several international treaties and pacts relating to it, the latest and the most comprehensive being the Convention on Biological Diversity (CBD). The CBD was signed at the Earth Summit in Rio de Janeiro in 1992 by 155 nation states and came into force in 1993. This legally binding treaty obliges ratifying countries to protect biodiversity, to move towards the sustainable use of biological resources and to ensure that benefits from such use are shared equitably across local, regional, national and global societies. India ratified this Convention in 1994. As a signatory to the Convention, India is committed to take appropriate legal and administrative steps to follow its provisions.

There are many laws in India that directly or indirectly provide for biodiversity conservation. More specifically, the following are the relevant laws:

- Indian Forest Act (1927)
- Forest Conservation Act (1980)
- Wildlife Protection Act (1972) as amended from time to time
- Biological Diversity Act (2003)
- Convention on Bilogical Diversity (1992)
- Convention on International Trade in Endangered Species (CITES)

Many of the benefits of biodiversity conservation that we have discussed in this chapter are global environmental values. These benefits include global climate regulation, pharmaceutical uses, option values and existence value. Because the opportunity costs of ecosystem preservation fall mainly on low-income countries, it seems clear that some sort of international transfer mechanism is required to provide developing countries with the incentive to preserve biodiversity, over and above the amount that is efficient from their own point of view.

The Global Environmental Fund provides financial support to developing countries for biodiversity conservation. Debt-for-nature swaps express the willingness of rich countries to pay for endangered biological resources of poor countries. Under these swaps, some rich countries purchase an amount of the discounted national debt of a poor country with the agreement that the country then places an amount equal to the debt purchased into a special account or fund (usually in local currency) that will be used to manage protected areas, or for biodiversity conservation, carbon off-sets and the purchase of set-asides to store carbon in tropical forests are other indicators of the value placed on ecosystem protection. Given that primary and secondary forests can contain as much as 200–300 metric tonnes of carbon per ha, the value of carbon stored could be considerable (Schneider 1993; Brown et al. 1993). However, none of these are real measures of the intrinsic value of biodiversity. The best approach is to avoid irreversible losses and species extinction following the SMS criterion.

12.6.8 The Precautionary Principle

A problem that is difficult to analyse is the existence of discontinuities or 'threshold effects' in the behaviour of ecosystems. Thresholds are defined as critical values for populations or natural cycles at which the ecosystem loses resilience and hence the capacity to maintain its order. This means that a marginal change in one of the parameters of an ecosystem may lead to vast social and economic costs, if the result is a collapse in the ecosystem. The crux of the problem lies in the fact that the critical values for an ecosystem cannot be observed until the moment at which the collapse takes place. Therefore, considerable uncertainty remains as to the threshold values of some of the most important ecosystems.

The uncertainty regarding the extent to which ecosystems, including the global ecosystem, can be depleted of their constituent parts before their integrity and viability is put at risk, has led to calls for a 'precautionary principle' to be employed when taking decisions involving ecosystem destruction. This principle implies, among other things, postponing actions whose effects are uncertain, but which could be very damaging, until the uncertainty is reduced.

The possibility of sudden, dramatic changes in the structure of ecosystems has led Ehrlich and Ehrlich (1981) to liken the process of species extinction to the progressive removal of rivets from an aircraft in flight. While no particular rivet is essential, they say, as each one is removed the likelihood of disaster increases.

The National Environment Policy 2006 recommends the adoption of this principle for protection of environment. More specifically, it stipulates: 'Where there are credible threats of serious or irreversible damage to key environmental resources, lack of full scientific certainty shall not be used as a reason for postponing cost-effective measures to prevent environmental degradation'.

12.7 BIODIVERSITY CONSERVATION POLICY AND PROGRAMMES OF INDIA

Of late, there has been a spectacular growth in public awareness about the adverse environmental impacts of economic growth and the demand for public intervention to control the increasing air and water pollution, soil erosion, depletion of groundwater aquifers, denudation and degradation of forests, increasing waterlogging and soil salinity in canal command areas, growing desertification, and extinction or threat of extinction to many valuable plant and animal species. Accordingly, the government has responded by enacting laws, framing rules and regulations, and initiating a number of programmes for control of pollution, improving the environment and protection and conservation of endangered species of plants and animals. Besides, the growing awareness of, and concern over, environmental degradation are also reflected in many popular movements such as *Chipko*, *Appiko*, and *Narmada Bachao*, extensive media coverage of environmental issues, and emergence of numerous non-governmental organisations (Singh 1994a: 21–23).

India has adopted a policy known as the Protected Area (PA) approach to biodiversity conservation. By PAs, we mean areas notified as protected (against human interference) under the Wildlife (Protection) Act 1972. The Act provides for setting up of national parks and wildlife sanctuaries with a view to afford varying degrees of protection to a whole range of animal species. The Act has since been amended in 1982, 1986 and 1991. The 1991 amendment affords protection to scheduled plants and prohibits commercial felling in wildlife sanctuaries.

Duly recognising the importance of and need for PA approach, the Government of India, Ministry of Environment and Forests has recently launched an Ecodevelopment Project in seven selected PAs in India. The selected PAs are Buxa (West Bengal), Gir (Gujarat), Nagarhole (Karnataka), Palamau (Bihar), Pench (Madhya Pradesh), Periyar (Kerala) and Ranthambhore (Rajasthan). The Project is financially supported by the Global Environment Facility (GEF) and the International Development Association (IDA) (World Bank 1996: i–iii). Earlier, a pilot project titled 'Strengthening Wildlife Management and Ecodevelopment Planning Capabilities' was executed by the Wildlife Institute of India, Dehra Dun, in 10 selected PAs. The Project was a collaborative endeavour of the Government of India (Ministry of Environment and Forests) and the United Nations Development Programme (UNDP 1992). The project envisaged collaboration with various governmental and non-governmental agencies engaged in rural development in the selected PAs. In particular, it was envisaged that the

PA authorities would seek functional collaboration with the district level government departments dealing with income and employment generating activities, poverty alleviation, dry farming, soil and water conservation, animal husbandry, sericulture, pisciculture, non-conventional energy and rural industries and mobilise and utilise their funds for implementing ecodevelopment projects. The project employed the PA approach to biodiversity conservation and participatory ecodevelopment in and around PAs as an instrument of achieving the goal of biodiversity conservation.

The PA approach is not new to India. The recorded history of protection of animals, fish and forests in India dates back to 252 BC, the era of Emperor Ashok (Panwar and Mathur 1992: 3). Setting aside sacred (forest) areas as sanctuaries as distinct from exclusive hunting reserves is even older. Now, it is proposed under the Project to expand and strengthen the PA system and manage it scientifically.

The network of PAs comprising national parks (NP) and wildlife sanctuaries (WLS) has steadily grown from 10 NPs and 127 WLSs covering an area of about 2.50 million ha in 1970 (before the enactment of the Wildlife (Protection) Act 1972) to 92 NPs and 492 WLSs covering about 14.5 million ha (about 4.3 per cent of India's total geographical area) in 2004 (Table 12.3). It is planned to expand the PAs further to cover 183,574 km^2 (5.6 per cent of India's total geographical area) in keeping with the global trends in wildlife and biodiversity conservation. The project represents an important step forward in that direction.

A recent development in the field of biodiversity conservation is the formulation of the National Biodiversity Strategy and Action Plan (NBSAP) under the auspices of the Ministry of Environment and Forests (MoEF), Government of India. In 1998, the MoEF applied for funding to the Global Environment Facility through United Nations Development

Table 12.3 Number and Estimated Area Under Selected Biodiversity Conservation Measures

Sl. No.	Particular	Number	Area Covered (km^2)
1.	National Parks	92	38,570
2.	Wildlife Sanctuaries	492	117,077
3.	Tiger Reserves	28	37,761
4.	Biosphere Reserves	13	54,810
5.	Ramsar Sites	19	648,507
6.	Hot Spots	02	112,450

Source: Kotwal et al. (2005), Biodiversity in IIFM Campus, Indian Institute of Forest Management, Bhopal.

Programme (UNDP) to formulate a Comprehensive Biodiversity Strategy and Action Plan. The central concern for such an action plan and strategy was that it should be consistent with the ecological, social, cultural and economic framework of the country. In 1999, GEF/UNDP approved a grant of almost one million dollars (about Rs 4.3 crore). The process of formulating the NBSAP was started in January 2000 and the first draft of the National Action Plan was ready in November 2002 and the final draft was submitted to the MoEF in late 2003.

The NBSAP takes a holistic view of the term, biodiversity, and encompasses all its components, namely, natural and agricultural ecosystems, species of wild plants and animals, micro-organisms, crop and livestock systems, and the genetic diversity within these. Besides, aspects of conservation, sustainable use of biological resources and issues of economic and social equity are also covered in it. It focuses on achieving the twin goals of ensuring the ecological security of the country and the livelihood security of communities dependent on biodiversity. To achieve these goals, it recommends a series of measures including a major reorientation of the process of economic development and the system of governance of natural resources, such that the integrity of critical ecosystems and wildlife habitats, and security of livelihoods of biomass-dependent communities, become central to all development planning. It provides for, *inter alia*, formulation of a national land and water use plan, ecoregional planning, expanding the network of conservation sites including PAs, biosphere reserves, oral reefs, mangroves, and scared groves, strengthening of Environmental Impact Assessment procedure, and creating and strengthening of the institutions of decentralised governance (Kothari and Kohli 2005: 86 & 95–96).

12.8 MAIN POINTS

The following are the main points made in this chapter:

- India has an impressive diversity of crop species and varieties. It is rated as one of the 12 mega diversity countries in the world accounting for 60–70 per cent of the world's biodiversity. It has two of the world's 25 biodiversity hotspots, namely, Western Ghats and Eastern Himalayas. Biodiversity depends, to a large extent, upon the type and status of natural ecosystems, which are important not only for agriculture, but also for sustainable development.
- Biodiversity and the ecosystems in which it is contained represent the foundation of all life, including human life. Biodiversity performs several direct and indirect functions and provides several

services that support life support systems. Identification and economic valuation of benefits from biodiversity conservation is one of the most intractable and controversial issues in environmental and ecological economics. Some of the benefits from biodiversity conservation can be measured by the use of travel cost and contingent valuation methods. But it is generally believed that benefits from biodiversity conservation far exceed the costs.

- Biodiversity in India has been under great biotic pressure for decades now. India's high levels of human and domestic animal populations, their high density and rapid growth, high rate of urbanisation and industrialisation, commercialisation of agriculture, high incidence of poverty and high level of illiteracy have all contributed to degradation of natural resources and environment, and loss of biodiversity.

- Many plant and animal species are on the brink of extinction. It is high time that India adopted a responsible national policy of natural resources management and biodiversity conservation, which is in tandem with its economic and social development policies and implements it faithfully using appropriate measures.

- The major policy instruments of biodiversity conservation include the creation and assignment of property rights, internalisation of benefits from biodiversity conservation, education and national and international laws, regulations and conventions.

- A comprehensive strategy of ecosystem-based development planning and management is necessary for biodiversity conservation. Initially, such a strategy may be adopted in selected Protected Areas in India, as is being already done now, and lessons learned from those projects may be incorporated in formulating programmes for eco-development and biodiversity conservation.

- In the short run, the goals of sustenance of poor people depending on common pool natural resources and of biodiversity conservation are conflicting. But in the long run, it is possible to reconcile these goals through integration of eco-development and biodiversity conservation projects with various ongoing rural development programmes, such that the poor are able to benefit from the latter and their dependence on common pool natural resources for their survival is reduced. To make eco-development and biodiversity conservation projects self-sustaining, people's participation in their formulation and implementation is a must.

- The National Biodiversity Strategy and Action Plan needs to be implemented faithfully so as to protect and preserve biodiversity through appropriate policies and programmes.

12.9 DISCUSSION QUESTIONS

1. How does the increasing loss of biodiversity over time affect the environment? Illustrate your answer with an example.
2. Visit a National Park (NP) or a Protected Area (PA), talk to the forest officer-in-charge, a few visitors, and a few people living in the vicinity of the NP or PA about the benefits and costs of NP/PA and answer the following questions:

   (a) What are the tangible benefits of the NP/PA and to whom they accrue?

   (b) What are the costs—direct and indirect of establishing and maintaining the NP/PA and who bears them?

   (c) Based on your answers to (a) and (b), identify those who benefit most and who bears most of the costs.

   (d) Is it possible to compensate those who bear the loss and tax those who benefit? Yes/No, and why?

   (e) What is the best way of financing biodiversity conservation?

3. Why is the participation of local people necessary for biodiversity conservation?
4. Can the Biodiversity Act alone ensure biodiversity conservation? For details of the Act see Website: http://www.envfor.nic.in.
5. Critically examine the National Biodiversity Conservation Action Plan and list its strengths and weaknesses. For details of the plan see Kothari and Kohli (2005).

13 Climate Change and Environment

The term, climate, is generally used to connote a complex natural phenomenon comprising such variables as air temperature and humidity, wind, and precipitation. It is a complex system representing cumulative effects of regional or weather patterns. Solar energy is the driving force in the earth's climate. Although the climate remains fairly stable on the human time scale of decades or centuries, it fluctuates continuously over thousands or million of years and is affected by a large number of variables (Cunningham et al. 1999: 195). There have been perceptible changes in the climate all over the world, particularly in the last two decades or so. Studies have shown that human activity may cause large disturbances in regional and global climate. Such disturbances include global warming and acid rains.

The climate change and its adverse impacts on the environment, human health and the economy have recently risen to the top of economic and political agenda in various national and international forums and meetings on the environment. As some of the climatic changes are attributable to human activities, a change in human behaviour can be an important instrument of minimising the extent of those changes in the climate which have harmful effects. The most important climatic changes that have come to the fore recently and that are harmful include acid rain, global warming and depletion of the stratospheric ozone shield or layer. Besides, such climatic aberrations as floods, droughts, cyclones and tsunamis also cause serious damage to humans and have adverse effects on local, regional and global climate.

In this chapter, we will define and briefly discuss the causes, effects and remedies of acid rain, global warming and depletion of the ozone layer. In addition, we also examine the incidence of such climatic aberrations as floods, droughts and cyclones and their effects. This chapter is largely based on Internet sources and published literature available on the subject.

13.2 ACID RAIN

The problem of acid rain started long ago when the Industrial Revolution commenced. Acid rain is one of the most dangerous and widespread forms of pollution. Sometimes called 'the unseen plague,' acid rain can go undetected in an area for years. Technically, acid rain is rain that has a larger amount of acid in it than what is normal. The acidity of rain in parts of Europe and North America has dramatically increased over the past few decades.

13.2.1 Causes of Acid Rain

Acid deposition in the atmosphere occurs due to the release of sulphur oxides and nitrogen oxides in the atmosphere. Motor vehicles are a major source of nitrogen oxides, and electrical power plants and indus-trial boilers are the main sources of sulphur dioxide emissions. The acid deposition occurs when sulphur oxides and nitrogen oxides react with water to produce dilute solutions of sulfuric acid (H_2SO_4), nitric acid (HNO_3) and nitrous acid (HNO_2). Sunlight increases the rate of most of these reactions. Rainwater, snow, fog and other forms of pre-cipitation containing those mild solutions of sulfuric and nitric acids fall on to the earth as acid rain. The process of formation of acid rain is depicted in Figure 13.1.

Water moves through every living plant and animal, streams, lakes and oceans in the hydrologic cycle. In that cycle, water evaporates from the land and sea into the atmosphere. Water in the atmosphere then condenses to form clouds. Clouds release the water back to the earth as rain, snow or fog. When water droplets form and fall to the earth they pick up particles and chemicals that float in the air. Even clean, unpol-luted air has some particles such as dust or pollen. Clean air also

Figure 13.1   The Process of Formation of Acid Rain

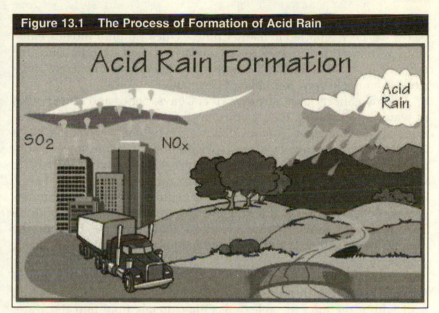

Source: http://en.wikipedia.org/wiki/Ozone_layer

contains naturally occurring gases such as carbon dioxide. The interaction between the water droplets and the carbon dioxide in the atmosphere gives rain a pH of 5.6, making even clean rain slightly acidic. Other natural sources of acids and bases in the atmosphere may lower or raise the pH of unpolluted rain. However, when rain contains pollutants, especially sulphur dioxide and nitrogen oxides, the rain water can become acidic.

Acid rain can be carried over a long distance by atmospheric winds, so much so that one country can export acid emissions to another. Due to its movement from the locations of its origin to other places within and across nations, the problem has become too complex and highly politicised to be resolved. There is no agreement among nations on sharing of the cost of abatement of acid rain.

13.2.2 Effects of Acid Rain

Acid rain adversely affects plants, fish and birds and corrodes metals and building materials. The effects of acid rain have been recorded in parts of the United States, the erstwhile Federal Republic of Germany, former Czechoslovakia, the Netherlands, Switzerland, Australia, former Yugoslavia and elsewhere. It is also becoming a significant problem in

Japan and China and in Southeast Asia. Rain with a pH of 4.5 and below has been reported in many Chinese cities. Sulphur dioxide emissions were reported in 1979 to have nearly tripled in India since the early 1960s, making them only slightly less than the then-current emissions from the Federal Republic of Germany.

Acid rain affects lakes, streams, rivers, bays, ponds and other bodies of water by increasing their acidity until fish and other aquatic creatures can no longer live. Aquatic plants grow best between pH levels of 7.0 and 9.2. As acidity increases (pH numbers become lower), submerged aquatic plants decrease and deprive waterfowl of their basic food source. At pH 6, freshwater shrimp cannot survive. At pH 5.5, bottom-dwelling bacterial decomposers begin to die and leave undercomposed leaf litter and other organic debris to collect on the bottom. This deprives plankton—tiny creatures that form the base of the aquatic food chain, so that they too disappear. Below a pH of about 4.5, all fish die.

As undecomposed organic leaf litter increases, owing to the loss of bottom-dwelling bacteria, toxic metals such as aluminum, mercury and lead within the litter are released. Other metals flow into the water from the soils in the surrounding watershed. These toxic metals are bad for human health; high lead levels may harm people who drink such water and people who ingest mercury in tainted fish suffer serious health problems. Most of the frogs and insects also die when the water reaches pH 4.5. Some fish and animals, such as frogs, have a hard time adapting to and reproducing in an acidic environment. Many plants, such as evergreen trees, are damaged by acid rain and acid fog. You also might notice how acid rain has eaten away the stone in some cities' buildings and stone artwork (see http://ga.water.usgs.gov/edu/acidrain.html).

Besides the aquatic life, acid rain also harms vegetation. The forests of Germany and elsewhere in Western Europe, for example, are believed to be dying because of acid rain. Scientists believe that it damages the protective waxy coating of leaves and allows acids to diffuse into them, which interrupts the evaporation of water and gas exchange so that the plant can no longer breathe. This stops the plant's conversion of nutrients and water into a form useful for plant growth and affects crop yields.

Toxic metals such as lead, zinc, copper, chromium and aluminum are deposited in the forest from the atmosphere. Acid rain releases these metals and they stunt the growth of trees and other plants and also that of mosses, algae, nitrogen-fixing bacteria and fungi needed for forest growth.

While there are no estimates of the economic loss due to acid rain available for Asia, economic losses from it in the United States provide a glimpse of such costs. According to one report, for example, the losses due to acid precipitation are of the order of $13,000 million annually in the eastern part of the nation and could cause $1,750 million yearly in forest damage, $8,300 million in crop damage in the Ohio River basin alone by about the year 2000 and $40 million in health costs in the State of Minnesota. The only cost-effective solution to the problem, according to many people, is to reduce emissions at their point of origin (Friedman and Friedman 1988).

13.2.3 Solutions to the Acid Rain Problem

Acid rain is a big problem, but it is not uncontrollable. The environment can generally adapt to a certain amount of acid rain. Often soil is slightly basic (due to naturally occurring limestone, which has a pH of greater than 7). Since bases counteract with acids, these soils tend to balance out some of the acid rain's acidity. However, in areas where limestone does not naturally occur in the soil, acid rain can harm the environment.

If the amount of sulphur dioxides and nitrogen oxides in the air is reduced, then acid rain will be reduced. There are many helpful things that 'normal' people (people who aren't part of a power company or the government) can do. First of all, conserve energy and pollute less! Use less electricity, more carpools and public transportation, or walk when you can. This will help more than one might think. When less energy is used and less coal is burnt, there is less acid rain. Experts say that if energy was used more carefully, we could cut the amount of fuel burned by half.

Also, if coal was cleaned before it was burnt, the dangerous pollutants that cause acid rain would be cleaned away. If coal is crushed and washed in water, the sulfur washes out. However, this is a very costly method, and many power companies and governments do not want to spend their money cleaning coal.

13.3 GLOBAL WARMING

According to the National Academy of Sciences, the Earth's surface temperature has risen by about 1° F in the past century, with accelerated warming during the past two decades (Figure 13. 2). In 1980, the mean global temperature was 15.18° C; it increased to 15.38° C in 1990, 15.39° C in 1995 and 16.04° C in 2005. In fact in the northern hemisphere, 2005

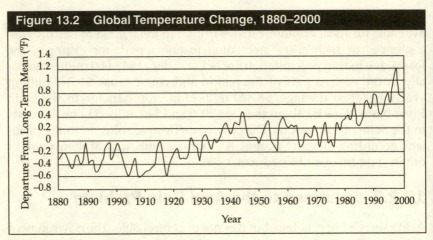

Figure 13.2   Global Temperature Change, 1880–2000

Source: U.S. National Climatic Data Centre, 2001.

is likely to go down as the warmest year ever recorded with an increase in the mean global temperature of the order of + 0.6.5° C. Increasing concentrations of greenhouse gases are likely to accelerate the rate of climate change. Scientists expect that the average global surface temperature could rise 0.6–2.5° C in the next 50 years, and 1.4–5.8° C in the next century, with significant regional variations. Evaporation will increase as the climate warms, which will increase average global precipitation. Soil moisture is likely to decline in many regions, and intense rainstorms are likely to become more frequent.

13.3.1 Causes of Global Warming

There is new and stronger evidence that most of the global warming over the last 50 years is attributable to human activities. Human activities have altered the chemical composition of the atmosphere through the build-up of greenhouse gases—primarily carbon dioxide, methane and nitrous oxide. Since the beginning of the Industrial Revolution, atmospheric concentrations of carbon dioxide have increased nearly 30 per cent, methane concentrations have more than doubled, and nitrous oxide concentrations have risen by about 15 per cent. These increases have enhanced the heat-trapping capability of the earth's atmosphere. The heat-trapping property of these gases is undisputed although uncertainties exist about exactly how the earth's climate responds to them.

The U.N. Inter-Governmental Panel on Climate Change (IPCC) (1995) reported that human-produced air pollutants have played the key role in recent climate change. The IPCC, based on studies by numerous scientists, had projected a 1° C to 3.5° C increase in global temperature by the year 2100 (Raven et al. 1998: 461). Global warming is caused by concentration in the atmosphere of carbon dioxide and certain other trace gases including methane, nitrous oxide, chlorofluorocarbons (CFCs) and stratospheric ozone. The concentration of atmospheric carbon dioxide has increased from about 28 parts per million (ppm) over the last 200 years or so to 361 ppm in 1995 and is increasing year after year (Raven et al. 1998: 462). This is largely due to the rapidly increasing number of motor vehicles. Global warming occurs because carbon dioxide and other gases trap the sun's radiation and then dissipate the heat into space, leading to an increase in the atmospheric temperature. Some of the atmospheric heat is transferred to the ocean and raises its temperature as well. As the atmosphere and ocean warm, the overall global temperature rises. As CO_2 and other gases trap the sun's heat in much the same way that glass does in a greenhouse, global warming produced in this manner is called the *greenhouse effect* (Figure 13.3).

Why are greenhouse gas concentrations increasing? Scientists generally believe that the combustion of fossil fuels and other human activities are the primary reason for the increased concentration of carbon dioxide. Plant respiration and the decomposition of organic

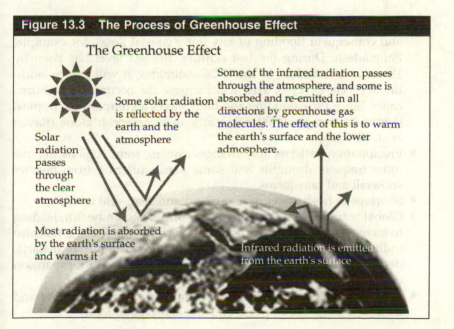

Figure 13.3   The Process of Greenhouse Effect

The Greenhouse Effect

Some solar radiation is reflected by the earth and the atmosphere

Solar radiation passes through the clear atmosphere

Some of the infrared radiation passes through the atmosphere, and some is absorbed and re-emitted in all directions by greenhouse gas molecules. The effect of this is to warm the earth's surface and the lower admosphere.

Most radiation is absorbed by the earth's surface and warms it

Infrared radiation is emitted from the earth's surface

matter release more than 10 times the CO_2 released by human activities; but these releases have generally been in balance during the centuries leading up to the Industrial Revolution with carbon dioxide absorbed by terrestrial vegetation and the oceans.

What has changed in the last few hundred years is the additional release of carbon dioxide by human activities. Fossil fuels burned to run cars and trucks, heat homes and businesses, and power factories are responsible for about 98 per cent of US carbon dioxide emissions, 24 per cent of methane emissions, and 18 per cent of nitrous oxide emissions. Increased agriculture, deforestation, landfills, industrial production and mining also contribute a significant share of emissions. In 1997, the United States emitted about one-fifth of total global greenhouse gases.

Estimating future emissions is difficult, because it depends on demographic, economic, technological, policy and institutional developments. Several emissions scenarios have been developed based on differing projections of these underlying factors. For example, by 2100, in the absence of emissions control policies, carbon dioxide concentrations are projected to be 30–150 per cent higher than today's levels.

13.3.2 Effects of Global Warming

Global warming has the following effects:

- Thawing of glaciers and polar ice caps leading to rise in sea level and consequent flooding of low lying coastal areas, for example, Bangladesh. During the last century, the sea level has risen by 18 cm and according to the IPCC estimates, it will rise by additional 50 cm by 2100. This will increase the occurrance of hurricanes. Since 1970, flooding and high waves accompanying tropical storms have caused 300,000 deaths in Bangladesh alone (Raven et al. 1995: 465).
- Precipitation patterns may change, causing some regions to have more frequent droughts and some areas suffering from heavier snowfall and rainstorms.
- Shortage of fresh water in many arid and semi-arid areas.
- Global warming will also adversely affect human health, leading to increase in heat-related diseases and deaths. Besides, it will also indirectly affect human health due to higher incidence of malaria, dengue, yellow fever and viral encephalitis caused by expansion of mosquitoes and other disease carriers to warm areas.
- Adverse effect on agricultural production due to droughts and increased incidence of pests, causing shortage of food.

Like acid rain, global warming is a complex international issue having several political, economic and social dimensions. Greenhouse gases are primarily produced by developed nations but developing countries may experience the greatest impact of global warming. This has led to tensions between the developed and developing nations.

13.3.3 Managing Global Warming

There are three ways of managing global warming, namely, prevention, mitigation and adaptation. Prevention can be accomplished by preventing the build-up of greenhouse gases in the atmosphere. For example, this could be done through development of alternatives to fossil fuels and levying taxes on greenhouse gases. Mitigation is moderation or postponement of global warming. It could be achieved through planting more trees to serve as carbon sinks. Adaptation is responding to changes brought about by global warming. This could be achieved through shifting agricultural zones or changes in crop-pattern.

13.4 OZONE DEPLETION

Within the stratosphere, a concentration of ozone molecules make up the ozone layer. Around 90 per cent of the ozone is within the ozone layer. There are several layers surrounding the earth's atmosphere. The layer that is around us is called the troposphere. A level higher is known as the stratosphere. Stratospheric ozone is a gas which occurs naturally. The ozone layer could be thought of as the earth's sun-glasses, protecting life on the surface from the harmful glare of the sun's strongest ultraviolet rays, which can cause skin cancer and other maladies. The stratospheric ozone layer filters ultraviolet (UV) radiation from the sun. As the ozone layer is depleted, more ultraviolet radiation reaches the earth's surface (Raven et al. 1995: 471–75).

13.4.1 Causes of Ozone Depletion

The ozone layer can be depleted by free radical catalysts, including nitric oxide (NO), hydroxyl (OH), atomic chlorine (Cl) and bromine (Br). While there are natural sources for all of these catalysts, the concentrations of chlorine and bromine have increased markedly in recent years due to the release of large quantities of man-made organohalogen compounds, especially chlorofluorocarbons (CFCs) and bromofluorocarbons. These highly stable compounds are capable of surviving the rise to the stratosphere, where Cl and Br radicals are liberated by the action of ultraviolet light. Each radical is then free to initiate and catalyse a chain reaction capable of breaking down over 10,000 ozone molecules. Ozone levels, over the northern hemisphere, have been dropping by 4 per cent per decade. Over approximately 5 per cent of the earth's surface, around the north and south poles, much larger (but seasonal) declines have been observed; these are the *ozone holes*.

There are reports of large ozone holes opening over Antarctica, allowing dangerous UV rays through to earth's surface. Indeed, the 2005 ozone hole was one of the biggest ever, spanning 24 million sq km in area, nearly the size of North America. While the ozone hole over Antarctica continues to open wide, the ozone layer around the rest of the planet seems to be on the mend (Source: http://www.sciencedaily. com/releases/2006/05/060527093645.htm).

13.4.2 Effects of Ozone Depletion

Over-exposure to UV rays may cause several health hazards for humans. Skin cancer is the most widely known. In addition, over-exposure to UV rays can also cause cataracts. Therefore, it is wise to protect yourself when you go out in the sun for extended periods of time. Always use sunscreen and check that you are using sunscreen with proper SPF rating. A good pair of sunglasses with 100 per cent UVA and UVB protection are also important to protect the eyes.

Since the ozone layer has depleted, protecting your health is the first priority. However, preventing ozone depletion is everyone's responsibility. The CFCs released in the past have caused ozone depletion. CFCs were mainly used as refrigerants. Avoid using products that contain CFCs when possible.

There is need for more research to learn more about the ozone layer and how you can protect yourself when enjoying the sun outside. Also, learn how you can help prevent further ozone depletion.

13.4.3 Regulation of Ozone Depletion[1]

People were understandably alarmed in the 1980s when scientists noticed that man-made chemicals in the atmosphere were destroying

---

[1](http://en.wikipedia.org/wiki/Ozone_layer).

this layer. Governments quickly enacted an international treaty, called the Montreal Protocol, to ban ozone-destroying gases such as CFCs then found in aerosol cans and air conditioners.

On 23 January 1978, Sweden became the first nation to ban CFC-containing aerosol sprays that are thought to damage the ozone layer. A few other countries, including the United States, Canada and Norway, followed suit later that year, but the European Community rejected an analogous proposal. Even in the US, chlorofluorocarbons continued to be used in other applications, such as refrigeration and industrial cleaning, until after the discovery of the antarctic ozone hole in 1985. After negotiation of an international treaty (the Montreal Protocol), CFC production was drastically cut down beginning in 1987 and phased out completely by 1996.

On 2 August 2003, scientists announced that the depletion of the ozone layer may be slowing down due to the international ban on the CFCs, and chemical compounds containing chlorine, fluorine and carbon. Three satellites and three ground stations confirmed that the upper atmosphere ozone depletion rate has slowed down significantly during the past decade. The study was organised by the American Geophysical Union. Some breakdown can be expected to continue due to CFCs used by nations which have not banned them, and due to gases which are already in the stratosphere. CFCs have very long atmospheric lifetimes, ranging from 50 to over 100 years, so the final recovery of the ozone layer is expected to require several lifetimes.

Compounds containing C-H bonds are being designed to replace the function of CFCs, since these compounds are more reactive and less likely to survive long enough in the atmosphere to reach the stratosphere where they could affect the ozone layer.

The following are the major international treaties and protocols designed to protect the ozone layer:

1. **The Vienna Convention on the Protection of the Ozone Layer**: This was signed in 1985. This treaty is the precursor to the Montreal Protocol.
2. **The Montreal Protocol on Substances that Deplete the Ozone Layer**: This was adopted on 16 September 1987 and has been amended four times as follows:
   - London Amendment (1990)
   - Copenhagen Amendment (1992)
   - Montreal Amendment (1997)
   - Beijing Amendment (1999)

This treaty is the basis on which Title VI of the Clean Air Act was established.

There are several international organisations engaged in actions aimed at protecting the ozone layer. A few of them are listed here (http://www.epa.gov/ozone/intpol/index.html).

UNEP Ozone Secretariat

The Ozone Secretariat coordinates implementation of, and meetings under, the Montreal Protocol.

OzonAction

UNEP TIE's OzonAction Programme provides the industry, government and other stakeholders in developing countries with information exchange services (including a Website), and training and networking of ODS Officers. In addition to these core clearinghouse services, the programme also provides assistance with Country Programmes and Institutional Strengthening projects. OzonAction also provides the Information Clearinghouse, a computer programme that contains several databases of contacts and technical information.

Technology and Economic Assessment Panel (TEAP)

The TEAP, organised under UNEP, is responsible for issuing regular reports on progress on implementing the programmes of phasing out of ozone-depleting substances, including assessments of alternatives and emissions reduction.

The United Nations Development Programme (UNDP)

The UNDP helps countries implement national programmes to phase out CFCs, halons and other ODS through: (a) national country programme formulation; (b) technical training and demonstration projects; (c) institutional strengthening/national capacity building; and (d) technology transfer investment projects.

World Bank

The World Bank coordinates the efforts of staff and local partners to help countries meet their obligations under the Montreal Protocol.

For the last 10 years or so, worldwide ozone has remained roughly constant, halting the decline first noticed in the 1980s. The question is why? Is the Montreal Protocol responsible? Or is some other process at work?

It is a complicated question. CFCs are not the only things that can influence the ozone layer; sunspots, volcanoes and the weather also play a role. Ultraviolet rays from sunspots boost the ozone layer, while sulfurous gases emitted by some volcanoes can weaken it. Cold air in the stratosphere can either weaken or boost the ozone layer, depending on altitude and latitude. Whatever the explanation, if the trend continues, the global ozone layer should be restored to 1980 levels sometime between 2030 and 2070. By then even the Antarctic ozone hole might close—for good (Source: http://www.sciencedaily.com/releases/2006/05/060527093645.htm).

13.5 CLIMATIC ABERRATIONS

There have been many climatic aberrations and natural catastrophes in the world in the last one century or so. As we stated in Section 13.3, the global mean surface temperatures have increased by about 1° F in the past century. The 20th century's 10 warmest years all occurred in the last 15 years of the century. Of these, 1998 was the warmest year on record. The snow cover in the Northern Hemisphere and floating ice in the Arctic Ocean have decreased. Globally, sea level has risen 4–8 inches over the past century. Worldwide precipitation over land has increased by about 1 per cent. The frequency of extreme rainfall events has also increased in many countries of the world. This has led to droughts in some parts of the world or even within the same country and floods in other parts over the same period of time. A few examples of extreme climatic aberrations in the last few years are presented in Box 13.1.

Box 13.1   A Few Examples of Recent Extreme Weather Patterns in the World

- The first monsoon rains between 25 June and 4 July 2005 claimed no fewer than 200 lives in the state of Gujarat. About 400,000 people had to be evacuated, and insured losses amounted to approximately US$ 50 m.
- On 26 and 27 July 2005, the heaviest rainfall ever recorded in India fell in the state of Maharashtra, including the financial and commercial centre, Mumbai. A precipitation depth of 944 mm

(Box 13.1 Contd.)

(Box 13.1 Contd.)

was recorded in just 24 hours—surpassing the previous record for one single day in India.

- In 2006, there were unprecedented floods in Barmer district of western Rajasthan, where the average annual rainfall is hardly 120 mm.
- Between October 2004 and June 2005, the total volume of precipitation in western France, Spain, Portugal and the United Kingdom was only half the long-term average. As a consequence, Spain and Portugal suffered their worst drought since the 1940s, resulting in many wildfires. And that only two years after the hot and dry summer of 2003.
- With an anomaly of +1.75° C in the first five months, 2005 was the hottest year in Australia since recordings began in 1910.
- There was hardly any rain in Brazil in 2005, leading to extreme dryness in the south (Rio Grande do Sul) and the Amazon region, producing the worst drought in the last 60 years.

Source: Annual Review: Natural Catastrophes 2005, Topics Geo, Knowledge Series, Munich Re Group, Germany (http://www.munichre.com).

Table 13.1 presents the type and number of natural catastrophes in the world by region and the losses caused by them for the year 2005. The total number of catastrophes was 243, total fatalities caused by them 91,364, and total losses of US\$ 172,200 million. This estimate is only for one year. More or less, losses of the same order occur almost every year. The situation is indeed alarming and calls for urgent global action to manage it.

Now some action is being taken by all countries at every level to reduce, to avoid and to better understand the risks associated with climate change. Many countries have prepared policies and programmes for mitigating the harmful effects of extreme climatic changes.

At the international level, the US Global Change Research Programme coordinates the world's most extensive research effort on climate change. In addition, the Environment Protection Agency (EPA) and other federal agencies are actively engaging the private sector, states and localities in partnerships based on a win-win philosophy aimed at addressing the challenge of global warming and at the same time, strengthening the economy.

At the global level, countries around the world have expressed a firm commitment to strengthening international responses to the risks

Table 13.1   Great Natural Catastrophes in the World, 2005

Region	Number	Loss event	Fatalities	Overall Losses US$ (in million)	Insured Losses US$ (in million)
India	30	Floods	1,150	5,000	770
USA	37	Hurricane Katrina	1,322	125,000	60,000
USA	41	Hurricane Rita	10	16,000	11,000
Middle America	44	Hurricane Stan	840	3,000	100
Pakistan, India	45	Earthquake	88,000	5,200	NA
Mexico, USA, Caribbean	46	Fatalities	42	18,000	10,500
All	243	–	91,364	172,200	82,370

Source: Annual Review: Natural Catastrophes 2005, Topics Geo, Knowledge Series, Munich Re Group, Germany (http://www.munichre.com).

of climate change. The US is working to strengthen international action and broaden participation under the auspices of the United Nations Framework Convention on Climate Change (Source: http://yosemite. epa.gov/oar/globalwarming.nsf/content/actions.html).

In India, natural disasters have been a bane of the economy since time immemorial. In ancient Indian literature, there are references to natural disasters such as prolonged droughts, flash floods, hailstorms, landslides, cyclones and forest fires. About 60 per cent of the landmass in India is vulnerable to earthquakes; over 40 million hectares (ha) is prone to floods;[2] about 8 per cent of the total area is prone to cyclones; and about 68 per cent of the total area is susceptible to droughts. The 8,000 km long coastline is prone to severe cyclonic formations. About 55 per cent of the total area lies in Seismic Zones III–V and is vulnerable to earthquakes. Sub-Himalayan regions and Western Ghats are vulnerable to landslides (GoI 2004a: 32; Kanwar 2001: 7). In Chapter 9, Section 9.3.7, we have briefly discussed the problems of droughts and floods in India and their effects. Here we present in Box 13.2, a case of floods in India's commercial capital, that is, Mumbai.

[2]India is one of the most flood prone countries in the world and accounts for one fifth of the global death count due to floods. Over 30 million people are displaced annually due to the floods.

Box 13.2   Flood in Mumbai in 2005

The precipitation pattern in India is primarily governed by the monsoons. The southwest or summer monsoon that blows inland from the sea between June and October brings copious rainfall to most parts of the country. The largest volumes of rain are recorded on the west coast, in the Western Ghats, on the slopes of the Himalayas, and in Northeast India (Cherrapunji: 11,000 mm/year). On 26 and 27 July, the heaviest rainfall ever recorded in India fell in the state of Maharashtra, including the financial and commercial centre, Mumbai. A precipitation depth of 944 mm was recorded in just 24 hours—surpassing the previous record for one single day in India (Cherrapunji, 1910). About 94 per cent of this amount (885 mm) fell in just 12 hours (between 11.30 a.m. and 11.30 p.m. on 26 July). The downpour was accompanied by heavy thunderstorms and storm gusts. The meteorological reasons for this particularly extreme event are still uncertain. The entire system had an expanse of only 20–30 km, but radar measurements put the height of the cloud towers at 15 km.

The torrential rain swamped many districts of the city up to a depth of 3 m. Schools, banks, the stock exchange, and the airport had to be closed. Traffic came to a standstill and suburban and long-distance rail links were cut. Over 150,000 people were stranded in railway stations. The situation was particularly critical in the area around Bhiwandi in the northeast of the city, where large warehouses were badly damaged. Bhiwandi is an important terminal for goods and cargo intended for Mumbai and the western Indian states.

The situation deteriorated east of Mumbai when the upriver dams were opened, causing the river to rise by about 2 m within the space of an hour. Conditions in the slums, where about 30 per cent of the city's population live, were catastrophic. Countless huts were so flimsy that they collapsed, and the occupants lost all their worldly possessions. The immense volumes of rain triggered scores of landslides. Many people were electrocuted, buried under collapsing walls or drowned in flooded vehicles. The death toll in Maharashtra was about 1,100. Hundreds of cases of gastrointestinal diseases like cholera and dysentery were registered because the water was contaminated. With the warehouses in Bhiwandi damaged, there were inadequate supplies of medication for the people.

Source: Adapted from Annual Review: Natural Catastrophes 2005, Topics Geo, Knowledge Series, Munich Re Group, Germany (http://www.munichre.com).

According to an estimate made by the Ahmedabad-based Disaster Management Institute (DMI), India has suffered direct disaster losses of US\$ 30 billion over the last 35 years, that is, almost US\$ 1 billion a year. On average, almost 2 per cent of India's GDP is lost in disasters every year. A disaster like the Gujarat Earthquake of 2001 or Orissa Super Cyclone of 1999 can slow down the growth rate to up to 2 per cent in the year immediately following the disaster. In droughts, due to the lack of water for irrigation, crops in the field perish, resulting in the fall of crop production and consequent loss of income to farmers. For example, in Gujarat, an estimated loss of agricultural production worth Rs 40,000 million during the drought of 2000 was reported (IRMA–UNICEF 2000: 5). There is a large scale destabilisation of economy because of the loss of agricultural production and incomes, resulting in the overall fall in other rural economic activities allied to agriculture. The plight of daily wage labourers becomes distressing. According to an estimate made by the DMI based on micro-studies, up to 10 per cent of the rural poor suffer the loss of work and employment or assets due to disasters every year in India.

In the post-Independence era, until recently, natural disaster management was considered a post-disaster activity, focusing mainly on rescue, relief and rehabilitation. In the recent past, there has been a paradigmatic shift in India's approach to disaster management. The new approach is multisectoral, multidisciplinary, holistic and proactive, and disaster management is now sought to be built into the development planning process itself. As it is the poor and underprivileged, who are most vulnerable to disasters, and hence are worst affected by them, the strategy is pro-poor. This new approach has been incorporated into a National Disaster Framework, or a Road Map, prepared by the Natural Disaster Management Division of the Ministry of Home Affairs (GoI 2004a). However, despite its importance, the subject of disaster management does not find any mention in any of the three lists included in the 7th Schedule of the Constitution of India, nor is there a law to provide an appropriate legal framework for disaster management.

13.6 MAIN POINTS

- There have been perceptible changes in the climate all over the world, particularly in the last two decades or so. The major changes include acid rains, global warming, depletion of ozone layer and increased incidence of drought, floods, cyclones and hailstorms.
- Acid rain is one of the most dangerous and widespread forms of pollution. It can be carried over long distances by atmospheric

winds so much so that one country can export acid emissions to another. The acidity of rain in parts of Europe and North America has dramatically increased over the past few decades. It has harmful effects on plants, fish and other forms of aquatic life.

• Acid rain is a big problem, but it is not uncontrollable. The environment can generally adapt to a certain amount of acid rain due to soils which are slightly basic. However, in areas where limestone does not naturally occur in the soil, acid rain can harm the environment. If the amount of sulfur dioxides and nitrogen oxides in the air is reduced, then acid rain will be reduced. To do this, we should use less electricity; more carpools and public transportation, or walk when we can.

• Global warming is indicated by an increase in the mean global temperature. There has been a marked increase in the mean global temperature in the last two decades or so. Increasing concentrations of greenhouse gases are likely to accelerate the rate of global warming. Scientists expect that the average global surface temperature could rise 0.6–2.5° C in the next 50 years, and 1.4–5.8° C in the next century, with significant regional variation.

• There is new and stronger evidence that most of the global warming over the last 50 years is attributable to human activities. Human activities have altered the chemical composition of the atmosphere through the build-up of greenhouse gases.

• Global warming adversely affects human health, leading to an increase in heat-related diseases and deaths. Besides, it also has an adverse effect on agricultural production due to droughts and increased incidence of pests, causing shortage of food.

• Like acid rain, global warming is a complex international issue with several political, economic and social dimensions. Greenhouse gases are primarily produced by developed nations but developing countries may experience the greatest impact of global warming. This has led to tensions between the developed and developing nations.

• Stratospheric ozone is a gas which occurs naturally. The ozone layer could be thought of as the earth's sunglasses, protecting life on the surface from the harmful glare of the sun's strongest ultraviolet rays, which can cause skin cancer and other maladies. The stratospheric ozone layer filters ultraviolet radiation from the sun. As the ozone layer is depleted, more ultraviolet radiation reaches the earth's surface.

• The ozone layer can be depleted by free radical catalysts, including nitric oxide (NO), hydroxyl (OH), atomic chlorine (Cl) and

bromine (Br). While there are natural sources for all of these catalysts, the concentrations of chlorine and bromine have increased
markedly in recent years due to the release of large quantities of
man-made organohalogen compounds, especially chlorofluorocarbons (CFCs) and bromofluorocarbons.

- Over-exposure to ultraviolet rays may cause several health hazards for humans including skin cancer and cataracts.
- Now governments all over the world are concerned over the
increase in man-made chemicals in the atmosphere which are
destroying the ozone. There is an international treaty, called the
Montreal Protocol 1987, to ban ozone-destroying gases such as
CFCs. Besides, several other international organisations are also
making special efforts to protect the ozone layer.
- There have been many climatic aberrations and natural catastrophes in the world in the last one century or so. The global mean
surface temperatures have increased by about 1° F in the past century. The snow cover in the Northern Hemisphere and floating ice
in the Arctic Ocean have decreased. Globally, sea level has risen
4–8 inches over the past century. Worldwide precipitation over
land has increased by about 1 per cent. The frequency of extreme
rainfall events has also increased in many countries of world.
This has led to droughts in some parts of the world or even
within the same country and floods in other parts over the same
period of time.

13.7 DISCUSSION QUESTIONS

1. The greenhouse gas concentrations have been increasing, leading to global warming. In 1997, the United States emitted about
one-fifth of total global greenhouse gases. However, the harmful
effects of global warming are not confined to US or the other
developed countries responsible for much of the global warming.
What policy instruments could be used to persuade the US and
other developed countries to compensate other countries who
suffer from the global warming caused by them?

2. Fossil fuels burned to run cars and trucks, heat homes and businesses, and power factories are responsible for most of the carbon
dioxide emissions. Increased agriculture, deforestation, landfills,
industrial production and mining also contribute to a significant
share of the emissions. One simple solution to the problem is to
reduce the number of cars and trucks. But in India, the number of

motor vehicles has been increasing at an enormous rate. Discuss how this trend could be reversed.

3. Talk to some knowledgeable and elderly people in your area and find out their perception about the change in the climate over their life time. Prepare a note based on your findings and support with empirical data wherever possible.

4. Do the problems of global warming, acid rain and depletion of the ozone layer pose immediate problems for India? Yes/No, and why or why not?

5. Critically examine the National Environment Policy 2006 with reference to its provisions for controlling global warming and depletion of ozone layer and prepare a short note suggesting what additional provisions it should make.

14 An Ideal Environment Management Policy

14.1 INTRODUCTION

The term 'policy' may be defined as a definite course of action selected by a government, an institution, a group or an individual, from among alternatives and in light of given conditions to guide and usually to determine present and future courses of action. The most common social and political usage of the term 'policy' refers to a course of action or intended course of action conceived of as deliberately adopted after a review of possible alternatives and pursued or oriented to be pursued. The policy process is the formulation, promulgation and application of these courses of action. Here, we will concern ourselves with public environment policy, by which we mean the actions taken by the government in pursuit of certain objectives of improving the quality of environment and its conservation.

It is important to distinguish at the outset between (i) policy, (ii) programme, and (iii) project. Policy is a comprehensive term and connotes, as mentioned earlier, a set of intended actions. It subsumes programmes which are narrower in scope than policy but more specific with regard to what is to be done, how, by whom and where. A policy has to be translated into a number of programmes before it can be implemented. A project is highly specific and detailed in terms of its objectives, location, duration, funds and executing agency and lends itself to planning, financing and implementation as a unit. A programme may consist of several projects (Singh 1999a: 113). An environmental project may be defined as an investment activity where resources are expended to protect, improve and conserve the environment with a view to realise environmental benefits over an extended period of time.

It is increasingly evident that poor environmental quality has adversely affected human health. Environmental factors are estimated as being responsible in some cases for nearly 20 per cent of the burden of diseases in India and a number of environment-health factors are closely linked with dimensions of poverty (for example, malnutrition, lack of access to clean energy and water). It has been established that interventions targeted at environment management—for example, reducing indoor air pollution, protecting sources of safe drinking water, sanitation measures, improved public health governance—offer tremendous opportunities in reducing the incidence of a number of critical health problems. It is also evident that these environment protection measures would be difficult to implement without extensive awareness-raising and education (MoEF 2006).

Given the above-stated importance of the environment, it is but necessary that it should be managed professionally. As we all depend on the environment for our survival and growth, it is in our collective interest to protect, conserve and improve its quality. However, individually, we are helpless to protect and improve the environment and hence there is need for government intervention or a public policy to manage the environment in the interest of society at large.

In this chapter, we first attempt to present the basic elements of an ideal policy for environment management, drawing upon various ideas, economic theories, analytical conclusions and real world experiences presented in this book. Finally, we present a critique of India's National Environment Policy 2006, in the light of basic elements of an ideal policy. The main objective of the chapter is to enhance the ability and skills of students to synthesise various ideas, theories and real world experiences into a coherent policy framework.

14.2 NEED FOR AN ENVIRONMENT POLICY

The farther we move away from a largely rural population engaged in simple, small scale handicraft industry and self-contained and subsistence agriculture towards complex, modern, large scale capital intensive industries, commercialised agriculture and a large proportion of urban population, a greater need develops for public policy in the economic field and as also to protect the environment from various negative externalities generated in the process of economic growth. The individual, as a producer and as a consumer, depends more and more upon the general conditions of the market: this affects and is affected by the actions of other individuals.

Environmental degradation can occur where there is too little of economic development as well as where there is too much of it. Under the condition of too little of economic development, poverty and population pressure often combine to force people to overexploit and degrade the natural resources and the environment to eke out subsistence living. On the other hand, too much of economic development, characterised by growing urbanisation, industrialisation and proliferation of infrastructure development projects, can also lead to the problem of over-crowding, congestion, air, water and land pollution and increased incidence of diseases. In both the cases, the solution lies in a well-designed national environment policy that seeks, *inter alia*, well-planned, balanced and sustainable development.

Some specific reasons favouring government intervention in the field of environment are discussed below.

14.2.1 Increasing Population of Human Beings and Animals

India's total human population increased from 299 million in 1951 to 1,027 million in 2001, registering more than a three-fold increase over the 50-year period. India accounts for about 16 per cent of the world's population but for only about 2.4 per cent of the total geographical area of the world. Similarly, the country has a very large animal population. It ranks first in the world in terms of population of cattle and buffaloes. According to the Livestock Census 2002–03, the country had 185 million cattle, 98 million buffaloes, 61.5 million sheep, 124 million goats, 14 million pigs and 489 million poultry birds (GoI 1998: 318). Both, the human and livestock population, exert high pressure on the country's natural resources, particularly land and water resources, and degrade the environment.[1]

---

[1] Raising of livestock requires land for producing feed and fodder, water for drinking and washing purposes, and air for breathing. Livestock raising and processing livestock products generate wastes in the form of solids, liquids and gases. All these wastes are either dumped on land or released into water-bodies or emitted into airsheds, which are all parts of our environment. Perhaps the greatest environmental threat that livestock poses arises from peri-urban livestock enterprises located in close proximity to urban areas (ILRI 2000).

As we know, Planet Earth and every individual nation state has a finite carrying capacity in terms of its ability to support the population of human beings, animals and other living organisms. More specifically, the input provisioning and waste assimilation capacity of our environment is limited. There is evidence to prove that in many areas in India, this capacity has been exhausted due to increasing population of human beings and animals and there are signs of unduly high stress on the environment there. In view of this, there is need to regulate the population of both human beings and livestock so as to minimise their pressure and harmful effects on the environment.

14.2.2 Growing Chemicalisation of Agriculture

Driven by the need to increase agricultural production at a faster rate to meet India's growing requirement for food and raw materials, there has been a growing chemicalisation of India's agriculture, particularly after the Green Revolution which was ushered in the mid-1960s. This is reflected in the increased use of chemical fertilisers and pesticides. For example, the total fertiliser consumption in India in terms of NPK nutrients increased from 2.18 million tonnes in 1970–71 to about 18.4 million tonnes in 2004–05. Food grains production also increased from 124.32 million tonnes to about 204.6 million tonnes over the same period of time. Similarly, the consumption of pesticides also registered significant increase over this period of time. The increased use of chemical fertilisers and pesticides has led, albeit unintentionally, to pollution of water-bodies and land degradation in many areas. There is need to regulate their use and replace them by eco-friendly bio-fertilisers and bio-pesticides over a period of time through a deliberate policy.

14.2.3 Growing Urbanisation and Industrialisation

India's urban population has been growing at a very rapid rate for the last two decades or so. In 1981, its share in the total population was about 20 per cent but increased to 23 per cent in 1991 and further to 28 per cent in 2001. This is due largely to the increased migration of poor people to urban areas in search of jobs. Chopra and Gulati (2001: 65), in a study conducted in India's arid and semi-arid regions, found that out-migration was largely due to the push factors operative at the place of origin such as environmental degradation process and shrinkage of CPRs. The urban public services, particularly waste disposal, sanitation and supply of drinking water, have not increased commensurate with the increase in urban population. Consequently, there are environmental problems of congestion, air pollution, water pollution and encroachment and pollution of common public lands.

In urban areas the most potent cause of air pollution is the growing number of two wheelers, cars, jeeps, buses and trucks. As of 31 March 2003, there were over 64 million vehicles in the country; with the highest number per lakh of population being in Punjab (12,527), followed by Gujarat (11,599) (TSL 2005: 137–38). Taking note of the recent reports on health hazards posed by vehicular pollution in New Delhi, the Supreme Court of India gave directions to address the problem. On 18 November 1996, the court directed the Secretary-cum-Transport Commissioner of the Delhi Government to notify various unions of motor vehicles, including three-wheelers and taxis, to submit proposals by 28 November to check air pollution. Earlier, the court suggested various means like suspension of licences, scrapping licences of vehicles more than seven years old, no renewal of licences of three-wheelers and keeping one-third of the existing vehicles off the roads (*Down to Earth*, November 1996).

Like urbanisation, there has also been rapid growth of industrialisation in India over the last two decades or so. This has also caused problems of air and water pollution and land degradation. In many industrial belts, the quality of air has deteriorated markedly and groundwater and surface water has become unfit for human consumption due to discharge of toxic wastes into water-bodies. There is need to regulate the location of industries and the technologies used so as to minimise the extent of pollution caused by them.

14.2.4 Unregulated International Trade in Agricultural Commodities

In the wake of the new world trade regime ushered in by the World Trade Organization (WTO) in 1995, international trade is intended to be liberalised and freed from various kinds of regulations. India, being a member of WTO, is bound to abide by the new rules of the international trade. International trade in agricultural commodities affects the environment directly and indirectly. By inducing export demand, it provides incentives to producers through increased prices to increase their production. Producers normally respond by using chemical fertilisers, pesticides and irrigation water at higher rates to increase their production. This degrades the quality of our natural resources and environment. It is a bit too early to assess the impact of liberalised international trade in agricultural commodities on environment in

India. However, the evidence available to us proves that the export-led increase in the catch of fish and in rice production have both had an adverse effect on the environment.[2]

The increase in rice production, especially fine variety rice such as *basmati*, in response to the export-promoting measures taken by the government has led to the problems of waterlogging and soil salinity in many areas in Punjab, Haryana and Western Uttar Pradesh, which produce fine variety rice for export. In view of this, there is need for government action to regulate international trade in those agricultural commodities whose production leads to environmental degradation, directly or indirectly (Singh 1994c: 89–102).

Besides, international economic relationships also pose a particular problem for poor countries trying to manage their environment, since the export of natural resources constitutes a large part of their economies, especially those of developing nations. The processing of certain raw materials—pulp and paper, oil and alumina, for example, can have substantial environmental side-effects. Industrial countries have generally been more successful than developing ones in seeing to it that export product prices reflect the cost of environmental damage and of controlling that damage. Thus, in the case of exports from industrial countries, these costs are paid by consumers in importing nations, including those in developing countries. However, in the case of exports from developing countries, such costs continue to be borne entirely domestically, largely in the form of damage costs to human health, property and ecosystems.

14.2.5 High Discount Rates and Myopic Planning Horizon

Natural resources, environment conservation and sustainable development ultimately involve a sacrifice of present consumption for the promise of future benefits. Because of time preference of people in developing countries like India, such an exchange appears unattractive unless one rupee of sacrifice today yields more than one rupee of benefits tomorrow. Future benefits are discounted, and the more heavily they are discounted, the less attractive they are. A high rate of discount may discourage conservation altogether.

Environmental and market uncertainties, coupled with a short and uncertain life-span, lead people to adopt myopic time horizons and discount rates which result in short-sighted decisions in pursuit of survival or quick profits at the expense of long-term sustainable benefits.

---

[2]For the effect of export of fish on the environment, see Chapter 11, Section 11.5 of this book.

At subsistence levels of living, when people's very survival is at stake, a 'hand-to-mouth' economy prevails in which exploitation of natural resources and under-investment in their conservation and regeneration ultimately leads to their depletion. The high cost of rural credit from informal sources, in the absence of institutional credit, also leads to high rates of discount. Conservation projects that would have been profitable at 10 per cent or 15 per cent interest rates are not profitable at 50 per cent or even 100 per cent rates charged by informal credit sources. Again, there is scope for government intervention to induce longer time horizons and lower discount rates (through increased savings), to regulate resource extraction and to invest in the conservation and regeneration of resources according to the society's true time preference. Society, because of its continuity and risk pooling capacity, tends to be less myopic than individual members.

14.2.6 Uncertainty and Risk Aversion

Environment conservation and management is about the future, a future which is beset with uncertainties and risks. A situation is said to involve uncertainty if more than one outcome is (or is perceived to be) possible from any given action and no objective probability can be assigned to any of the possible outcomes. Two types of uncertainty may be distinguished: (a) environmental uncertainty arising from factors beyond the decision-maker's control, for example, weather, epidemic diseases and technological discoveries; and (b) market uncertainty arising from a market failure to provide information (prices) required for decisions affecting the future (absence of future markets). The longer the time horizon, the further into the future forecasts need to be made and the greater the uncertainties involved. While uncertainty affects all sectors of the economy, natural resource sectors are more seriously affected for a variety of reasons. Some of the reasons are uncertainty about the ownership and access to natural resources, higher potential negative externalities from other activities, longer gestation periods and more violent fluctuations in their prices than those of other commodities and constant threat of substitution from cheaper substitutes, developed by continuous but unpredictable technological change.

In contrast to uncertainty, risk is a situation where the general level of probability of each outcome can be inferred, although known probabilities cannot be precisely assigned. In everyday use, a situation is said to be risky if one of the outcomes involves losses to the decision-maker. Thus, the risk of loss to a firm or a farm may be defined as the probability that profits will be less than zero or the probability that returns will fall below some 'disaster level' of income. Risks may be reduced through diversification of activities with negatively correlated outcomes. Risks in one activity may also be reduced by pooling them with risks from other independent activities. Where risks are of a given type (for example, independent of the actions of the decision-maker), risk-pooling or insurance markets have often emerged to exploit these possibilities. Individuals transfer their risks to an insurance company by paying an insurance premium which, in a perfect insurance market, would equal the administrative costs of the company plus the cost of any remaining risk.

However, not all risks are insurable. Insurance markets fail to appear when the outcome is not external to the policyholder, the risk affects all policyholders in a similar way or the probabilities of the various outcomes are difficult to assess. For example, a farm cannot insure itself against the risk of losses whose profitability is as much a function of the farmer's actions as it is of environmental uncertainty (like weather). Similarly, a poultry farm cannot insure itself against the risk of an epidemic such as bird flu because such risk would affect all poultry farms in a similar way, reducing the benefits from risk-pooling. In such cases, government intervention is needed to insure farmers against such risk or compensate them for the losses suffered by them.

Risks may be objective or subjective. Objective risks are calculated on the basis of the probability of occurrence of the adverse outcome. Attitudes towards risk differ among individuals based on sociocultural and economic factors. In general, risk aversion tends to be stronger among poor people because their survival is at stake.

14.2.7 Irreversibility

Market decisions about the future (such as, consumption vs. investment) are made with the best available, yet incomplete information about future developments, on the assumption that such decisions can be reversed if they prove to be unwise in the light of new information. This assumption of irreversibility does not hold in many decisions involving natural resources. Consider the choice between preserving a tropical rainforest with some unique features and clear-felling it for logging and mining. If the social benefits from logging and mining development exceed the social benefits from conservation even marginally, we should choose logging and mining, except for the fact that logging and mining can be irreversible, while conservation is not. Choosing logging and mining forecloses our options, if we or future generations were to have a change of mind there would be no way to reproduce the uniqueness and authenticity of the original species that became extinct. In contrast, choosing conservation preserves our option to reverse our decision. Clearly, there is a social value or shadow price for the preservation of options (option value), though it is difficult to estimate. However, there are reasons to favour 'high' value. On the one hand, technical change is asymmetric: it expands our ability to produce ordinary goods, the products of development, but does little to improve our ability to produce natural environments, the products of conservation. On the other hand, consumer preference tends to shift in favour of environmental services relative to ordinary goods. In conclusion, we could say that if certain economic decisions have an impact on the natural environment that is both uncertain and irreversible, there is a value to retaining an option to avoid the impact.

14.2.8 High Vulnerability to Natural Disasters

Natural resources and the environment are highly vulnerable to natural disasters such as prolonged droughts, flash floods, hailstorms, landslides, cyclones and forest fires. More specifically, about 60 per cent of the landmass in India is vulnerable to earthquakes; over 40 million hectares (ha) is prone to floods; about 8 per cent of the total area is prone to cyclones; and about 68 per cent of the total area is susceptible to droughts. The 8,000 km long coastline is prone to severe cyclonic formations. About 55 per cent of the total area lies in Seismic Zones III-V and is vulnerable to earthquakes. Sub-Himalayan regions and the Western Ghats are vulnerable to landslides (GoI, 2004: 32; Kanwar 2001: 7). Given the high vulnerability of the environment to natural disasters and its open access nature, there is need for a public policy to protect and conserve the environment.

14.3 THE VISION, GOALS AND OBJECTIVES OF ENVIRONMENT POLICY

The first logical step in the process of formulation of an environmental policy is to evolve a shared vision of a desirable 'managed' state of the environment in future, say, by the year 2015. A vision is necessary to serve as a guidepost for planning and implementation. Planning without a vision is like shooting without an aim. A vision has an element of a dream but it is not wishful thinking. It requires looking into the future objectively, based on the past experience and future perspective.

To be actualised, a vision has to be translated into goals and objectives, which could serve as guideposts for action required for realising the goals and objectives of the policy.

14.3.1 An Environmental Vision for India

Based on the India's current state of the environment, it seems realistic to construct 'India Environmental Vision 2015' as follows: 'In the year 2015, every person living in India is aware of the critical importance of the environment for survival of all living beings and for sustainable development of the country, and of the need for its protection, conservation, improvement and judicious management at the household, firm, industry and other higher levels. Everybody's basic needs for clean air, safe water and environmental services are fully met at affordable cost and nobody suffers from environmental pollution-induced diseases. People at the local level fully participate in and contribute to judicious management of the environment through appropriate organisational/institutional structures, customs, traditions and locally evolved and self-enforced norms. In a nutshell, everybody is environmentally secured on a sustainable basis'.

14.3.2 The Goals

The goals of public policies are determined by what people desire and the measures of policies by what people think the government can and ought to do to bring about the desired change. This is the theory of public policy. Changes are desired only when people do not like the way things are going. Pressure for public action arises when people feel that they, individually, cannot bring about the desired adjustments. They have in mind some 'norm', some image of an ideal situation towards which they strive. These norms become the goals of policy towards which objectives of specific programmes or projects are directed. In our opinion, the main goal of an environment policy should be to improve the overall quality of life in the country on a sustainable basis through restoration, protection, conservation, improvement and judicious utilisation and management of the environment.

More specifically, an ideal environment policy should have the following major goals (Singh 1994a: 313–14):

1. *Survival of Human and other Life Systems*: First and foremost, an ideal environment policy should have survival of human and

other life systems in perpetuity as its primary goal. No other goals or concerns could be superior to this basic tenet in any region, culture and time period.

2. *Sustainability and Efficiency*: Second, to achieve the first goal of survival of human and other life systems, it will be necessary to restore, enhance, conserve and utilise all natural resources including the environment sustainably and efficiently. By 'sustainable' we mean using the resources in such a way that the natural resource base of production of the basic necessities of life can produce socially optimum quantities of various commodities in perpetuity with no irreversible damages to the physical environment and without the imposition of significantly greater risks on future generations. To the extent sustainability subsumes socially optimum rate of resource use in perpetuity, it also satisfies the goal of economic efficiency. However, maximisation of economic efficiency in the short run may conflict with the goal of sustainability, but the latter is superior to the former as a goal of environment policy.

3. *Intergenerational Equity*: Third, an environment policy should provide for equitable distribution of benefits and equitable sharing of costs of environmental development projects among all of its present and future stakeholders. Many environmental development projects have failed in the past because they ignored equity considerations in their design and implementation and did not legitimise the local users' rights. Availability of benefits and their equitable distribution should be guaranteed through appropriate legal provisions. Similarly, cost-sharing arrangements should also be legitimised to reduce or eliminate the problems of free-riding and shirking by the users.

4. *Nationalistic Stance*: Last, but not the least, a pragmatic environment policy in the contemporary context must have a nationalistic stance, that is, it should attach higher weight to national concerns and priorities than international ones. This is so because the possibilities of international determination and coordination of resource use and management policies, or for that matter, any policies seem remote at present. However, this does not mean that a nationalistic stance or perspective excludes any considerations of the rest of the world. Growing international interdependence through trade, investment, technology transfers, cultural and educational exchange programmes, and open access natural resources must be recognised and given due weightage in determining national policies.

The present day consensus about the goals of an ideal environment policy reflects three foundational aspirations of people. First, human beings should be able to enjoy a decent quality of life. Second, that humanity should become capable of respecting the finiteness of the biosphere. Third, that neither the aspiration for the good life, nor the recognition of biophysical limits should preclude the search for greater justice in the world (GoI 2006).

All these goals seem to us to be appropriate for an ideal environment management policy.[3] They should be used for evaluating the performance of environmental programmes and projects. The goal of survival of all living beings on this earth is a universal goal of common concern to mankind and, therefore, deserves the highest priority. The efficiency criterion can help ensure that the present systems of use and management of environmental goods and services are most efficient and that any proposed change in the existing use and management system is not likely to make a few or most of the stakeholders better off without making any one worse off. The sustainability criterion makes sure that the existing or enhanced flow of benefits from the environment can be maintained for ever, that is, production of goods and services/amenities does not lead to degradation and depletion of natural resources, including the environment. The equity criterion makes sure that each member of the group contributes his fair share to the maintenance/management of the environment and gets returns/rewards commensurate with his contribution.

In view of the above, all these goals seem to be worthwhile and therefore deserve serious pursuit by policy makers. However, to be of any use to society, these goals should be translated into concrete objectives, which in turn, should be translated into specific programmes and projects that are manageable under the existing conditions. Many environmental problems are complex and require combinations of various sets of means or instruments and are limited by various political, legal and socioeconomic conditions. To resolve such problems, we must design several programmes or projects. For each programme, a clearly defined objective may be designated which a particular government agency should pursue. The programme measures can then be identified and appraised as to whether they are appropriate and efficient in serving the objective and adapted to the conditions outside the influence of that particular programme. These conditions are often the decisive factors determining whether or not a certain programme is 'administratively' feasible.

---

[3]India's National Environment Policy 2006 also lists some of these goals but under the heading 'Objectives' (NEP 2006).

14.3.3 The Objectives

The objectives of the National Environment Policy 2006 (MoEF 2006: 8) are as follows:

1. *Conservation of Critical Environmental Resources*: To protect and conserve critical ecological systems and resources and invaluable natural and man-made heritage which are essential for life-support, livelihoods, economic growth and a broad conception of human well-being.

2. *Intragenerational Equity or Livelihood Security for the Poor*: To ensure equitable access to environmental resources and quality for all sections of society and in particular, to ensure that poor communities, which are most dependent on environmental resources for their livelihoods, are assured secure access to these resources.

3. *Intergenerational Equity*: To ensure judicious use of environmental resources to meet the needs and aspirations of present and future generations.

4. *Integration of Environmental Concerns in Economic and Social Development*: To integrate environmental concerns into policies, plans, programmes and projects for economic and social development.

5. *Efficiency in Environmental Resource Use*: To ensure efficient use of environmental resources in the sense of reduction in their use per unit of economic output to minimise adverse environmental impacts.

6. *Environmental Governance*: To apply the principles of good governance (transparency, rationality, accountability, reduction in time and costs, and participation) to the management and regulation of use of environmental resources.

7. *Enhancement of Resources for Environmental Conservation*: To ensure higher resource flows, comprising finance, technology, management skills, traditional knowledge, and social capital, for environment conservation through mutually beneficial multi-stakeholder partnerships between local communities, public agencies and investors.

These objectives are all worthwhile but strictly speaking, they are not worded in operational terms. They seem to be an amalgam of goals and objectives.

14.4 MANAGEMENT SYSTEMS FOR ENVIRONMENT POLICY

A pragmatic environment policy should specify a particular organisation structure and a management system or a combination of management systems appropriate for fulfilling its goals. The management system subsumes implementation and monitoring functions also. *A priori*, any one or a combination of centralised public management and collective/cooperative management could be used to achieve the goals of environment policy. In practice, both the systems coexist in most situations and there is no single best system of management that will work successfully in all situations and at all times. The choice of a system will depend on the particular setting in question and often requires an interdisciplinary approach, use of traditional knowledge and modern scientific knowledge and consultation with local people and government functionaries. Based on a survey of literature, the following general guidelines/principles are laid down to help determine an appropriate management system. The guidelines are organised under two heads, namely, centralised public management and decentralised collective management (Singh 1994a: 314–18).

14.4.1 Centralised Public Management

Under centralised public management or nationalisation, the central government fully owns and manages the environmental conservation programmes directly through the Ministry of Environment and Forests (MoEF). The underlying rationale of nationalisation is that a national government can better serve the interest of people at large, can raise investment funds more easily and has a longer planning horizon and hence, a lower discount rate than individuals. The experience with nationalisation of common pool and open access natural resources has been mixed; there have been failures as well successes. However, nationalisation seems to be an appropriate system given the strategic importance of the natural resources and environment to India (ibid. 58–63).

14.4.2 Decentralised Collective Management

An increasing number of scholars now advocate that decentralised collective management of natural resources, including environment conservation by their co-users, is the most appropriate system. Cases of success in collective management of common natural resources by their co-users abound in the literature on management of natural resources. Collective management is likely to succeed under the following conditions (Singh 1994a: 63–70):

1. If the community of users of common pool natural resources in an ecosystem is small, well-defined, homogeneous, self-conscious, self-governing with political and economic independence to manage the ecosystem as it sees fit, and organised formally into some association which is headed by an enlightened leader.

2. Access to and use of the resources of the ecosystem are both regulated by a set of rules that are compatible with the technical and physical characteristics of the resource and the local setting and that are mutually accepted, enforced and monitored by the resource users themselves rather than an external superordinate authority.

3. Rules for equitable sharing of benefits and costs are incorporated in the bye-laws of the resource users' association, have a legal back-up, are easy to understand and enforce, and are enforced and monitored by the CPR users themselves.

4. There exists a system of sanctions against violation of rules and free-riding or shirking that is mutually accepted by all the users of environment and is enforced by them voluntarily.

5. The government is willing and able to help the resource users with needed funds, technical information, training, provision of basic infrastructure, including marketing and processing facilities and facilitating legal and political environment.

6. Last, but not the least, expected private benefits to each individual resource user from collective management not only markedly exceed the expected private costs of his participation in the collective management, but are also assured by an honest and benevolent local leader or an external authority having high credibility among the environment users.

An ideal environment policy should provide for effective implementation and regular monitoring of various project activities and establishment of a computerised management information system for the purpose. Some general guidelines for environmental project implementation and monitoring are given below. The guidelines are based on a survey of the literature available on the subject.

1. Prepare a plan for project implementation which should, at the minimum, specify what is to be done, who is to do it, when and where it is to be done and how it is to be done.

2. Provide for the maintenance of a continuing dialogue between environment policy makers and analysts, and for communication and flow of information both ways, from policy makers to analysts and back to policy makers.

3. Involve all major stakeholders in implementing and monitoring of environmental projects on a continuous basis, which is best done when they are organised into small and homogeneous groups and are properly conscientised, motivated and empowered through provision of technical information, training and financial incentives.

4. Educate politicians, policy makers and other stakeholders and provide them complete and unbiased information about various aspects of environment management so that they are able to take the right decisions.

5. Blend conventional wisdom with knowledge of modern technologies in designing and implementing environmental projects.

6. Build up an adequate environmental database and set up a computerised National Environmental Information System (NEIS). The Planning Commission has already sponsored a number of pilot projects in Natural Resources Information System (NRIS) and has set up an Inter-agency Expert Committee to formulate policies and oversee the implementation of NRIS. This needs to be strengthened in respect of environmental data and user organisations enabled to have access to and use the NRIS.

7. Keep the formats of monitoring reports simple and their contents brief and precise.

8. Link the monitoring system to the responsibility centres in the project organisation concerned. A responsibility centre is simply a unit of an organisation headed by a responsible manager who is accountable for the work done by his unit. The manager should be provided with the information that he needs for decision-making, control and remedial action.

9. Use collegial sanctions against poor work and communicate directly with the area where the bottleneck has occurred.

The NEP-2006 takes note of the fact that the poor enforcement of environmental regulations is largely due to inadequate technical capacities, monitoring infrastructure and trained staff in enforcement institutions. In addition, there is insufficient involvement of the potentially impacted local communities in the monitoring of compliance and absence of institutionalised public-private partnerships in enhancement of monitoring infrastructure.

The NEP-2006 proposes the following two measures to improve the enforcement and monitoring of environmental regulations:

1. Give greater legal standing to local community-based organisations to undertake monitoring of environmental compliance, and report violations to the concerned enforcement authorities.
2. Develop feasible models of public-private partnerships to leverage financial, technical and management resources of the private sector in setting up and operating infrastructure for monitoring of environmental compliance, with iron-clad safeguards against possible conflict of interest or collusion with the monitored entities.

14.5 INSTRUMENTS OF ENVIRONMENT POLICY[4]

Given the goals of an environment policy and the choice of a particular management system to pursue the goals, the next logical question relates to what instruments should be used to achieve the given goals within the framework of the chosen management system. The choice of instruments should be consistent with the goals or objectives of the environment policy on one hand, and with the technical, physical, economic, political, institutional, sociocultural and managerial conditions under which the policy is to be promulgated, on the other.

The instruments of environment policy could broadly be classified into four categories, namely, institutional changes, direct controls, money and credit and public finance. Creation of new institutions, modification of existing institutions, changes in existing systems of property rights, enacting new laws, imposing new taxes, and provision of newly introduced subsidies, belong in the category of institutional changes. Use of these instruments usually requires a change in the laws and hence they take a long time to be effective. Such measures are required more in developing countries like India, where various structural problems render the use of other policy instruments ineffective, than in developed countries. We will now briefly discuss some important policy instruments that are currently in use in India and/or that could be used in future.

14.5.1 Institutional Instruments

Article 48-A of the Constitution of India also provides that the state shall endeavour to protect and improve the environment and to safeguard

---

[4]For details of instruments, see Chapter 7 of this book.

the forest and wildlife of the country. Article 51-A imposes, as one of the fundamental duties on every citizen, the duty to protect and improve the natural environment, including forests, lakes, rivers and wildlife, and to have compassion for living creatures. The present legislative framework for environment management in India is broadly contained in the umbrella Environment Protection Act 1986, the Water (Prevention and Control of Pollution) Act 1974, the Water Cess Act 1977 and the Air (Prevention and Control of Pollution) Act 1981. The laws in respect of management of forests and biodiversity are contained in the Indian Forest Act 1927, the Forest (Conservation) Act 1980, the Wild Life (Protection) Act 1972 and the Biodiversity Act 2003. There are several other enactments which complement the provisions of these basic enactments.

India has a large number of environmental acts and regulations. Pollution limits for various industries have been prescribed in the Environmental Protection Rules 1986. Environmental clearance from the Union Ministry of Environment and Forests is mandatory for setting up new industries in many sectors. A list of major environmental Acts and Rules now in force in India is given below (see also: http://www.envfor.nic.in).

- Indian Easement Act, 1882
- The Water (Prevention and Control of Pollution) Act, 1974
- The Water (Prevention and Control of Pollution) Rules, 1975
- The Water (Prevention and Control of Pollution) Act, 1977
- The Water (Prevention and Control of Pollution) Rules, 1978
- The Air (Prevention and Control of Pollution) Act, 1981
- The Air (Prevention and Control of Pollution) Rules, 1982–83
- The Environment (Protection) Act, 1986
- The Environment (Protection) Rules, 1986
- The Hazardous Wastes (Management and Handling) Rules, 1989
- Manufacture, Storage and Import of Hazardous Wastes Rules, 1989
- Manufacture, Use, Import, Export and Micro Cess Rules, 1989
- The Public Liability Insurance Act, 1991
- The Public Liability Insurance Rules, 1991
- Environmental (Protection) Rules—'Statement', 1992–93
- Environmental (Protection) Rules—'Standards', 1993
- Environmental (Protection) Rules—'Clearance', 1994
- The National Environment Tribunal Act, 1995

All these Acts and Rules seek to provide incentives for reducing pollution from various sources and disincentives for those firms which pollute. What is needed, however, is more strict enforcement of all these Acts and Rules.

The present approach to dealing with environmentally unacceptable behaviour in India has been largely based on criminal processes and sanctions. Although criminal sanctions, if successful, may create a deterrent impact, in reality they are rarely fruitful for a number of reasons. On one hand, giving lower level officials the power to institute criminal prosecutions may provide fertile opportunities for rent-seeking. Civil law, on the other hand, offers flexibility, and its sanctions can be more effectively tailored to particular situations. The evidentiary burdens of civil proceedings are less daunting than those of criminal law. It also allows for preventive policing through orders and injunctions to restrain prospective polluters. Accordingly, the NEP-2006 recommends a judicious mix of civil and criminal processes and sanctions in the legal regime for enforcement through a review of the existing legislation. Civil liability law, civil sanctions and processes would govern most situations of non-compliance. Criminal processes and sanctions would be available for serious and potentially provable infringements of environmental laws, and their initiation would be vested in responsible authorities. Recourse to the relevant provisions in the Indian Penal Code and the Criminal Procedure Code is also possible.

As we know, most of the problems of environmental degradation arise because of the open access or common pool nature of the environment. In view of this, where technically feasible and economically viable, transforming the open access and common pool environmental resources into some sort of state or private property through the creation of property rights could resolve the problems of environmental degradation. In Chapter 8, Section 8.4.3, we have shown how privatisation of degraded revenue lands (state property) and village common lands (CPRs) in West Bengal through granting of land *pattas* (leases) to individuals helped resolve the problem of their degradation and transformed those lands into productive private property.

14.5.2 Direct Controls and Regulation

Direct controls include quantity quotas, seasonal restrictions, safe minimum standards, price controls, prohibition of certain socially undesirable practices by government and courts, and so on. They are powerful tools of environment management, can take effect quickly, and can be selective. They are good for use in dealing with short-term environmental problems but less effective in resolving long-term or structural problems. Their enforcement and monitoring could be very costly and could lead to corruption.

Conventionally, direct controls or regulations are given effect through governmental orders or pronouncements by judiciary. In certain cases, laws are also enacted which stipulate that, for instance, you are not allowed to pollute the air above a certain level and if you do, you will be fined or imprisoned, or both. This form of intervention has high costs of administration and compliance, and is often inflexible providing little incentive for innovation to reduce environmental degradation. For all these reasons, the use of regulatory instruments in isolation from other measures is unlikely to be the least-cost method of achieving environmental objectives in many cases. Control and regulation compares unfavourably with the use of market-based approaches such as taxes and emission charges. Despite its weaknesses, control and regulation is still the predominant instrument for addressing environmental problems in most countries, including India.

Several significant orders have been issued by the Supreme Court (SC) of India and the High Courts from time to time, directing the Union and State Governments to take action to protect the environment (see for details, Chapter 7, Section 7.4.5 (iii) of this book). The court orders have, in fact, been more effective than the government fiats in most of the cases.

14.5.3 Environmental Standards

Environmental standards refer both to the acceptable levels of specified environmental quality parameters at different categories of locations (ambient standards), as well as permissible levels of discharges of specified wastes into streams by different classes of activities (emission standards).

It is now well understood that environmental standards cannot be universal, and each country should set standards in terms of its national priorities, policy objectives and resources available. These standards could be revised to become more stringent, as a country develops, and has greater access to technologies and financial resources for environment management. Environmental standards also need to relate to other measures for risk mitigation in the country, so that a given societal commitment of resources for achieving overall risk reduction yields the maximum aggregate reduction in risk.

Specific considerations for setting ambient standards in each category of location (residential, industrial and environmentally sensitive zones) include the reductions in potential aggregate health risks (morbidity and mortality combined in a single measure) to the exposed population; the risk to sensitive, valuable ecosystems and man-made assets; and the likely societal costs of achieving the proposed ambient standard.

Similarly, emission standards for each class of activity need to be set on the basis of general availability of the required technologies, the feasibility of achieving the applicable environmental quality standards at the location (specific or category) concerned with the proposed emissions standards, and the likely unit costs of meeting the proposed standard. It is also important that the standard is specified in terms of quantities of pollutants that may be emitted, and not only by concentration levels, since the latter can often be easily met through dilution, with no actual improvement in ambient quality. The tendency to prescribe specific abatement technologies should also be eschewed, since these may unnecessarily increase the unit and societal costs of achieving the ambient environmental quality, and in any case because a technology that is considered ideal for meeting a given emission standard may not be acceptable on other relevant parameters, including possibly other sources of societal risk.

The NEP-2006 advocates the following three specific measures to improve the effectiveness of environmental standards:

1. Set up a permanent machinery comprising experts in all relevant disciplines to review notified ambient and emission standards in the light of new scientific and technological information as they become available, and changing national circumstances, ensuring adequate participation by potentially impacted communities, and industry association.
2. Strengthen the network for monitoring ambient environmental quality, including monitoring through participation by local communities, and public-private partnerships.
3. Progressively ensure real-time, and on-line availability of the monitoring data.

14.5.4 Economic Instruments[5]

This set of instruments affects costs and benefits of alternative actions open to economic agents, and thereby influences the behaviour of decision makers in such a way that alternatives are chosen that lead to an environmentally more desirable situation than in the absence of the instrument. Economic instruments aim to bridge the gap between the

[5]For details of economic instruments, see Chapter 7 of this book.

private and social costs by internalising all external costs to their sources, namely, the producers and consumers of resource depleting and polluting commodities. Such instruments are often referred to as market-based instruments, as they work by using market signals such as prices, emission charges/taxes and subsidies to encourage socially better decisions.

14.5.5 Education[6]

This instrument seeks to change perceptions and priorities of users of environmental resources and services by internalising environmental awareness and responsibility into individual decision-making. Besides education and persuasion, this instrument could also take the form of provision of information and training as well as forms of 'moral suasion' such as social pressure and negotiation. They can complement economic and regulatory instruments and assist in their successful implementation.

14.6 ENLISTING STAKEHOLDERS' PARTICIPATION

Viable and sustainable conservation of the environment requires the participation of multiple stakeholders, particularly local people's participation in planning, implementation and monitoring of environmental projects. They may bring to bear their respective resources, competencies and perspectives so that the outcome of partnerships are superior to those of each acting alone. For this to happen, it is essential that all major stakeholders are organised into formal or non-formal homogeneous groups, conscientised about the need for environmental protection and conservation, empowered through education and training, and motivated and guided preferably by local NGOs. There are many factors that affect people's participation in collective action of the type required for environmental protection and conservation. The most important among them is that the expected private benefits from participation must markedly exceed the expected private costs and that the expected benefits must be assured and equitably distributed among participants in proportion to contribution in the form of labour, cash or both. Singh (1991: 278–86) identifies various factors that affect people's participation in natural resource management. They include project design, characteristics of the resource, characteristics of local people, type and orientation of project personnel, and institutional arrangements and incentives for people's participation.

---

[6]For details of economic instruments, see Chapter 7 of this book.

Implementing and policy making agencies of the Government at the Central, State, Municipal and Panchayat levels; the legislatures and judiciary; the public and private corporate sectors; financial institutions; industry associations; academic and research institutions; independent professionals and experts; the media; community-based organisations; voluntary organisations; and multilateral and bilateral development partners may each play an important role in partnerships for the formulation, implementation and promotion of measures for environmental conservation.

In seeking to realise partnerships among the diverse stakeholders, it is essential on the part of the government agencies involved to eschew the confrontational posturing adopted in many cases in the past. While it is not possible that the interests and perceptions of all stakeholders will converge in each case, nevertheless, it is necessary to realise that progress will be seriously impeded if the motives of other partners are called into question during public discourse. It is also essential that all partnerships are realised through, and are carried out in terms of the principles of good governance, in particular, transparency, accountability, cost effectiveness and efficiency.

The NEP 2006 identifies a number of specific themes for partnerships, a few of which are stated below:

1. *Public-Community Partnership*: This is intended to seek the cooperation of public agencies and local communities in the management of a given environmental resource, each partner bringing agreed resources, assuming specified responsibilities with defined entitlements. The Joint Forest Management programme is an example of this kind of partnership.
2. *Public-Private Partnerships*: In this arrangement, specified public functions with respect to environment management are contracted out competitively to private providers, for example, monitoring of environment quality.
3. *Public-Community-Private Partnerships*: In this system, the partners assume joint responsibility for a particular environmental function, with defined obligations and entitlements for each, with competitive selection of the private sector partner, for example, afforestation of degraded forests.
4. *Public-Voluntary Organisation Partnerships*: These are similar to public-private partnerships, in respect of functions in which voluntary organisations may have a comparative advantage over others, the voluntary organisations, in turn, being selected competitively, for example, environmental awareness raising.

5. *Public-Private-Voluntary Organisation Partnerships*: In this arrangement, the provision of specified public responsibilities is accomplished on a competitive basis by the private sector, and the provision is monitored by competitively selected voluntary organisations, for example, 'Build, Own, Operate' sewage and effluent treatment plants.

14.7 INSTITUTIONAL MECHANISM FOR INTEGRATION

In this section, we will briefly describe an institutional mechanism that, to us, seems appropriate for coordination and integration of the NEP 2006.

14.7.1 Integration at the National Level

Environment/ecology and forestry are in the Concurrent List and agricultural and rural development in the State List of the Constitution of India. This means that policies for the former are made by both the Central and State governments and for the latter by State governments. The Central government plays an important role by way of providing policy guidelines and sponsoring and funding programmes of national importance. So, to be meaningful, the process of integration should start at the Central government level. At the national level, Union Ministries of Environment and Forests, Agriculture, and Rural Development are primarily responsible for planning and programming in their respective fields. The Planning Commission also plays an advisory and coordinating role in these exercises. So, the first step in the process of integration is to make a clear policy statement that every agricultural and rural development programme will have an Environmental/Ecological Impact Statement (EIS) built into it and that no programme will be approved for funding until and unless such a statement is incorporated. For overall coordination, guidance and monitoring of the compliance with this requirement, a small Standing Committee of Secretaries representing the Union Ministries concerned and Members incharge of the relevant portfolios in the Planning Commission may be constituted. The Committee may be headed by the Union Minister of Environment and Forests (MoEF)/Vice Chairman, Planning Commission and the Secretary, Ministry of Environment and

Forests may be its Member-Secretary. The Committee may meet at least once every three months and convene one National Consultation Meet of all the Chief Wildlife Wardens of the states where eco-development projects are underway once every year to review the progress and problems of the projects and chalk out a programme for the coming year.

A multidisciplinary cell comprising specialists in forestry, ecology, agriculture, animal husbandry, natural resource economics, environment engineering, management, sociology, rural development and development planning may be set up within the MoEF to assist the Committee and to provide technical guidance to the participating State Forests Departments on a regular basis. Such an administrative procedure will need to be backed up by an appropriate legislative measure as has been done in USA under their National Environment Policy Act of 1969. In India, the Environment (Protection) Act of 1986 provides such a back-up. Many other countries have also formalised incorporation of EIS in their development programmes. A typical EIS would include information on the following:

- A brief description of the proposed project.
- A description of the environmental features likely to be affected by the proposed project.
- An analysis of likely environmental consequences of the project.
- A description of the measures envisaged to mitigate those consequences.
- A review of the relationships between the project and the existing policy.

Care should be taken that compliance with EIS requirement should not result in unnecessary delays, rigidity and increase in the cost, as has been the case in USA and other developed countries. Preparation of EIS is a technical job which should be done by well trained ecologists/environmental scientists with the help and close cooperation of the project personnel.

14.7.2 Integration at the State Level

A mechanism similar to the one proposed for the national level will need to be established at the State level. The Standing Committee of Secretaries and Members of the State Planning Commission concerned may be headed by the Chairman, State Planning Commission. At the State level, besides the agricultural and rural development programmes with EIS incorporated therein, separate projects for eco-development of PAs may be prepared and launched.

14.7.3 Integration at the Protected Area Level

In the context of ecosystem-based development planning and management, PA constitutes the basic planning unit. At the PA level, a Co-ordination and Monitoring Committee representing the following departments/disciplines may be constituted:

1. President(s) of the *Zila Parishad*(s) in whose jurisdiction the PA in question lies.
2. District Collector(s) in whose jurisdiction the PA lies.
3. District Head of Department of Agriculture/Soil and Water Conservation.
4. District Head of Department of Rural Development/District Rural Development Agency.
5. District Head of Animal Husbandry Department.
6. Environmental scientist/Ecologist.
7. Socio-economist.
8. Development banker.
9. The Divisional Forest Officer (DFO).

The Committee may be headed by the President, *Zila Parishad* or the District Collector and the DFO concerned may be its Member-Secretary. The Committee should be responsible for integrating agricultural/rural development programmes with the eco-development plan of the PA under consideration. Ideally, there should be only one comprehensive integrated plan for overall development of the PA. A format and guidelines for preparing such a plan will need to be developed by the Coordinating and Monitoring Committee. Guidelines prepared by Pabla et al. (1994) seem to be an important step forward in this direction. All the funds earmarked for agricultural/rural development, animal husbandry and dairy development, forestry, irrigation, watershed development and infrastructure development in the area should be placed at the disposal of this Committee.

Similar committees may be constituted at the sub-divisional and block levels, if necessary. The sub-divisional level committee may be chaired by the Sub-Divisional Officer and the block level committee by the Block Development Officer concerned, the Assistant Conservator of Forests and the Range Forest Officer concerned may be the Member-Secretary of the Committees respectively.

14.8 A CRITIQUE OF INDIA'S ENVIRONMENT POLICY

The present national policies for environment management are contained in the National Forest Policy, 1988, the National Conservation Strategy and Policy Statement on Environment and Development, 1992; and a Policy Statement on Abatement of Pollution, 1992. Some sector policies such as the National Water Policy, 2002, have also contributed towards environment management. Despite these policy documents a need for a comprehensive policy statement had been evident for some time in order to infuse a common approach to the various sectoral, cross-sectoral, including fiscal, approaches to environment management. With the changes in India's development challenges over time, and increase in our understanding of the centrality of environmental concerns in development, a need was felt to review the earlier objectives, policy instruments and strategies. The MoEF responded to this need by formulating a draft National Environment Policy (NEP 2004). This was also in compliance with India's commitment to a clean environment, mandated in the Constitution of India under Articles 48 A and 51 A (g), strengthened by judicial interpretation of Article 21. It is recognised that maintaining a healthy environment is not the state's responsibility alone, but also that of every citizen.

The draft National Environment Policy (NEP) dated 15 August 2004 was put up on the website of the Ministry of Environment and Forests (MoEF) with a deadline (extended) for public responses by 31 December 2004. The draft NEP is an important document, especially because it articulates the government's view on the relationship between the environment and development. The draft after certain changes was approved by the Cabinet on 18 May 2006.

We now present a critique of the NEP 2006 in light of the basic elements of an ideal national environment policy, presented in the preceding sections.[7]

At the outset, we would like to state that bringing out the NEP 2006 in and by itself represents a big achievement on the part of the MoEF. A national environment policy was badly needed and the MoEF has filled in this void and therefore deserves full credit for this. Also, there are many positive elements in the NEP 2006, such as the enunciation of

[7]In an Open Letter to the Ministry of Environment and Forests dated 29 October 2004, citizens' groups across the country had expressed serious reservations about the process and substance of the draft NEP. We have taken the liberty to draw upon some of their views on the draft NEP. The discussion on the draft had provoked concern from hundreds of organisations and individuals across India prompting the National Advisory Council to discuss it further.

a few principles including the Precautionary principle, the 'Polluter Pays' principle and the Equity principle, that should guide formulation of environmental programmes and projects. Besides, the Doctrine of Public Trust, the need to review macroeconomic policies and securing *adivasi* rights over forests and other natural resources are other good features of the NEP. However, all these good elements will remain on paper unless they are woven within an overall context and operative framework of environment protection, conservation and management. Who will do this, how, and when, is not specified in the policy.

The NEP has a few drawbacks, which are briefly stated in the following paragraphs.

Lack of Transparency and Participatory Approach

The process of policy formulation followed by the MoEF has been opaque and undemocratic, despite the Ministry's claim to have had extensive consultations. NGOs known for their environmental record, or communities with maximum dependence on the environment have not been part of the process of formulating the NEP, nor is the current process of seeking public inputs genuinely participatory, since the draft was available only on a Website, and that too only in English and for a limited period of 45 days. Besides, there were no known plans for consultations with local communities, although a consultation with corporates and bureaucrats had been planned.

Lack of Statement of a Vision and Clearly Defined Goals and Objectives

The NEP falls short of the essential elements of a policy statement. A policy must start with a clear statement of a long-term vision, goals and objectives, identification problems it seeks to address, and what state of affairs it aims to create. It must then refer to other existing policies on the subject, analyse their successes and failures, and indicate the need for the new policy statement based on this analysis. The policy document needs to be brief, essentially laying down the broad principles that would determine decision-making, investment and action rather than go into details—such as the mentioning of specific sites—that change ever so often. A sound policy also needs to indicate the interfaces with other related policies (in this case with sectors like energy, water, agriculture, forestry, transport, infrastructure and tribal affairs), in particular to highlight the over-riding importance that the environment should be given in relation to such policies. The NEP is lacking on most of these counts.

Lack of Specification of an Organisation Structure and Governance System

The NEP does not specify any particular organisation structure or management system for implementing the policy and monitoring its progress, nor has it a coherent vision of genuine decentralised governance and grassroots empowerment. Though it says a few general things in this direction, the operative strategies and actions have hardly anything on how the proposed natural resource governance system would be administered, or how current structures that centralise all powers in the hands of a small bureaucracy are to be changed. While it declares that the government is only a custodian of India's environment, holding it in trust for citizens, it does not go into how this can be operationalised through a truly public-controlled decision-making process. In the absence of a concrete framework to ensure accountability and public participation at state and local levels, the NEP's attempt to decentralise project clearances and other decisions to these levels may sound progressive but will, in fact, be a dangerous gamble. The provisions of the NEP actually go against the spirit of the government holding the environment in trust.

The NEP highlights the need to 'reduce delays' in environmental clearances of projects but ignores the fact that most delays are caused by inadequate, incorrect or improper fulfilment of the mandatory requirements under the Environment Protection Act or Forest Conservation Act. It is ironic that the NEP condones the view that environmental legislations are to blame for delaying developmental processes, sidelining the fact that unsustainable 'development' processes destroy the environment. There is an urgent need for a comprehensive strengthening of the Environment Impact Assessment procedures by making it mandatory from the very start of the project planning stage, ensuring meaningful public participation and making all decisions transparent to the public.

Materialistic and Anthropocentric Stance

Environment is a multifaceted phenomenon and therefore solution of environmental problems requires a holistic perspective. However, the NEP displays a predominantly materialistic and anthropocentric view of the environment, ignoring the basic ethical imperative of conserving nature, and leaving out any discussion of the moral and cultural relations of humans with nature. It displays a very strong 'economic fundamentalist' approach, which assumes that market and economic instruments will solve basic environmental problems. This is also reflected in the proposed monitoring of the NEP by the Cabinet

Committee on Economic Affairs rather than by a professional environmental agency. It could pave the way for weaker regulatory measures, including impact assessment and coastal zone notifications. It is also scientifically and technically unsound, leaving huge gaps in conservation measures and ignoring many technological innovations.

It is also very weak on indigenous approaches to environment, including knowledge, innovations, traditions, practices and technologies, mentioning only one or two specific facets of these.

Failure to Incorporate Lessons from the Past Experience

It is a sad commentary that the government does not learn from its own experience. A glaring example of this is the fact that not long before the announcement of the NEP, the MoEF followed a participatory and transparent approach for the preparation of the National Biodiversity Strategy and Action Plan (NBSAP). This process deliberated on many of the above substantive points, and came out with detailed strategies and actions in the draft national plan prepared jointly with communities most dependent on nature and natural resources. It accorded a high priority to ecological security and to the livelihood security of such communities, also what any NEP should focus on. Both the process and the outcomes of the NBSAP seem to have been totally ignored by MoEF while finalising the NEP.

Lack of a Gender Perspective

Last, but not the least, there is no mention of gender in the entire NEP. This is despite the fact that it is the women who interact with the environment most frequently and most intensively while they fetch water, collect fuelwood and fodder, and tend animals. Environment cannot be improved on a sustained basis unless it is considered a joint responsibility shared by women and men. A gender perspective emphasises the relations between men and women and the relationship they have with their social and natural environment. It recognises that the success of environmental projects largely depends on the extent to which both women and men participate in project design, planning, implementation and monitoring. There are many ways of institutionalising a gender-sensitive approach to environment management. The first and foremost requirement is the policy of equal involvement of both men and women in environmental projects. Next, women should be assigned specific roles, responsibilities and rights in making various decisions, rather than simply attending project meetings. Besides, the whole project team has to be sensitised to gender issues if gender awareness is to be encouraged.

The whole team also has to be trained and made responsible for the implementation of the gender-sensitive approach.

14.9 MAIN POINTS

The following are the main points made in this chapter:

- Given the increasing levels of air, water, land and noise pollution, loss of biodiversity, and degradation of forests and common pools marine and inland fisheries in India due to a variety of reasons, there is need for a pragmatic national environment policy to protect, conserve and improve the environment. Conservation of the environment is also necessary for survival of human beings and all other living beings on this planet.
- An ideal environment policy should place the environment (including biodiversity and wildlife) and livelihoods based on natural resources as the central concerns of India's planning and development process. It should have a long-term vision of ensuring environment security and aim at ensuring the socially efficient use and management of natural resources and the environment on a sustainable basis as well as inter-generational equity. Besides, it should also specify the policy instruments appropriate for achieving its goals and objectives, and an appropriate management system for its implementation, coordination and monitoring.
- Some of the major instruments useful for environment management include environmental laws, rules and regulations, safe minimum standards, emission charges/taxes, subsidies and education.
- The Ministry of Environment and Forests, Government of India announced its first draft National Environment Policy in August 2004 and the Cabinet passed it on 18 May 2006. Prior to that there was no comprehensive integrated national policy for the environment. What existed was an assortment of a few sectoral policies such as National Agriculture Policy, National Water Policy and National Forest Policy. In many cases, objectives of one programme conflict with those of others and there is no institutional mechanism for reconciling the conflicts. Consequently, many programmes have not only failed to produce the intended benefits but have also negated, *albeit*, unintentionally, the positive impacts of many other programmes.
- The NEP 2006 has several good features such as the enunciation of principles like the Precautionary Principle, 'Polluter Pays'

principle and Equity principle. They would help guide the formulation of environmental programmes and projects. Besides, the Doctrine of Public Trust, the need to review macroeconomic policies, and securing *adivasi* rights over forests and other natural resources are also its good features.

- The NEP 2006 suffers from several drawbacks. Its overall orientation and its actual operative part are largely 'business as usual', which will hardly help to reverse the country's environmental crisis or to safeguard the interests of either wildlife or the millions of people who depend directly on the natural environment.
- The NEP 2006 rightly emphasises the need for empowerment of *Panchayats* and the Urban Local Bodies, particularly in terms of functions, functionaries, funds and corresponding capacities for operationalising some of its major provisions. However, it does not specify who will do that, how, and why.
- The NEP 2006 duly acknowledges the need for integration of environmental concerns in all relevant development processes but does not specify how the proposed integration would be achieved.
- However, we must appreciate the fact the the NEP 2006 is a good step forward in the direction of environmental protection and conservation, and hope that it is implemented faithfully.

14.10 DISCUSSION QUESTIONS

1. In India, we already had a National Forest Policy, a National Agriculture Policy, a National Water Policy and a Marine Fishing Policy. Why, then, was a separate Environment Policy needed and formulated in 2006, and what is the guarantee that it would not remain as ineffective as other policies?
2. The objectives of the NEP 2006 could be realised only by concrete actions in different areas relating to key environmental challenges. A large number of such actions are currently underway, and have been for several years, in some cases, for many decades. But they have not produced the desired outcome. Why?
3. The NEP 2006 stipulates that action plans would be prepared on identified themes by the concerned agencies at all levels of Central, State/UT and Local governments. In particular, the State and Local governments would be encouraged to formulate their own strategies or action plans consistent with the National Environment Policy. But given the lack of requisite expertise and

skilled man-power at the district and village levels, discuss how such expectations can be realised?

4. Discuss why a gender perspective should be incorporated in the NEP 2006. Will its incorporation make the policy more effective? Yes/No, and why?

5. Why is the materialistic and anthropocentric stance of the NEP not desirable?

Glossary

Like any other field of study, environmental economics also uses numerous concepts and technical terms. A clear understanding of those basic concepts and terms is necessary for the student to be able to make further progress. Here, we present definitions of most commonly used concepts and terms of environmental economics. The definitions used here are compiled from various sources, the most prominent being Grafton et al. (2001).

Abatement: This term is used to connote a method or process that is used to control or reduce pollution, or any other environmentally hazardous effects of an activity.

Ability-to-pay principle: This is an important concept frequently used in welfare economics and environmental economics. It implies that publicly provided goods and services should be priced on the basis of what potential consumers are able to pay. See also *willingness-to-pay*.

Abiotic factors: This term is used to mean non-living components of the natural environment such as land and water.

Acid rain: Technically speaking, acid rain is rain that has a larger amount of acid in it than what is normal. The acidity of rain in parts of Europe and North America has dramatically increased over the past few decades. Acid rain can go undetected in an area for years.

Adaptability: This term is used to connote the ability of a population or species to adjust to changes or shocks in the environment. See also *resilience*.

Afforestation: This term is used to mean plantation of trees on lands which are degraded, or marginal agricultural lands or wastelands.

Agenda 21: A document that outlines policies to help achieve sustainable development. It was released at the 1992 Rio de Janeiro Earth Summit. See *United Nations Conference on Environment and Development*.

Agro-forestry: By this term, we mean the practice of growing of trees in agricultural lands, jointly with crops or alone.

Air: A common name for the constituent gases in the earth's atmosphere that consists of nitrogen (78.08 per cent), oxygen (21.95 per cent), argon (0.93 per cent) and trace gases, including greenhouse gases.

Airshed: This term refers to a geographic area, delineated on the basis of local atmospheric conditions. The term is used in the context of control of air pollution.

Altruism: The term connotes a personal attribute and implies a deliberate act of an individual undertaken for the benefit of others without expecting any benefits in return.

Ambient: The background level of an environmental measure, such as the air temperature or the level of particulate matter in the air.

Amenity value: This refers to the non-market value attached to an environmental asset, such as the value of walking in a forest.

Amortisation: This term means making a provision for repayment of a debt (such as a mortgage) over time.

Annuity: This term refers to a constant annual payment of a benefit such as pension. Annuities can be obtained by paying a lump-sum to a financial institution in return for a constant and certain stream of annual payments.

Anthropocentric (ethics): This term is used to describe a set of human beliefs and associated behaviours that are focused upon the well-being of human beings, to the possible exclusion of other species.

Anthropogenic: This term refers to an object which is of human origin. For example, anthropogenic greenhouse gas emissions arise from human activity, such as the burning of fossil fuels.

Aquaculture: The term is used to connote a managed system of raising and harvesting of fish and shellfish.

Aquifer: A porous body of rock or sediments capable of storing water. Over-use of aquifers by withdrawing more groundwater than is replenished naturally is a major concern in many countries.

Arable land: The term refers to land suitable for the cultivation of crops.

Average variable cost: The term refers to costs of production that vary with output. It is computed by dividing the total variable cost of production by total output.

Averting expenditures: Market costs incurred in averting the effect of deterioration in the environment. For example, the purchase of bottled water, because of concern over the quality of drinking water, represents an averting expenditure.

Avoidance costs: The term includes costs involved in preventing degradation of a natural resource including environmental quality.

Benefit-cost ratio: The present value of benefits from an investment or project divided by the present value of the costs associated with the project.

Bequest value: The term is used to describe a value that individuals may place on the environment that represents their consideration for its use by future generations.

Biological diversity or biodiversity: The total variation in all forms of life on earth or within a given area or ecosystem, typically expressed as the total number of species found within the area of interest or the genetic diversity within a species.

Carbon sequestration: The process by which the uptake of carbon dioxide in carbon sinks is increased, such as by planting trees, increasing the growth rate of trees, or by ocean fertilisation. Sequestration may also involve the long-term storage of carbon or carbon dioxide in underground sites.

Catchment: An area of land which drains into a water system, such as a stream or river.

Civil society: A term used to describe the non-governmental organisations and individuals that contribute their time and resources for the benefit of others, as well as the good of society.

Classical economics: A term used for the body of thought developed mainly by British economists in the late 18th to the mid-19th centuries. The best known classical economist was Adam Smith who published his *Wealth of Nations* in 1776.

Climate: The term is generally used to connote a complex natural phenomenon comprising such variables as air temperature and humidity, wind and precipitation. It is a complex system representing cumulative effects of regional or weather patterns.

Closed economy: An economy which has very little or no trade with other countries.

Club of Rome: A group of people who brought their collective skills and experience together to examine the state of humanity and the earth. A famous publication of the group was the book *Limits to Growth* that predicted the medium- and long-term supply and use of natural resources.

Coase Theorem: Theorem named after Ronald Coase, a Nobel Laureate in Economics. Coase examined how the assignment of property rights can be used to overcome the problems of pollution. The Theorem is commonly interpreted as stating that the assignment of a property right can be used to internalise an externality and it does not matter, in terms of economic efficiency, which party (the polluter or persons suffering from the pollution) is assigned the right.

Collective rights: The traditional rights to a resource, area, or practice held by a community or people but which may not formally be recognised.

Command and control system: An approach to pollution prevention and natural resource management that relies upon direct regulations and standards with enforcement and fines.

Commons: A popular term for common-pool resources. Sometimes the term is interpreted as a common pool resource (CPR) to which users have no property rights or a CPR over which there exist community rights.

Common pool resources (CPR): Natural resources that are used in common by a group of identifiable people, irrespective of whether they have property rights in the resource or not.

Common property resources (CPR): Natural resources that are used in common by a group of identifiable people, who have property rights in the resource.

Compounding: This is a method of converting a stream of costs into current rupees. For example, if the interest rate is 'r' per year, then the cost of Rupee 1 incurred n years ago is worth: $A/(1 + r)^n$ in current rupees, after compounding.

Cost-benefit analysis: A methodology for determining whether a project or activity generates a positive net benefit for society by evaluating all the costs and benefits over time.

Damage function: A function that relates the level of emissions or discharges to the associated environmental or social costs.

Debt-for-nature swaps: Agreements wherebs countries or conservation groups buy some of the existing debt owed by a developing country which, in return, agrees to set aside a given area of land for conservation purposes.

Degradation: The diminution in value or output. Environmental degradation is the state in which the environment has been altered in some way, rendering it less productive or valuable from any perspective, for example, economic, ecological or spiritual.

Depletion costs: The reduction in value of a non-renewable resource that results from a fall in the total quantity available due to extraction.

Depreciation: The physical loss and/or financial loss over time associated with the use of an asset.

Desalinisation: A process for removing salt from water or soil. Desalinisation of soil can involve better drainage and the 'flushing' of soil with water with low levels of sodium. Desalinisation of sea-water is an important source of drinking water in some countries, such as Saudi Arabia.

Desertification: Process by which the moisture in the soil over an area of land and vegetative cover declines over time. Desertification can be caused by both natural (for example, climate change) and anthropogenic factors (for example, deforestation).

Discounting: This is a method by which future costs and benefits are converted into current rupees. For example, if the discount rate is 'r' per year, then a payment of Rupee 1 after n years is worth: $A/(1+r)^n$ in current rupees, after discounting.

Discount rate: This is a numeric value that serves to convert a future value to a present value.

Ecology: This is a discipline which deals with the study of life and interactions between organisms, and between organisms and their biotic and abiotic environment.

Ecological balance: The condition in which a community of organism or an ecosystem is in dynamic equilibrium, within which genetic species, and ecosystem diversity remain relatively stable over time.

Ecological carrying capacity: The ecologically determined maximum sustainable stock (like animals, humans, etc.) that can be supported by a given unit of habitat.

Ecological economics: A branch of economics that explicitly recognises environmental limits, and the interactions between human activities and the environment.

Economic rent: The return over and above that necessary to ensure the supply of a factor of production.

Emission/effluent charge: A pollution charge or tax levied on an emitter based on the amount of pollution emitted.

Emission permit: A permit or property right which allows the holder to emit or release a given quantity of a pollutant in a defined period of time. Tradable emission permits allow different parties to sell and buy permits such that those who can meet the emission limits at low cost can sell some of their permits to others who are only able to meet their obligations at a high cost.

Entropy: The level of disorder in a system that, in a closed system, represents the amount of unavailable or bound energy. Living organisms (including human beings) try to maintain, or at least slow down, an increase in their own entropy by using low entropy materials in their environment. Economic activity can be broadly characterised as the transformation of low entropy natural resources (such as oil) into higher entropy forms, such as wastes.

Environment: The natural environment encompasses all the abiotic and biotic elements that form our surroundings, that is, the air, land, the water, the forests, the seas, the animals, and all other living and non-living elements of this Planet Earth.

Environmental amenities: The term refers to the utility enhancing attributes of the natural environment. Usually, amenities refer to non-extractive, consumption attributes (for example, site attributes, air quality, views, etc.).

Environmental economics: The application of economic principles to the management of environmental quality. Environmental economics differs from resource economics in that it focuses on the valuation and management of environmental quality and not just resource stocks.

Environmental Impact Assessment (EIA): A detailed accounting of the impacts on the environment that would be expected given a proposed development. The findings of the EIA are presented in an environmental impact statement (EIS).

Environmental Kuznets Curve: An inverted U-shaped functional form relating levels of environmental degradation with income. The curve suggests that environmental degradation first increases as countries start to develop, reaches a turning point, and then subsequently declines as countries become wealthier.

Estuary: The lower part of a river or stream that enters the ocean and is influenced by tidal waters.

Exchange rate: The price of a currency in terms of other countries' currencies, or the rate at which one can exchange one currency for another.

Exclusive Economic Zone (EEZ): A zone of extended jurisdiction up to 200 nautical miles from the shores of coastal states.

Externality: This term connotes an unintended side-effect of the actions of an individual, company or community on others or the environment, and these effects are not taken into account in the decision making of the parties causing them.

Fallow: Land that is left uncultivated for one crop season or two. The land may or may not have been previously cropped.

Farm forestry: By this term, we mean the practice of growing of trees in privately-owned agricultural lands.

Fixed costs: Costs of production that do not vary with the level of output.

Flood plain: The area of land surrounding a water channel that is subject to flooding.

Free good: Goods that are so abundant that they have no market price. Paradoxically, free goods can be the most essential, such as the air we breathe.

Free-rider: An individual who benefits from the actions and efforts of others without contributing to the costs incurred in generating the benefits.

Free riding: Using a public good without contributing toward its cost.

Global warming: The term implies an increase in the mean global temperature. There has been marked increase in the mean global temperature in the last two decades or so. Increasing concentrations of greenhouse gases are likely to accelerate the rate of global warming.

Green accounting: Approaches to national income accounting in which an attempt is made to account for changes in the quality of the environment in physical and/or value measures.

Green GDP: The conventional measure of gross domestic product adjusted for changes in values of the environment.

Greenhouse gases (GHGs): Molecules in the atmosphere which are able to absorb the thermal radiation emitted from the earth. The most important greenhouse gases include carbon dioxide, water vapour, methane, nitrous oxides and chlorofluorocarbons.

Gross National Product (GNP): A measure of the total value of goods and services produced in an economy in a year, including net income paid to foreigners less net income paid to domestic nationals.

Groundwater: Water contained in rocks and soil beneath the earth's surface which has precipitation as its source of replenishment.

Growing stock: The volume of merchantable trees that are still actively growing within a forest area.

Hedonic pricing: A method of evaluating the economic value of goods based on econometric techniques that identify and quantify the utility of various attributes of the good inherent in its surrounding environment.

Human capital: The term is used to refer to the learned and inherent abilities that are embodied in individuals.

Indigenous knowledge: The body of knowledge of local inhabitants regarding the physical functions, uses, and interdependence of resources and living organisms found within their environment.

Input-output analysis: A method of modelling an economy by specifying the relationship between inputs, intermediate outputs, outputs and final demands in an economy.

In situ: This is a Latin term used for the natural state. It connotes the attributes and characteristics of a natural resource or environmental asset that arise from its current state. For example, a growing forest provides *in situ* value in terms of carbon sequestration.

Intangible benefits: Benefits that accrue to individuals that cannot be quantified in financial terms.

Intergenerational equity: The notion that the present generation should consider the needs of future generations in current decision making. Intergenerational equity is a fundamental feature of sustainable development.

Internalisation: The terms refers to the process by which individuals or firms explicitly consider the costs or benefits that they impose, unintentionally, on others from their actions or decisions.

Internal rate of return (IRR): The discount rate in cost-benefit analysis at which the present value of benefits equal the present value of costs.

Intrinsic value: Value of a good, asset or aspect of the environment that is separate from its value in use.

Institutional economics: A sub-discipline of economics that emphasises the importance of institutions and social structures and their affect on economic performance.

Irreversibility: The term refers to a state of a change, or a process that is impossible to be restored. For example, the extinction of a species is irrevocable.

Life expectancy: The age that half the population is expected to live to or beyond.

Morbidity: This is a measure of the incidence of disease. A morbidity rate is usually defined as the number of reported cases of a disease in a population per 100,000 people in a given period of time.

Natural resource economics: A sub-discipline of economics concerned with the allocation, use, and management of renewable and non-renewable resources.

Natural resources: Commodities or assets with some economic value which exists without any effort of mankind, that is, those assets which are not man-made. They are used for direct consumption as well as in producing other goods. They may be renewable or non-renewable. The examples include air, water, natural forests, mineral deposits, and so on.

Neoclassical economics: The term is used to refer to the most popular mode of economic analysis at present. It is based on the premises of rational behaviour by economic agents, that is, individuals and firms who try to optimise their utility/profit, given their constraints.

Net domestic product (NDP): The gross domestic product less an allowance for depreciation of the capital stock.

Net national income (NNI): The net national product plus subsidies but less indirect taxes (such as value-added taxes). See *net national product*.

Net national product (NNP):The gross national product less an allowance for capital depreciation.

Net present value (NPV): The sum of the discounted net benefits (benefits minus costs) in each time period, over the lifetime of the investment.

Nistar: The term connotes a set of rights granted under the Indian Forest Act 1927 to forest dwellers and villagers living within the radius of five km from forests. Under the Nistar system, the Forest Department is mandated to provide the eligible persons with certain specified forest products such as poles, fuelwood and bamboo at concessional rates, or free of charge.

Open access: The term is used to describe the lack of property rights over resources whereby no controls exist over the number of users or how much of the resource they may extract. In other words, open access resources are nobody's exclusive property.

Opportunity cost: The term refers to the cost of an economic activity in terms of the other goods and services, in the next best alternative, that must be forgone to be able to undertake the activity. For example, an opportunity cost associated with the time of a person spent in visiting a recreation site is the value of the forgone production that would otherwise have occurred if the person had, instead, invested his time in producing some good.

Option value: A value, beyond an expected use value, derived from the willingness to pay for the option of using a resource at a future date.

Ozone depletion: Stratospheric ozone is a gas which occurs naturally. The ozone layer could be thought of as earth's sunglasses, protecting life on the surface from the harmful glare of the sun's strongest ultraviolet rays, which can cause skin cancer and other maladies. The ozone layer can be depleted by free radical catalysts, including nitric oxide (NO), hydroxyl (OH), and atomic chlorine (Cl) and bromine (Br). As the ozone layer is depleted, more ultraviolet radiation reaches the earth's surface.

Ozone hole: Region first discovered over Antarctica where, in the spring, a significant reduction in stratospheric ozone occurs due to chemical reactions between chlorofluorocarbons (CFCs) and halons and ozone. A so-called ozone hole has also been discovered over the extreme northern latitudes.

Pareto criterion: A social welfare criterion, according to which a change in the state of the world is socially desirable if, for every individual, the expected utility that results from the change is at least equal to the status quo level of utility, and strictly greater for at least one individual.

Pareto improvement: A change in the state of the world in which the expected utility of every individual in the new state is at least equal to the status quo level of utility, and strictly greater for at least one individual.

Pareto optimality: Allocation of resources or goods in which there exists no other feasible allocation that could improve the utility of one individual without diminishing the utility of at least one other individual.

Pigouvian tax: Tax named after the economist A.C. Pigou. A Pigouvian tax (commonly a per unit charge) is a tax applied to emissions or pollution and is designed to internalise an environmental externality.

Price support: The payment by the government or a state enterprise of a minimum price for a good irrespective of the market price. Price supports most commonly exist for agricultural products.

Private costs: Money costs of the production (like the costs of labour, material, electricity and other production inputs).

Producer's surplus: This is a measure of returns over and above those necessary to compensate a firm to supply a given quantity of a good or service.

Property rights: A bundle of rights that have legal recognition. The rights include the right to consume, sell, exchange, bequeath.

Public good: A pure public good is non-exclusive (anyone can use it) and non-rivalrous (the number of users does not affect the benefits derived from its consumption). Public goods may be publicly provided (such as national defence) or may be privately provided (such as a lighthouse).

Purchasing power parity (PPP): A method of comparing the value of currencies across countries using a suitable basket of goods and services. For example, if the basket of goods costs A$ 400 in Australia and US$ 200 in the United States then the purchasing power parity is A$ 2 for US$ 1. The PPP may differ from the actual exchange rate.

Pure existence value: The value ascribed to a good solely for its existence and divorced from any possible *in situ* use value it might have.

Quota: A regulated amount of a good that can be produced, imported or exported by a firm or country.

Referendum: A question format in contingent valuation surveys in which the respondent is asked to respond 'yes' or 'no' to a hypothetical trade-off between some amount of an environmental good or service and something else of value (especially money).

Resilience: This term is used to refer to the ability of natural populations to return to their previous state following a shock.

Riparian rights: The property rights associated with the access to, and use of, streams, lakes and rivers.

Riparian water doctrine: A system of property rights in which access to water (from a natural water course) requires ownership, or other tenure, of land adjacent to that water.

Royalty: A payment made to the owner of a natural resource for exploiting the resource, and that is based on the value of the resource extracted.

Run-off: The water that is transported across the land and deposited into water-bodies such as rivers and lakes. Run-off from urban centres may also include a variety of contaminants, including oils and particulates.

Satellite accounts: Financial accounts, especially in systems of national accounts, that consider economic and physical stocks and flows (for example, the value of oil reserves) that relate to traditional accounts (for example, gross domestic product), but are not considered part of the system of core accounts.

Scarcity: A situation when demand for a good/service is greater than its supply at zero price.

Social capital: The institutions and norms of behaviour that facilitate social and economic cooperation. Social capital is important in explaining economic performance and environmental quality.

Social benefits: The total value of an economic activity that accrues to society as a whole and thus leads to an increase in the social welfare. In effect, it is the sum of two benefits: (*a*) the benefit to the agent performing the action (producer's surplus, profit made), and (*b*) the benefit accruing to society as a result of action, for example, increase in tax revenue.

Social cost: The total costs to society of an economics activity, that is, private costs plus value of externalities.

Social forestry: This term is used in India to refer to the practice of growing of trees in community/common pool lands.

Socially optional use: The allocation of resources that will yield the highest possible benefit for society as a whole, taking into account all costs and benefits.

Social welfare: A measure of the collective well-being of a society.

Strategic bias: This is a term used in contingent valuation. This connotes the potential that a respondent's stated willingness to pay (or accept) may be different from her true willingness to pay (or accept) if she believes that her answer will influence the provision of the good or service in question.

Stratosphere: A region in the earth's atmosphere from 10 to 50 km above the earth's surface (as low as 8 km in polar regions and as high as 15 km in tropical regions) and which contains the ozone layer that helps shield the earth's surface from ultraviolet radiation.

Strong sustainability: The principle that there should be no net depletion of natural resources from economic activity. This contrasts with weak sustainability, which allows for the conversion of one type of capital stock into another type, so long as the aggregate value of the net capital stock does not decrease.

Stumpage rate: The charge that is paid to the owner for the right to harvest a given volume of wood from a forest.

Stumpage value:The value placed upon a tree on the stump. Generally, stumpage is the market value of a log less transportation, milling and harvesting.

Sustainable development: A term popularised by the United Nations in the report, *Our Common Future*. The term is defined in many different ways. It is commonly defined as a process by which current generations meet their needs and care for the environment in ways that do not compromise the needs of future generations.

Sustainability: This is a characteristic of a system. In the context of the environment, it implies that the natural capital stock remains constant over time. Differences in what constitutes the natural capital stock and what exactly remains constant over time have led to a number of different definitions of sustainability.

Tariff: A tax imposed on imports that is often based as a percentage of the import price.

Terms of trade: Ratio of export prices to import prices. A long-term decline in the terms of trade reduces the ability of countries to pay for their imports.

Territorial User Rights in Fisheries (TURFs): This is a term coined by Francis Christy to denote areas of the ocean or sea floor to which individuals or groups of individuals have property rights in terms of the harvest of marine animals. TURFs are not widely used in fisheries although they do exist for some shellfish.

Thermodynamics: A field of study that deals with different forms of energy, and especially the conversion of heat into other forms of energy, and vice versa.

Time preference: A preference in terms of relative weight given to consumption in the present rather than in the future.

Total allowable catch (TAC): The term is used in fisheries to denote the total permissible catch of the fishing fleet in a given period of time, usually a fishing season. The TAC is used to ensure the sustainability of the resource.

Total dissolved solids (TDS): A measure of the total quantity of solids dissolved in a solution. This is an indicator of the level of water pollution.

Total economic value: The total willingness to pay to preserve, maintain or possess a natural resource or environmental good. The total economic value includes use and non-use values.

Total factor productivity (TFP): A broad measure of productivity defined as a ratio of output(s) to all inputs.

Trade-off: A conscious decision to forgo the benefits of one resource, good or service, in order to enjoy those of another exclusive resource good or service.

Transactions costs: The costs incurred in exchanging and enforcing property rights. High transactions costs can be a major impediment to trade and exchange.

User cost: The future cost, in terms of increased extraction costs in the future, and lost market opportunities from extracting an extra unit of a resource at present.

Use value: The term is used to refer to an individual's willingness to pay for the *in situ* use of a natural resource or an environmental good.

Usufruct rights: Rights to use land or any other natural resources that are contingent on its use, irrespective of the person or entity, who legally owns the resource. Usufruct rights may be conferred on a particular individual, or a group of individuals, or any organisation such as a Water Users Association.

Utility: The term is used to connote the well-being, or satisfaction, associated with the consumption or use of a commodity, or a resource. Utility theory forms the basis of many economic models of consumer behaviour.

Utility function: A relationship where utility is a function of the quantities consumed of various goods and services.

Value added: The difference between the value of a good after a production process, less the value of all the inputs in producing the good.

Value added tax (VAT): A tax on the value added from one stage of the production and distribution process to another that is imposed as a percentage of the price of the good or service.

Vulnerability: This is a measure of the extent to which an ecosystem, or species is threatened or endangered by natural, or man-made changes.

Watershed: The term refers to an area that is the drainage basin of a defined stream or river, or any other water body. The surface run-off of rain water from the area is generally drained to the water body through a common outlet.

Weak sustainability: The notion that the environment or natural capital is, to some extent, a substitute for human-made capital. See *strong sustainability*.

Welfare economics: A branch of economics, which deals with the principles and criteria of evaluating alternative economic states and policies from the viewpoint of 'efficiency or social welfare'.

Willingness-to-Accept (WTA): The compensation required to return an individual to his or her original state of economic well-being following some change (possibly hypothetical) in the world. In many cases, a willingness to accept measure is considered to be inferior to the willingness to pay measure of welfare change.

Willingness-to-Pay (WTP): This refers to the willingness of an individual to pay (that is, give up part of one's budget) in order to secure a good or service. Willingness-to-pay is often used to refer to the amount that a consumer would pay for a hypothetical good, service, or change in some state of the world, particularly as described in a contingent valuation survey.

Woodlot: A forested area of community-owned land used for harvesting trees for the benefit of the community.

World Trade Organization (WTO): The successor to the GATT that was established in 1995, is mandated to expand multilateral trade. WTO has a dispute resolution mechanism to help prevent restrictive trade practices.

Zero sum game: A mathematical construction of a set of choices where the outcomes are symmetrically opposed such that the total benefits received by one party are equivalent to the losses borne by the other.

References
and Select
Bibliography

Ahmad, Yusuf J., Salah El Serafy and Ernst Lutz. 1989. *Environmental Accounting for Sustainable Development*. Washington, D.C.: The World Bank.

Allaby, M. (1996). *Basics of Environmental Science*. London: Routledge.

Anderson, M.S. 1994. *Governance by Green Taxes: Making Pollution Prevention Pay*. Manchester: Manchester University Press.

Anderson, S.H. 1999. *Managing Our Wildlife Resources*. Upper Saddle River, New Jersey: Prentice-Hall.

Anderson, Terry L. 1982. 'The New Resource Economics: Old Ideas and New Applications', *American Journal of Agricultural Economics*, 64: 928–34.

Arnold, J.E.M. and J.G. Campbell. 1986. 'Collective Management of Hill Forests in Nepal: The Community Forest Development Project', in *Proceedings on the Conference on Common Property Management*, 425–54. Washington, D.C.: National Academy Press.

Arnold, J.E.M. and W.C. Stewart. 1991. 'Common Property Resource Management in India', Tropical Forestry Paper No. 24. Oxford: Oxford University and Oxford Forestry Institute.

Arrow, K. and A. Fisher. 1974. 'Environmental Preservation, Uncertainty and Irreversibility', *Quarterly Journal of Economics*, 88(1): 312–19.

Australian Bureau of Agricultural and Resource Economics. 1997. *The Economic Impact of International Climate Change Policy*. Canberra: Commonwealth of Australia.

Axelrod, Robert. 1984. *The Evolution of Co-operation*. New York: Basic Books.

Ayyappan, S. and M. Krishnan. 2004. 'Fisheries Sector in India: Dimensions of Development' Keynote paper, *Indian Journal of Agricultural Economics*, 59(3): July–September: 392–412.

Azad, K.C., R. Swarup and B.K. Sikka. 1988. *Horticultural Development in Hill Areas: A Study of Himachal Pradesh'*. Delhi: Mittal Publications.

Bahuguna, Sunderlal. 1989. 'Environment Conservation for Survival', *Indian Journal of Public Administration*, (3593), July–September.

Balakrishnan, Suresh, Katar Singh and Mukunda V. Das. 1992. 'Interventions in Common Pool Resource Management: A Case Study of Marine Fisheries in Kerala', Paper presented at the Workshop on Co-operatives for Natural Resources Management, 7–11 December 1992, Institute of Rural Management, Anand.

Bali, J.S. 1988. 'A Critical Appraisal of Past and Present Policies and Strategies of Watershed Development and Management in India and Role of Governmental and Non-Governmental Organisations in Small Scale Watershed Development'. Mimeo. New Delhi: Society for Promotion of Wastelands Development.

Balooni, Kulbhushan. 1997. 'Financing of Afforestation of Wastelands', unpublished Ph.D. Dissertation, Department of Economics, Sardar Patel University, Vallabh Vidyanagar, India.

Balooni, Kulbhushan and Katar Singh. 1994. 'Economics of Farm Forestry: A Case Study in Shankerpura Village, District Panchmahal, Gujarat', Working Paper No. 61, Institute of Rural Management, Anand.

———. 2003. 'Financing of Wasteland Afforestation in India', *Natural Resources Forum*, 27(3), August.

Bannock, Graham, R.E. Baxter and Evan Davis. 1998. *Dictionary of Economics*. London: The Economist Book.

Barbier, Edward. B. (ed.). 1993. *Economics and Ecology*. London: Chapman and Hall.

———. 1997. 'Introduction to the Environmental Kuznets Curve Special Issue', Summaries, *Environment and Development Economics*, 2.

Barbier, E.B., J. Burgess and C. Folke. 1994. *Paradise Lost? The Ecological Economics of Biodiversity*. London: Earthscan Publications Ltd.

Barkley, Paul W. and David W. Seckler. 1972. *Economic Growth and Environmental Decay: The Solution Becomes the Problem*. New York: Harcourt Brace Jovanovich, Inc.

Bartelmus, Peter. 1997. 'Whither Economics? From Optimality to Sustainability', *Environment and Development Economics*, 2(3): 323–45.

Baumol, W.J. and W.E. Oates. 1988. *The Theory of Environmental Policy*. (2nd edn). Cambridge: Cambridge University Press.

Bell, Simon and Stephen Morse. 1999. *Sustainability Indicators: Measuring the Immeasurable?* London: Earthscan Publications Ltd.

Berkes, Fikret. 1986. 'Marine Inshore Fishery Management in Turkey', *Proceedings of the Conference on Common Property Resource Management, National Research Council*. Washington, D.C.: National Academy Press.

Bhattacharya, R.N. (ed.). 2002. *Environmental Economics: An Indian Perspective*. New Delhi: Oxford University Press.

Bierman, H.S. and L. Fernandez. 1993. *Game Theory with Economic Applications*. Reading, MA: Addison-Wesley Publishing.

Brackley, Peter. 1988. *Energy and Environmental Terms: A Glossary*. Aldershot, U.K.: Gower Publishing.

Braybrooke, David. 1985. 'The Insoluble Problem of the Social Contract', in Richard Campbell and Lanning Sowden (eds), *Paradoxes of Rationality and Co-operation*. Vancouver: University of British Columbia Press.

Bromley, D.W. 1991. *Environment and Economy: Property Rights and Public Policy*. Oxford: Basil Blackwell.

———. (ed.). 1992. *Making the Commons Work*. San Francisco: ICS Press.

———. (ed.). 1997. *The Handbook of Environmental Economics*. Cambridge, USA: Blackwell.

Brown, G. and R. Mendelsohn. 1984. 'The Hedonic Travel Cost Method', *Review of Economics and Statistics*, 66: 427–33.

Brown, K., D. Pearce, C. Perrings and T. Swanson. 1993. 'Economics and the Conservation of Global Biological Biodiversity', Global Environment Facility, Working Paper No. 2, Washington, D.C.: UNDP/UNEP/World Bank.

Brown, L.R. et al. 1993. *State of the World 1993*. London and New York: W.W. Norton.

Callan, S.J. and J.M. Thomas. 2000. *Environmental Economics and Management: Theory, Policy and Applications*. Orlando, Florida: The Dryden Press.

Campbell, Richmond and Leanning Sowden. (eds). 1985. *Paradoxers of Rationality and Co-operation: Prisoner's Dilemma and Newcomb's Problem*. Vancouver: University of British Columbia Press.

Campbell, J.Y. 1992. 'Joint Forest Management in India', *Social Change*, 22(1): 36–54.

Carson, R.T., N.E. Flores, K.M. Martin and J.L. Wright. 1996. 'Contingent Valuation and Revealed Preference', *Land Economics*, February, 72(1): 80–99.

Chandrasekharan, C. 1996. 'Cost, Incentives and Impediments for Implementing Sustainable Forest Management', paper published in the proceedings of the workshop on financial mechanisms and sources. Project report prepared for MoEF, India.

Chaturvedi A.N. 1994. 'Sequestration of Atmospheric Carbon in India's Forests' *Ambio* 23: 460–61.

Chopra, K. and G.K. Kadekodi. 1997. 'Natural Resource Accounting in the Yamuna Basin: Accounting for Forest Resources'. Project report prepared for MoEF, India.

Chopra, Kanchan and S.C. Gulati 2001. *Migration, Common Property Resources and Environmental Degradation: Interlinkages in India's Arid and Semi-arid Region*. New Delhi: Sage Publications.

Christy, F.T. Jr. 1982. 'Territorial Use Rights in Marine Fisheries: Definitions and Conditions', FAO Fisheries Technical Paper No. 227, Food and Agriculture Organization of the United Nations, Rome.

Ciriacy-Wantrup, S.V. 1952. *Resource Conservation: Economics and Policy*. Berkeley: University of California Press.

———. 1955. 'Benefit Cost Analysis and Public Resource Development', *Journal of Farm Economics*, 37(4): 676–89.

———. 1968. *Resource Conservation: Economics and Policies* (3rd edn). Berkeley: Division of Agricultural Sciences, University of California.

Ciriacy-Wantrup, S.V. and R.C. Bishop. 1975. 'Common Property as a Concept in Natural Resources Policy', *Natural Resources Journal*, 15: 713–27.

Clark, C. 1990. *Mathematical Bioeconomics* (2nd edn). New York: John Wiley & Sons.

Coase, R.H. 1960. 'The Problem of Social Cost', *Journal of Law and Economics*, 3: 1–44.

Cohen, J. and I. Stewart. 1994. *The Collapse of Chaos*. New York: Penguin Books.

Colborn, T., D. Dumanoski and J.P. Myers. 1997. *Our Stolen Future*. New York: Plume/Penguin.

Common, Michael. (1996). *Environmental & Resource Economics: An Introduction*. UK: Longman Addison Wesley, Ltd.

Conrad, J. 1995. 'Bioeconomic Models of the Fishery', *The Handbook of Environmental Economics*. Cambridge, MA: Basil Blackwell.

Cornes, R. and T. Sandier. 1996. *The Theory of Externalities, Public Goods and Club Goods* (2nd edn). Cambridge: Cambridge University Press.

Costanza, R., O. Segura and J. Martinez-Alier. 1996. *Getting Down to Earth*. Washington, D.C.: Island Press.

Cropper, M. and F.G. Sussman 1990. 'Valuing Future Risks To Life', *Journal of Environmental Economics and Management*, 20(2): 160–74.

Cruz, Wilfrido D. 1986. 'Overfishing and Conflict in a Traditional Fishery: San Miguel Bay, Philippines', in: Proceedings of the Conference on Common Property

Resource Management. National Research Council, National Academy Press, Washington, D.C.

CSE. 1996. *Down to Earth*. New Delhi: Society for Environmental Communications, Centre for Science and Environment, November issue.

———. 2001. *Down to Earth: Survival Primer*. New Delhi: Society for Environmental Communications, Centre for Science and Environment.

CSO. 1989. *Sources and Methods*. New Delhi: Central Statistical Organisation, Ministry of Statistics and Programme Implementation, Government of India.

———. 2002. *National Accounts Statistics*. New Delhi: Central Statistical Organisation, Ministry of Statistics and Programme Implementation, Government of India.

———. 2004. *National Accounts Statistics*. New Delhi: Central Statistical Organisation, Ministry of Statistics and Programme Implementation, Government of India.

Cunningham, William, Terrance, H. Cooper, Eville Gorham, Malcolm T. Hepworth (eds). 1999. *Environmental Encyclopedia*. Mumbai: Jaico Publishing House.

Daly, Herman E. 1973. 'The Steady-State Economy: Toward a Political Economy of Biophysical Equilibrium and Moral Growth', in H.E Daly (ed.), *Toward a Steady-State Economy*. San Francisco: W.H. Freeman and Company.

———. 1990. 'Toward Some Operational Principles of Sustainable Development', *Ecological Economics*, 2: 1–6.

———. 1996. 'Consumption: Value Added, Physical Transformation, and Welfare', in R. Costanza, O. Segura and J. Martinez-Alier (eds), *Getting Down to Earth*, 49–59. Washington, D.C.: Island Press.

Dasgupta, Partha. 1982. *The Control of Resources*. Cambridge, MA: Harvard University Press.

De Bruyn, S.M. 2000. *Economic Growth and the Environment: An Empirical Analysis*. Dordrecht: Kluwer Academic Publishers.

Deaton, M.L. and J.J. Winebrake. 2000. *Dynamic Modelling of Environmental Systems*. New York: Springer-Verlag.

Devlin, R.A. and R.Q. Grafton. 1998. *Economic Rights and Environmental Wrongs: Property Rights for the Common Good*. Cheltenham, UK: Edward Elgar.

Dixit, A. and V. Norman. 1980. *International Trade: Theory of International Trade: A Dual, General Equilibrium Approach*. Welwyn, Herts: J. Nisbet.

Dixon, John A, Louise Fallon Scura, Richard A. Carpenter and Paul B. Sherman. 1994. *Economic Analysis of Environmental Impacts*. London: Earthscan Publications Ltd. in association with the Asian Development Bank and the World Bank.

DoES, M.P. 2003. *Estimates of State Domestic Product of Madhya Pradesh (1993–94 to 2001–02)*. Bhopal, Madhya Pradesh: Directorate of Economics and Statistics.

Dorfman, R. 1974. 'The Technical Basis for Decision Making', in Haefele T. Edwin (ed.), *The Governance of Common Property Resources*. Baltimore and London: The Johns Hopkins Press for the Resources for the Future.

Duraiappah, A.K. 1993. *Global Warming and Economic Development*. Boston: Kluwer Academic Publishers.

Editorial (2004). 'Ethics and Short Cuts', *The Hindu*, 15 December 2004.

Eggertsson, T. 1990. *Economic Behavior and Institution*. Cambridge, UK: Cambridge University Press.

Ehrlich, Paul. 1968. *The Population Bomb*. New York: Ballantine Books.

Ehrlich, P.R. and A.H. Ehrlich. 1981. *Extinction: The Causes and Consequences of the Disappearance of Species*. New York: Random House.

Ekins, P. 2000. *Economic Growth and Environmental Sustainability: The Prospects for Green Growth*. London: Routledge.

FAO. 1989. *The State of Food and Agriculture 1989*. Agriculture Series No. 22, Food and Agriculture Organization. Rome, Italy: FAO

————. 2001. *Global Forest Resources Assessment 2000*. Main Report. FAO Forestry Paper 140. Rome: FAO.

————. 2003. *Review of the State of World Fishery Resources: Inland Fisheries*. Fisheries Circular No. 942, Rev. 1., Food and Agriculture Organization, 60p. Rome: FAO.

Feeny, D., S. Hanna and A.F. McEvoy. 1996. 'Questioning the "Tragedy of the Commons" Model of Fisheries', *Land Economics*, May, 72(2): 187–205.

FES. 2002. *Annual Report 2001–2002*. Anand: Foundation for Ecological Security, NDDB Campus.

————. 2005. *Annual Report 2004–2005*. Anand: Foundation for Ecological Security, NDDB Campus.

Field, Barry C. 1997. *Environmental Economics: An Introduction*. USA: Irwin-McGraw-Hill.

————. 2000. *Natural Resource Economics: An Introduction*. Boston, MA: McGraw-Hill.

Fisher, Anthony C. 1995. *Environmental and Resource Economics*. Cheltenham, UK: Edward Elgar.

Folmer, Henk, H. Landis Gabel and Hand Opschoor (eds). 1995. *Principles of Environmental and Resource Economics—A Guide for Students and Decision-Makers*. Cheltenham, UK: Edward Elgar.

Folmer, Henk, H. Landis Gabel, Shelby Gerking and Adam Rose (eds). 2001. *Frontiers of Environmental Economics*. Cheltenham, UK: Edward Elgar.

Freeman III, A. Myrick. 1993. *The Measurement of Environmental and Resource Values: Theory and Methods*. Washington, D.C.: Resources for the Future.

Friedman, Alan E. 1971. 'The Economics of the Common Pool: Property Rights in Exhaustible Resources', *UCLA Law Review*, 18 May, 855–87.

Friedman, Sharon M. and Kenneth A. Friedman. 1988. *Reporting on the Environment: A Handbook for Journalists*. Published by the Asian Forum of Environmental Journalists in Cooperation with The United Nations Economic and Social Commission for Asia and the Pacific, Bangkok, Thailand.

FSI. 1997. *State of Forest Report 1997*. Dehra Dun: Government of India.

————. 1999. *State of Forest Report 1999*. Dehra Dun: Government of India.

————. 2001. *State of Forest Report 2001*. Dehra Dun: Government of India.

Gajja, B.L. and R. Prasad. 1998. 'Approaches to Financing of Operation and Maintenance Costs of Kakrapar Irrigation Projects', *Current Agriculture*, 22(1–2): 55–67.

Gale, R.P. and S.M. Cordray. 1994. 'Making Sense of Sustainability: Nine Answers to "What Should Be Sustained"', *Rural Sociology*, 59(3): 311–32.

Garrod, G. and K.G. Willis. 1999. *Economic Valuation of the Environment: Methods and Case Studies*. Northampton, MA: Edward Elgar.

Gillis, M., D. Perkins, M. Roemer and D. Snodgrass. 1997. *Economics of Development* (5th edn). New York: W.W. Norton.

Government of India. 1952. *The National Forest Policy 1952*. New Delhi: Ministry of Agriculture and Forestry.

————. 1976. *Report of the National Commission on Agriculture 1976, Part II: Policy and Strategy*. New Delhi: Ministry of Agriculture and Irrigation.

————. 1991. *Waterlogging, Soil Salinity & Alkalinity. Report of the Working Group on Problem Identification in Irrigated Areas with Suggested Remedial Measures*. December. New Delhi: Ministry of Water Resources.

————. 1998. *India*. New Delhi: Ministry of Information and Broadcasting.

————. 1999. *Integrated Water Resources Development: A Plan for Action, Report of the National Commission for Integrated Water Resources Development, Volume I*. New Delhi: Ministry of Water Resources.

Government of India. 2000. *Forest Statistics of India 2000*. Ministry of Environment and Forests, Government of India, Office of the Deputy Inspector General of Forests.

Government of India. 2002a. *National Water Policy 2002*. New Delhi: Ministry of Water Resources.

————. 2002b. *Annual Report 2001–2002*. New Delhi: Ministry of Rural Development.

————. 2004a. *Disaster Management in India: A Status Report*. New Delhi: Natural Disaster Management Division, Ministry of Home Affairs.

————. 2004b. *Marine Fishing Policy 2004*. New Delhi: Department of Animal Husbandry and Dairying, Ministry of Agriculture.

————. 2006. *National Environment Policy*. New Delhi: Ministry of Environment and Forests.

Government of Kerala. 1983. *The Acts and Ordinances of Kerala 1981*. Trivandrum: The Law Department.

Gordon, H. Scott. 1954. 'The Economic Theory of a Common Property Resource: The Fishery', *Journal of Political Economy*, April: 124–42.

Grafton, R.Q. 2000. 'Governance of the Commons: A Role for the State?', *Land Economics*, November, 76(4): 504–17.

Grafton, R.Q. and J. Silva-Echenique. 1997. 'How to Manage Nature? Strategies, Predator-Prey Models and Chaos', *Marine Resource Economics*, 12: 127–43.

Grafton, R.Q., D. Squires and K.J. Fox. 2000. 'Private Property and Economic Efficiency: A Study of a Common-Pool Resource', *The Journal of Law and Economics*, 43(2): 679–713.

Grafton, R.Q., L.K. Sandal and S.I. Steinshamn. 2000. 'How to Improve the Management of Renewable Resources: The Case of Canada's Northern Cod Fishery', *American Journal of Agricultural Economics*, 82: 570–80.

Grafton, R.Q., Linwood H. Pendelton, and Harry W. Nelson. 2001. *A Dictionary of Environmental Economics, Science and Policy*. Cheltenham, UK: Edward Elgar.

Grafton, R.Q. and R.A. Devlin. 1996. 'Paying for Pollution: Permits and Charges', *Scandinavian Journal of Economics*, 98: 275–88.

Grafton, R.Q. and T.C. Sargent. 1997. *A Workbook in Mathematical Economics for Economists*, New York: McGraw-Hill.

Green Media: A daily E-news letter devoted to compiling and disseminating environment reporting in selected Indian newspapers, brought out by the Centre for Media Studies and Supported by: ENVIS Secretariat, Ministry of Environment & Forests, GoI.

Greene, W.H. 1997. *Econometric Analysis*. Upper Saddle River, New Jersey: Prentice-Hall.

Hanley, N., J.F. Shogren and B. White. 1997. *Environmental Economics in Theory and Practice*. New York: Oxford University Press.

Haque, M.S. 1997. 'Development of India's Wastelands through Institutional Credit—A 15-Year Plan' in T.K. Sarkar, R.C. Vaish, V. Verma and S.P. Gawande (eds), *Advances in Wastelands Development*, 155–59. New Delhi: Soil Conservation Society of India.

Hardin, Garett. 1968. 'The Tragedy of the Commons', *Science*, 162: 1143–248.

Hardin, Russel. 1982. *Collective Action*. Baltimore: Johns Hopkins University Press.

Haripriya, G.S. 2000. 'Estimates of Biomass in Indian Forests', *Biomass and Bioenergy*, 19: 245–58.

Hartwick, J.M. and N. Olewiler. 1998. *The Economics of Natural Resource Use*. Reading, MA: Addison-Wesley.

Hazilla M. and R.J. Kopp. 1990. 'The Social Cost of Environmental Quality Regulations: A General Equilibrium Analysis', *Journal of Political Economy*, 98(4): 853–73.

Hicks, John R. 1939. 'The Foundations of Welfare Economics', *The Economic Journal*, 49: 696–712.

Hicks, John R. 1941. 'The Rehabilitation of Consumer's Surplus', *Review of Economic Studies*.

Hirshleifer, Jack. 1987. 'Evolutionary Models in Economics and Law: Co-operation versus Conflict Strategies' *in* Jack Hirshleifer (ed.), *Economic Behaviour in Adversity*. Chicago: University of Chicago Press.

Holling, C.S. 1973. 'Resilience and Stability of Ecosystems', *Annual Review of Ecology and Systematics*, 4: 1–23.

Holmberg, J., K. Robert and K. Erikson. 1996. 'Socio-Ecological Principles for a Sustainable Society', in R. Costanza, O. Segura and J. Martinez-Alier (eds), *Getting Down to Earth*, 17–48. Washington, D.C.: Island Press.

Houghton, J. 1997. *Global Warming: The Complete Briefing*, (2nd edn). Cambridge, UK: Cambridge University Press.

Howe, Charles W. 1979. *Benefit Cost Analysis for Water Systems Planning*. Washington D.C.: American Geophysical Union.

Hughes et. al. 2001. *Environmental Health in India: Priorities in Andhra Pradesh*. Environment and Social Development Unit, South Asia Region, World Bank quoted in NEP 2006.

ICFRE. 2001. *Forestry Statistics of India*. Dehra Dun: Indian Council of Forestry Research and Education.

IIFM. 2000. 'Operational Strategy for Sustainable Forestry Development with Community Participation in India: A Project Proposal submitted by the Government of India to the International Tropical Timber Organization'. Bhopal: Indian Institute of Forest Management.

International Institute for Sustainable Development. 2000. *Environment and Trade: A Handbook*. Winnipeg, Manitoba: International Institute for Sustainable Development.

ILRI. 2000. *ILRI Strategy to 2010: Making the Livestock Revolution Work for the Poor*. Nairobi, Kenya: International Livestock Research Institute.

IRMA-UNICEF. 2000. *White Paper on Water in Gujarat*. Anand: Institute of Rural Management and UNICEF.

Iyer, Ramaswamy R. 2003. *Water: Perspectives, Issues, Concerns*. New Delhi: Sage Publications.

John, M. Kerr, Dinesh K. Marothia, Katar Singh, C. Ramasamy and William R. Bentley. 1997. *Natural Resource Economics: Theory and Application in India*. New Delhi: Oxford and IBH Publishing Co.

Joshi, M.V. 2001. *Theories and Approaches of Environmental Economics*. New Delhi.: Atlantic Publishers and Distributors.

Joshi, P.K., and D. Jha. 1991. 'Farm Level Effects of Soil Degradation in Sharda Sahayak Irrigation Project.' Working Paper on Future Growth in Indian Agriculture. Washington, D.C.: Central Soil Salinity Research Institute, Indian Council of Agricultural Research and the International Food Policy Research Institute.

Just, R.E., D.L. Hueth and A. Schmitz. 1982. *Applied Welfare Economics and Public Policy*. Englewood Cliffs, NJ: Prentice-Hall.

Kanwar, Rakesh. 2001. 'Disaster Management', *The Administrator*, Vol. XLIV, December, 96–110.

Karpagam, M. 1991. *Environmental Economics: A Textbook*. Madras: Sterling Publishers P. Ltd.

Katiha, Pradeep K. 2006. 'The Status of and Prospects for Inland Aquaculture and Culture-based Fisheries in India', Unpublished paper included in the *Compendium of Abstracts: Water and Equity*, presented at the 5th IWMI-Tata Annual Partners Meet, 8–10 March 2006, Institute of Rural Management, Anand.

Katz, M.L. and H.S. Rosen. 1998. *Microeconomics* (3rd edn). Boston, MA: Irwin McGraw-Hill.

Kerr, John M., Dinesh K. Marothia, Katar Singh, C. Ramasamy and William R. Bentley (eds). 1997. *Natural Resource Economics: Theory and Applications in India*. New Delhi: Oxford and IBH Publishing Co. Pvt. Ltd.

Khanna, Pradeep. 2004. 'Governance in Forestry Sector: Opportunities and Constraints', Paper presented in the workshop on 'Governance in Forestry Sector' held at the Institute of Rural Management, Anand, 14–19 December.

Kimmins, J.P. 1997. *Forest Ecology: A Foundation for Sustainable Management* (2nd edn). Upper Saddle River, New Jersey: Prentice-Hall.

King, M. 1995. *Fisheries Biology, Assessment and Management*. Osney Mead, England: Fishing News Books.

Kishor Vimal. 2000. 'Problems and Prospects of Watershed Development in India'. Occasional Paper 12. Mumbai: National Bank for Agriculture and Rural Development.

Kolstad, Charles D. 2000. *Environmental Economics*. USA: Oxford University Press.

Kothari, Ashish and Kanchi Kohli. 2005. 'A National Plan Process, Built from Below: The National Biodiversity Strategy and Action Plan, India' in Nirmal Sengupta and Jayanta Bandyopadhyay (eds), *Biodiversity and Quality of Life*. Delhi: Macmillan India Ltd. Published for the Indian Society for Ecological Economics (INSEE).

Kotwal, P.C., R.P. Mishra and D. Dugaya. 2005. *Biodiversity in IIFM Campus*. Bhopal: Indian Institute of Forest Management.

Krugman, P. and M. Obstfeld. 1997. *International Economics: Theory and Policy*. Reading, MA: Addison-Wesley Longman.

Krutilla, J.V. and A.C. Fisher. 1975. *The Economics of Natural Environments: Studies in the Valuation of Commodity and Amenity Resources*. Baltimore, MD: The Johns Hopkins University Press.

Kumar, Praduman and V.C. Mathur. 1996. 'Agriculture in Future: Demand-Supply Perspective for the Ninth Five Year Plan', *Economic and Political Weekly*, 28 September.

Kuznets, Simon. 1955. 'Economic Growth and Income Inequality', *American Economic Review*, 49: 1–28.

Kyrklund B. 1990. 'The Potential of Forests and Forest Industry in Reducing Excess Atmospheric Carbon Dioxide', *Unasylva*, 41: 12–14.

Lange, Glenn-Marie. 2003. *Manual for Environmental and Economic Accounts for Forestry: A Tool for Assessing Cross-Sectoral Policy Impacts of Forestry*. New York: Centre for Economy, Environment and Society, The Earth Institute at Columbia University.

Laughland, A.S., W.N. Musser, J.S. Shortle and L.M. Musser. 1996. 'Averting Cost Measures of Environmental Benefits', *Land Economics*, February, (72)1: 100–112.

Lesser, A. Jonathan, Daniel E. Dodds and Richard O. Zerbe, Jr. 1997. *Environmental Economics and Policy*. New York: Addison-Wesley.

Lewis, Tracy R. and Margaret Slade. 1985. 'The Effects of Price Controls, Taxes, and Subsidies on Exhaustible Resource Production', in Anthony Scott (ed.), *Progress in Natural Resource Economics*. Oxford: Clarendon Press.

Libecap, G.D. 1989. *Contracting for Property Rights*. New York: Cambridge University Press.

Lovejoy, Thomas E. 1980. 'A Projection of Species Extinction', in Gerald O. Barney (ed.), *The Global 2000 Report to the President: Entering the Twenty-first Century*. Vol. 2. Washington D.C.: Council on Environmental Quality, US State Department.

Magrath, William B. 1986. 'The Challenge of the Commons: Nonexclusive Resources and Economic Development: Theoretical Issues', Working Paper, World Resources Institute, Washington, DC.

Manoharan, T.R. 2000. 'Natural Resource Accounting: Economic Valuation of Intangible Benefits of Forests'. Research and Information System for the Non-aligned and other Developing Countries (RIS), New Delhi.

Markandya, Anil and Julie Richardson (eds). 1992. *The Earthscan Reader in Environmental Economics*. London: Earthscan Publications Ltd.

McConnell, K.E. 1983. 'Existence and Bequest Value', in R.D. Rowe and L.G. Chestnut (eds), *Managing Air Quality and Scenic Resources at National Parks and Wilderness Areas*. Boulder: Westview Press.

McKibben, W. 1989. *The End of Nature*. New York: Random House.

McNeely, Jeffrey A. 2005. 'Conservation and the Future: Trends and Options Toward the Year 2005' in Nirmal Sengupta and Jayanta Bandyopadhyay (eds), *Biodiversity and Quality of Life*. Delhi: Macmillan India Ltd. Published for the Indian Society for Ecological Economics (INSEE).

Meadows, D.H., D.L. Meadows, J. Randers and W.W. Behrens III. 1972. *The Limits to Growth: A Report for the Club of Rome's Project on the Predicament of Mankind*. New York: Universe Books.

———. 1974. *The Limits to Growth: A Report for the Club of Rome's Project on the Predicament of Mankind* (2nd ed). New York: Signet.

Metrick, A. and M.L. Weitzman. 1996. 'Endangered Species Preservation', *Land Economics*. February, 72(1): 1–16.

MoEF. 1999. *National Forestry Action Programme - India* (Volume 2), Executive Summary. New Delhi: Ministry of Environment and Forests, Government of India.

———. 2006. *National Environment Policy 2006*. New Delhi: Ministry of Environment and Forests, Government of India.

Moench, Marcus and Dinesh Kumar. 1997. 'Distinction between Efficiency and Sustainability: The Role of Energy Prices in Groundwater Management' in Anil Agarwal (ed.), *The Challenge of the Balance: Environmental Economics in India, Proceedings of a National Environment and Economics Meeting*. New Delhi: Centre for Science and Environment.

Morris, P. and R. Therivel. 1995. *Methods of Environmental Impact Assessment*. Vancouver: UBC Press.

Murakami, T. (nd), 'Fishery Co-operatives Expected to be Viable Models for Future Development: Resources Management in Japan', Mimeo, National Insurance Federation of Fishery Co-operatives, Japan.

NABARD. 2001. *Report of the Expert Committee on Rural Credit*. Mumbai: National Bank for Agriculture and Rural Development (NABARD).

Nadkarni, M.V., John M. Kerr and M. Ravichandran. 1997. 'Economics of Externalities and Pollution Control in India', in Chapter 7 in John M. Kerr et al. eds., *Op.cit.*

Nair, N. Balakrishnan. 1989. *Report of the Expert Committee on Marine Fishery Resources Management in Kerala*. Trivandrum: Government of Kerala.

Nair, Ram Mohan and Katar Singh. 1992. 'The Marine Fishermen Co-operative Societies in Kerala: An Exploratory Study', Paper presented at the Workshop on Co-operatives for Natural Resources Management, 7–11 December 1992, Institute of Rural Management, Anand.

National Research Council. 1999. *Sharing the Fish: Toward a National Policy on Individual Fishing Quotas*. Washington, D.C.: National Academy Press.

Negi, S.S. 1991. *Environmental Degradation and Crisis in India*. New Delhi: Indus Publishing Co.

Nelson, Robert H. 1995. *Public Lands and Private Rights*. Lanham, MD: Rowman and Littlefield.

Neumayer, E. 1999. *Weak Versus Strong Sustainability: Exploring the Limits of Two Opposing Paradigms*. Cheltenham, UK: Edward Elgar.

Nigam, Ashok, Biksham Gujja, Jayanta Bandhopadhyay and Rupert Talbot. 1998. *Fresh Water for India's Children and Nature—Learning from Local-level Approaches*. New Delhi: United Nations Children's Fund (UNICEF) and World Wide Fund for Nature (WWF).

Nordhaus, W.D. and E.C. Kokkelenberg. 1999. *Nature's Numbers: Expanding the National Economic Accounts to Include the Environment*. Washington, D.C.: National Academy Press.

Norgard, R.B. 1984. 'Co-evolutionary Agricultural Development', *Economic Development and Cultural Change*, 32(3): 193–205.

Olson Jr., Mancur. 1971. *The Logic of Collective Action: Public Goods and the Theory of Groups*. Cambridge, MA: Harvard University Press.

Ostrom, E. 1990. *Governing the Commons: The Evolution of Institutions for Collective Action*. Cambridge, MA: Cambridge University Press.

Ostrom, E., R. Gardner and J. Walker. 1994. *Rules, Games and Common-Pool Resources*. Ann Arbor: The University of Michigan Press.

Pabla, H.S., Sanjeeva Pandey and Ruchi Badola. 1994. 'Guidelines for Ecodevelopment Planning', Draft Mimeo, WII-UNDP/FAO Project IND-92/007, Wildlife Institute of India, Dehra Dun.

Panayotou, Theodore. 1992. 'The Economics of Environmental Degradation: Problems, Causes and Responses', in *Green Markets: The Economics of Sustainable Development*. San Francisco, USA: ICS Press for International Centre for Economic Growth.

Pandey, Sanjeeva. 1992. 'Ecodevelopment at its Best: A BMS Experience', *WII Newsletter*, April–June, 73(2): 29–31.

Panwar, H.S. and V.B. Mathur. 1992. 'Protected Area Network in India: A Review', Paper presented at the IV World Congress on National Parks and Protected Areas, 10–12 February, Caracas, Venezuela.

Patel, H. 1990. *Financial Working of Irrigation Projects—A Case Study of Four Projects in Gujarat*. Vallabh Vidyanagar, Gujarat: Department of Economics, Sardar Patel University.

Pathak, Anil. 2004. 'First Tree Census: 25 Crore Trees in State's Non-Forest Areas', *The Times of India*, Ahmedabad, 18 October.

Pearce, David W. 1976. *Environmental Economics*. London: Longman.

Pearce, David. W. and C.A. Nash. 1981. *The Social Appraisal of Projects: A Text in Cost-Benefit Analysis*. London: Macmillan.

Pearce, David. W. and R. Kerry Turner. 1990. *Economics of Natural Resources and the Environment*. Baltimore, Maryland, USA: The Johns Hopkins University Press.

Pigou, A.C. 1920. *The Economics of Welfare*. London: Macmillan.

———. 1962. *The Economics of Welfare* (1920 Reprint). London: The English Language Book Society and Macmillan.

Prakash, T.N. and David W. Pearce. 2001. 'Resilience as a Measure of Environmental Sustainability: The Case of Karnataka Agriculture, India'. London: University College London, Department of Economics.

Prest, A.R. and R. Turvey. 1965. 'Cost-Benefit Analysis: A Survey', *The Economic Journal*, 75(3): 683–735.

Randall, A. 1975. 'Property Rights and Social Microeconomics', *Natural Resources Journal*, 15: 729–40.

———. 1987. *Resource Economics: An Economic Approach to Natural Resource and Environmental Policy*. New York: John Wiley & Sons.

Rao, P.K. 2000. *Sustainable Development—Economics and Policy*. Maiden, MA: Basil Blackwell.

Raven, Peter H., Linda R. Berg and George B. Johnson. 1998. *Environment* (2nd ed). New York: Saunders College Publishing, Harcourt Brace College Publishers.

Rawls, J. 1971. *A Theory of Social Justice*. Cambridge, MA: Harvard University Press.

Ray, D. 1998. *Development Economics*. Princeton, New Jersey: Princeton University Press.

Reynolds, Jack and Celeste K. Gaspari. 1985. 'Cost Effectiveness Analysis, Primary Health Care Operations Research (PRICOR)', Monograph Series, Methods Paper 2. Chevy Chase, Maryland: Centre for Human Services.

Richards, Michael, Jonathan Davies and Gil Yaron. 2003. *Stakeholder Incentives in Participatory Forest Management: A Manual for Economic Analysis*. London: ITDG Publishing.

Robbins, L.C. 1935. *An Essay on the Nature and Significance of Economic Science*. London: Macmillan.

Romer, D. 1996. *Advanced Macroeconomics*. New York: McGraw-Hill.

Rosen, S. 1974. 'Hedonic Prices and Implicit Markets: Product Differentiation in Pure Competition' *Journal of Political Economy*, 82: 34–55.

Ross, M.R. 1997. *Fisheries Conservation and Management*. Upper Saddle River, New Jersey: Prentice-Hall.

Sankar, U. (ed.). 2001. *Environmental Economics: Readers in Economics*. New Delhi: Oxford University Press.

Saxena, N.C. 1992. 'Farm Forestry and Land Use in India: Some Policy Issues', *Ambio* 21(6): 420–25.

Saxena, Rakesh. 1996. 'The Vatra Tree Growers' Co-operative Society,' in Katar Singh and Vishwa Ballabh (eds), *Co-operative Management of Natural Resources*. New Delhi: Sage Publications.

Schneider, R. 1993. 'Land Abandonment, Property Rights, and Agricultural Sustainability in the Amazon'. LATEN Dissemination Note No. 3, Washington, D.C.: The World Bank.

Schumacher, E.F. 1973. *Small is Beautiful: Economics as if People Mattered*. New York: Harper and Row.

Seers, Dudley. 1969. 'The Meaning of Development'. Paper presented at the Eleventh World conference of the Society for International Development, New Delhi.

Sehgal, J. and I.P. Abrol. 1994. *Soil Degradation in India: Status and Impact*. New Delhi: Oxford and IBH.

Sengupta, Nirmal and Jayanta Bandyopadhyay (eds). 2005. *Biodiversity and Quality of Life*. Delhi: Macmillan India Ltd. Published for the Indian Society for Ecological Economics (INSEE).

Sengupta, Nirmal. 2005. 'Economics of Indigenous/Traditional Knowledge About Biodiversity', in Nirmal Sengupta and Jayanta Bandyopadhyay (eds), *Biodiversity and Quality of Life*. Delhi: Macmillan India Ltd. Published for the Indian Society for Ecological Economics (INSEE).

Serageldin, I. 1995. *Toward Sustainable Management of Water Resources. Directions in Development Series*. Washington, D.C.: The World Bank.

Shah, Tushaar. 1993. *Groundwater Markets and Irrigation Development: Political Economy and Practical Policy*. New Delhi: Oxford University Press.

Sharma, Vinod K. 2003. 'Disaster Management—Approach and Emerging Strategies in India', *VISION: The Journal of Business Prespective*, January–June 2003.

Shishodia, Anil. 1994. 'Some Economic and Environmental Aspects of Conjunctive Water Use in the Mahi Right Bank Canal Command, Gujarat'. Unpublished Ph.D. Thesis, Vallabh Vidyanagar, Gujarat: Department of Economics, Sardar Patel University.

Simon, J.L. and H. Kahn (eds). 1984. *The Resourceful Earth: A Response to Global 2000*. New York: Basil Blackwell.

Singh, Ghanshyam N., T.V. Varagunasingh, N. Manonmoney and Kanti Singh (eds). 1991. *Environmental Economics*. New Delhi: Mittal Publications.

Singh, Katar. 1988. *Managing Dry Land Watershed Development Programmes: Lessons of Karnataka Experience*, Research Paper No. 1, Anand: Institute of Rural Management.

Singh, Katar. 1990. 'Expanding and Intensifying Work Opportunities Through Watershed-based Development in Rain-fed Areas', *IASSI Quarterly*, 9(1&2), July–December.

———. 1991a. 'Dryland Watershed Development and Management: A Case Study in Karnataka', *Indian Journal of Agricultural Economics*, 46(2), April–June: 121–31.

———. 1991b. 'Determinants of People's Participation in Watershed Development and Management: An Exploratory Case Study', *Indian Journal of Agricultural Economics*, 46(3).

———. 1993. Cooperative Sea Tenure as an Instrument of Managing Marine Fisheries: Lessons of Kerala's and Japan's Experiences, *Indian Journal of Agricultural Economics*, 48(3): 536–42.

———. 1994a. *Managing Common Pool Resources: Principles and Case Studies*. New Delhi: Oxford University Press.

———. 1994b. 'Marine Fishermen Cooperatives in Kerala', in S. Giriappa (ed.), *Role of Fisheries in Rural Development*. Delhi: Daya Publishing House.

———. 1994c. *International Trade in Agricultural Commodities: Some Implications for Environment and Sustainable Development*. Research Paper 13. Anand: Institute of Rural Management.

———. 1995a. 'Planning and Funding Eco-development Projects in and around Protected Areas in India'. Unpublished Report. Dehra Dun: Wildlife Institute of India/New Delhi: Food and Agriculture Organization (FAO).

———. 1995b. 'The Watershed Management Approach to Sustainability of Renewable Common Pool Natural Resources: Lessons of India's Experience'. Research Paper 14'. Anand: Institute of Rural Management.

———. 1997. 'Property Rights and Tenures in Natural Resources', in John M. Kerr et al. (eds), *Natural Resource Economics: Theory and Application in India*. New Delhi: Oxford and IBH Publishing Co.

———. 1998. 'Cooperative Property Rights as an Instrument of Managing Groundwater', in Marcus Moench (ed.), *Groundwater Law: The Growing Debate*. Ahmedabad: Vikram Sarabhai Centre for Development Interaction-VIKSAT, and Nehru Foundation for Development.

———. 1999a. *Rural Development: Principles, Policies, and Management* (2nd ed). New Delhi: Sage Publications.

———. 1999b. 'Sustainable Development: Some Reflections'. Presidential Address, *Indian Journal of Agricultural Economics*, 54(1), January–March: 6–41.

———. 2001. 'An Evaluation of Some Selected Social Forestry Models Adopted in India', *Indian Journal of Agricultural Economics*, 55(3), July–September.

———. 2005. *Forest Resource Valuation and Accounting: A Critique of the Conventional Method and a Framework for a New System*. Bhopal: Indian Institute of Forest Management.

Singh, Katar and S. Bhattacharjee. 1991. *Privatisation of Common Pool Resources of Land: A Case Study in West Bengal*, Case Study 6. Anand: Institute of Rural Management.

Singh, Katar and R.N. Ghatak. 1995. 'Pricing of Canal Irrigation Water: An Application of the Contingent Valuation Method', *Artha Vikas*, July–December.

Singh, Katar and V. Ballabh. Forthcoming. 'Incidence, Impacts and Management of Droughts in India: An Overview', in Jasween Jairath and Vishwa Ballabh (eds), *Droughts and Integrated Water Resource Management in South Asia — Issues, Alternatives, and Futures*. New Delhi: Sage Publications.

Singh, Katar and Vishwa Ballabh (eds). 1996. *Cooperative Management of Natural Resources*. New Delhi: Sage Publications.

Singh, Katar and Kulbhushan Balooni. 1997. 'Tree Growers' Co-operatives: Farm Forestry in India,' *Journal of Forestry*, 95(10).

Singh, Katar and K.K. Gupta. 1998. *The Sadguru Model of Community-Based Natural Resources Management*. Occasional Publication No. 14. Anand: Institute of Rural Management.

Singh, R.B. (ed.). 2000. *Disaster Management*. Jaipur & New Delhi: Rawat Publications.

Smith, R.L. and T.M. Smith. 2000. *Elements of Ecology*. San Francisco: Addison-Wesley Longman.

SPWD. 1984. *Society for Promotion of Wastelands Development*. Monograph. New Delhi: Society for Promotion of Wastelands Development.

Stavins, Robert. 2001. *Environmental Economics and Public Policy*. Cheltenham, UK: Edward Elgar.

Stern, David I. 1998. 'Progress on the Environmental Kuznets Curve?' *Environment and Development Economics*, 3.

Studenmund, A.H. 2001. *Using Econometrics: Practical Guide* (4th edn). Boston, MA: Addison-Wesley Longman.

Subbiah, A.R. 2004. *Natural Disaster Management, State of the Indian Farmer: A Millennium Study*, 21. Academic Foundation, New Delhi for the Department of Agriculture and Cooperation, Ministry of Agriculture, Government of India, New Delhi.

Swaminathan, M.S. 1996. 'Science and Technology for Sustainable Food Security,' *Indian Journal of Agricultural Economics*, 51(1&2): 60–75.

Swanson, T. 1993. *The International Regulation of Extinction: An Economic Analysis of the Forces Causing and Controlling the Extinction of Species*. London: Macmillan Press Ltd.

Tewari, D.D. and Katar Singh. 1996. *Principles of Microeconomics*. New Delhi: New Age International Publishers.

Thornton, J. 2000. *Pandora's Box: Chlorine, Health, and a New Environmental Strategy*. Cambridge, MA: MIT Press.

Tietenberg, T.H. 1994. *Environmental Economics and Policy*. New York: HarperCollins.

Tietenberg, T.H. 1996. *Environmental and Natural Resource Economics* (4th edn). New York: HarperCollins.

Tinbergen, Jan. 1952. *On the Theory of Economic Policy*. Amsterdam: North Holland Publishing Company.

TOI. 1997. 'Ground Realities: Soil Degradation', *The Times of India*, 25 August 1997.

———. 1998. 'Alarming Rise in Salinity', *The Times of India*, 22 May 1998.

TSL. 2005. *Statistical Outline of India 2004–2005* Mumbai: Tata Services Limited, Department of Economics and Statistics.

UNDP. 1990. *Human Development Report 1990*. United Nations Development Programme. New York: Oxford University Press.

———. 1991. *Human Development Report 1991*. United Nations Development Programme. New York: Oxford University Press.

———. 1992. 'Project of the Government of India: Project Document', IND/92/007/A/01/99. Strengthening Wildlife Management and Ecodevelopment Planning Capabilities, New Delhi, 28 May (Confirmed copy).

———. 1995. *Human Development Report 1995*. United Nations Development Programme. New Delhi: Oxford University Press.

———. 1996. *Human Development Report 1996*. United Nations Development Programme. New Delhi: Oxford University Press.

———. 2005. *Human Development Report 2005*. United Nations Development Programme. New Delhi: Oxford University Press.

United Nations. 2000. *Integrated Environmental and Economic Accounting: An Operational Manual*. Handbook of National Accounting, Series F. No. 78. New York: United Nations.

Van Kooten, G.C. 1993. *Land Resource Economics and Sustainable Development: Economic Policies and the Common Good*. Vancouver, BC: University of British Columbia Press.

Van Kooten, G.C. and E.H. Bulte. 2000. *The Economics of Nature*. Oxford: Blackwell Publishers.

Verma, Madhu. 2000. *Himachal Pradesh Forestry Sector Review Annexes: Economic Valuation of Forests of Himachal Pradesh*. International Institute for Environment and Development (IIED) in collaboration with Himachal Pradesh Forest Department, Indian Institute of Forest Management, Bhopal.

Vivekanandan, V. 1991. 'Problems and Prospects of People's Participation in Marine Fisheries Management: The Case of Artificial Reefs at Valiathura, Kerala'. Paper presented at a Workshop on People's Participation in Natural Resource Management, 25–30 November, 1991, Institute of Rural Management, Anand.

Vogler, J. 2000. *The Global Commons: Environmental and Technological Governance* (2nd edn). Chichester, UK: John Wiley & Sons Ltd.

Wimpeny, J.T. 1991. *Values for the Environment: A Guide to Economic Appraisal*. London, UK: Overseas Development Institute, HMSO.

Wolf, Peter and Rolf Hubener. 1999. 'Irrigation in the World — The Future will not be like the Past', *Natural Resources and Development*, 51, Institute of Scientific Co-operation, Tubingen.

World Bank. 1996. *Staff Appraisal Report: India Ecodevelopment Project*. Report No. 14914-N, South Asia Department II, Agriculture and Water Division. Washington, D.C.: The World Bank.

———. 1988. *India: Wasteland Development Review*. Washington, D.C.: The World Bank.

———. 1996a. *India Ecodevelopment Project*. Report No. 14914-N, South Asia Department II, Agriculture and Water Division. Washington, D.C.: The World Bank.

———. 1996b. *World Development Report 1996: From Plan to Market*. Washington, D.C.: The World Bank and Oxford University Press.

———. 1998. *World Bank Atlas 1998*. Washington D.C.: The World Bank.

World Commission on Environment and Development. (WCED) 1987. *Our Common Future: Report of the World Commission on Environment and Development*. Oxford: Oxford University Press.

World Commission on Forests and Sustainable Development. 1999. *Our Forests, Our Future*. Cambridge, MA: Cambridge University Press.

WRI. 1992. *World Resources 1992–93: A Report by the World Resources Institute (WRI)*. Oxford: Oxford University Press.

WRI. 1998. *World Resources 1998–99: A Guide to Global Environment*. The World Resources Institute. Oxford: Oxford University Press.

WSSCC. 1999. 'Water for People: Vision 21: A Shared Vision for Water Supply, Sanitation, and Hygiene and a Framework for Future Action'. Review Version, Water Supply and Sanitation Collaborative Council, Stockholm, August.

Zerbe, R.O. and D.D. Dively. 1994. *Benefit–Cost Analysis in Theory and Practice*. New York: HarperCollins.

Internet Resources

Acid rain: http://www.geocities.com/narilily/acidrain.html

Action for dealing with climate change: http://www.yosemite.epa.gov/oar/globalwarming.nsf/ content/actions.html

Biodiversity hot spots: http://www.conservation.org

Climate change: http://www.yosemite.epa.gov/oar/globalwarming.nsf/content/climate.html

Data relating to agriculture, cooperation, national income etc: http://www.agricoop.nic.in/statatglance2004/AtGlance.pdf

Effects of acid rain: http://www.epa.gov/maia/html/acid-rain.html

Economic Survey (of India), 2005–2006: http://www.indiabudget.nic.in

Global atmospheric changes: http://www.Saundern college.com/literci/environment.

Global warming: http://www.epa.gov/ozone/intpol/index.html

International organisations engaged in protecting the depletion of ozone layer: http://www.epa.gov/ozone/intpol/index.html

Ministry of Environment and Forests, Government of India: http://www.envfor.nic.in

National Environment Policy 2006: http://www.envfor.nic.in/nep/nep2006.html

National Wastelands Identification Project (NWIP): NAEB Home Page, http://www.envfor.nic.in/naeb/naeb.html

Ozone layer depletion: http://www.en.wikipedia.org/wiki/Ozone_layer

Index

About the Authors

Katar Singh is Honourary (Founder) Chairman, Indian Natural Resource Economics and Management (INREM) Foundation, a non-governmental, academic organisation, committed to promoting teaching, training and research in natural resource economics and environment management, and improving natural resource management policies and programmes. He was Director and RBI Chair Professor at the Institute of Rural Management, Anand (IRMA), India, and also had a short stint as Director, Bankers Institute of Rural Development, Lucknow. He has also taught at GB Pant University of Agriculture and Technology, Pantnagar, India.

Dr Singh holds a Ph.D. degree in agricultural economics from the University of Illinois at Urbana-Champaign, USA, and has done post-doctoral research in natural resource economics. He has over 45 years of experience in teaching, training, research and consulting in the areas of agricultural and rural development, and natural resource and environmental economics and rural management.

He has coordinated and conducted several research and consultancy projects funded by national and international agencies. A prolific writer, he has published over 120 articles and papers in reputed journals and authored/co-authored eight books, including *Rural Development: Principles, Policies and Management, Second Edition* (Sage, 1999), and

Managing Common Pool Resources: Principles and Case Studies (Oxford, 1994). He has also co-edited three books: *Co-operative Management of Natural Resources* (Sage, 1996), *Natural Resource Economics: Theory and Application in India* (Oxford & IBH, 1997), and *Designing and Managing Rural Development Organisations* (Oxford & IBH, 2000).

Anil Shishodia is Senior Lecturer in the Department of Economics, Sardar Patel University (SPU), Vallabh Vidyanagar, Gujarat. He was a World Bank Post-Doctoral Research Fellow in Environmental Economics at the Colorado State University, Fort Collins, USA, from August 1999 to May 2000, where he credited and audited a number of advanced courses in natural resources and environmental economics, including a course in environmental ethics. At SPU, he was instrumental in designing and offering a post-graduate level course in Environmental Economics. He has about 11 years of experience in teaching and research, and has published a number of articles on the subject.